CORN KINGS & ONE-HORSE THIEVES

CORN KINGS & ONE-HORSE THIEVES

A Plain-Spoken History of Mid-Illinois

JAMES KROHE JR.

Southern Illinois University Press
Carbondale

Southern Illinois University Press
www.siupress.com

Some material in this book appeared in very different form in *Illinois Times* and *Illinois Issues* and is used with permission.

Printed in the United States of America

20 19 18 17 4 3 2 1

Cover illustrations: bird's-eye view of Mattoon, Illinois, 1884, Library of Congress Geography and Map Division, LCCN 73692308; cornfield (cropped as silhouette), TVAllen_CDI, photographer, iStock.

Library of Congress Cataloging-in-Publication Data

Names: Krohe, James, author.
Title: Corn kings and one-horse thieves : a plain-spoken history of mid-Illinois / James Krohe Jr.
Description: Carbondale : Southern Illinois University Press, 2017. | Includes bibliographical references and index.
Identifiers: LCCN 2016046480 | ISBN 9780809336029 (paperback) | ISBN 9780809336036 (e-book)
Subjects: LCSH: Illinois—History. | BISAC: HISTORY / United States / State & Local / Midwest (IA, IL, IN, KS, MI, MN, MO, ND, NE, OH, SD, WI).
Classification: LCC F541 .K76 2017 | DDC 977.3—dc23 LC record available at https://lccn.loc.gov/2016046480

Printed on recycled paper. ♲

This paper meets the requirements of ANSI/NISO Z39.48-1992 (Permanence of Paper) ♾

To three hundred generations of mid-Illinoisans
for making a history worth telling,

and to L. for making it possible to tell it

CONTENTS

ILLUSTRATIONS

CORN KINGS & ONE-HORSE THIEVES

Map of mid-Illinois. TOM WILLCOCKSON / MAPCRAFT CARTOGRAPHY.

In the Middle of Everywhere: An Introduction to Mid-Illinois

> Corn pressed in on Hope like a tame jungle.
>
> —Carl Van Doren, recalling his Vermilion County hometown

Say "Illinois" to people from other places, and most of them will think first of one of two things—corn and Abraham Lincoln. Both the staple and the statesman were products of the place, and since each is unlikely to have developed in quite the same way anywhere else, neither can be perfectly understood without knowing the middle part of the state that is the middle of the Middle West.

Like Lincoln, corn was a homely product of the countryside that grew into something unexpectedly important to Illinois and the nation. Its cultivation transformed what at one time might have been dismissed as thirty thousand square miles of weeds into one of the globe's most productive agricultural empires. Where mid-Illinois farmers once cultivated corn using horses and mules, their descendants do it in air-conditioned machines steered by satellites and sensors. These modern tractors can vary the application of chemicals row by row to match variations in soil quality, the better to nurture bug-repelling plants that yield twice the kernels with half the water of those that sustained Great-Grandpa. Such technological miracles have more of Silicon Valley than Sunnybrook Farm about them, and many of them were invented or perfected in the middle part of the state.

Lincoln too was bred to flourish here, where Southerners' tolerance for treelessness, flatness, and cold overlapped most Northerners' tolerance for Southerners. People from half a hundred different places brought to mid-Illinois nearly that many different ideas about God, humanity, and government and the proper relation of each to the others. Imported sectional rivalries manifested themselves politically in not-always-civil wars between Democrats and Whigs, states-righters and abolitionists, Copperheads and Unionists. What better place for a future president in the 1850s to prepare to lead a divided nation?

For decades, the Illinois period in the rail-splitter's life was dismissed by biographers who saw as unimportant its relative uneventfulness compared with his career as president and commander in chief. Most writers saw Lincoln's years in Springfield as merely a prolonged pupation during which a hack lawyer, snug in his cocoon, awaited the miraculous transformation into a leader that could only occur in Washington. The history of the region itself therefore is widely regarded as interesting only to the extent Lincoln once was part of it. A case can be made, however, that Lincoln was interesting because so much of mid-Illinois was a part of him.

Mid-Illinois is the territory that lies wholly or in part between the Indiana state line and the Mississippi River and between interstates 70 and 80. It sprawls across twenty-nine thousand square miles, an area larger than Ireland, much larger than the Netherlands, Belgium, or Denmark, and twice as large as Switzerland. These are the corn latitudes, whose climate and geology are so perfectly suited to its cultivation that any seed seems to come up corn. Nearly everywhere in this expanse the prominences on the landscape are the interstate overpass and the occasional coal mine slag heap. The glaciers' meltwater laid down mud and gravels so smoothly atop most of mid-Illinois that a person could see on Wednesday who was coming to dinner on Friday. That part of eastern mid-Illinois once known as the Grand Prairie is one of the flattest parts of a famously flat state. (There really is a Flatville, Illinois, a hamlet about ten miles northeast of Urbana.) A mid-Illinois vista thus is all foreground. Only occasionally, as during a storm, does the modern Illinoisan feel that dread of exposure reported by so many travelers left adrift on the prairie 170 years ago; even such trees as grew here at settlement didn't offer much shelter, as they tended to hide themselves (from prairie fires, mainly) in the creek bottoms.

Whether and in which ways such a setting shaped the culture that took root there has been debated for decades, and it will not be settled in these pages. Transplanted Vermonter Stephen A. Douglas said that his mental horizon had been widened by the unadorned prairies, which relieved his eyes of the cramp of hills and mountains they were used to back home.[1] If pioneer reminiscences are to be believed, many more people found all that space discomfiting and, turning their backs on it, developed a crabbed and inward frame of mind. In a place so exposed, it was probably inevitable that isolationism should become a persistent strain of thought.

Unfortified by mountains or deserts or forest, mid-Illinois always was open to settlement by what one historian describes as "diverse, entangled peoples."[2] Native American peoples from the eastern and northern forests shared the region for more than a century with French fur traders and priests and British soldiers and colonial administrators. The arrival in the latter 1700s of settlers from the east (mostly Kentuckians) began the Euro-American era.[3] Arriving by wagon and flatboat in the 1830s were emigrants from mid-Atlantic states and their western outposts such as Pennsylvania and Ohio. They in turn were joined by Yankees and, later, northern Europeans (mainly Germans, Swedes, and Irish) pushing south from Chicago after voyages by boat through the Erie Canal and the Great Lakes. The railroads later brought African Americans from the Deep South and refugees from a dozen unhappy countries in eastern Europe and the Mediterranean.

Springfield was typical of mid-Illinois's larger towns and cities. Its founders hailed from Kentucky, Virginia, and Connecticut, and its most prominent early businessman was a former New Jerseyan. The authors of a 1920 social survey of the capital noted that because it stood about midway between the northern and southern states and near the center of population of the country, "[Springfield] has shared in the cross-currents of political, social, and economic forces of the East and the West, the North and the South."[4] Not everyone agreed that this cross-breeding produced a superior hybrid. John Hay famously said that Springfield combined "the meanness of the North with the barbarism of the South."[5]

Geographer Douglas Meyer would later make the point more circumspectly when he noted of the region that "cultural coherence was not the norm."[6] One might think that a stew with so many flavors in it would be spicy indeed, but the result is just the opposite. Mid-Illinois's architecture, for instance, is a bland blend, and its residents' indeterminate patterns of speech make them sound like people you've heard everywhere and nowhere. (Springfield, according to that 1920 study, "may hardly be regarded as a city of many extremes; it is rather a city of many averages."[7])

Mid-Illinois is thus defined by its lack of definition. The region as a whole lacks Chicago's and southern Illinois's self-consciousness as a place. Quincy and Macomb (the latter the home of Western Illinois University) consider themselves emphatically part of western Illinois, but the rest of state is so little aware of the region that disgruntled locals in the 1970s began referring to it as Forgottonia. "Eastern Illinois" also scarcely exists as a popular term of identification, in spite of the fact that, smack in the middle of it, in Charleston-Mattoon, there is Eastern Illinois University; instead, eastern Illinois is generally considered to be part of "central Illinois," which on the maps is actually east-central Illinois. Thus this book's resort to "mid-Illinois," a term that while unfamiliar to some locals at least has the merit of coherence.[8]

In sum, mid-Illinois is a mini-Illinois. Only in this part of Illinois did the mix of immigrant populations achieve the same proportions as those in the state as a whole; its averageness, its lack of a specific identity, its unambiguous ambiguity, its Illinois-ness, is mid-Illinois's true identity—the region of Illinois that is both the most and the least like itself.

CHAPTER ONE

A Classic Mixing Zone: The Peopling of Mid-Illinois

> I am getting skeery about them 'ere Yankees; there is such a power of them coming in that they and the Injuns will squatch out all the white folks.
>
> —An old Tennessee woman, quoted in Christiana Holmes Tillson, *A Woman's Story of Pioneer Illinois*

At the end of Peoria's Caroline Street, where it overlooks Peoria Lake near the entrance to the Detweiller Marina, is a plaque. Placed there in 1992 by the Pimiteoui chapter of the Illinois Society of Colonial Dames, it marks the site of the first European settlement in the Illinois Country—a French fort built in 1691 to protect the fur trade along the Illinois River. The French named the fort after St. Louis, as they had an earlier structure atop Starved Rock upriver, but this new fortification was probably more widely known as Fort Pimiteoui. A settlement of French traders and missionaries accreted around that post, which in turn attracted Native Americans of various bands who set up their villages nearby.

No physical evidence of Fort Pimiteoui had survived at the surface of modern Peoria, and the archeological record that might reveal the location of the fort was imprecise. Finally, in 2001, archeologists Robert Mazrim and Dave Nolan found evidence of a fence and a cabin of types known to have been built by the French of the period, which they conjectured to be the remains of the quarters of a French or mixed-blood voyageur or of a slave whose owner's house stood nearby.

While French in construction, the house was not otherwise very French, or indeed very European. Some two hundred miles to the south of Peoria Lake, in the French towns along the Mississippi River across from today's St Louis, settled, respectable people grew wheat and corn and livestock in commercial quantities on fields like those remembered from northern France. In contrast, the Canadian Frenchmen at Peoria had been not settlers but sojourners who traded for food rather than growing it. They not only bartered with native peoples but also lived among them, speaking their languages and raising families with them. In cultural terms the traders were probably as much Native American as French, as were, in genetic terms, their children by Indian wives, the mixed-bloods known as *métis*. The barren earth at his cabin site confirmed Mazrim's guess that, French or not, the people who had lived in it were not what is usually thought of as European. The Colonial Dames would have been disappointed.[1]

SLICING THE CAKE

Measured by the duration of Native Americans' tenancy, mid-Illinois is an Indian land. If we imagine the human occupation of the region to have consumed but one hour, Euro-Americans did not arrive until fifty-eight minutes had passed, and the newcomers did not fully dispossess the peoples now called Native Americans until thirty seconds before the hour.

Wherever archeologists have looked in mid-Illinois (usually where someone wants to build a road), they have found signs of this former human occupation. When the Central Illinois Expressway (today's Interstate 72) was laid out from Jacksonville to Quincy in the 1970s, archeologists discovered along the way evidence of nearly six hundred prehistoric villages, special-purpose camps, and burial grounds.[2] Fulton County is thought to harbor the greatest concentration of prehistoric archaeological sites in Illinois—the remains of some three thousand mounds and villages from all phases of the state's prehistoric occupation. One of the signal artifacts of Midwest prehistory is the Macoupin Creek Figure Pipe, a stone effigy carved from reddish-brown bauxite or fireclay mined in eastern Missouri; it was found in a stone-box grave along the bluffs of Macoupin Creek north of Plainview in 1876 or 1877.[3]

Mid-Illinois moreover is the site of two of the most important Native American archeological sites on the continent. Several archaeological and cultural "traditions"—the term used to denote the complex of tool-making techniques, building styles, and the like by which various people make themselves known to us in the absence of a written record—were originally defined using artifacts and other data from the region.

No archeological site in North America has contributed more chapters to the narrative of prehistoric mid-Illinois than the farm of Theodore and Mary Koster. American Indians used this site in the lower Illinois River valley six

Digging not only down but also backward in time. The famous archeological excavation at the farm of Mary and Teed Koster in Greene County revealed remains of eleven settlements spanning more than six thousand years. New discoveries about ancient death rituals, food preparation, and the domestication of animals made there earned the dig site a place on the National Register of Historic Places. PHOTO BY DEL BASTON. COURTESY OF THE CENTER FOR AMERICAN ARCHEOLOGY.

miles south of Eldred in southwest Greene County with only a few interruptions from eighty-seven hundred years ago until around eight hundred years ago. They left behind remnants of their stays, covering the discarded with the new, each buried in turn by mud or refuse until there accumulated a layer cake of human debris more than thirty feet deep.

Digging from 1968 until 1979, scientists from the Center for American Archeology and from Northwestern University found traces of at least fifteen successive Indian communities. The site harbored no temples, no graves filled with gold or jewelry, only the discarded leftovers from mundane activities such as farming, hunting, and toolmaking. These humble items proved more valuable to archeologists than symbols of wealth and power. That North America's indigenous peoples had elaborate and organized social structures and a continental trade network was understood; the results of excavation at the Koster farm suggested that each of these traits of a complex civilization had evolved much earlier than previously thought. The earliest evidence of permanent houses yet known in North America (around 4000 B.C.), of domesticated dogs, of the use of stone grinders to prepare food, and of the use of a cemetery to dispose of the deceased were all found at Koster. One town, which for a time (around 800 A.D.) numbered more than one thousand inhabitants, was built before the builders had mastered what we know as agriculture—a contradiction of the long-held assumption that the concentrated populations of town could be sustained only by cultivated plants.

STRONGHOLDS OF THE PLAIN

The Illinois territory described by the first Europeans was dotted with earthen mounds that plainly were (to quote one local history) the product of the "labors of an ancient people."[4] Mounds were especially numerous on the bluffs along the Illinois and Mississippi river valleys and up and down the Macoupin Creek valley. Some of the Midwest's best examples of circular earthworks, flat-topped pyramids, and conical mounds survive in Quincy's Indian Mounds Park.[5] Beardstown took root on the spot that French explorers had named "Beautiful Mound Village." Rockwell Mound in Havana—the second-largest Indian mound in the Midwest—covers nearly two acres and today stands fourteen feet high.[6] Many other earthen structures are known.

The artifacts dug up from inside some of the mounds made plain their human origins, but their age and purpose remained mysterious, as did the identity of their builders. Puzzled Euro-Americans often refused to believe that ancestors of the Indians they knew could have constructed such large structures; they credited them instead to a more sophisticated race long vanished. (To some extent, this conclusion was convenient, the Indians' evident fall from grace justifying their expulsion by white people.) As for the local Native Americans, they were as mystified by the mounds as seventeenth-century inhabitants of Egypt must have been by the stone pyramids in their midst.

Poets were inspired to explain what science could not. William Cullen Bryant saw mid-Illinois in 1832 when he visited relatives around Jacksonville. The experience inspired a poem, "The Prairies," in which he imagined that the region's mound builders had been vanquished by roaming hunter tribes, "warlike and fierce."

> The platforms where they worshipped unknown gods,
> The barriers which they builded from the soil
> To keep the foe at bay—till o'er the walls
> The wild beleaguerers broke, and, one by one,
> The strongholds of the plain were forced, and heaped
> With corpses.

Much of the story that Bryant imagined has since been told more accurately by anthropologists relying on the only historical record these preliterate societies left behind—stains in the soil, bone fragments in long-cold fires, broken pots. Their version is less romantic and more complicated. The mounds were built over millennia not by a single people but by several, for purposes that evolved with the cultures of the people who built them. Some mounds were built for communication, some for defense, some for ritual; some mounds might have served all three ends. Many mounds simply accumulated over time as dead from a village were buried one atop another, but the largest ones housed complex tombs or served as platforms for ceremonial buildings—undertakings possible only in organized societies with surplus labor.

Alas for future anthropologists, the relics excited more than curiosity among Euro-Americans. Burial mounds in the latter 1800s were targeted by collectors who prized as curios the pots and bowls and necklaces that Native Americans often had interred with the dead. A veterinarian from Chandlerville was said to have taken so many rare unbroken pots from mounds in Fulton County that he filled an old high-sided farm wagon three times. The great mound at Beardstown was made less great by hunters of arrowheads and trinkets. In McDonough County's Bethel Township, a group of mounds yielded bones, stone hatchets, spear and arrow heads "and occasionally some trifling ornament, which were evidently used for burial purposes."[7]

Scientific investigations of these mounds did not begin until the 1920s, when archaeologists from the University of Chicago were attracted to a group of about thirty mounds at what they dubbed the Ogden-Fettie site in Fulton County. Excavation revealed them to have been built during the Middle Woodland period that lasted roughly two millennia and ended some two thousand years ago. The innovations of the Woodland culture were transformative, ranging from making pottery to cultivating and processing plants for food. Burial rituals suggest the Woodland people had an evolved spiritual life, and they engaged in trade on the continental scale. Remains of the dead at Ogden-Fettie were placed in open tombs with log walls, which were then roofed over and buried. In addition to crematory basins filled with the ashes of many individuals, the largest of these tombs contained the skeletal remains of a male buried with necklaces of pearl, bone, and shell beads and copper tools of materials from the Gulf of Mexico and the northern Great Lakes.[8]

"Mississippian" is the name given to the culture of a later people who flourished in western mid-Illinois and the rest of the Mississippi River valley seven to eight hundred years ago. The Mississippians' mastery of maize agriculture generated food surpluses that freed labor sufficient to build the sprawling Indian metropolis of Cahokia on the Illinois side of the Mississippi River floodplain near modern St. Louis.[9] Emigrants from Cahokia founded new mid-Illinois settlements in the valleys of the middle Illinois and the Spoon Rivers, and established ones were reshaped by contact with these urban, sophisticated people.

One of these outposts was in Fulton County. A sprawling burial mound containing the remains of perhaps three thousand people was created on the crest of a bluff more than ninety feet above the Illinois River valley floor by Mississippian people living in villages in the bottomland. Eight hundred years later it became the property of the Dickson family. Pots and jewelry from Indian burials were coveted locally, but the bones of the dead that accompanied them usually were regarded as little more than trash. Don Dickson, however, was a chiropractor and found such remains professionally fascinating. He carefully exposed the burials of 234 individuals for study, for the most part leaving the bones as he found them. His private explorations in what became known as Dickson Mounds anticipated later science, which learned to derive from bones not only the deceased's age and sex but also his or her diet, disease history, and likely cause of death.

Dickson Mounds overlooks the spot at which the Spoon River empties onto the Illinois. The origin of the former river's name is ultimately Indian, as the mussels whose shells they used to dip food grew plentifully there. Modern Euro-American peoples know the Spoon River as the setting for one of the best-known works of verse in the United States, *Spoon River Anthology*, by Edgar Lee Masters. As anyone who survived high school lit class knows, *Anthology* is a collection of more than two hundred apocryphal epitaphs from the graveyard of an imagined Spoon River town. As anthropologist Robert L. Hall explains in *An Archaeology of the Soul*,

> There are . . . pre-Columbian American Indian cemeteries in the Spoon River country that are next to unknown in literary circles, but whose stories are every bit as poignant as those from the graves to which Edgar Lee Masters . . . called attention. The Dicksons were able to convey the picture of pre-Columbian Indians as human beings who lived in families, loved, laughed, cried, prayed, and believed in a divine creator and an afterlife, and for many white visitors to Dickson Mounds this came as an unexpected revelation.[10]

The burials at Dickson Mounds stopped at about the same time that Cahokia and its satellite towns along the Illinois River went into decline. Why the Mississippian culture collapsed is unknown, although debate on the topic remains lively. (Religious or political upheaval, warfare, climatic shifts, and

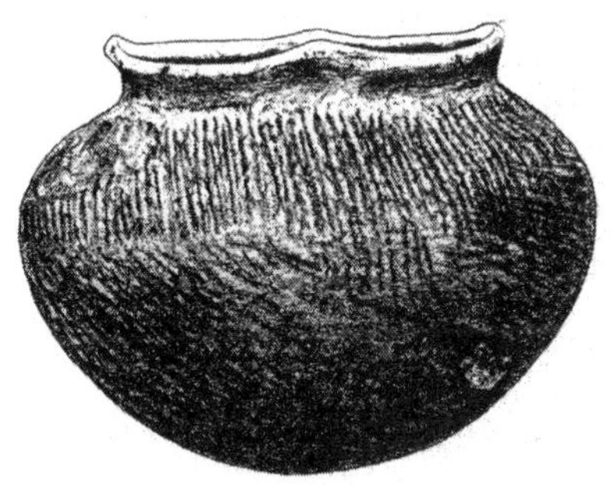

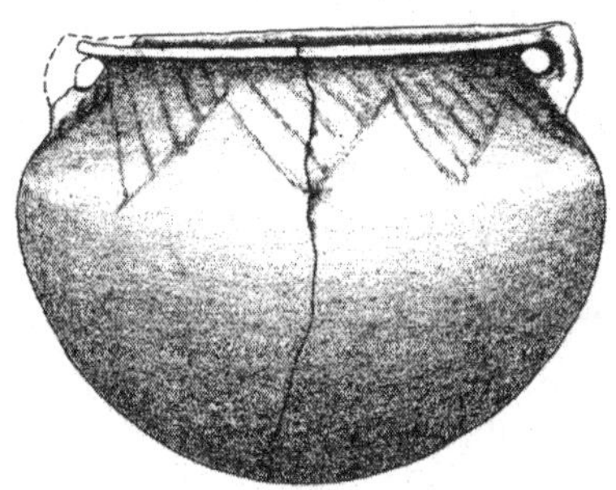

Dickson jars. Jars and beakers of fired clay were often buried with the dead in Dickson Mounds. These were not specially made symbolic funerary vessels but everyday ceramics, apparently intended for use by the dead in the afterlife. FROM *THE PREHISTORY OF DICKSON MOUNDS: THE DICKSON EXCAVATION* BY ALAN D. HARN, 2ND ED. (SPRINGFIELD: ILLINOIS STATE MUSEUM, 1980), 109. COURTESY ILLINOIS STATE MUSEUM.

disease have been suggested.) The demise of the culture, after having dominated this part of Illinois for some three hundred years longer than the tenure to date of the most recent wave of people, the Euro-Americans, might be the most valuable of the lessons they have to teach us.

"HISTORICAL" NATIVE AMERICANS

The story of Illinois's more recent Indian past has not yet found its Gibbon, unfortunately, as the history of these people is as complex, if acted out on a smaller scale, as that of Europe in its more unsettled eras. When Euro-Americans began trekking into mid-Illinois from eastern states in the 1820s, they encountered not only relics of societies long dead but also people who were very much alive. After the Mississippian cultural blossoming faded, the region was unsettled in every sense. Newcomers from west of the Mississippi showed up after a climate shift turned much of mid-Illinois into a version of the grasslands that these people had learned how to exploit. Warfare between these Oneota people and remnant Mississippians from roughly 1200 to 1400 A.D. appears to have left mid-Illinois largely vacant of permanent occupiers. The cultural ancestors of the people the French encountered were a forest people from the east; they had traded with the Oneota, learned from them how to hunt bison, and in time themselves pushed west into mid-Illinois around 1500.

These were the native peoples from whom the modern State of Illinois takes its name (via a French rendition). The Illiniwek[11] (also known as the Illini or Illinois) were a confederation of five main groups the French called *familles* based on culture and kinship ties. In the middle part of the state these included the Peoria, Tamaroa, Kaskaskia, and Cahokia. Aggressive, prosperous, and proud, they had adapted intelligently to the opportunities offered by a new terrain and new game in an empty land, and they were the proprietors, if not the rulers, of much of the mid-continent in the seventeenth century. The Illinois River valley was the center of the Illiniwek realm, and it was there that fur trader Louis Jolliet and missionary Jacques Marquette encountered them in 1673 as those Frenchmen canoed through the region.

White men's diseases and wars with the Iroquois over control of the fur trade decimated the Illiniwek. Perhaps fifteen thousand strong at their peak, they numbered six thousand in 1700 or so, and in 1736 the French counted fewer than three thousand. By the summer of 1832, it is thought that the once great Illiniwek nation had been reduced to two tribes totaling fewer than two hundred people.[12] The survivors became idle, dependent, and dissolute. (Edgar Lee Masters's grandmother recalled Indians begging at her back door in the years before their final exodus to new lands in the western states.) Their past is largely forgotten in their former domain, even at the principal university of the city named after the Peorias, whose students cheer their Bradley Braves on the sports fields.

The Illiniwek lands were soon occupied by people from the north and east who had themselves been unmoored from their homelands by the white presence in eastern North America. The Native Americans resident in mid-Illinois at the time of American settlement thus were as demographically diverse as the Euro-Americans. Some twenty tribe-like bands are known to have hunted, farmed, and sometimes battled in mid-Illinois in what Euro-Americans know as the historic era. The Miami and Potawatomi settled in the eastern parts of mid-Illinois along the Kankakee River, where they were joined by bands of the Ottawa and Chippewa nations. The Illinois River was rich in food, and it was a convenient thoroughfare for cross-continental travel and trade, so its banks too were much used for village sites. Local histories describe the Illinois River bottomland between California Bend on the Spoon River and Liverpool as one continuous campsite for the Sauk, Fox, Chippewa, Kickapoo, and Potawatomi.

The Indians of the historic period were as prone to factionalism as old-time Baptists. The Kickapoo in Illinois had divided into two self-governing bands, separated mainly by their views on whether and to what degree to accommodate white people. The Prairie Band occupied a stretch of mid-Illinois in today's Logan, McLean, and DeWitt counties running from the headwaters of the Sangamon River in modern-day McLean County westward to Peoria Lake. The Prairie Kickapoo had several villages, but their principal town was the fortified Grand Village that is thought to have stood about five miles northeast of the McLean County village of LeRoy.

The other Kickapoo faction was known as the Vermilion Band, who maintained a village where the Middle Fork and Salt Fork Rivers meet in today's Vermilion County. The leader of that band was Kennekuk, a medicine man also known as the Kickapoo Prophet. He was among the Native American leaders who encouraged peaceful resistance to white encroachment. As we will see in chapter 6, Kennekuk borrowed from Christian sects as they borrowed from each other, and urged on his people meditation and abstinence from the liquor that had proven a fatal vice to so many Indians.

Lottie E. Jones, in her 1911 history of Vermilion County, observed of the Potawatomi that their manners and dialect were rough and barbarous compared with those of other Algonquin tribes[13] (an opinion echoed by many of their countrypeople back east when describing most early American settlers). By 1810 the territory of the Potawatomi stretched down the Illinois River to

Peoria Lake and along the Kankakee and upper Wabash Rivers. Between the Illinois and Mackinaw Rivers in present Tazewell County there were at least three villages; one, at the head of Peoria Lake where Chillicothe now stands, was the village of Gomo, an influential chief. Another Potawatomi town stood near Cayuga, now an unincorporated community in Livingston County northeast of Pontiac.[14] The most extensive of the Potawatomi settlements along the Kankakee was Rock Village, inside the present-day Kankakee State Park.

This last, a village of fifty warriors, was led by the war chief Main Poc, or Withered Hand, who was implacably anti-American. The families of the state's transplanted Tennesseans, Kentuckians, and Ohioans had been fighting Indians for land for generations. In mid-Illinois they confronted Native Americans resentful of the loss of their lands to dubious treaty makers and the loss of their ways to whiskey. The result was sporadic skirmishing along the frontier that extended to captive taking and the burning of crops and houses by both sides. In the end, white people's guns drove the native peoples from mid-Illinois, not because white people used them against Indians but because Indians used them against game animals. The latter's traditional ways had begun to collapse soon after their first contact with this European technology, because while guns brought plenty at first, their use resulted in the eventual overhunting of game on which they had come to depend.

Widespread hunger was not the only result. Without furs all the Indians had left to trade for guns and kettles and axes was land. Title to Indian lands in mid-Illinois had been ceded to the Americans by the Kaskaskia in the Treaty of Vincennes in 1803. However, the Kickapoo, with the Peoria, complained that the Kaskaskia had no authority to treat for them. A subsequent pact, signed in Edwardsville in 1819 by Indians claiming to be Vermilion Kickapoo chiefs, relinquished the former's rights in exchange for an annuity and land in Missouri. That agreement proved as momentous for mid-Illinois history as it did for the Kickapoo. By clarifying land ownership, this cession, plus a similar cession by the Peoria, opened up to white settlement more than eight million acres of mid-Illinois that included the future sites of Decatur and Danville, Peoria and Springfield, Bloomington and Jacksonville.

Extinguishing Indian title to mid-Illinois land did not immediately end the Indians' presence, in spite of treaty language that obliged them to leave. As late as 1828, Kickapoo and Delaware still dwelt in villages about three miles south of the eventual site of Lexington in McLean County. As its name commemorates, Indian Grove Township in Livingston County was the site of a Kickapoo village, this one home to more than six hundred persons in

1828–30. In the early 1830s, Kickapoo also camped around a spring in the vicinity of what is now Second Street and Springfield Avenue in Champaign. In Vermilion County, Kickapoo gathered in a village near the confluence of Salt Fork and the Middle Fork of the Vermilion on land that today is the site of Kennekuk County and Kickapoo State Parks.

Kennekuk's Vermilion band were peaceful farmers, and for years American authorities did not press them to go. The outbreak in northern Illinois and Wisconsin of the Black Hawk War in 1832 made it impolitic to treat so generously any Indian band in mid-Illinois, however pacific, and Kennekuk was pressed to sign a new treaty that obliged the Vermilion Kickapoo to leave immediately for Kansas. That march west was the final farewell of the Native Americans dwelling in the region.

The physical remains of the long occupation of historic Native Americans in mid-Illinois are scattered and sparse, but their presence is colorfully recalled in local place names. Maroa, Chebanse, Senachwine, Minonk, Onarga, Pesotum, Tuscola, and Wauponsee add poetry to the dull prose of white place names.[15] In Lincoln the Logan County Chamber of Commerce maintains its office on Kickapoo Street. Indian Field Cemetery in McLean County's Lexington Township was named after a nearby Indian cornfield noted in an 1824 land survey. The name Macoupin comes from the Indian word *macupiana*, or "white potato," for the wild artichoke that grew along the banks of the county's waterways. Shick Shack Hill in Menard County was named for a neighborly Potawatomi chief who, according to Edgar Lee Masters, used chants and incantations to protect the white man's crops from corn borers.

FRANCE ON THE ILLINOIS

The state now known as Illinois was revealed to Europe by Frenchmen. The governor of New France, as that nation's North American possessions were known, sought a Northwest Passage across the North American continent to the Orient. Among the explorers who pushed south and west to find it from the French stronghold on the St. Lawrence River were Jolliet and Marquette. In 1673 the pair—the first but not the last of those who would pass through Illinois looking for riches to the West—paddled through Peoria Lake on their way back from their explorations of the Mississippi River.

As noted, Peoria, a city with a Native American name and an all-American reputation, was one of the earliest outposts of French (and thus European) civilization in mid-America. In 1679 two of Illinois's great men—René-Robert Cavelier, Sieur de La Salle, and Henry de Tonti (also *Tonty*)—ventured down the Illinois River with thirty other men to establish trading posts. A location on Peoria Lake had much to recommend it. The larger French trading system was anchored by Montreal and New Orleans, and Peoria offered easy water access to both. The traders attracted Native Americans, and over a century the French built several forts to, variously, defend against hostile Indians, to protect Indians against other Indians, and later to protect both against the British. The Americans would do the same in time, when they defended the area against the British during the War of 1812.

The first of the Peoria forts was built in the winter of 1680 on the southeast bank of the Illinois River just below Peoria Lake. Meant as a base for a French expedition to the Gulf of Mexico, it was christened by LaSalle Fort Crevecoeur, or "broken heart." Descriptions of it as one of the first permanent European buildings in the middle of America are generous; Fort Crevecoeur was damaged by mutinous workmen only three months after it was built, and the wreckage was later burned by Indians. In its impermanence, and in the violence it inspired, the fort is a fair symbol of the European effort to bring their civilization to the Illinois country.

A decade after Fort Crevecoeur had been abandoned, in the winter of 1691–92, Tonti returned to the area. La Salle in 1683 had based his operation upriver at Fort St. Louis at Starved Rock, near an Illiniwek town whose population had stripped the area of game and wood for fires. Tonti built a new Fort St. Louis, today remembered as Fort Pimiteoui, whose protection attracted local Indians being menaced by marauding Iroquois and who in turn attracted missionaries. The construction of Tonti's fort gave Peoria a past that was a century old by the time the recording of history is usually reckoned to have started in the rest of the state when Euro-American settlers began to arrive in substantial numbers in the early 1800s. Certainly few other Illinois towns are entitled to put on a tercentenary celebration, as Peoria did in 1991.

All the outposts at this spot on the Illinois, be they fort, trading post, or village, proved evanescent. Their populations ebbed and flowed with the seasons and with trade and, just as often, the temper of the surrounding Indians. Fort Pimiteoui languished after a few years of prosperity and was abandoned; from its stump was thought to have sprouted a settlement known as the Old Village, which in 1750 was home to twelve hundred Native Americans tended by a small Jesuit mission.

The Illinois country had become nominally British in 1763 after the British victory in the French and Indian War gave them possession of that part of New France, but British rule had little effect on life at the French enclave at Peoria until the American War for Independence. Then the Old Village was attacked by Native Americans siding with the American rebels. The original settlement, which was dwindling in any event, was abandoned around 1796.

George Rogers Clark, whose Virginia militia had captured the Illinois territory for that colony, appointed French trader Jean Baptiste Maillet the military commander in 1778. Maillet built a stockaded house a mile and a half south of the Old Village, approximately where downtown Peoria is today, thus founding the fourth of the known Peoria habitations. The new one was known by the French variously as *Au Pied du Lac* (at the foot of the lake) and *La Ville de Maillet*. Gradually, the inhabitants of the Old Village joined Maillet there, and a thriving community of mostly traders and boatmen took root for a time. Laid out and built in the French style, the village included in its essential infrastructure a winepress, an underground wine vault, and a Catholic chapel.[16]

Future commentators would hold up Peoria during the French interregnum as an early and successful working out of what is now known as multiculturalism. Historian James Davis describes the hybrid French and Indian world at the foot of Peoria Lake as a middle-ground culture based on accommodation rather than annihilation. What moderns find admirable was not thought so by many Americans of the time, however. Ann Durkin Keating, in her history of the Indian uprising in Illinois during the War of 1812, points out that American militia in the area regarded the distinction between French Canadian traders and the Native Americans to be meaningless,[17] targeting both indiscriminately. La Ville de Maillet was wrecked in fighting between American militiamen and Indians allied with the British during the War of 1812 and was never rebuilt. Indeed, one of the reasons no permanent settlement took root at Peoria between 1680 and 1813 was the tendency of the area to explode in violence. One fortified structure after another had to be built in the area during that period, because one faction after another kept wrecking them. The last fort was burned down in 1818 and never replaced, it being thought no longer necessary.

The end of formal hostilities between Americans and British after the War of 1812 allowed the resumption of commerce at Peoria, but now it was the new Americans (specifically John Jacob Astor's American Fur Trading Company) who were behind the counter. A few French traders lingered in the area until the Illinois government expelled all Native Americans after the 1832 Black Hawk War,[18] after which the French, who once dominated this part of the state, were relegated to being just another immigrant group. Apart from a few relics and some hard-to-pronounce place names, little evidence of the pioneering French immigrants has endured beyond the invaluable records of the encounters by French explorers, missionaries, and traders with Native Americans.

A CLASSIC MIXING ZONE

Light-skinned people first came to stay permanently in mid-Illinois at the dawn of the nineteenth century, but Indian claims on the land and the fighting that attended the War of 1812 stymied mass migration by Euro-Americans. As a result, at statehood in 1818 the region averaged fewer than two residents per square mile. Most of those early arrivers were poor hunter-farmers who cleared and plowed their way from the south up the valleys of the Illinois River's tributary creeks into Greene and Macoupin Counties. Most numerous in the region by 1850 were Kentuckians, followed by Virginians, Tennesseans, and North Carolinians. Their Southern roots show in the names they gave to the region's new places. Pike County was named by nostalgic immigrants from Pike County, Kentucky. When Warren County was split in 1841, residents of the new county voted to name it Henderson, since many of them were late of Henderson, Kentucky. Wataga, in Knox County, is a corruption of town names in Tennessee and North Carolina. One could go on.

"Southerner" is an imprecise term when applied to mid-Illinoisans from south of the Ohio River. Geographer John C. Hudson mapped the birthplaces of the early migrants to Sangamon County and found that while most of 245 single individuals and heads of families who settled there before 1830 were born south of the Mason-Dixon line, their families' American sagas had begun in the East. After arriving via the ports of Philadelphia or Baltimore, these ancestors settled first in southeastern Pennsylvania, then migrated down the Great Valley, as the Shenandoah Valley in Virginia was known; after they entered the continent's interior through the Roanoke Gap they made farms on the Carolina Piedmont before moving on to the Bluegrass region of Kentucky.[19]

Southerners predominated in mid-Illinois for only a few years, but the cultural influence of those founding settlers proved durable. Novelist and critic Floyd Dell grew up in the Pike County town of Barry at the end of the nineteenth century. He described it as "vaguely permeated by Southern influences—a touch of laziness, quite a lot of mud, and, like the scent of honeysuckle, a whiff of the romantic attitude toward life."[20]

Better wagon roads and the opening of the Erie Canal in 1825 opened mid-Illinois to less romantic immigrants coming from the east and north. Conspicuous among these later newcomers were the "Yankees." This term too was used loosely; to many Southerners, anyone not from the South was a Yankee. True Yankees from New England clustered in mid-Illinois towns they

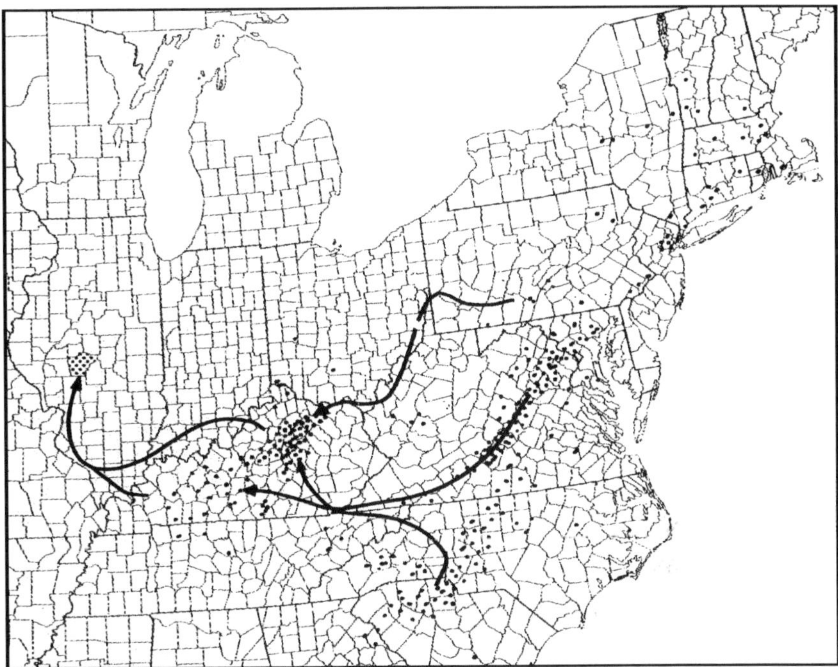

Sangamon County in-migration map. Dots indicate the birthplaces of 245 heads of families and single individuals who settled in Sangamon County before 1830. The arrows show the migration routes they and many others followed over generations as they worked their way west toward mid-Illinois. ADAPTED FROM *MAKING THE CORN BELT: A GEOGRAPHICAL HISTORY OF MIDDLE-WESTERN AGRICULTURE*, BY JOHN C. HUDSON (BLOOMINGTON: INDIANA UNIVERSITY PRESS, 1994). REPRINTED WITH PERMISSION OF INDIANA UNIVERSITY PRESS.

gave names like Pittsfield and Quincy. Stonington, in Christian County, was settled by families from Stonington, Connecticut, who arrived in 1837. Delavan in Tazewell County was named for founder Edward Cornelius Delavan, a land promoter and temperance advocate from Rhode Island. The first settlers in Waverly were New Englanders who arrived in Morgan County during the early 1830s. The Yankee presence is betrayed architecturally as well; the town squares and spired churches of several towns in western mid-Illinois reflect the founders' intentions to re-create the life they knew back home in the new land; the historic Alexis Phelps House, built in 1832–33 in Oquawka, is only one of many New England–style houses in the region.

Southerners and Yankees were the most culturally distinct of mid-Illinois's American transplants, but the most numerous immigrants were harder to characterize. These were the Midlanders, or immigrants raised in what has been called the Midland-Midwest culture—Ohioans, Pennsylvanians, New Yorkers, Indianans, New Jerseyans.[21] Jersey County was named after the state from which many of the early settlers emigrated. Beardstown's Thomas Beard was an Ohioan. The Montgomery County town of Litchfield honors the wonderfully named Electus Bachus Litchfield of New York, where he must have been missed.

Most of the newcomers, Northerner, Southerner, or Midlander, came from settled societies where their neighbors had been people more or less like themselves. That made them more or less unlike most of their new neighbors in mid-Illinois. Apart from a shared devotion to business, for instance, true Yankees and immigrants from the mid-Atlantic states were as unlike as each was from the French and the Indians who had previously occupied the territory. But they were more like each other than either were like the Southerners, traditionalists who resisted, indeed resented, the trends toward modernization that began in mid-Illinois in the latter 1830s. They were devoted to clan rather than community, and most were suspicious of commerce and institutions. Yankee and Southerner in particular differed over slavery, kinships, church, marriage, farming, money, politics, manners, drinking, government, taxes, even what to have for supper.

Today, historians of that period laud the Southern-bred pioneers for their hardiness and their courage, but travelers and immigrants from other places found them lazy and dissolute. Southerners squatted without qualm on government land. They ignored laws banning the selling of liquor to Indians. As for their personal habits, Eliza Farnham describes her visit to a cabin in Tazewell County occupied by a Southern man and wife and their children. "I have never seen more utter poverty or filth," she reported. "Had such physical degradation been the result of extreme poverty, the case would have excited compassion, instead of curiosity or disgust. But it was not so."[22] Miller Wetmore was an upstate New Yorker who in 1836 settled in Knox County when Galesburg was still a-building. "We are pleasently [*sic*] situated at a Mr. Roundtrees," he wrote his wife that June. "He is a Kentuckian but a verry [*sic*] fine Man."[23]

This antagonism, which was noted in almost every traveler's guide, memoir, letter home, and early history, was mutual. Among the many faults Southerners saw in Yankees was sharpness in business dealings to the point of dishonesty. Nor did the Yankees' social and religious creeds impress locals, whose views on such matters were decidedly rough-hewn. In the 1840s a journalistic rival of Jacksonville's Jonathan Baldwin Turner scorned the transplanted Massachusettsan in print as a "crack-brained, gaping, half-witted theorist

Yankee."[24] Linking Lake Michigan to the Illinois River via the Illinois and Michigan Canal was opposed by politicians of Illinois's lower latitudes out of fear that it would provide Yankees with a too-convenient path into the state's interior.

The Reverend Peter Cartwright, the fabled circuit-riding Methodist who came to Pleasant Plains by way of Kentucky, understood the antagonism in terms of the old East versus the new West rather than Yankee versus Southerner, but no Yankee needed a map to know who Cartwright was talking about. In an 1831 sermon, Cartwright said of Eastern men, "They represent this country as a vast waste, and people as very ignorant; but if I was going to shoot a fool, I would not take aim at a Western man, but would go down by the sea-shore and cock my fusee at the imps who live on oysters."[25]

Early mid-Illinois society was more a mix of North and South than a blend, and so were a lot of its people. Typical of these cultural cross-breeds was lawyer Andrew Johnston, one of Quincy's leading lights. A scion of slave-owning Virginia planters, Johnston coedited a Whig newspaper with a Connecticut native, and he introduced to the law there his nephew, who became famous as a Confederate general.

Many an Andrew Johnston made homes in antebellum mid-Illinois. John Hallwas notes helpfully that the social clash between Southern and Yankee settlers was embodied by the political clash between Stephen A. Douglas, a Vermonter, and Abraham Lincoln, a Kentuckian, but not in the ways one might expect. Lincoln was a Whig rather than a Democrat like most Southerners, he did not drink the whiskey that his fellow Kentuckians swilled like water, and he advocated Yankee values on such issues as slavery and economic development. Douglas—a whiskey-drinking New Englander who was tolerant of slavery—became the chief spokesman for the agrarian traditionalism espoused by Tennessean Andrew Jackson.[26] Such political mongrels were peculiarly qualified to be community leaders in places whose residents collectively mirrored their own complex cultural heritage.

As for the purebred Southerners and Yankees, they persisted as separate streams occupying the same space, much as the turbid Mississippi River and the clear-running Ohio do for several miles after they meet at Cairo. Members of each subculture tended to dominate their own political parties or factions as well as the professions and trades that their talents and attitudes made congenial. The Yankees often stuck to business in the towns, while many Southerners persisted in subsistence farming, often in backwaters like Macon County's Whistleville, a community of Kentucky hill people on Big Creek.

Wood mansion, 1930s. Built in 1838, the house of Quincy town builder John Wood was perfect for a mid-Illinois grandee: a Southern-style mansion built mostly by German immigrant craftsmen for the New York–born founder of a city named for a Massachusettsan. PHOTO BY PIAGET–VAN RAVENSWAAY. COURTESY LIBRARY OF CONGRESS, HISTORIC AMERICAN BUILDINGS SURVEY, HABS ILL,1-QUI,2–1.

A WELCOME EXOTICISM

Beginning in the 1830s, a fourth migration further enriched the cultural pot. Land and the prospect of a better life attracted people to mid-Illinois from places that offered little enough of either, such as northern Europe. State-backed railroad and canal building in the 1840s, for example, attracted laborers from Ireland ("vast hordes of brawny Irish"[27] in the words of Arthur Charles Cole) who were fleeing the potato famine back home. Germans settlers, arriving by river from New Orleans via St. Louis or by land or canal from Chicago, began landing in mid-Illinois beginning in the 1830s; they were followed in the 1840s by Swedes who spilled into the region from northern Illinois.

Because its biggest town was a river entrepôt, Cass County had an especially large proportion of foreigners—more than 30 percent of its population in 1850. Its main town, Beardstown, was a "foreign country," writes Douglas Meyer, where more than half the townspeople were foreign-born, two-thirds of them German.[28] The German migration into Macoupin County began in 1846; when a new courthouse was erected there in 1867, the Holy Bible placed in the cornerstone was printed in both English and German. The German craftsmen imported from St. Louis by town founder John Wood to build his grand new house blazed a trail followed by so many countrymen that as many as 80 percent of the families in today's Quincy can trace their ancestry to them wholly or in part. Chebanse, in Iroquois County, was mostly German in the years just after its founding, notwithstanding its Potawatomi name; residents of nearby Buckley (also known as Bulkley) recall how men gathered around the pot-bellied stove to converse with each other in German at the Klann Grocery while their wives shopped.[29]

Golden windmill. Immigrants to mid-Illinois built their houses and barns in the styles they knew back home. German Henry Emminga built this "Dutch smock" windmill near the Adams County town of Golden. The grindstones were quarried in Germany and shipped to Golden by steamship and ox-drawn sled. The mill remained a working one into the 1930s. COURTESY OF THE GOLDEN HISTORICAL SOCIETY.

Illinois thought it was done officially with the French after 1812, but the French were not quite done with Illinois. About 1830 fur trader Francoise Bourbonnais settled at a spot on the Kankakee River that came to be known as Bourbonnais Grove. Two years later Noel LeVasseur, a Quebec-born trader for the American Fur Company, became that area's first permanent nonnative American settler. When the area's Potawatomi were finally pushed west by the U.S. government, LeVasseur turned real estate promoter, persuading a number of his fellow French Canadians to emigrate in the 1830s and 1840s. The Bourbonnais settlement spawned similar ones nearby—St. Anne, St. Mary, L'Erable, and Papineau—in which French was still being spoken as late as World War II.[30]

After the 1830s, immigrants of any accent usually traveled in family groups, and tended to settle (often by prearrangement) near other people of like background. Enough Irish clustered around Merna in Towanda Township in McLean County to support their own church, and the distinctive music of spoken Welsh could be heard in the speech of many people living northeast of Lexington.[31] Germans made the area around Colfax and Anchor in that county distinctive in their way; East Frisians from the northwesternmost part of Germany established a settlement at Golden, near Quincy, in 1848, and by 1852 the fourteen families there formed a Lutheran congregation.[32]

New Englanders had established the colony of Andover in Henry County in 1835, but newly arriving Swedes quickly outnumbered the founders and turned it into a Scandinavian outpost. (In 1854 the Lutherans there dedicated a church they named the Jenny Lind Chapel after the famous "Swedish nightingale" who made a sizeable contribution to its construction.) Donovan, in Iroquois County, was settled substantially by Swedish immigrants; so was Paxton, the Ford County seat. Swedes settled around Kelly Township in Warren County too; in his memoir, *An America That Was*, Albert Britt recalled that they were regarded as "different and slightly amusing, but not necessarily inferior" by citizens of British stock, even if the Scandinavians spoke a queer language and had peculiar tastes in food.[33] What the Swedes thought of English food we must guess.

Galesburg's founding population was exclusively New Englanders, but in 1857 a large number of Swedes from the faltering Bishop Hill colony relocated there and were later joined by kin from the old country. (Chapter 6 has more about the Swedes at Bishop Hill.) The economy of early Illinois was more open to immigrants like the Swedes than was the region's social life, and their skills and habits made them valuable workers. In Galesburg they were fixtures at George Brown's corn planter works and on railroad crews. (Carl Sandburg's father worked in the local shops of the Chicago, Burlington, and Quincy Railroad.) Within a few years, one-sixth of the population of Galesburg was Swedish, to the consternation of local postal workers; in the 1860s the city's postmaster invented the "Swedish roll"—a revolving barrel on which letters addressed to Swedes were displayed to potential addressees, each of whom identified his or her letters to the mail clerks.

Most Galesburg Swedes went home at night to what the local histories carefully call a Swedish residential "district" or "quarter" east and north of Main Street. The Swedish district persisted well into the middle years of the twentieth century, long after housing in the rest of the city was open to Swedes.[34] Self-conscious and compact, the Swedish community was able to sustain its own church, newspaper (said to be the first Swedish-language newspaper of any kind in America), fraternal lodges, even a bank.

Most of the region's larger towns and cities had within them ethnic enclaves of this sort. A rope-making firm had promised Portuguese immigrants work on a hemp plantation outside Jacksonville that never was built. The people of Jacksonville welcomed the exiles anyway, who prospered in the Madeira and Portuguese Hill neighborhoods. Germans who lived in northeast Pekin gardened so industriously that the neighborhood became known as *Bohnen Fertel*, or Bean Town. In Quincy, new German residents clustered on the south side of town, but in this case they had not been banished there by prejudice; town founder John Wood had paid the German craftsmen who built his mansion on Twelfth Street with free or cheap lots.[35]

CHICAGO IN THE CORNFIELDS

The industrialization of the mid-Illinois economy after the Civil War altered the pace and the source of immigration. This is usually the point in Illinois histories when the focus shifts to Chicago, but immigration to mid-Illinois at the end of the nineteenth century left its cities resembling Chicago in every way but size. In his autobiography, *Always the Young Strangers*, Carl Sandburg recalled how in the Galesburg of the 1890s, then a town of twenty thousand or so, he met Swedish politicians and Irish railroad switchmen, German Jewish hoteliers and African American shoe shiners and the Italian priest at the Corpus Christi Church. The poet reported that he didn't get to know any Poles, Bohemians, Slovaks, Russians, Hungarians, Spanish, Portuguese, Mexicans, South Americans, or Filipinos—one of the few ways in which his Galesburg education was insufficient—but it was not for lack of opportunity.

The Chicago and Alton Railroad shops in Bloomington not only repaired but also built that railway's locomotives and cars, work that required skilled workers recruited from Europe. As the twentieth century began, thirteen of every hundred citizens in Springfield were foreign-born white people drawn to that city's mines and factories; in 1920 the largest foreign-born groups in the city were Germans, Russians, Britishers, and Finns.[36] However, if one counts the children of immigrants, the foreign cultural presence in the capital was more substantial, enough to leave some natives uneasy.

Coal mining attracted an especially polyglot workforce to mid-Illinois. The men who did this work around Streator and Braidwood, for example, were largely English, Irish, Scottish, and Welsh immigrants, many of whom had been miners in their native lands.[37] A now-vanished coal town in Livingston County was named Cardiff; the mining community of St. David in Fulton County was founded by a Welshman, who named it for the patron saint of Wales. Britons also made up much of the population of the mining town of Colchester in McDonough County. Society in such towns in the mid-1800s had a distinctly British tone—literally, as local custom included sing-alongs in the saloons.

Many of the thousands of immigrants pouring into Illinois from southern and eastern Europe during the closing decades of the nineteenth century had come from peasant backgrounds and were much more familiar with plows than picks and shovels. But hundreds of them, finding farmland too dear, had to seek their living underground plowing up coal seams instead. Even skilled craftsmen, who had been kept from their original trade by barriers of language or prejudice, joined the pit crews. British miners in the Colchester area were joined by Irish and Croatians, among others. In Sangamon County, as in the rest of the state, the largest single immigrant group in the mines was the Italians, but their numbers were approached by the Lithuanians. Riverton, now a suburb of Springfield, began life as a settlement of Italian coal miners and their families. Of the fifteen hundred people living in the Montgomery County town of Panama in 1910, the predominant ethnic group was Italian, but well over a dozen other nationalities were present too. In the 1890s the workforce of the McLean County Coal Company, on Bloomington's west side, included English, French, Irish, Italian, Polish, Russian, and Swedish miners.[38] The African American father of popular cabaret singer Bobby Short came to Vermilion County from Kentucky to work in coal. The name of Belgium in Vermilion County honors the homeland of its predominant early ethnic group, imported to work the mines there.

In Macoupin County's coal district, Staunton and Mt. Olive were known as German towns, as was Nokomis in Montgomery County. Throughout that two-county area, businessmen advertised in German, and public speeches were often delivered in German until well into the twentieth century.[39] Victor Hicken, a historian of the mining towns in Montgomery and Macoupin Counties, notes that, thanks to the Germans, the best bootleg beer after 1925 was thought to come from Mt. Olive. Hicken added that the best wine and pasta came from the Italians of Benld; the best home-cooked candies came from Witt, where scores of English families had settled; and the Scots in Gillespie offered the best scones and tea cakes.[40]

The noted theologian Reinhold Niebuhr was reared in Lincoln, but he was unusual only in his subsequent fame; one-third of Lincoln's nine thousand or so residents in 1900 were either born overseas or were children of immigrants, and roughly two-thirds of that group were Germans like the Neibuhrs.[41] In Tazewell County, both of the parents of future U.S. senator Everett McKinley Dirksen were born in East Frisia.[42] Longtime Republican whip of the House of Representatives Leslie Arends, raised in nearby Melvin, also had East Frisian ancestry—one biographer fancied he saw a shared East Frisian world view in the simple conservatism of both men.[43]

As a sizeable factory city that was easy to reach by river from both St. Louis and Chicago, Peoria was a popular destination for immigrants. By 1850, immigrants made up more than a quarter of the population in the county and more than a third of the city proper, which gave the Peoria area the most numerous aggregation of foreigners in the valley of the middle and lower Illinois River. Germans in particular were as important to young Peoria as the Irish were to Chicago. In the early 1900s a significant portion of Peoria's large German-speaking business community was East Frisian. Many Frisians worked in the wagon and plow works of Smith, Velde, and Company (owned by a compatriot), and there they amassed the capital to establish themselves as farmers in nearby Logan County.[44] One of the first *Turnvereine* in Illinois booked music concerts, lectures and debates, and other improving entertainments in Peoria beginning in 1851.[45] Perhaps more significant, southern Germans introduced to Peoria the craft of beer making, which gave the young city an industry and, later, an identity.

SOUTHERNERS OF COLOR

The first African American settlers in the region arrived with the first white settlers, but they cannot be said to have migrated there. Rather, they were brought as slaves or indentured servants. True, a few freedmen had made their way north, but they were never numerous in the decades before the Civil War, as Illinois was then far from welcoming to people of color.

William de Fleurville was a Haitian who came to the capital by way of Baltimore, New Orleans, and New Salem, the last being where he met and was befriended by the young Lincoln. In the capital, de Fleurville (who was more widely known as Billy Florville) was well known and respected as a musician and active church member and investor; when Lincoln left for Washington in 1861, he bade "Billy the Barber" a personal good-bye.[46] Florville is the only African American resident of Springfield mentioned in the best-selling Lincoln biographies of their respective generations, Benjamin Thomas's *Abraham Lincoln* and Stephen Oates's *With Malice toward None*. However, when Lincoln left Springfield for the White House in 1861, African Americans there numbered more than two hundred, or about 5 percent of the population.

Historians of the period have begun to look again at these black Springfieldians because of the role they might have played in Lincoln's evolving understanding of the race issue in America. Springfield historian Richard E. Hart notes that Lincoln was the friend and neighbor of some of these people, the lawyer for others, and the employer of yet others. Jamieson Jenkins was a freeman originally from North Carolina, who moved to Springfield in the mid-1840s. He lived a half-block south of the Lincolns on Eighth Street. He is best known to history as the man who drove Lincoln's carriage to the train on the day he left Springfield, but perhaps Jenkins ought to be remembered for helping convey runaway slaves from Springfield to Bloomington on their way to Canada.

African American immigrants tended toward the towns, where they lived amicably enough because their small numbers posed no threat to their white neighbors. African American freedman Frank McWhorter (also *McWorter*) was unusual in seeking a rural life. "Free Frank," an industrious and ambitious man who had purchased the freedom of the rest of his entire family, in 1830 bought a farm in Pike County's Hadley Township and in 1836 platted 144 lots three miles east of Barry, composing a town he called New Philadelphia. McWhorter's settlement is probably not the first black-founded town in the United States, if by "town" one means an incorporated place.[47] However, any settlement developed by a black man was rare. (See chapter 4 for more on McWhorter.)

In 1860 a significant part of Illinois's African American population of under eight thousand people lived in mid-Illinois. Of the only nine towns in the state that year with at least one hundred black residents, five were in the region—Springfield, Jacksonville, Quincy, Bloomington, and Peoria. Postwar industrialization and the adoption of the Thirteenth Amendment after the Civil War (which forced the repeal of the State of Illinois's racist black codes) caused the region's black population between the end of the Civil War and the start of World War I to boom. Jacksonville, Danville, and Peoria were among the cities that saw a rapid increase in black residents from 1900 to 1910.

Antebellum mid-Illinois had no black ghettoes, there being not enough black people to fill one. (Many African Americans lived in white neighborhoods as servants in the houses of their employers.) As their numbers rose, African Americans, like other ethnic groups, tended to gather in racially distinct neighborhoods. In Jacksonville, that neighborhood was the district southwest of the square known locally as Africa; in Springfield it was the Black Belt east of downtown; in Galesburg it was the Negro quarter.[48]

In each such community there evolved a parallel society that mirrored the larger white society from which black people had been largely excluded. It had its own schools and social clubs, its own fraternal organizations and churches, indeed its own economy, which created opportunities for black businesspeople from saloon keepers and barbers to undertakers. But while proportionately larger than it had been, the region's new African American population was still relatively modest, as the rate of white in-migration outpaced the black one during the years of the latter's growth.

VARIANT CULTURES

Is it possible to detect some characteristic traits of the mid-Illinoisan that owes to the region's peculiar mix of populations? This mingling had resulted in fruitful social and cultural cross-fertilization long before the Euro-Americans showed up. The people whose remains were found in the Dickson Mounds area had been relatively primitive Late Woodland peoples who had adopted many aspects (such as ceramics technology) of the more advanced Mississippian culture.[49] The result was what anthropologists call a variant culture, not quite like either of the two cultures that created it. The historic Illiniwek are thought to have added traditions of the Siouan peoples of the Plains—bison hunting, the calumet ceremony—to their own Algonquin ways from the forested Great Lakes and became a people who lived and looked like neither, to the confusion of French explorers.[50]

In his fine study of the cultural origins of the Corn Belt, geographer John C. Hudson pointed out that Corn Belt farmers who came to mid-Illinois from the Upland South—farmers who were themselves ultimately of English, Scotch-Irish, or German backgrounds—brought half the world on their wagons to mid-Illinois.

> They built cabins, barns, corn cribs, smokehouses, and a variety of other small buildings in the fashion of log pens, following the practices brought to North America by the Savo-Karelian Finns who came to New Sweden on the Delaware River in the 1640s. Their cattle and swine included breeds that had come to the New World with the Spanish years before English colonies were planted. . . . And, most distinctively, this group of migrants threading the gaps leading west from the Great Valley carried sacks of Dent corn, the high-yielding Mexican race that was probably [also] introduced to the southeastern United States by the sixteenth-century Spanish.[51]

Mid-Illinoisans learned to accommodate each other over time, often unwittingly, sometimes begrudgingly. The later Yankees were obliged to shape their rather narrow notions of community to the individualistic, egalitarian society of the West. The Southerners had to adapt to the social forces unleashed by unbridled commerce that made money rather than kinship the basis of relations. Americans of whatever origin had to accustom themselves to different languages and different religions. This was not always done with grace, but it was done, and the result was a new culture whose distinctiveness lay in its lack of distinctiveness.

CHAPTER TWO

Eden Despoiled: Nature's Economy in Mid-Illinois

> There has been a wicked destruction of the forest trees in Vermilion county during the past thirty years.
> —Lottie E. Jones, *History of Vermilion County, Illinois*, 1911

John Burlend came from Yorkshire to Pike County with his wife Rebecca and their five children in 1831. Recalling the forests of that spot, Rebecca wrote, "Every thing here bears the mark of ancient undisturbed repose. . . . [W]hen the woodman with his axe enters these territories for the first time, he cannot resist the impression that he is about to commit a trespass on the virgin loveliness of nature, that he is going to bring into captivity what has been free for centuries."[1]

Trespass they did nonetheless. Early travelers to the region in the new nineteenth century saw all of mid-Illinois as a sort of new Eden (to borrow a phrase historian Robert P. Howard used to describe the Sangamon River valley), because all that humans needed was free for the taking. The region had rivers like the Illinois that were teeming with fish and turtles, meadows in which deer traveled in herds, forests festooned with berry bushes and trees that yielded firewood, nuts, honey hives, sugary sap, and—to the extent that hogs found rich pickin's on the forest floor—pork.

The Native Americans knew all that, of course; their culture for thousands of years revolved around the annual cycle of collecting these riches, and even after they mastered rudimentary farming, they continued to add to the pot with annual winter hunting trips and harvests of nuts and sugar. The early Euro-Americans' economy was only relatively more sophisticated. Skilled tradesman practiced handcrafts in the towns and cities, but the only economic enterprises done on a large scale before the 1850s or so were based on the simple harvesting of the wealth that nature provided—taking rather than making. Frontiersmen and women grazed cattle on prairie grasses, collected salt from saline springs, gathered honey and berries, netted fish, cut down local woods for lumber and firewood, and tapped sweet sap from groves of sugar maples.

Collectively these enterprises were not industries; individually each barely qualified as a business. They were more like hunting and gathering, Euro-American style. Capital requirements were few, seldom extending beyond some iron kettles, an ax or a saw, a flat-bottomed boat, and some second-hand nets. Whatever the product, the harvesting was heedless and often frenetic and usually led to the exhaustion of the resource and the collapse of the trade. This cycle, in its brevity and its heedlessness, would characterize much of the region's later industrial phase.

THE FIRST COMMODITY

The first commodity sold in quantity in mid-Illinois was mid-Illinois. Surveying the land, financing its purchase, recording its sale, outfitting and sheltering travelers looking for land, then supplying the tools needed to turn raw land into homesteads—for years the land itself nourished the region's rudimentary economy as richly as it nourished its people.

The contrast of the region's riches to the guttered and exhausted soils of Illinois's southern counties was unknown to all but a few cattle herders and traders until the War of 1812. Militiamen who traipsed into mid-Illinois in pursuit of Britain's Indian allies that year spread the word, and when Indian resistance to white encroachment collapsed, the wagons started rolling north. However, it was not until 1814 that any land could be purchased from the government in Illinois, its sale having to wait until the land was properly surveyed, which took years.

Until the surveyors finished with their chains, the one thousand or so people living in Morgan County in 1823 were, like so many of their neighbors across the region, technically squatters.[2] While the newcomers had no official rights to the land they occupied, they enjoyed unofficial squatter's rights, conferred by the custom of the locals. Any family that hacked a field out of woods and built a house on it was considered to have thus earned ownership, and anybody who tried to buy it out from under them would have to answer to the neighbors, most of whom had taken possession of their plots in the same way.

In 1813 Congress acknowledged these realities by decreeing that settlers who had actually inhabited and cultivated a tract of land in the territory were granted the right to buy as much as a quarter section of it at the minimum official price once public sales commenced. The problem was a lot of those people either lacked the money (the frontier had a practically cashless economy) or balked at buying land they had come to regard as theirs by right. They were even less inclined to surrender the land when it was purchased by others.

Those others often were speculators. An impecunious Congress had awarded to veterans of the War of 1812 warrants in lieu of cash that would be redeemed for three and a half million acres in fourteen counties west of the Illinois River. Few veterans were willing or able to farm land so remote from the rest of the country, and most sold their right to it for as little as sixty cents an acre. Congress in 1850 gave millions more acres of unsellable "swamp lands" to state governments; lacking the means to drain them, the states, including Illinois, sold off those lands to speculators at bargain prices.

Most of the early encomiums to the health, the climate, and the scenery of mid-Illinois were written by speculators trying to persuade someone to buy their piece of it. John Mason Peck quotes from a Springfield booster in 1837: "The country here is beautiful—equal in native attractions though not in classic recollections to the scenes I visited and admired in Italy. The vale of Arno is not more beautiful than the valley of Sangamon, with its lonely groves and murmuring brooks and flowing meads."[3] The prospect of purchasing flowing meads at the government price would excite anyone—and the prospect of selling them at a higher price excited them even more.

To aid in the construction of the Illinois Central (IC) Railroad's Centralia-Chicago route through the then largely desolate Grand Prairie, Congress in 1850 granted to the State of Illinois a lavish subsidy in the form of 2.5 million acres of public land in eastern mid-Illinois, to be granted to the IC to sell and thus defray construction costs. Much of this land the firm sold outright to homesteading farm families at prices low enough to entice settlement, but the company also invited capitalists to purchase from this treasure without limit, and many did, anticipating making fortunes by renting it out to tenant farmers.

Economists have long debated whether such speculation was good or bad for development. In 1853–54, when the IC Railroad tracks reached Danville, sales of once-remote government land in the area skyrocketed to nearly a half million acres a year and area populations rose with them. (In 1833 neighboring Iroquois County had a population of 350; in 1860 it boasted 16,000.) In other parts of mid-Illinois, however, land held off the market in anticipation of a rising price retarded settlement. Archibald Campbell, a Scot who settled in Cass County outside Virginia, explained in a letter to a friend back home why that small town had not grown any bigger by 1852. "About sixteen years ago a Gentleman, Mr. Hall. . . . bought nearly all the land around it at Congress price. . . . He died four or five years ago and the land can't be legally sold till his widow dies, which has prevented Farmers from settling close to town."[4]

Speculation often had baleful effects on the speculators too. Certainly many of them went bust waiting for prices to rise. However, speculation paid off for the prudent, the smart, and the lucky, and it is the rare mid-Illinois "first family" that did not attain its status as a result of the rise in land values pushed by speculation in the nineteenth century.

LIVING ON THE EDGE

What trees there were at settlement were clustered in ravines and on wettish stream and river bottoms, where they were protected from fire and drought. Trees also were found, anomalously, in groves on open uplands otherwise the province of grasses. The groves probably were remnants of much larger and older forests that had shriveled as the postglacial climate grew drier. A grove seen from a distance reminds the viewer of a herd of bison, huddled together against a blizzard. As were the trees, in a way, huddled against a blizzard of fire.

Long Grove, a strip of timber perhaps three-fourths of a mile wide, ran along the southern edge of its namesake township in Macon County. Morgan County had a Diamond Grove, Sangamon an Island Grove. In Champaign County the leafy landmarks included Bouse Grove, Lynn Grove, Big (some sixty-four hundred acres) Grove about four miles northeast of Urbana, and, in the northern section of the county, Buck Grove, so named for its abundance of deer. (The edges of prairie groves were perfect deer habitat, offering both shelter and forage to these animals.)

Prairie groves decorated the landscape especially prettily in McLean County, if we can believe pioneer accounts. Scattered clumps of timber—mostly white and burr oak, hickory, sugar maple, and elm—covered perhaps one-eighth of the landscape thereabouts. The result put many observers in mind of a park. One of those was Bloomingtonian Jesse Fell. Fell planted towns, and where he planted towns he planted trees. He is said to have planted more than ten thousand in Normal alone,[5] and Bloomington followed his example so avidly that it earned the nickname Evergreen City. (Bloomington was named for the nearby Blooming Grove.) The result of such efforts was the eventual transformation of the towns of mid-Illinois into artificial groves, islands of wooded land in a denuded landscape.

The groves were pantries for local people. Paul Mowrer, a famous reporter in public life and a poet in his private one, remembered "nutting time" each fall in his native McLean County, when his father

. . . drove us
Out to the fabulous grove where fat-jowled squirrels,
Running from oak to hickory, butternut, walnut,
Angrily chided.[6]

The forest also produced a wide variety of fruit: raspberries, mulberries, may apples, and wild strawberries in spring, blackberries and wild plums in summer; and come fall, paw paw, persimmon, crab apple, wild cherry, red and black haw, and wild grape.

Sugar maples were common in most groves and along creek bottoms, as Illinois's many Sugar Creeks attest. Maple sugar was, with molasses, the common sweetener on the frontier, and so valued that it was a common medium of exchange. Native peoples had long practiced the craft of making sweet syrup from sap, indeed had taught it to European newcomers, beginning with the French. As carried on in places like Sugar Hollow in Jersey County near Otterville, sugar making was a sophisticated form of husbandry. Sugar groves were maintained by clearing brush (to allow easy access to trees) and burning out exhausted sugar maple trees to nurture vigorous new ones.

Groves served cruder needs in the decades before the Civil War. Native peoples made their houses from a few wooden poles and woven reed mats, but Euro-Americans needed logs to build and warm their houses. Native peoples air-dried their meats, Euro-Americans cured them using smoke from burning logs. Indians did not herd animals, and thus had no need for fences, but the Euro-American newcomers did. Livestock roamed at will here as elsewhere in early Illinois, so crops, not animals, had to be put behind protective fences. Since cheap barbed wire would not be available until the mid-1870s, the alternative was rail fences made from crudely split logs. Making them was hard work, but paying others to do it added more to capital costs than most farmers could afford, as it took as much as $300 worth of rails to enclose a forty-acre field around 1840.

Mid-Illinois's famous soils made farming profitable, but it was its trees that made it possible. One early Sangamon County settler thought Island Grove ought to have been called Lost Grove "because there was not more than enough timber for one family, and as one family could not live alone, it would be lost." He bought bottomland nearby instead, but worried that he "would cut the last stick of his timber in twenty years, and he would have to leave the country."[7]

The manifold advantages of having trees nearby explains why the wooded edges of the prairies were usually the first places occupied by farmers.[8] Later arrivals, obliged to build farms in the open countryside, which lacked timber, found themselves at a serious disadvantage. The aforementioned Mr. Campbell wrote to a friend in 1852, "All around the timber has been settled up first and the Farmers in the Prairie generally complain of having so far to haul wood."[9]

If a farmer didn't have trees on his property, he took someone else's. Land belonging to the federal government or other absentee owners was regarded by the neighbors as common property. When Abraham Lincoln joined his stepbrother John Johnston and his cousin John Hanks to build a flatboat in 1831 for their new employer, merchant Dennis Offut, they used trees felled on federal land. The noted land historian Paul W. Gates tells the story of Romulus Riggs of Philadelphia, who had acquired 256 quarter-sections of land (nearly forty-one thousand acres) in the Military Tract during the 1830s. "When he discovered the Illinois Suckers' propensity for hooking or stealing timber from nonresident or speculator-owned land he decided that action was necessary or else his investment might become worthless." Suing the locals just angered them, so Riggs struck a bargain with squatters that allowed them to farm some of his land if they stopped felling trees on the rest of it. "A little later he induced squatters to agree to pay the taxes. Then, when their improvements such as a one-room log house, a little fencing, and a few acres of cultivated land represented sufficient labor and investment to put them in a receptive mood, Riggs demanded a cash rent in excess of the taxes. Thus was tenancy born on the frontier."[10]

THE WAR AGAINST TREES

As people do, those living in mid-Illinois in the early 1800s assumed that the bounty of trees was inexhaustible because they had not been able to exhaust it. Their optimism was uninformed. Among the possible explanations for the collapse of the great Indian city at Cahokia was that its inhabitants, needing wood for stockades and fires, had stripped the local woods like locusts strip a field; one of the reasons the Illiniwek established new villages at Peoria Lake in the 1690s, remember, was that they had done the same around their great settlement near Starved Rock.[11]

Salt was an essential raw material in the rudimentary economy of the Euro-American era, used not as flavoring but as a preservative in the days before mechanical refrigeration. (Salt is what meat-packers packed meat in.) Long before European newcomers named it, the Salt Fork of the Middle Fork River, which drains the eastern part of the old Grand Prairie into the Wabash River, was known as a source of salt. Kickapoo people had long collected it from saline springs bubbling from the stream's north bank where it enters the Middle Fork in Vermilion County. French explorers had noted the presence of the springs early in the 1700s, as did an interpreter for General William Henry

Harrison, then the territory's governor. That the Americans did not at first exploit the springs owed to what a contemporary account described as "the extreme hostility of these [Kickapoo] Indians."[12]

The expulsion of the Kickapoo opened the salines to exploitation by Euro-American settlers. They boiled this briny groundwater in large iron kettles to concentrate its salt, which was then dried for shipping. In the 1820s it was no more fanciful to describe kettles of boiling water in the woods as an industrial facility than it was to call Illinois a state. The settlement that accreted around the thriving saltworks consisted of twelve cabins and a tavern (a rather higher proportion of residential buildings to taverns than would be found in later Illinois mining camps). The settlement was substantial enough in any event to be proposed as a county seat.

By 1848 the Salt Fork operation had as many as eighty kettles boiling at once, and it yielded a total of 120 bushels of salt each week, for which customers often rode many miles. Alas, as a geologist reported in 1870, the Salt Fork springs were but "feebly impregnated with salt,"[13] and so yielded as little as a fifth as much salt per gallon of brine as did the mines that then were being opened in far southern Illinois. To recover a bushel of Vermilion County salt one had to boil away one hundred gallons of water, which meant burning away a lot of wood. Keeping the kettles boiling required three men to fell and haul trees from ever greater distances.[14] Other saltworks could do it cheaper, and when their salt became available in mid-Illinois the Salt Fork works was closed down. Today the only physical evidence of this protoindustry is historic bric-a-brac like the fragment of a kettle on display at the Salt Kettle rest area on I-74 West near Oakwood.

Water boiled by wood fire also powered steamboats. The early versions of these vessels that worked the region's two big rivers burned thirty to forty cords of wood per day. Most of it was cut from bottomland woods by farmers and commercial woodcutters who sold it for a dollar to five dollars per cord. Supplying that wood was hard work, indeed a hard life, as traveler Edmund Flagg reported from the Illinois River in 1838. He was dismayed by "the miserable cabin of the woodcutter, reared upon the very verge of the water, surrounded on every side by swamps, and enveloped in their damp dews and the poisonous exhalations rising from the seething decomposition of the monstrous vegetation around."[15]

By the latter 1800s, both train locomotives and riverboats were burning coal rather than wood, but railroads still needed track ties and trestles, so timber cutting along the Mississippi and Illinois continued. Flagg's "monstrous vegetation" was no match for men like James L. Seago, the Jersey County farmer who in the 1860s began amassing 360 acres of fine stock land in English Township, most of it originally festooned by trees that he happily sold for lumber to the Chicago and Alton Railroad.[16]

Mature trees had always been used to build with, at least by the Euro-Americans. The hewn timber used in the crudely worked log house is the most familiar result, but affluence gradually created a market for milled hardwood lumber. The handsome Woodford County courthouse in Metamora, built in 1844–46 from timber felled nearby (much of it black walnut), is one of the few survivors of many buildings so constructed.[17] Sawmills built on local creeks near Big Grove made it possible to convert about twelve thousand acres of oak, walnut, hickory, linden, elm, ash, and sycamore into fine houses in Champaign and Urbana.[18] Funks Grove, among the largest prairie groves in the region, proved to be a gold mine to its owner, so keen was the demand for its timber. It has been estimated that more than a million dollars' worth of building materials, fencing, ties, and fuel wood were taken from it by 1903. So intense was this mining of wood that the estimated three thousand acres of trees that composed the original grove shriveled to only twelve hundred acres.

NATURE'S BOUNTY

Among the Euro-Americans attracted to mid-Illinois in 1673 was the French Catholic missionary who wished Indians to trade their traditional spirit beliefs for Christian salvation. Another was the trader who wished them to trade their furs for kettles, knives, and guns. The latter acquired the richer harvest.

Trapping muskrats, skunks, minks, and raccoons and preparing their skins for shipment was the first industry in this part of what was then French-run Upper Louisiana. In 1816 the American Fur Trading Company established its own fur-trading posts along the Illinois River; one was a few miles below Peoria Lake, in what today is East Peoria, and another was at the mouth of Bureau Creek, in the county of the same name.[19] (The creek, like the county, is named for the French trader Pierre de Beuro, who had operated a post there in the 1700s.)

In one year, proprietors of fur-trading posts along the Illinois River collected ten thousand deer pelts, three hundred bear, ten thousand raccoon, thirty-five thousand muskrat, four hundred otter, three hundred pounds of beaver, five hundred cat and fox, and one hundred mink.[20] Even the Illinois's fabled fecundity could not long sustain exploitation at that pace, and the variety and value of the pelts soon declined. Where beaver and otter once had been common, soon only muskrat were to be had.[21] Overhunted, furbearers became harder to find, and the Indian economy collapsed.[22]

The first of the Euro-Americans who ventured into mid-Illinois also hunted, but for meat; indeed many found themselves in mid-Illinois because they had followed game into the region from the south. Such men hunted to live, and only incidentally to trade. The first Euro-American in the Sangamon valley was North Carolinian Elisha Kelly, who spent two winters in what became Macoupin County and trailed deer into Sangamon County. Kelly later brought

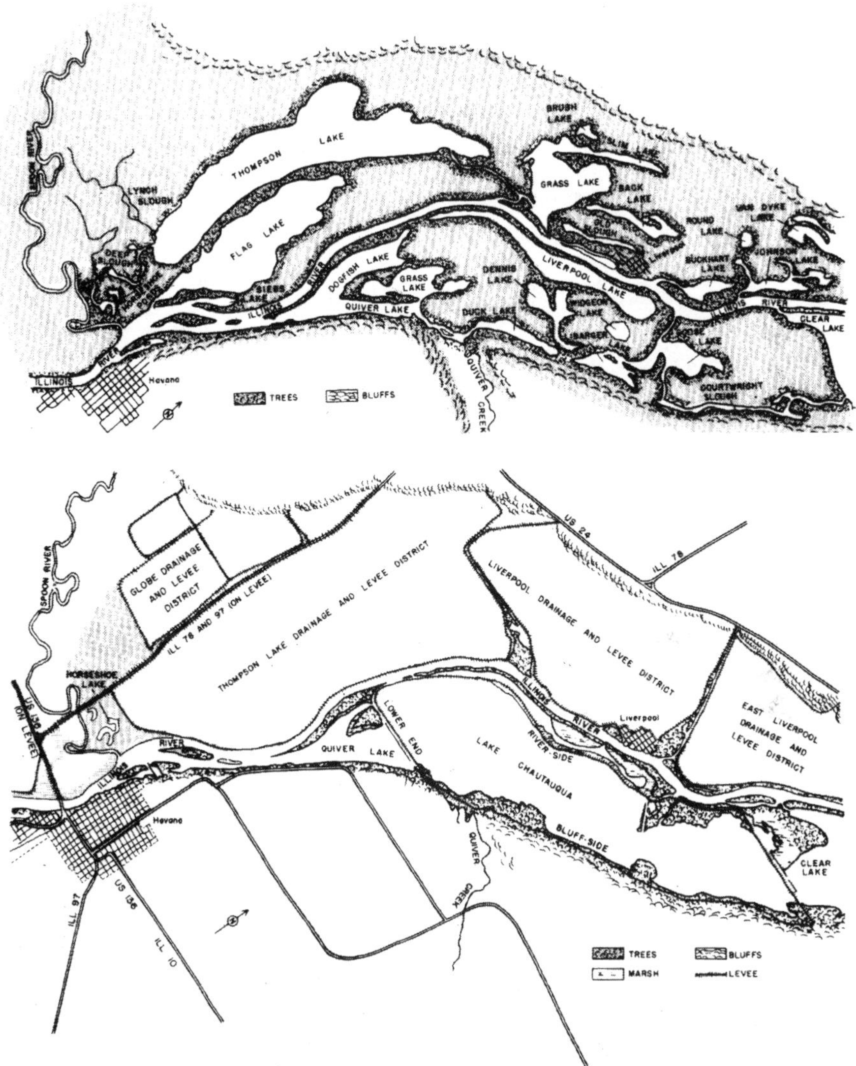

Floodplain change. Maps show the Illinois River floodplain upriver from Havana as it appeared before 1912 (*top*) and in the 1960s, after its conversion from bottomland to farmland (*bottom*). Areas on the latter marked "Drainage and Levee District" had become dry farmland. FROM "A BIOLOGICAL INVESTIGATION OF THE FISHES OF LAKE CHAUTAUQUA, ILLINOIS," BY WILLIAM CHARLES STARRETT AND ARNOLD W. FRITZ, 1965, PAGE 29. COURTESY OF THE ILLINOIS NATURAL HISTORY SURVEY, A DIVISION OF THE UNIVERSITY OF ILLINOIS PRAIRIE RESEARCH INSTITUTE.

Duck hunter. Newly flooded bottomlands along the mid and lower Illinois valleys created new habitat for migrating waterfowl and game fish and new recreational opportunities for outdoorsmen who in the early part of the twentieth century traveled from as far as two hundred miles away, like this hunter in his blind near Bath. COURTESY LIBRARY OF CONGRESS, LC-USZ62–98539.

his family to live there; as others followed his example, the animal population was pushed into the less inhabited corners of the region.

One such corner was the marshy bottomlands of the Illinois River valley from Peoria to the Mississippi. After paddling through it in 1673, Father Marquette wrote in his diary, "We have seen nothing like this river that we enter, as regards its fertility of soil, its prairies and woods, its cattle, elk, deer, wildcats, bustards, swans, ducks, parroquets, and even beaver."[23] This cornucopia was still filled a half-century later. "The Illinois is by many considered the *belle rivière* of the Western waters," reported Edmund Flagg after a visit in the late

1830s, "and, in a commercial and agricultural view, is destined, doubtless, to occupy an important rank."[24]

It occupied that rank for nearly another century. The marshes around old Chicago had helped feed that city, but as they were drained and built on, local suppliers had to look farther afield for product. Most of the Illinois's bottomlands, however, were undrainable and unbuildable, and these backwater lakes and woods remained prodigious animal factories well into the twentieth century. Commercial or market hunters fell on the flocks of big canvasbacks, mallards, and Canada geese that settled along the Illinois to rest and feed each fall; millions of waterfowl were crammed into iced barrels and shipped out by rail.

The hunters' methods were crudely industrial. Diving ducks, for instance, were ambushed dozens at a time from "sneak boats" using "punt guns," multibarreled shotguns that each spewed up to two pounds of shot at a time. Trios of professional hunters were reported to have killed 2,200 ducks in three weeks near Browning in 1900 and 3,008 ducks in eight days below Bath in the fall of 1901.[25] So comprehensive was the slaughter that authorities had to impose restrictions to preserve the flocks. Punt guns were banned in 1910. Changes in the daily limits—fifty ducks a day in 1903, thirty-five in 1905, twenty in 1907—tell a tale of resource exhaustion. Because the limits were widely ignored, the federal Migratory Bird Act made market hunting of waterfowl illegal altogether in 1913.

CHARACTERISTIC DISREGARD

To lawfully exploit the riches offered by the land, one had to own it. Not so the riches that one could harvest from mid-Illinois's common waters. Principal among these were the Mississippi and Illinois Rivers and their backwater lakes. Freshwater mussels, for example, grew nearly as luxuriantly on the beds of the pristine Mississippi and lower Illinois Rivers as grasses grew on the upland soils that lined them. Never craved as a food source, the bivalves had long been harvested for their shells. Native Americans made tools and eating utensils from them; the Spoon River, which ambles through Stark, Knox, and Fulton Counties and was immortalized by poet Edgar Lee Masters, was so named because the mussels whose shells were so used grew profusely there.

In the 1890s it was not as utensils but as raw material for buttons that Euro-Americans coveted mussels from mid-Illinois's two big rivers. Mussels were harvested and cleaned locally, and rounds of shell known as blanks were drilled or sawn from shells in "factories" (in fact small shops) before being shipped to real factories that made them into buttons. The upper Mississippi River itself was perfect mussel habitat, and in 1891 a button factory was set up in Muscatine,

Musseler's camp. Harvesting and cleaning mussel shells to make buttons created boom times in Illinois River towns for a few years before World War I —and so depleted the populations of the shellfish that they have yet to fully recover. USED WITH PERMISSION OF U.S. FISH AND WILDLIFE SERVICE UNDER CREATIVE COMMONS LICENSE 2.0 (HTTPS://CREATIVECOMMONS.ORG/LICENSES/BY/2.0/LEGALCODE).

Iowa. When the beds near Muscatine were picked clean, the hunt simply moved downstream. In Hancock County, Warsaw had a blank-sawing shop from 1907 to 1935. Upstream at Oquawka, making pearl button blanks was the main local industry as recently as the 1940s; Oquawka had so many spent shells lying about that it crushed them and surfaced its riverfront streets with them.

The harvesting moved into mid-Illinois streams in 1906 after hundreds of professional shellers had picked clean not only the Mississippi but also the Wabash and the Rock Rivers.[26] Shelling was also done in a smallish way in the Sangamon, Kaskaskia, Spoon, Embarrass, and Okaw, but it was the Illinois River that sustained the next big boom. In 1907 a blank-cutting shop was opened at Beardstown. In 1908 a second opened at Meredosia. By 1909, the peak year, as many as twenty-six hundred launches and johnboats between Peoria Lake and Grafton were kept busy supplying the button makers.

In its peak years the Wilbur E. Boyd Button Factory in Meredosia employed thirty-four people, which as a percentage of the population was the equivalent of nearly eighteen hundred people in a place the size of Springfield. Howard Edlen, whose family was involved in the business, recalled that Meredosia button cutters got paid by the piece, "so the harder you worked the more you earned. . . . Each week your buttons were weighed and tested for quality and size. If they did not meet requirements the cutter would be docked. If you docked a cutter too much he sure didn't hesitate to tell you so." Nonetheless, standing all day while drilling holes in shells at piecework rates was considered a good job.[27]

Meredosia's musseling operation was only a slightly more evolved version of the many woodcutters' camps, saltworks, and coal towns that popped up to exploit those riches. The flesh of the animals that made them first had to be removed, which was done in outdoor camps on the banks. Some of the flesh was sold to local farmers, who fed it to their hogs, but most of it was simply thrown aside. In warm weather, the stench of rotting meat could make a visiting Chicagoan long for the sweet air of home. Eventually Meredosia officials required that mussel shellers dispose of the waste by hauling it out to midriver.

By late 1911 the Illinois River became the most productive water body per river mile in shelling history. Great middens of shells piled up on the Illinois's banks. (A house in Liverpool was shingled with them.) Then the mussel harvest crashed in a matter of months. Twenty-five shellers worked the river between Peoria and Pekin in 1910, ten shellers in 1911, and only two in 1912. Downriver, two hundred regular shellers operating between Meredosia and Naples gathered one hundred rail carloads of shells during 1909; in 1912 only thirty-five regular shellers found it profitable to work the river, and they gathered only fifteen rail carloads. At Montezuma only four musselers worked where forty boats had operated two years earlier.[28]

The immediate cause of the decline was overharvesting. Far more shellfish were removed from beds than could be sold; millions that were too small or had no commercial value were discarded and died. Worse, shells were routinely taken during the spawning season so this season's harvest came at the expense of future seasons' yields. One fisheries expert who surveyed mussel fishing warned of such practices as early as 1898. "The history of the fishery up to this time," he wrote, "shows the disregard for the future which has come to be regarded as characteristic of fishermen."[29]

FISHY BUSINESS

The Illinois also teemed with fish that the open-minded found palatable enough to pay for. The region's river people of all eras had always fished for sustenance, but the recreational angler in the Euro-American era could, with the purchase of some extra equipment, go commercial, and hundreds of river folks did just that. Railroad access to growing urban markets turned fishing on the Illinois into a quasi-industry that offered livings to more than two thousand commercial fishermen and helped sustain such towns as Pekin, Havana, Beardstown, and Meredosia.

In the early years of the twentieth century, the biggest fish company in Beardstown reported daily catches as large as fifty thousand to one hundred thousand pounds, mostly of channel catfish, common carp, and smallmouth buffalo. Eel, frogs, and turtles were shipped fresh for the table, and even the river's lowliest creatures were coveted; gizzard shad were sold for bait or smoked. By 1900 the catch up and down the river was eight million pounds a year; by 1908 it was nearly twenty million. Fully 10 percent of the nation's catch of freshwater fish was harvested from the Illinois between Hennepin and Grafton in that period, making the mid-Illinois reaches of the river the second most important river fishery in the nation, after the salmon fishery of the Columbia River.

The fish were shipped either dead and gutted on ice in barrels or alive in water tanks fitted into railcars. (Packing those barrels created a secondary industry; vast quantities of ice were harvested from the backwater lakes of the area.) The fish went to such cities as New York, Boston, Philadelphia, Atlanta, Memphis, and of course Chicago. In 1782 French fur trader Pierre Delliette had reported that in good weather, an Illiniwek Indian could spear "as many as sixty [fish] in a day"; in one day in the 1920s, a Meredosia dealer loaded sixty thousand pounds of live carp in tanker cars for shipment to Philadelphia.[30]

The commercial fishermen on the river made the same kinds of mistakes as did the musselers—perhaps inevitably, they often being the same men. The biggest hauls of such profitable species as buffalo were made when the fish were spawning, because that was when they were easiest to catch; in the process the fishermen destroyed uncounted millions of eggs on which their future catches depended.

THE INDUSTRIAL RIVER

Heedless exploitation was not the only cause of the decline of the region's fisheries. The middle Illinois valley was the scene of a fateful contest between the old mid-Illinois and the new, between nature's Illinois River—substantially unchanged since Marquette and Jolliet saw it in 1673—and industry's Illinois. Industry won, hands down. Fish spawning grounds were flooded by the higher flows and pollutants that came downriver when Chicago started flushing garbage from its riverside factories. So copiously were topsoils washed into them by the constant plowing of farm fields on the uplands along the river that the backwater lakes where fish bred and where fish and waterfowl fed gradually turned into land. Massive navigation dams that deepened the water sufficiently to float big barges drowned wetlands flanking the main stream, turning marshes into lakes too deep to be of use to spawning fish or feeding waterfowl. Timbered wetlands that harbored fur-bearing animals also were submerged, and all the low areas were polluted by waterborne wastes. Other backwater lakes were barricaded behind levees and then drained so they could be farmed. To add injury to insult, the German carp, a species introduced in the 1880s to sustain a commercial industry that had overfished the native buffalo to the point of depletion, itself depleted the wealth of native aquatic plant species on which waterfowl fed.

The changes cost the nation one-fifteenth to one-twentieth of the nation's wildlife resources, according to an estimate of the U.S. Division of Migratory Water Fowl. The avian ecosystem had been put on what amounted to artificial life support. Sportsmen were willing to pay to guarantee something to shoot come fall. The choicest bottomlands were purchased for conversion into private rod and gun clubs. By 1918 these sportsmen's paradises occupied a nearly unbroken thirty- or forty-mile stretch of overflowed bottoms and backwaters above and below Beardstown.

Barge lock. Cargo barges and towboat pass through the La Grange Lock and Dam on the Illinois River at Versailles in Brown County. Such dams converted the free-flowing Illinois into a series of ponds, with unhappy effects on the riverine ecosystem. PHOTOGRAPH BY BRIAN GROGAN. COURTESY LIBRARY OF CONGRESS, HISTORIC AMERICAN ENGINEERING RECORD, HAER IL-164-A-6.

Many of the stockholders in such enterprises were business and professional men who lived in the region's biggest cities such as Springfield, Bloomington, and Decatur, but some came from as far as Chicago, Indianapolis, and St. Louis. The private clubs fitted their preserves with cabin boats and duck blinds and fitted their members with lodges that offered all the comforts. They also fitted them with ducks. Local businessman Morris Bell recalls that local residents known as pushers would take Al Capone and his people out to the prime hunting locations in the area around Snicarte and Bath and teach them how to hunt. "If the gang members didn't shoot any ducks on their own, the pushers would kill some so the gangsters could go back to Chicago and gloat about their 'catch.'"[31]

In a 1930 survey for a conservation-minded sporting group, ecologist Aldo Leopold reported that clubs in the area spread up to 430 bushels of corn per acre to attract mallards—the output of perhaps fifteen acres of cornfields. Such baited spots were surrounded by blinds, behind which as many as ten gunners waited in ambush, and as many as two or three parties of shooters were rotated through each such killing station each day. Leopold called Beardstown "the baiting capital of America." Baiting birds in this way was legal but not universally regarded as sporting, and the practice was banned in 1934.

The private clubs were welcomed by locals because they provided jobs as guides, caretakers, and caterers, but they were sources of social tension too. The clubs' appropriation of land for the private pleasure of rich out-of-towners was resented by residents accustomed to treating the bottomland as a commons from which anyone might take fish and game. Happily, the well-to-do hunter was only one of the classes of visitors drawn to the Illinois between 1900 and the early 1920s. Each summer, day-trippers and vacationing families by the hundreds rented cottages in ad hoc settlements, sustaining hotels, dance pavilions, and boat liveries in nearby Havana and at such riverside villages as Quiver, Matanzas, Liverpool, Bath, and Kampsville. For a time (beginning roughly when working families were able to buy automobiles) catering to the summer outdoorsman brought more money into the local economy than commercial fishing. Alas, television and air-conditioning proved as fatal to the resort trade as baiting bans.

UNRESTRAINED USE

Generations of river people have placed the collapse of once-thriving river trades squarely on Chicago's big shoulders. The reality, like most realities, was more complex. Yes, when Chicago reversed the flow of the Chicago River in 1900 to flush its sewage and industrial waste down the Illinois (an estimated 75 to 80 percent of the river's pollution load), it severely damaged the river ecosystem. But historical geographer John Thompson notes that the dead fish and decomposing garbage and vegetation that soured the summer air at Beardstown in 1889 had been dumped on the town's watery margins by its own residents; at Peoria, the river was burdened with slop from distilleries and manure from stockyards.[32] In all, 17 percent of the stream's pollution load was contributed at Peoria and Pekin, and it degraded river life downstream as far as Havana. The valley's farmers played a part too. Between the 1890s and 1930, more than 183,000 acres of Illinois River floodplain was drained so it could be reliably farmed; more than twenty-one thousand of those acres had been backwater lakes much used by spawning fish.

Science had also reaped a rich harvest along the Illinois. "Within a very short distance of almost any town, tracts of virgin forest, prairie, marsh, or other undisturbed habitats could be reached with little effort," explained one history of the Illinois Natural History Survey. "As a result, the State Laboratory insect collections . . . became the finest which had ever been assembled for any one state, and early in the twentieth century the collections of fishes and certain other groups were equally fine." Unfortunately the pickings got slim soon thereafter, leaving the state's public scientists to sing a familiar lament around their campfires. "Many of the old virgin landscapes which were the type localities of Illinois species are now either flooded by artificial lakes, under cultivation, or covered by urban developments. Most of the marshes, which were once commonplace, have been drained."[33]

In short, Chicago sewage authorities and bargemen and levee builders proved no less heedless than the river people themselves to the consequences of exploitation of the river system. "It was accepted that individuals who lived by the axe, trap, shotgun, seine, or sheller's gear, like the plowman, pursued what they perceived as their natural rights in harvesting the bounty of the floodplain and river," writes Thompson. "Use of the gifts of nature was unrestrained."[34]

THE UNPRAIRIE STATE

The natural resource that was most reduced was the one that covered most of mid-Illinois—the prairie. Before it began growing corn, mid-Illinois soil grew grass. Illinois at its founding was the Prairie State in nature as well as name, and no part of Illinois was more festooned with prairie than its middle third. The easternmost counties of mid-Illinois encompass what used to be known, with reason, as the Grand Prairie. Here the grasses did not merely rule; they dominated. Government land office surveyors around 1820 found that prairie covered 90 percent or more of the future McLean, Grundy, and Champaign

Counties. In Ford County the figure was 96 percent, making it the least sylvan county in frontier Illinois.

The root zone of a tallgrass prairie hosts a microbial world that rivals the Amazon rainforest in complexity. (One gram of prairie loam is estimated to contain as many as two million protozoans and another fifty-eight million bacteria.) The massive root systems were a jungle belowground too, and when they died their decay gradually enriched the soil to depths measured in feet. The resulting landscape was no village greensward; the specimens of Logan County prairie grass that Mt. Pulaski's John Buckles sent to the world's fair in Chicago in 1893 were nine feet tall.[35]

While there were half-hearted attempts to cut and dry prairie sod for use as a fuel, and cattle were grazed on some of it, most of the prairie was simply destroyed to get at the soils that lay beneath it. Never having seen one, most Illinoisans have come to use "prairie" to refer to any flattish landscape unadorned by trees, whether it supports corn or coneflowers. (In ecological language the term "prairie" refers to a kind of plant community, not a kind of terrain.) The Federal Writers' Project's *Illinois: A Historical and Descriptive Guide* reported that in the 1930s between Kankakee and Mattoon "no hill breaks the prairie,"[36] but, strictly speaking, no prairie by then broke the prairie there either.

The price of buying unspoiled land was diligently recorded in ledgers. The cost of spoiling land by turning it into farms and towns was not. Prairie plants held topsoil in place; corn did not. In 1950, Illinois State University geography professor Arthur W. Patterson estimated that from the time the prairie sod was broken in McLean County, one inch of topsoil had been lost locally every ten years from exposed plowed land. That topsoil clogged streams, and the plant nutrients it carried turned reservoirs into algae-rich soups unfit for fish.

Today, it is easier to find a square-dancing Shorthorn than to find a bit of surviving prairie much larger than a lawn anywhere in mid-Illinois. Champaign County for example contained more than 592,000 acres of prairie when Euro-Americans began settling it; as of the late 1990s only one acre of high ecological quality was known to exist. Pristine prairie remnants persist only where they are safe from plows, such as on steep creek banks or railroad embankments. (Sparks from locomotives periodically set the latter afire, thus achieving the same ecological effect as the vanquished prairie fires of presettlement days.) Prairie also grows, ghostlike, in pioneer cemeteries. At the Prospect Cemetery Prairie Nature Preserve in Ford County, for instance, a five-acre remnant of black soil prairie has been growing in protected ground since the graveyard was opened in 1859. Twenty-one of the cemetery's nearly eighty species of native herbaceous forbs and grasses occur nowhere else in the county. What more apt resting place for a dead ecosystem than a graveyard?

CHAPTER THREE

"Wondorous plant": The Industrialization of Nature in Mid-Illinois

> If a cornfield of several thousand acres is not "a symbol of the infinite," I should like to know what is.
>
> —Sara Jane Clarke Lippincott, after a visit in 1871

The presence of a cornfield in the middle of town is the sort of thing that Chicagoans expect to see when they venture downstate. On Gregory Drive in Urbana, across from Mumford Hall at the heart of today's University of Illinois's main campus, stands the Morrow Plots. In 1876 George Morrow (later the U of I's first dean of agriculture) and ag professor Manley Miles divided a field on what was then the edge of the campus into ten half-acre test plots. Each was a miniature cornfield. On some of these plots, agronomists planted corn year after year, alternated it with other crops on others, and let the soil lie fallow in still others, with the intention of measuring the effects of each practice on yields.[1]

The Morrow Plots today offer little to entice any traveler who is not a corn borer moth. Over the years the growing university cannibalized the ten original half-acre plots until only three remain, totaling six-tenths of an acre. They are no longer of much use to researchers in an era when such investigations are conducted with computers rather than campus real estate. Nevertheless, one of those plots is by now the oldest "continuous corn" test plot in the world—the reason why the plots were designated a National Historic Landmark in 1968, and why, when the university needed to build a new undergraduate library next door, it ordered architects to construct it underground, lest the building cast an inhibiting shadow on the plants.

Morrow Plots. James H. Pettit (*left*) of the Agricultural Experiment Station and Cyril G. Hopkins of the Department of Agronomy take soil samples in 1904 at the agricultural experiment fields on the Urbana campus of the University of Illinois. Known as the Morrow Plots, these are the only cornfields to be designated a National Historic Landmark. COURTESY OF THE UNIVERSITY OF ILLINOIS AT URBANA-CHAMPAIGN ARCHIVES, IMAGE 0002623.TIF.

NINE FEET TALL

Nature made all of mid-Illinois a perfect corn laboratory. After repeated advances and retreats, the continental ice sheets that first reached the region about seventy-five thousand years ago withdrew for good roughly sixty thousand years later, chased back north by a climate turned less clement for ice. These events are so recent in geologic terms that, were this a battlefield, the ruins would still be smoking. The ice spread out over these latitudes uncountable tons of pulverized Canada. It was a mineral legacy of incalculable richness, perfectly suited to the cultivation of grains on the township scale by machines as big as the log houses of the region's pioneer farmers.

Mid-Illinois soils (especially the younger soils of the former Grand Prairie) are among the richest in the world in terms of their store of trace minerals, their benign pH, and their ability to retain moisture. It was not the prairie on which mid-Illinois societies took root, nonetheless. The land was marvelously fertile, yes, but it was not hospitable to humans. Wood for building and burning was scarce, for one thing. Much of it was ill-drained. Greenhead flies swarmed in open prairies for six weeks or so each summer in such profusion that traveling had to be done at night. "It is impossible to now conceive of the great annoyance of the flies," recalled one Champaign County historian in 1878. "Instances were numerous of stock being so depleted of blood, and torn by their exertions in fighting them that death resulted."[2] Prairie sod, as Bloomington novelist Harold Sinclair remarked in *American Years*, "was tougher than the back pastures of hell."[3] One Vermilion County settler recalled that when his oxen team turned the earth there for the first time it was "like ploughing through a heavy woven door-mat."[4] Plowing up doormats was a job for expensive specialists, as it required small herds of draft animals pulling special equipment.

No wonder then that the country's newest westerners were slow to adapt to life on what one modern writer calls the "much dreaded prairies."[5] The Grand Prairie in particular was the last large bit of Illinois to be settled. As late as 1850 there were but two towns between Urbana and the Illinois-Michigan Canal corridor, ninety miles to the north—one reason why two counties that now lay in that tract, Ford and Douglas, were the last counties to be formed in Illinois.

"TOO LOW, NO"

Transforming open prairie into farms was as much a triumph of technology as pluck. Three inventions proved essential. One was cheap, easy-to-maintain fencing in the form of barbed wire, which was needed to protect crops from roaming livestock. Another was a self-scouring steel plow capable of slicing cleanly through sticky prairie soils. A third invention has been less celebrated but was no less crucial to mid-Illinois's agricultural development—the ceramic drain tile.

Rainwater and snowmelt did not run off the prairie's flat surface, and clay subsoils kept that water from seeping away below it. The result was land that lay wet for as many as eight months of the year. The folks in the Champaign County town of Tolono probably made up the story that a band of Native American hunters declined to camp there, declaring it, "Too low; no."[6] The judgment is sound in any event. Virtually all the forms in which fresh water can gather to make life inconvenient to humans—marshes, potholes, backwater lakes, sedge meadows, swamps—sprawled across hundreds of square miles of mid-Illinois. An ambitious farmer encountering that vast and swampy tract must have felt like an idealist considering a career in Illinois politics.

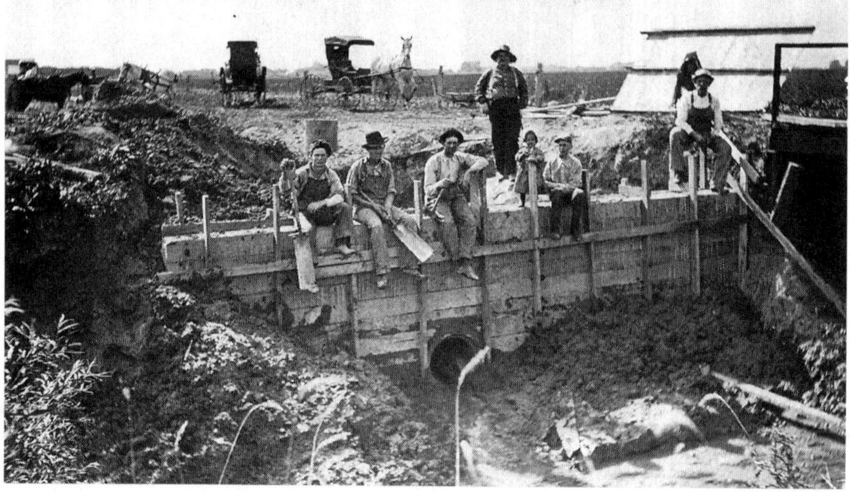

Tile crew. A crew installing field drains in Moultrie County at the dawn of the twentieth century takes a break. The ceramic drain tile was nearly as important as the plow in converting ill-drained prairie land into some of the most productive farmland in the world. COURTESY OF THE ARTHUR PUBLIC LIBRARY, ARTHUR, ILLINOIS, NOEL DICK COLLECTION.

Bogged-down wagons and flooded fields were not the worst of the problems caused by poor surface drainage. Mosquitoes that bred in wetlands would have been merely a nuisance like the greenhead flies but for the fact that they carried the dreaded ague, or malaria. Malaria was to nineteenth-century Illinois what boredom is to the late twentieth, meaning so many people suffered from it that nobody noticed it. You could tell an Illinoisan in those days by the way he shook—not the way he shook hands, but the way he shook all over, from the ague. (The disease was known as the Illinois shakes.) As mid-Illinois was one of the wettest parts of the state, so were its citizens among the sickest of the state.

If the virgin terrain was ill-suited to being farmed, so were many of its farmers ill-suited to farm it, at least until the migration into the area of German and Dutch farmers experienced at cultivating soggy paradises. The Iroquois County village of Danforth was settled by thirty families from the Netherlands brought there by a promoter to farm some of his twenty-seven thousand acres of what was officially designated swampland. From the late 1850s through the 1870s, the Danforthians were joined by immigrants from other damp, flat places. Germans from East Frisia settled near Benson in Woodford County in 1858. Members of an earlier Frisian settlement in Adams County came to the future towns of Flatville and Gifford in Compromise Township in Champaign County in the winter of 1869; the land the latter chose was so marshy that they had to move to it in the middle of the night when it was frozen hard enough to support wagons.[7]

Landowners who tried to build unnatural streams in the form of ditches to drain fields left wet by nature quickly learned why nature hadn't bothered. George and Asa Danforth of Tazewell County in 1866 constructed twenty-five miles of drainage ditch using a bulldozer-like ditching machine that needed as many as forty oxen to budge.[8] That was a mere garden hoe compared with the ditching plow used by a big landowner in Livingston County; the contraption was eighteen feet long and needed sixty-eight oxen and eight men to operate.[9] An ingenious patented mole ditching machine debuted in the mid–Piatt County town of Monticello in 1856, which made tunnels by dragging a torpedo-shaped "shoe" through the subsoil. But these dirt water pipes were prone to collapse, and when they clogged they could not be unclogged.

William P. Pierson of the Iroquois County town of Onarga explained it all at the 1868 annual convention of the Illinois State Horticultural Society. "It is quite evident that our world was not finished on the day of creation," he said. "The job of finishing up this world of ours can never be completed until a considerable portion of it is well under-drained. . . . This is a task that has been assigned to man to do."[10] Drainage tiles of fired clay, buried in trenches along the perimeter of a field, formed a more durable tunnel that did not easily clog or collapse. Such tiles were cheap, but the labor to install them made tiling a large farm expensive. In 1881 Benjamin Gifford bought parts of the seventy-five-hundred-acre Wildcat Slough in Champaign County for as little as thirteen dollars per acre but had to spend forty dollars per acre to drain it.

Worse, it did no good to drain one's field if water from the neighbors' fields overflowed onto it. To effectively drain a field, the larger watershed of which it was a part had to be drained, and that required all the farmers in an area to act cooperatively. For that reason, the drying out of the low prairies did not begin in earnest until drainage districts were created and given the power to tax local land to pay for the work. (*That* had to await the passage of two state drainage laws and the adoption in 1878 of a state constitutional amendment that allowed their establishment.) In Champaign County alone, some 120 drainage districts eventually encompassed 85 percent of the county. Thanks to such reengineering, swamps became pasture, pasture became cropland, and farmers became as rich as farmers could get.

Chicagoans were to brag some years later about their engineering bravado in reversing the flow of the Chicago River, but mid-Illinoisans have a boast or two to make when it comes to rearranging nature on that scale. Historical geographer John Thompson has described the bottomland of the Illinois River between Peoria and St. Louis as having been "the last frontier in mid-Illinois" for agricultural development. Recurring overflows cost bottomland farmers nearly as many crops as they harvested. Drying out a river bottom field that in some years grew more carp than corn had to wait until the advent of steam-powered earthmovers and pumps. Such tools were used for the first time in the Midwest along the lower Illinois River valley. Between the 1890s and 1930 more than 183,000 acres of floodplain was thus stolen from nature by farmers, more than 21,000 of which had been not merely wet but completely covered by water.[11]

CATTLE KINGS

The woodless prairies of Illinois's middle third might have been daunting places for farmers, but for men looking for a place to graze livestock, those expanses of tall grass were heaven. Hundreds of thousands of acres of grassy lands still lay in public ownership; largely unpoliced, they constituted a sprawling commons on which one could pasture herds at little or no cost. As the French fur traders penetrated mid-Illinois in canoes, looking for furs, so herdsmen penetrated it on horseback looking for grass. Robert Pulliam, the man usually acknowledged as the first permanent Euro-American settler in what became Sangamon County in 1817, was only one of many who made such a trip.[12]

Mid-Illinois in those days had grass but no markets; in 1825 cattle fattened around Springfield had to be driven four hundred miles to Green Bay in Wisconsin to be shipped east. Many such prairie cattle men who started as drovers turned buyers, then invested their profits from the sale of cattle in land that could feed more. The profit that McLean County's Isaac Funk made from his livestock business helped him buy some twenty-two thousand acres in and around what became known as Funk's Grove. (Funks are still counted among the important landowners in that part of mid-Illinois.) John T. Alexander started with a five-thousand-acre estate in Morgan County, "then a cattle range bounded only by the horizon"[13]; for a time, the Wabash Railroad's stop on the Alexander farm shipped more cattle than any station in the world. Alexander went on to amass even larger holdings in eastern Illinois.[14]

Jacob Strawn, a Pennsylvanian cattleman who saw mid-Illinois on a stock-buying trip as a young man in 1828, decided to resettle his family in Morgan County. Admirers would write that at the peak of his operations, Strawn "personally bought and sold larger herds than any other man in the United States."[15] Hungry St. Louisans had reason to remember Jacob Strawn in their prayers, because for years he supplied booming St. Louis with nearly all its beef.[16]

The "Old Homestead" of cattle-and-corn king Jacob Strawn, Morgan County, 1872. Strawn owned tens of thousands of mid-Illinois acres; his home farm alone sprawled across eight thousand of them. *ATLAS MAP OF MORGAN COUNTY, ILLINOIS* (DAVENPORT, IOWA: ANDREAS, LYTER, AND COMPANY, 1872). COURTESY ABRAHAM LINCOLN PRESIDENTIAL LIBRARY AND MUSEUM.

The years immediately before and after the Civil War made millionaires of most of these men, who thus were able to live the lives of country squires. Strawn, who as a young man dwelt in a log house, could afford to send his children on the European grand tour. "A farm which one might walk over in a few minutes would not satisfy him," wrote one admirer; "he must have one which a day's ride on horseback would hardly encompass."[17] Like many successful persons, Strawn attributed his achievements to his own wisdom, which he was generous enough to share with others in printed form. These maxims—"Study your interests closely, and don't spend any time in electing Presidents, Senators, and other small officers, or talk of hard times, when spending your time in town whittling on store boxes, etc."—suggest that wisdom had less to do with his success than hard work, good timing, and a relentless focus.[18]

Mid-Illinois cattle ranchers first bred their own stock, feeding the calves to maturity on grass before selling them. That way of making meat takes time and a lot of pasture, and it proved to be uneconomic once demand for farmland pushed up the price of grassy land. (In 1838 John T. Alexander paid as little as eighty-seven cents per acre for land; in 1855 an acre cost him thirty dollars, and in 1857 fifty.) Most Illinois cattlemen eventually moved west in search of cheaper range, but many in mid-Illinois did not. Instead of changing addresses they changed the way they did business in order to extract more value from their land as costs rose.[19] At first they plowed up the native prairie grasses and replaced them with more nutritious European pasture grasses, but by 1880 or so Illinois cattlemen had quit raising their own herds on grass of any kind. Instead they began to put meat on the bones of scrawny young range-raised Texas cattle by feeding them corn they grew on their former pastures.

One of the masters of this new method was New Englander John Dean Gillett, who came to Logan County in 1838. At the time of his death, Gillett's land holdings totaled more than sixteen thousand acres, much of it in Sangamon and Logan Counties—this in a day when the ideal farm size in places like Illinois was one-hundredth that size. By then Gillett had become the "Cattle King of the World," or at least that part of the world inhabited by the London magazine writer who called him that because of his shipments of Shorthorn cattle to England.

Another big landlord was Decatur's Richard Oglesby. He was an adviser to Abraham Lincoln, a three-time governor of Illinois, and (just as crucially) a husband to John D. Gillett's daughter Emma. Admirers found Oglesby "widely traveled, widely read, well-spoken, well-connected, well-rounded in personality, experience and body."[20] When the Oglesbys arrived in Springfield in 1865 for the first of his gubernatorial stints, the governor found the executive mansion staffed with only a half-dozen servants; Oglesby felt obliged to add two more, paid for out of his own pocket, to keep up standards.

John Gillett. Logan County's John Dean Gillett was dubbed the "The Cattle King of the World" by the *London Gazette*. Gillett, a regular winner at Chicago livestock shows, poses with all thirty-two hundred pounds of two-time winner McMullin. COURTESY OF THE OLD GILLETT FARM, ELKHART, ILLINOIS.

The kind of people who live on the hill will congregate wherever a hill is. For a time, Elkhart Hill in Logan County—a forested pile of glacial rubble nearly two hundred feet high and some two miles long—was a social as well as a geologic high spot. Gillett had built a mansion on the northwest face of Elkhart Hill where (writes Paul W. Gates) "he could dwell in lordly splendor surrounded by vassals—tenants—who cared for his herds of cattle."[21] In 1890 Emma and "Uncle Dick" retired to a thirty-two-room mansion on the north side of Elkhart Hill they called Oglehurst. The hill afforded splendid views of nothing much but cornfields, but to men like Gillett and Oglesby, that must have seemed the handsomest scenery in the world.

AGRICULTURAL NAPOLEONS

After the cattle kings, then, came the corn kings. Matthew T. Scott's personal estate in McLean County covered five thousand acres, and he had a hand in developing more than forty-five thousand acres of farmland in the old Grand Prairie. He founded the town of Chenoa in 1855 as a commercial center for his enterprises, much the way businessmen with smaller horizons founded small-town banks. Michael L. Sullivant was an Ohioan who wanted more room to expand his operations, and he found the Grand Prairie "well suited to his notions of farming on a magnificent scale."[22] He developed the Broadlands Farm in Vermilion County, sold it in 1867, and bought forty-seven thousand acres in Ford County. The latter property, Burr Oaks, was eight miles square, and with the help of four hundred laborers Sullivant set about growing corn on what became known as the largest such farm in the world under one-man management.[23] It was said to take two hundred mules working all winter just to move his crop to market; the Sullivant farm was home, appropriately, to the world's largest corn crib, more than three hundred feet long and thirty-five feet tall, dimensions that earned it mention in Ripley's "Believe It or Not." Sullivant borrowed heavily to make such improvements, but poor harvests drove down the value of farmland and caused him to lose the farm to a creditor. He died in 1879, penniless.[24]

Hiram Sibley bought out much of Sullivant's holdings in Ford County and had a town there renamed after him. His eighteen-thousand-acre farm supported 146 families. Among the other large holdings in the region were the Vandeveer estate in Christian County, the C. H. Moore estate in DeWitt County, and the Hoge, Holderman, and Collins estates in Grundy County. By the mid-1800s about a third of Illinois was held by what historian Gates called "agricultural Napoleons."[25]

Some of these lords of land bought property intending to sell it rather than work it, but they found buyers scarce at the prices they demanded. To earn at least the taxes owed on it, owners rented it to farmers unable to buy land of their own. Whether it is more accurate to say that farmers rented the land of the owner or that such owners rented the labor of the farmers is arguable, but the system benefited both parties. Other owners at first tried to farm using paid labor but found it scarce (and thus pricey) and unreliable. Jacob Strawn turned hired hands into tenants by leasing them quarter-section chunks of his estate. McLean County's Isaac Funk did the same thing. He rented to tenants land not needed to pasture his own cattle. If they provided their own farming tools and teams, he provided housing for them and their animals and storage for their grain in return for two-fifths of the grain they produced; if Funk provided the tools and the teams his share of the grain rose to half.[26]

Tenancy was common, but it could not be called popular. Landlords were one of the things many people had come to mid-Illinois to escape. Well-heeled buyers drove up land prices beyond the reach of many a tenant saving up to buy his own ground, not that crop-share pacts left that tenant with much money to save. Tenancy that began as a short-term step toward independence for the small yeoman thus often became a permanent condition.

If tenancy diminished the prospects of would-be owners, it had worse effects on the land. Manuring, drainage improvements, crop rotation, fallowing fields, weed control—all steps that would maintain the long-term health of the land—were widely ignored under short-term leases, as renters sensibly concluded that it made little sense to protect at their expense the long-term viability of another man's investment. Happily, the best of the wealthy absentee landlords of mid-Illinois, such as Gillett, insisted that tenants use the best equipment and most modern farming methods as a condition of their leases, which made themselves and their tenants richer.

IRISH INCUBUS

Of all mid-Illinois landlords, none owned more land, caused more controversy, elicited more passionate complaint, and, in the opinion of some historians, was more unfairly condemned than William Scully. A member of a prominent land-owning family of Tipperary County, Ireland, Scully arrived in America as a landlord with a past. In 1870, Parliament passed a land act that (among other reforms) made it more difficult to push tenants off the land without compensating them for their improvements, something Scully had done often enough to make him one of the most hated men in Ireland among peasant farmers.

Scully learned that the law in America was as protective of landlords as it had been in pre-reform Britain, so he sought to re-create his former family estate abroad. He made massive purchases of mostly government land in four states, including Illinois, that totaled twenty thousand acres at a then-staggering cost of $1,350,000. The center of his Illinois purchases was Logan County, of which he eventually would own some thirty thousand acres. Scully ran his new estates in general accordance with the tenets of landlordism that so recently had become proscribed in the old country—not the first instance in which the new state of Illinois was not a laboratory for new ideas but the home of outmoded and discredited ones imported by its settlers.

Most tenant farmers were allowed to pay their crop rent in an agreed-upon number of bushels or, more often, a share of whatever was harvested. Scully, however, demanded cash.[27] He also decreed that tenants pay property taxes owed on the land they rented. This was a political as much as an economic policy. Tenants tended, as a class, to vote in favor of large taxes on property to pay for roads or schools, which benefited the tenants and his neighbors at the landlord's expense. By making tenants responsible for local property taxes, Scully removed their incentive to vote for local public improvements that he would have to help pay for. As a result, roads and schools in areas dominated by Scully tenants tended to be poorer quality than those elsewhere in Illinois.

Scully was loath to pay for even private improvements. "There is little hedging; the fences are poor, the houses the most comfortless in the county," reads one contemporary account of a Scully landscape. "There are no orchards, no barns to speak of, scarcely a tree of any description. Churches and schoolhouses, as may be supposed, are as cheap and far apart as in many regions we term 'heathen.'"[28]

Fairly or not, Scullyism, or at least the exaggerated version of Scullyism that was sometimes described in the press, was widely resented. "An incubus upon Logan County's development" is how Scully was described in 1886.[29] As Gates notes, Scully was seen as a monopolist of the same ilk as the railroad barons, then the target of ire among farmers because of overcharging on freight and other misdemeanors. Worse, he was an alien monopolist who managed his lands from Europe through agents. Scully also was a Roman Catholic. In the 1870s and 1880s Scully, who then had some three hundred farms rented out in Illinois, became a target of newspaper editorials and eventually of bills in the General Assembly.

One of the state representatives from Logan County successfully introduced into the Illinois General Assembly an anti-alien-landlord act of 1887 that banned noncitizens from owning farmland and further prohibited them from passing on the cost of their property taxes to their tenants.[30] Both restrictions proved easy to avoid. Scully took out citizenship papers in response to its first requirement and reworded his leases to comply with the second. To their dismay, farmers learned that lawmakers never intended the new law to actually reduce tenancy, merely to reduce the voters' annoyance with the General Assembly for not acting to reduce tenancy. (Such failures set off grumblings about the need for farmers to form their own political party to fight for their interests in Springfield, a story told in chapter 9.)

The quasi-plantation system eventually collapsed on its own, weakened by Illinois's periodic farm depressions and by chronic mismanagement. Thousands of acres gradually fell into the hands of banks and other creditors who did not want to farm but found it profitable to rent to those who did. Also, by the 1880s many of the region's first generation of settlers had begun to retire, and they held on to their land by renting it out to their children or neighbors. Nakedly exploitive tenancy thus decreased, but tenancy did not. According to Gates, Logan County in the late 1800s led the state in the proportion of farms worked by people who did not own them—52 percent. In second place was neighboring Mason County, with one-half of its farms in tenant hands, followed by Christian and Piatt Counties. In 1880 the practice was virtually unknown in Michigan, Wisconsin, and Iowa and concentrated only in small parts of central and southwestern Ohio and mid-Indiana; in virtually the whole of mid-Illinois, save for a few counties in the old Military Tract, from 30 percent to more than 40 percent of the land was being farmed by tenants.[31]

Governor John Peter Altgeld in 1897 warned the General Assembly that the rise of the absentee landlord meant the loss of the independent farmer who had built Illinois and threatened to create a rural underclass as had happened so often in Europe. That didn't happen, at least not quite. Tenants still failed, but most of them simply packed up their problems and found new land in the West or factory jobs in the cities. Illinois would have to deal with a disaffected peasantry, to be sure, but it would be in cities like Chicago rather than its rural districts.

COMMERCIAL CORN

The very first early Euro-American homesteaders were not the first farmers in the region. Perhaps seven thousand years ago native peoples began cultivating plants as well as gathering useful wild ones. Three such plants were the basis of mid-Illinois's earliest agricultural economy. Into ground worked with hoes made from bison horn or mussel shell was planted corn, squash, and beans, all of which were usually dried and stored in burial pits. This was done in large summer villages; when the season's crop was established it was left standing in the fields as the people left on a summer bison hunt; on their return the now-ripened crops were harvested and stored. The village then dispersed again for a winter hunt before returning in the spring to start the cycle again. The earliest Euro-Americans in the region also were as much hunters as farmers who grew only what they could not shoot. Their holdings were more like gardens than farms, and provided only a sustenance and maybe a small surplus—a hog this year, honey next—that could be sold or (more likely) bartered for tools and other goods.

With the shift from subsistence agriculture to commercial farming, independence on the frontier quickly ceased to be a matter of growing what one needed to eat and became a matter of selling what one didn't. Single-crop cash agriculture allowed farmers a different kind of independence (from toil, mainly) by enabling them to buy manufactured store goods rather than making their own.[32] For decades, that cash crop was not corn. In 1860 the leading wheat producer in the country was Illinois, and much of that wheat was grown in its middle part, which, had it been a state in itself, would have ranked as the fifth-largest wheat producer in the nation that year. The money in wheat sparked a search for new farmland and new varieties capable of growing on it, however, thus quickly shifting the wheat belt west to cheaper land in the Great Plains.[33]

Even if a mid-Illinois farmer in those decades made his money growing wheat, he—or rather they, because no farm could be managed without the labor of women as partners—survived on easy-to-grow corn. Years on the stump had perfected in Richard Oglesby the ability to say a great deal without saying a thing, as he famously proved in his oratorical tribute to corn in Chicago in 1894. Oglesby no doubt saw in the members of that city's Fellowship Club an audience that needed instruction on the topic, and he proceeded to give it to them hard. "The corn, the corn, the corn. . . . Look on its ripening waving field. See how it wears a crown, prouder than Monarch ever wore," he enthused. "Majestic, fruitful, wondorous [*sic*] plant."[34]

The plant yielded grain that was of limited value, being bulky to ship. But corn fed to livestock was converted into meat, a product of considerable value that also was easier to ship than raw grain. The successful farmer fattened both hogs and beef cattle that way. (More accurately, the farmer fed the cattle and the cattle fed the hogs, the latter feeding on the undigested corn that littered the feedlots in the manure of the cows.) Corn-and-livestock husbandry of this sort was efficient, prosperous, and flexible.

The corn-and-livestock husbandry that was perfected in mid-Illinois had been learned from farmers back east. The corn latitudes extended as far as

Pennsylvania, explains John C. Hudson in *Making the Corn Belt*, and it was there that the Illinois version of the system had been invented, and from where it was carried by migrants into Ohio and Tennessee and Kentucky. Many among Sangamon County's founding generation, for example, were from neither the slave-oriented lowlands nor the hardscrabble hill country, but had come to mid-Illinois looking for land of the sort they knew from home. No plant-with-a-pointed-stick pioneers, they were savvy husbandmen who had the tools as well as the ambition to exploit mid-Illinois's more plentiful land.[35] In short, argues Hudson, the soils and terrain of mid-Illinois did not turn immigrant husbandmen into successful corn farmers. Rather, successful corn farmers from other, similarly endowed regions to the east in Ohio, Pennsylvania, Tennessee, and Kentucky turned much of mid-Illinois into successful farms.

SOOTHSAYERS AND MEDICINE MEN

The corn-and-livestock system was an efficient way to use corn. More efficient ways to *grow* corn required innovations from other quarters. "During a fifty-year period [ending in 1890] Illinois agriculture experienced more changes than had occurred in all previous human history," wrote Fred Kohlmeyer in 1984. "Historians have coined terms like 'agricultural revolution' and 'rural transformation' to describe the process which centered in Illinois."[36]

That revolution was touched off not in the fields but in the workshop. The mechanization of farmwork dates back to the 1850s in Illinois. Most farmers were quick to adopt mechanical improvements whose benefits were immediate and whose workings they could comprehend. (Most farmers, then as now, were themselves tinkerers by necessity.) The manufacturers of the region obliged open-minded farmers with machine sheds full of new horse-age wonders, from binders, cultivators, and seed planters to stalk cutters and disc plows. These machines (abetted by terrain) made it possible for a single farm family to cultivate more acreage more intensively than ever. The machines made larger farms possible; larger farms made the machines necessary. By 1870 the federal farm census found thirty-two thousand-acre farms in all of Wisconsin, thirty-eight in Iowa, and seventy-six in Indiana; mid-Illinois alone counted nearly 250.[37]

Willing labor alone was no longer enough to provide for a family in Illinois. Anyone could farm, but commercial agriculture took brains plus machines and management skills. The State of Illinois thus had a need to both educate its best farmers to succeed and to train its less-than-best farmers for other kinds of work. The means of these transformations was the University of Illinois, which opened as the Illinois Industrial University in 1867. (See chapter 7 for

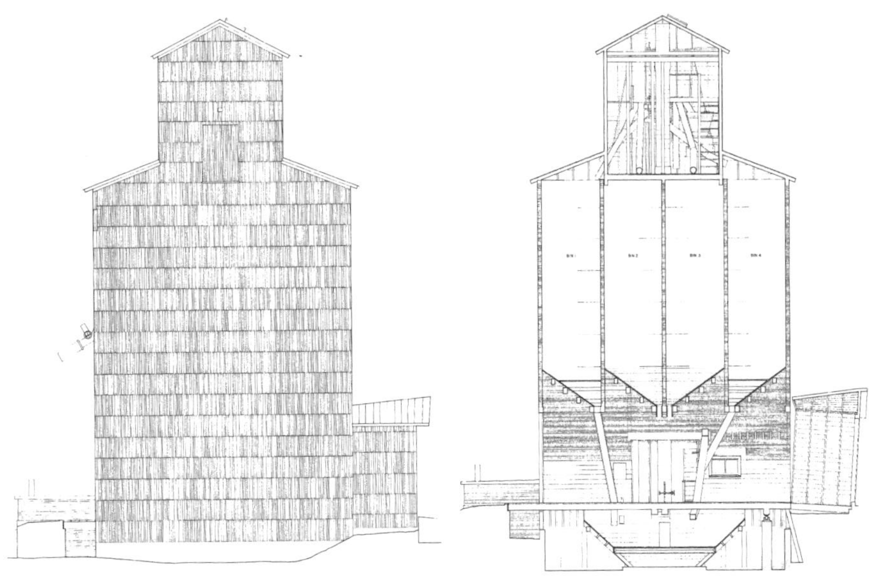

Grain elevator. The answer to every city dweller who ever asked, "Why grain *elevator*?," is this: Grain-filled wagons were driven into the Caldwell Elevator in Piatt County west of Seymour, then tilted so the grain flowed out into a basement bin. From there the grain was lifted to the top of the structure by bucket chain and distributed into bins for storage until it was unloaded via chutes into waiting rail cars. Built in 1917, this elevator was sheathed in corrugated metal to protect it from sparks from passing locomotives. COURTESY LIBRARY OF CONGRESS. ADAPTED FROM HISTORIC AMERICAN BUILDINGS SURVEY, HABS ILL,74-WHEA.V,1.

more about the university.) The university's motto celebrated the joining of learning and labor, but the pair remained as contemptuous of each other as ever. Few farmers wanted to become college students, and fewer college students wanted to become farmers. When Andrew S. Draper arrived as university president in 1894, the College of Agriculture of what had become the University of Illinois was moribund. The counsel of its staff was scorned as impractical by the region's farmers, and with some reason. Scientific knowledge did not begin to be adapted to Illinois conditions until the university's Agricultural Experiment Station was set up 1887 as a division of the agriculture college.[38]

By 1920, however, the College of Agriculture employed more than 180 faculty, enrolled more than 1,200 students, and commanded an annual budget of nearly $1 million.[39] That change owed much to Eugene Davenport, the man Draper named to run both the college of agriculture and the experiment station. A farmer himself, Davenport lobbied key farm associations to push in Springfield for greater state appropriations. (Any farmer would respect

Davenport's ability to increase yields from the stony ground of the legislature; from 1904 to 1920, the College of Agriculture's annual budget more than quintupled.) Better faculty were hired, and more modern facilities built, including an imposing new dairy barn that was as vital to the ag student as a lab is to the budding chemist.

Farmers needed the help. Mechanization had been welcomed by practical farmers, but they dismissed other improvements whose workings were more mysterious—basically, all the essentials of today's advanced row-crop agronomy, from soil conservation and fertilization to plant hybridization and what is now known as ecological approaches to pest control. Among Davenport's colleagues was Stephen A. Forbes, state entomologist from 1882 to 1917 and head of the Illinois Natural History Survey. Forbes, who also served as dean of the U of I College of Science, would later be recognized as one of the founders of the science of ecology. It was Forbes, wrote F. Garvin Davenport, who was able to convince at least a minority of farmers that the more practical features of science could be applied to agricultural economics. "He was a combined soothsayer, medicine man, educator, researcher and politician. He was closer to the people than any other scientist with the exception of the family physician."[40]

The university also built an efficient information transfer system to disseminate the results of its research in the form of a network of county extension agents. For more than a century now, the more adept mid-Illinois farmers have looked to "the boys down at the college" for advice on the latest methods. Thanks in no small part to these scientific missionaries, and to the training their sons and daughters have received at the hands of the university's wizards, the region's grain farmers have long been risk takers and early adopters, the high-tech geeks of the Corn Belt.

New methods had enabled the mid-Illinois farmer after the Civil War to raise more corn than ever. The problem was that his neighbors could too. The resulting bumper crops pushed down prices, which pushed up the pressure to get even more corn from each acre. One way to do that is to grow more plants per acre. Another is to harvest more corn per plant. Both required not just new corn-cultivation technology but also new corn.

Not surprisingly, mid-Illinois, whose farmers were the top corn producers in a top corn-producing state, was the site of much important research into higher-yielding crop varieties. At first, much of that research was done by farmers themselves. Golden Eagle, a popular open-pollinated variety of corn, was developed in 1871 by H. B. Perry, of Toulon in Stark County. In 1880 a standard variety called White Superior was developed by P. R. Sperry of Monmouth, and in 1890 H. Beagley of Sibley produced the Silver Mine.[41]

Identifying high-yielding varieties of corn is one thing; creating them quite another. Dr. J. R. Holbert was a Purdue-trained scientist who came to work for the Funk Brothers seed company near Bloomington. Holbert undertook to reinvent the plant. He interbred varieties capable of fending off disease and insect pests, of yielding more kernels per ear, and of standing upright against wind while awaiting harvest. One result was Funk's Tribred variety, which was marketed in 1916, the world's first recorded sale of hybrid seed corn.

Because the people who ran the early seed companies were or had been farmers themselves, farmers at first found it easier to trust the private seed companies rather than the public universities as the preferred source of scientific knowledge[42]—even though it was the discoveries of the professors that the private hybridizers exploited. In 1918 Holbert persuaded the U.S. Department of Agriculture to establish a disease and hybrid corn experiment station on Funk Farms, one of the many fertile hybrids of public institutions and private companies to grow in Illinois.[43] (Later that station was moved to the University of Illinois.)

The early hybrid corn varieties were not, as so often described, miracle crops. Their seeds returned only a few more bushels per acre than open-pollinated varieties and were more expensive. That suited certain high-volume producers, but it was not until the 1920s that double-cross hybrid seed corn began to show so much more potential than the familiar nonhybrids and thus the average farmer became willing to try it. In 1936 George Mecherle, founder of Bloomington's State Farm insurance companies, granted use of his home farm to the U of I for a field test. Mecherle had farmed that land nine miles east of Bloomington for decades, but while he had lavished care on it the farm had never produced hundred-bushel-per-acre corn, which then was considered the ultimate proof of virtue in both soil and farmer. A relentless drought that growing season shrank McLean County's average yield to twenty-five bushels per acre, but the five new hybrids planted on the Mecherle farm averaged more than one hundred. Not bread from stones, but close.

MIRACLE BEAN

While people do not eat many soybeans—not in bean form anyway—this high-protein miracle bean is nearly ubiquitous in the American diet as a food that goes into other foods. Satisfying this appetite has made soybeans a major commodity crop by every measure, and soybean fields are nearly as common in parts of mid-Illinois as lawns in a subdivision. It is astonishing to realize, then, that as recently as the 1920s the soybean as a commercial crop did not exist. As agricultural revolutions go, the beaning of mid-Illinois was rapid and comprehensive.

Growing corn year after year depletes the soil, and farmers wanted a second cash crop they could alternate with corn on those fields. Also, farmers had to devote many acres to growing the oats, alfalfa, and hay necessary to power the animals used to help plant, harvest, and move corn. When steam- and later petroleum-powered machines replaced animal machines in the barn, farmers were left with a lot of bare fields. The soybean had a lot to recommend it as a solution to both problems. It is well suited to mid-Illinois's climate. (Decatur lies at about the same latitude as Dairen, Manchuria, center of the soybean belt in the Old World.) Because the corn borer doesn't like soybeans, rotating fields between soybeans and corn disrupts that pesky insect's life cycle. And because soybean roots "fix" nitrogen from the air, the plant does not require the expensive nitrogenous fertilizers that corn does.

The soybean had been introduced to Illinois as early as 1851. However, early varieties were more vine than bush, which made their seeds hard to harvest. Worse, the oil extracted from crushed seeds tended to go rancid. Both problems were attacked by hybridizers. The result were upright, short-limbed varieties that obediently stand up to be raked clean at harvest by a combine. Meanwhile, new processing techniques rendered more of the bean usable. This transformation of a plant into a crop owed much to public research, some of which was performed early on at universities in Illinois. When Congress in 1935 wanted to set up a laboratory in the Midwest to learn more about the chemistry of the soybean with an eye toward finding new industrial uses for it, they put it at the University of Illinois, so the crop is firmly rooted in the agriculture of the state in every way.

Reinventing the soybean proved easier than persuading farmers to grow it, who, by the 1920s, had invested a lot of equipment and know-how in raising the old crops. They were no more eager to become bean farmers than laid-off auto workers are to become accountants. The soybean needed a Johnny Appleseed, and it got one in the person of August Eugene Staley, the founder and chief executive officer of the A. E. Staley Manufacturing Company. In 1922 Staley, eager to replace imported soybean products from China with his own firm's products, decided he would begin processing soybeans in his Decatur plant. Before Staley could crush beans in quantity, local farmers had to grow them in quantity. Fortunately (like many businessmen of the day) Staley had a little of the carnival huckster in him. He and the U of I sponsored a special educational train in 1927 (the Soil and Soybean Special) as part of a massive reeducation campaign to get the soybean accepted as a cash crop. Thanks to such efforts the farmers of the Grand Prairie undertook a massive shift in planting schemes, and what had been the nation's center of corn-and-livestock farming is today a center for corn-and-soybean farming. (See chapter 11 for more about Staley.)

THE EQUAL OF NEW JERSEY

In season, corn and soybeans dominate the mid-Illinois landscape, but lots of other crops tumble from the region's cornucopia. Watermelon and cantaloupe thrive in the sandy soils along the Illinois River. (Beardstown is proud to number itself among at least four watermelon capitals of the United States.) In Woodford County, Eureka owed its founding, the college that bears its name, and whatever reputation it has for fun to the family that founded the Dickinson Cannery in 1899. Dickinson contracted with area farmers to produce canned peas, sweet corn, and pumpkins. (Locals still tell of the pumpkin festival of 1947, when movie star and Eureka College grad Ronald Reagan came back to town and got to ride in a parade with the pumpkin queen and her court.[44])

The home orchard, a fixture on nineteenth-century farms, grew into commercial operations in mid-Illinois's western reaches. Liechtensteiner Alois Rheinberger set out a vineyard and built an arched wine cellar and pressroom near his house in 1851 on land that today is part of Nauvoo State Park. (The vines are still producing fruit.) The Baxter Winery on Nauvoo's Parley Street was founded in 1857 and was still in operation 160 years later, making it easily the oldest winery in Illinois. Adams and Pike Counties were major shippers of tree fruits. A traveler who signed himself *JBG* sent a dispatch from the first Illinois state fair to the *New York Tribune* in 1853, reporting, "Wm. Stewart & Son, of Quincy, Ill., have a hundred varieties of trees, and it is only candid to confess that, for apples, Illinois is more than the equal of New Jersey."[45] Fruit remained on the menu in that area until well into the twentieth century, when refrigerated railcars and trucks bearing imported fruit from distant growers wrecked the market for mid-Illinois fruit in places like Chicago.[46]

A commercial rose grower named Nelson began to turn Pana into the City of Roses in the early 1900s, after finding that the town had two advantages that uniquely suited it to the greenhouse business. For one thing, Pana enjoyed excellent rail links to the rest of the nation, which made the delivery of fresh flowers feasible. For another, a quirk in the climate was thought to make Pana one of the places in the country where hailstorms are least likely—important in the days when greenhouses consisted of fragile glass panes. At one time, six major wholesalers were hauling out of Pana nearly twenty million roses a year supplied by more than one hundred local greenhouses.[47] Pana's rose business wilted, alas, when the jet airplane gave low-cost South American growers access to international markets much the way the railroads had given Pana growers access to national ones.

Sorghums are grown for grain consumed by humans, for animal fodder, and for making molasses, but one variety, *Sorghum vulgare*, was widely cultivated in Illinois because its dried leaves make perfect bristles for brooms. Each region of Illinois in the 1800s had its own "broomcorn capital," but the largest producer was that part of Douglas County that rolls south from Arcola for twenty-five miles to Neoga. In the 1890s the Barnums in charge of the street fair in nearby Sullivan built a Broom Corn Palace at the intersection of Harrison and Main; covered and thatched with broomcorn, it was large enough that horse-drawn vehicles could pass through it. As recently as 1935, there were sixty thousand acres of broomcorn under cultivation in the Arcola area. But even today's nimble farm combines are not capable of the complex operations required for its harvest, and the rising cost of hand labor doomed local broomcorn cultivation.

LEAN AND MEAN

As noted, raw corn is bulky, and shipping it most years costs more than early mid-Illinois farmers could sell it for. Concentrate a corn crop in the form of live hogs, however, and you can walk it to market. The sight of herds of ham on the hoof being driven down the streets of meatpacking towns up and down the Illinois River must have been a spectacle bettered only by political parades.

Illinois's first hogs were a little like its first Euro-American settlers—nearly wild, and tending toward the lean and mean. Long-legged and good at jumping, with tusks on the males that could reach six inches in length, the animals were known variously as pointers or hazel splitters, razorbacks or scrub hogs, the last a reference to their favored environs. Hogs could be left untended in such woods or turned loose in a cornfield, where they would "hog down" ripened corn still on the stalk—in effect, a harvest and feed operation all in one. They would hog down a garden too, given a chance. In her memoir, *Life in Prairie Land*, Eliza Farnham writes that the absence of fences around the houses in Tazewell County "presented temptations which wrought lamentable corruption in the morals of the swine."[48]

In fact, the oinkers ate almost anything, which made them especially useful to have around an early Illinois farm. Hogs were also kept in towns, where they fed on garbage in the streets; as late as 1853 a visitor to Illinois's first state fair in Springfield reported, "Swine were more numerous in the streets of the City of Springfield than in the pens on the Fair ground."[49] Virtually every town had ordinances to control stray hogs, and it needed them. Left to run free, unclaimed hogs often became such pests that persons killing one were given half of the meat for doing a public service.[50]

Oscar B. Hamilton's history of Jersey County tells the story of the proprietor of a "grog-shop" in Grafton in the later 1850s, whose customers eagerly bought whiskey he had flavored by putting a bushel or two of ripe peaches into the barrel. When the barrel was empty

> he emptied the peaches upon the street, and the hogs, at large, ate greedily of the peaches, and in a very short time drunken hogs were staggering, squealing and performing various antics, to the great amusement of the small boys upon the street. The next day, after the hogs became sober, and for many days thereafter, the boys, to enjoy a repetition of the drunken performance, tried to drive the hogs back to the peaches, but they were not able to succeed; the hogs would not go near, much less eat them. How different from man! He will continue the repetition until drunkenness becomes a fixed habit. Not so with the swine.[51]

An animal so omnipresent in antebellum mid-Illinois was bound to figure in the life of the young Abraham Lincoln. When he first laid eyes on the Illinois River, in 1831, he did so in the company of live hogs, which composed part of the cargo aboard the flatboat he floated down to New Orleans.[52] As a lawyer Lincoln tried cases involving hog thieves, hog contracts, hog vandalism, even a hog-based slander. In a Taylorville courthouse Lincoln once had to ask the judge to issue a "Writ of Quietus" against the hogs outside, whose squealing was drowning out Lincoln's voice.

The practice of fattening hogs and cattle on corn was widespread in mid-Illinois by 1840 but was not perfected until breeders delivered animals capable of more efficiently converting that corn to meat. The Dorsey brothers of Pike County—Alexander, Bennett, and John—were typical of the more advanced stockmen of their day who introduced purebred animals to improve their herds. They specialized in new breeds like the Chester White from Pennsylvania, the Poland China from Ohio, and the Berkshire from England, each of which deserve to be listed among the region's more important immigrants. Illinois farmers improved not just hog bloodlines but their diet, and built facilities for feeding and confinement designed for the purpose. Each innovation upped output and quality and lowered costs.

The railroads had opened Europe to the products of mid-Illinois agriculture, and hogs were some of the region's first ambassadors. Carl Sandburg recalled that one of the houses on his paper route as a boy in Galesburg belonged to the Honorable Clark E. Carr, the Republican Party boss of Knox County. In the 1890s Carr served in the Benjamin Harrison administration as minister resident and counsel general to Denmark. Carl Sandburg recalled how Carr, whom Sandburg called "a waddly barrel of a man," worked out a deal that let American pork into Denmark at a lower tariff. "When I was the Minister to Denmark the American hog obtained recognition!" he said, then laughed at being his own punch line.[53]

THE UNPRAIRIE STATE

Agriculture since the Great Depression has continued down the road charted for it in the early years of the twentieth century. The farmer still has to plow and harvest, springs are still often too wet, the fall frost often comes too soon, and droughts still occur with a disheartening frequency. Farming still dominates the landscape of mid-Illinois (although it no longer dominates the economy) and row crops still dominate farming. But while the seasonal rhythms of farm life haven't changed, everything else has.

If the trend in the 1860s was to turn husbandmen into scientific farmers, the trend today is to turn scientific farmers into product engineers. The process of cultivating the soil and planting and harvesting crops has become not merely mechanized but also automated, with satellite-guided field equipment and computerized applications of chemicals. The more successful family farms have assets and gross receipts measured in millions. Metaphors of the garden have been replaced by images of the factory. At the start of the twenty-first century, the countryside of mid-Illinois was devoted to the production of the raw material for the production of sweeteners, engine fuels, and livestock feeds.

Not only the landscape but also rural society in mid-Illinois have been transformed by the advent of scientific agriculture. Farm populations peaked more than one hundred years ago in many mid-Illinois counties. Changes in farm methods that became widespread in that era made it possible for each new generation of farmer to cultivate more land than his or, lately, her predecessors. One result is that the number of people directly employed on the land is small, notwithstanding the fact that upwards of 90 percent of the land in some mid-Illinois watersheds is devoted to crops. In very few counties does the proportion of the total population engaged in farming reach three in twenty, and in most of them it is much less than that.

In recent decades, many of the region's rural counties have not kept pace with population growth elsewhere in the state. Illinois's population nearly quintupled between 1870 and 2000, but Ford County's population by 2000 was only half again as large as it had been 130 years earlier. Many rural counties in the region have actually lost people—often a great many people. Stark County numbered more than eleven thousand people in 1880 but in 2010 had about six thousand. Schuyler County had more than seventeen thousand residents in 1870; by 2010 it had lost ten thousand of them. In parts of today's mid-Illinois, the population per square mile meets demographers' definitions of a frontier zone. Here is nostalgia with a vengeance, a countryside that really is going back to the way things were in the old days.

CHAPTER FOUR

Town Mania: The Urban Frontier of Mid-Illinois

> The most matter-of-fact citizen who had paid six hundred dollars for a choice lot at the sales, could not but see his money doubled, interest included, within the first two years. Nearly every citizen owned one, two, or three such lots. . . .
>
> —Eliza Farnham, describing Tazewell County in the 1840s

The story is dubious but good enough that generations of tourists have believed it. In 1853 developers Robert Latham, John D. Gillett, and Virgil Hickox laid out a new town intended to exploit the presence of the new Chicago and Alton Railroad tracks being built through Logan County. They asked their attorney who drew up the papers, Abraham Lincoln, if they might name their town after him. According to one account, Lincoln at first demurred, saying, "I never knew anything named Lincoln that amounted to much."[1]

Lincoln the town did amount to something, a small city of some ten thousand people by World War I. Most town street grids in mid-Illinois, like those across the Midwest, were aligned by land surveyors with the cardinal compass points. When railroad companies laid out towns like Lincoln, however, the compasses they used all pointed to their tracks. For example, it is a sure bet that any town in this part of Illinois whose Main Street parallels the rails and whose north-south streets are numbered and whose east-west streets named for trees was laid out by the Illinois Central Railroad. That general town scheme was also used by other lines, including the C & A, which used it to lay out Lincoln. The new town thus was given a form that the authors of the 1939 Federal Writers Project guide to Illinois found to be "as familiar and recurrent in this area as the John Deere tractor and the Harvester plow."

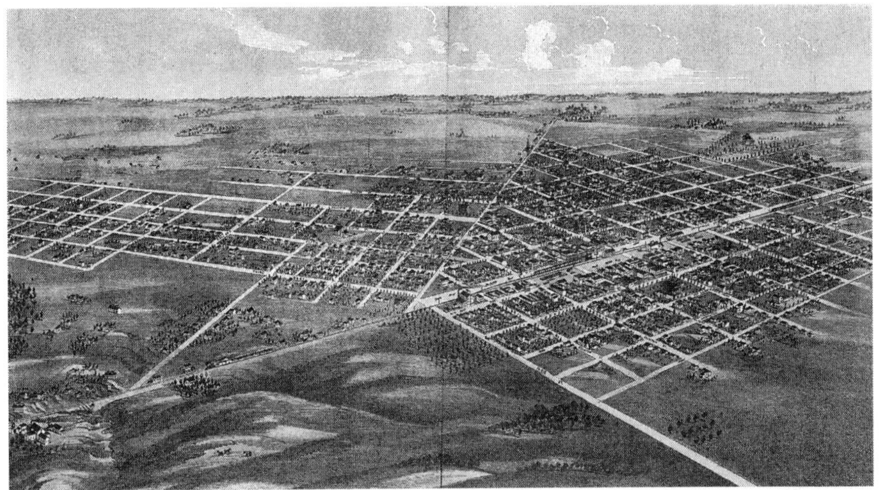

Street grid for Lincoln, Illinois, 1869. When the new town of Lincoln was laid out by developers in 1853, the streets were oriented to the tracks of the new Chicago and Alton Railroad, which ran northeast-southwest. The earlier town of Postville lay to the west; wagon town eventually met railroad town at Union Street. ADAPTED FROM A MAP BY A. RUGER (MADISON, WIS.: RUGER AND STONER, 1869). COURTESY LIBRARY OF CONGRESS, G4104.L6A3 1869 .R8.

Not far from early Lincoln stood the town of Postville. When it was founded in the pre-train era, seventeen years earlier, Postville's surveyors had aligned its streets east-west and north-south in the usual way. Lot by lot, Lincoln grew toward Postville, and when they met the two street grids had to be joined. The suturing of one town to the other left scars in the form of triangular blocks and dog-legged streets. (The same thing happened in downtown Champaign, among many others in mid-Illinois.) Driving down Lincoln's Union Street, where wagon town met railroad town, is a reminder that a town is an invention made for a purpose, whose physical form reveals much of its history.

FOCAL TOWNS AND GRAND VILLAGES

The building block of early mid-Illinois society is widely believed to have been the free-standing farm with rail fences and a log house, worked by the family that owned it or hoped to. Such farms could and did sustain families, but they could not by themselves sustain a society. That required a nearby place where farmers might trade, where residents might meet and talk and organize themselves to do the things that needed doing, from building a school to plowing a road: in short, a town.

Something like urban society could be found in mid-Illinois as long ago as eighteen hundred years, when Late Woodland people began to congregate in largish settlements for at least part of each year. These settlements were impermanent and inchoate in form, however, and the first towns in the modern sense did not appear until some seven hundred years later. They are thought to have served cultural and political purposes as well as economic ones. The Mississippian society in particular was organized into a distinctly urban hierarchy. At its apex were a few focal towns that lined the lower Illinois River valley every eighty miles or so. Each consisted of a central plaza (probably ceremonial in function) featuring one or more platform mounds, the plaza being surrounded by dwellings spread over ten to fifteen acres. Each such town was the center of a network of lesser villages that usually lacked temple mounds but still boasted central plazas.

At a farther remove from the focal town networks in both location and scale were smaller settlements that lacked the physical organization of towns; least permanent of all were many temporary sites that dotted the hinterlands, from winter-hunting and tool-making camps to fishing camps and gardens. The ancient peoples of the region thus arrayed themselves on the landscape much as would their Euro-American successors, whose urban

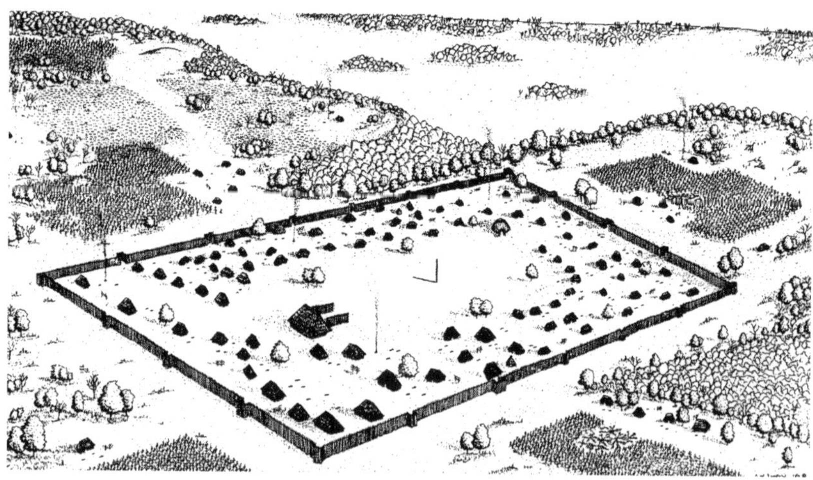

Orendorf Site. On the approximately twenty-acre Orendorf Site above Rice Lake in Fulton County are the remains of a temple village of Mississippian peoples of the thirteenth century. Nearly a hundred buildings stood within a stockaded square; many of them had been burned, contents intact, for reasons that are unclear. DRAWING BY KELVIN SAMPSON. COURTESY OF THE UPPER MISSISSIPPI VALLEY ARCHAEOLOGICAL RESEARCH FOUNDATION.

hierarchy consisted of cities, county market towns, summer resort towns, farm hamlets, and mining and logging "towns" that were in fact temporary work camps.

The Native Americans known to the region's first Euro-American visitors also made towns. The several tribes that made up the Illiniwek confederacy were semisedentary. Summer villages, located near rivers, were inhabited in April and May when corn was planted and again in late summer and fall, when corn was harvested. These towns were often quite large, some consisting of as many as 350 mat-covered communal longhouses, each of which housed about six families. The principal town of the Prairie Band of the Kickapoo, the aforementioned stockaded Grand Village in McLean County, was nearly on this scale,[2] as was a Kickapoo village in the future Indian Grove Township in Livingston County that was home to more than six hundred persons in 1828–30.

The populations of these places were surprisingly diverse. The several tribes within a language group were closely related culturally, and it was not unusual to find people from several tribes living together, along with slaves and possibly war captives from distant people adopted into the tribe. Outwardly so different, these villages in social terms were much like the mid-Illinois small town of the nineteenth century, in which the various tribes that made up the new American people—Yankee and Southerner, Baptist and Catholic, German and Irish, former peasants and former slaves—all lived in the same place.

The first Euro-American settlements in mid-Illinois date back to the first French explorations in the 1670s. People built cabins near forts served by a trading post, or trading posts protected by a fort, for convenience and safety. As noted in chapter 1, what is generally considered the first European town worthy of the name in Illinois was founded in 1778. That year Jean Baptiste Maillet, a French Canadian trader and Indian agent, laid out a street grid at a spot on Peoria Lake on which modern downtown Peoria now stands. Known variously as La Ville de Maillet or the New Village (to distinguish it from an earlier settlement some two miles upstream), the town had rectangular lots lining straight, narrow streets. In addition to houses and gardens of the inhabitants, the town had workshops for a carpenter, a blacksmith, and a cobbler as well as trading shops and a chapel with a large wooden cross on the roof and gilt lettering over the door. Over a period of years some fifty buildings were erected there,[3] which in the Illinois of the time made it a teeming metropolis. Modern Peoria did not grow from it—La Ville de Maillet was abandoned after fifty-one years—but it grew atop it.

LOT MANIA

As we have seen, in the 1820s and 1830s well-drained land near timber was coveted for farmsteads, and as government land in mid-Illinois came on the market these tracts were quickly bought up. Open prairie was all that was left at the low government price to later speculators. Because such holdings were remote from trees needed for fuel and timber, they offered as few natural advantages to the town maker as to the farmer. Their owners therefore sought to give them artificial advantages by establishing businesses that would draw people from surrounding farms to buy and trade.

Such artificial towns could be built almost anywhere, and they were. The result was what one historian called a sort of mania for laying out new towns—on paper. Companies by the dozen, maybe the hundreds, were organized to preempt the best available sites and make plats. In Sangamon County, speculators laid out at least twelve such paper towns from 1835 to 1838. In the same period, Stark County's plat books were enlarged by plans for a half-dozen towns, only two of which (LaFayette and Wyoming) managed the transformation from ink and paper to bricks and timber. Stark County thus had more "towns" in 1840, when its population was fewer than sixteen hundred people, than it did in 1910, when it had ten thousand.[4]

The mania for laying off town lots was nothing compared to the mania for selling them. German immigrant Frederick Julius Gustorf traveled from Philadelphia in 1836 to inspect the German settlements in Illinois and Missouri with an eye toward settling there. Peoria, he found, was "like the bourse in Vienna and Frankfurt am Main, where people by the thousands carry on trade without having a dime in their pockets," he wrote. "People are referred to as being very rich when they have bonds or deeds to a few town lots."[5]

Town making excited the same kind of fevers that today are usually associated with stock markets or lotteries. Jacksonvillian Joseph Duncan, the Whig, took time away from making land deals to run Illinois as its governor from 1834 to 1838. When he stood for election again in 1843, a Chicago newspaper snidely advised Duncan to campaign with a plat of his paper town of Illiopolis, which he had tried to have made the state capital.[6] In the 1830s the State of Illinois proposed to build a canal linking Lake Michigan to the Illinois River near Chicago, a waterway that would open the Illinois River and the adjacent countryside to the Great Lakes (and thus the East Coast). The canal talk touched off what Juliet E. K. Walker has called the most spectacular era in the history of Pike County town origins. Twenty-two towns were founded, nearly all on the Illinois River side of the county where canal boats would soon pass, and Pike's population almost doubled in anticipation of the boom sure to be brought by this access to wider markets. Alas, by the time the Illinois and Michigan Canal opened in 1848, industry was beginning to move on rails, not water. A few boats stopped at Pike, but the rest of the world passed it by.

Often smallish places laid out to serve one purpose became big by serving a wholly unexpected one. The towns of Ripley, White Hall, and Macomb, among others, were founded because the soil in that part of mid-Illinois was good for farming; only later did it become known that the earth in that area offered other commercially exploitable natural resources in the form of clays suitable for potting, a business that sustained the economy of those towns for years.

In Quincy the unexpected resource was human. John Wood and Willard Keyes were eager to earn back with profit the sixty dollars they had spent on a quarter section of land on that spot in 1822. Nature had given Quincy a steep-sided bank that made it the only spot on the Mississippi for 150 miles where the bigger steam-powered riverboats could dock in all seasons,[7] and Wood's astute politicking won Quincy's selection as the county seat (in 1825) and the government land office (in 1831). But Quincy also happened to develop at a time when political and social unrest sent thousands of Germans looking for new life in America. Hundreds of them sailed up the Mississippi River, and those that landed at Quincy gave the town an unexpected and stimulating transfusion of new blood. By 1850, German immigrants made up 40 percent of the town's population. The newcomers were notable practitioners of skilled crafts of all kinds and accounted for much of what passed for culture in Quincy. (They organized seven bands and choirs and a debating club, and founded no fewer than ten German parochial schools and three colleges by the time of the Civil War.[8]) Quincy's German citizens were an economic and cultural advantage that inland competitors could not match, and Quincy became the only real city for a hundred miles in either direction on the Illinois side of the Mississippi.

John Wood was only one of a generation of mid-Illinois town makers from the 1830s through the 1850s whose energy and guile matched their ambition. Galesburg's George Gale and Springfield's Elijah Iles merit mention in that company, but Bloomington's Jesse Fell might have been the region's town maker supreme. He planted towns like trees, cofounding the DeWitt County town of Clinton, establishing Livingston County, and investing in Pontiac, Lexington, Towanda, Clinton, LeRoy, and El Paso.[9]

Bloomington and its sister city now known as Normal were Fell's monuments. In 1837 the city nearest to Bloomington was St. Louis, which was not much closer than the moon in practical terms, being some 150 miles away. The only navigable river, the Illinois, lay more than thirty miles west at Pekin.

The prairie surrounding the spot was swampy much of the year, there was no known coal, no building stone, and limited water good enough to drink. As one chronicler later pointed out, unnecessarily, "This was not a very promising location for a town."[10] So Fell set out to make it one. Exploiting his political connections and a succession of boosting newspapers, he pushed for a public library, a produce market, a grist mill, and, later, for prohibition, firefighting equipment, sidewalks, sewers, and paved streets, and Fell's city got them all.

Fell and his like are long dead, but the boosting impulse survives. Few people outside Mattoon realize that it is "capital of the world" in no fewer than five realms—the "Expansion Capital of the World" during its boom days, "Amish Capital of the World" (because of its proximity to the colony at Arthur, just north of town), the "Tornado Capital of the World" (after a bad one struck in 1917), "Baseball Capital of the World" (because several minor-league teams once were based there), and, after the arrival of a Lender's Bagels factory in 1986, the "Bagel Capital of the World." Presumably it also is the Mattoon Capital of the World, but that is not offered as a distinction.

DOWN BY THE RIVER

Towns tended to sprout wherever people were. As noted, outlying farms and hamlets needed a nearby place with stables, a bank, warehouses, a tannery, and a mill, shops selling the things one could not make, and lawyers and doctors and blacksmiths selling skills one did not possess. Such towns had to lie within a day's ride of the farm families it served, which was not much more than fifteen miles by horse-drawn wagon. Farm towns thus necessarily were situated near where the farmers were, and before the railroad era the farmers were huddled along the forested edge of the prairies. Historian James Davis has calculated that in 1834, nearly all towns platted in the twenty-six counties roughly between Beardstown and Danville and Decatur and Ottawa lay not on the open prairie but near wooded lands. (Danville and Urbana were notable exceptions).[11]

People also congregated on the region's riverbanks at water-powered mills or river landings. Typical was Nimrod Phillips's ferry across the Illinois in Pike County. It began operation in 1822; Phillips Landing, eventually renamed Griggsville Landing, acquired a grist mill, warehouse, boatyard, and lime kiln. Juliet Walker describes how the process transformed places like this one.

> Produce awaiting shipment to New Orleans, eastern markets, or northern Illinois was stored in warehouses at the landings. Eventually, merchants there provided goods and services not only for farmers bringing their

produce to market but also for residents of outlying areas and for laborers from wharves and warehouses. Passengers who disembarked from the steamboats while farm produce was being loaded sometimes made their way to the local grocers, and westward moving pioneers were provisioned by merchants before crossing the Mississippi.[12]

Archeologist Robert Mazrim makes an important point about these early commercial towns in mid-Illinois: Whether they were creatures of convenience or design, they were not only places where business was done but also places where *only* business was done. The proprietors of many towns platted around or adjacent to mill seats sold commercial lots to accommodate distilleries, taverns, and dry goods stores to serve the customers of the mills, but the people who owned and used them continued to live and farm in the nearby countryside. Frontier-era towns in Illinois, Mazrim writes, thus were more akin to modern strip malls than traditional small towns.[13]

Torrence Mill on the south fork of the Sangamon River in Sangamon County's Cotton Hill Township, about 1900. Often, a motley collection of buildings accumulated at such mill sites, like downed trees caught on a sandbar; sometimes they grew into towns. COURTESY OF THE SANGAMON VALLEY COLLECTION, LINCOLN LIBRARY, SPRINGFIELD, ILLINOIS.

People and goods also moved to and fro across the interior of mid-Illinois on land by horse, wagon, and stagecoach, and many interior towns began where those conveyances regularly stopped for water or food. Pike County's Griggsville was platted on a crucial intersection of a road to Phillips Landing when that was the most important point of entry to Pike County from the east; the nearby town of Chambersburg, platted at about the same time three miles from the Illinois River, did not have Griggsville's road access and remained a local market town.[14]

Some towns just growed. Others were cultivated. Thomas Beard settled on a spot on the Illinois River in Cass County "on account of its being a valuable site for a town and a ferry."[15] Each fed the growth of the other. Beard's town soon had a City Hotel, which Beard built to shelter and victual travelers. By 1830 Beard's "city" boasted three stores, a steam-powered grain mill, a sawmill, and a distillery—all essential to a frontier metropolis.

Beard's town quickly became a flourishing trading post and steamboat port that rivaled Peoria. Beardstown was Springfield's Ostia, its Piraeus. One visitor recalled that in 1848 "a traveler between Springfield and Beardstown would rarely be out of sight of heavily loaded wagons carrying out the productions or bringing in the merchants goods"[16]; most of early Springfield's business district stretched along Jefferson Street because it was on that route that freight wagons arrived from Beardstown.[17] One Beardstown patriot recalled in a 1917 address that its businessmen were known as far away as Pittsburgh and New Orleans "while Chicago still lay in its infantile swaddling clothes."[18] Alas, the coming of the railroads took away much of Beardstown's trade. A town usually adopts a nickname when it believes that people have no other reason to remember it. Beardstown has taken several—Belle of the Bend, Friendliest Town in Illinois, Fun Capital of Illinois, Watermelon Capital of the Nation. For a brief but glorious moment, "Beardstown" was enough.

INTENTIONAL TOWNS

A few mid-Illinois towns were simply willed into being. The colony of Bishop Hill, described in chapter 8, was one such place. Another was the Mormon capital of Nauvoo. In three years Nauvoo grew from a hamlet into a city of some twelve thousand people, one of Illinois's biggest cities at the time, an urban blossoming matched in its speed only by Chicago later in the century. It was an impressive testament to the Saints' energy, determination, and faith in their prophet.

The town that Joseph Smith renamed Nauvoo had originally been named Commerce, which was ironic in a town that acquired almost overnight every accoutrement of an advanced town except an economy. The early arrivers made money selling lots to the later arrivals, of which there was a steady stream for a while. But there was no trade with the surrounding countryside, as everything that was made in Nauvoo was made for Nauvoo. By 1843 the Mormons' public and private finances had become so overextended and the prospects of paying off debts so remote that the Mormons resorted to repudiation and bankruptcy to extricate themselves. Had they not been driven out by vigilantes, the townspeople might well have been driven out by bankers.

The Mormons had in mind building a churchly empire. E. E. Malhiot, a wealthy sugar planter who also served in the Louisiana state assembly, dreamed of Mammon. Mid-Illinois being midcontinent, Malhiot in the 1850s envisioned a distribution point there from which products imported from his Southern plantation might be processed for sale to the north. He bought thirty sections of land in Christian County and urged 150 immigrants from his native lower Canada to move there in 1857. A town was platted close to Tacusa, which had been laid out earlier by the Illinois Central Railroad. (The two towns were eventually joined under the name Assumption, where French surnames still adorn both local businesses and notable families.[19]) But while Malhiot imported some sugar, the place never realized his ambitions for it.

No intention created more mid-Illinois towns than building, tending, and loading and unloading railroad trains. In Christian County, Pana's first building was a cabin on the Illinois Central tracks in which lived the grading contractor whose wife fed the workmen building the roadbed.[20] To supply itself with water and wood, the Illinois Central laid out towns every ten miles along its tracks; thus were added the names of Paxton, Peotone, Tolono, Tuscola, Neoga, Monticello, Deland and Weldon, Loda, Dwight, and others to the maps. Trains also had to stop frequently to deliver or pick up freight and passengers; Burtonview, Chesterville, Mountjoy, Narita, Skelton, and Union were just some of the many "grain stations" on the railroad lines in Logan County.

The railroads were not the only companies beguiled by the prospect of profits to be made by founding towns. Several of Pike County's larger farmers platted sections of their fields near where tracks ran, mindful that building lots brought a richer return than corn and only had to be harvested once. Their town cousins across the region were no less keen to seize the opportunity that was the first cargo carried by every new railroad; when the Illinois Central announced it would run its tracks two miles west of Urbana, merchants who smelled a profit filed a plat for a new town, to be called Champaign, before the IC had even secured land for its depot.[21] When a new line bypassed Henry County's Bishop Hill by seven miles in the 1850s, alert Bishop Hill residents bought land straddling the tracks and built stores, a hotel, and warehouses to handle their goods—thus was the town of Galva born.

With every town eager to have a rail connection, the railroads did good business extracting location incentives, or what a ruder age would have called bribes. The Iroquois County town of Gilman, for example, was founded where the new Peoria and Oquawka Railroad crossed the Illinois Central Railroad. In return for making Gilman a passenger and freight stop on the line, the railroad asked for and was given one half of all the lots in the town.[22] The lots were conveyed to the IC's chief engineer; as a rule, railroad companies in Illinois were forbidden by law to found towns themselves, so in such cases they merely arranged for lots to be given to an agent of the road instead.

COMPANY TOWNS

Railroads were not the only firms whose business plans included town making. Many coal mines were on the edges of towns, beyond the reach of streetcars. To accommodate miners, coal companies often built housing near the mine mouths. These coal hamlets were not, however, company towns on the model familiar from other industries and other states. Employees were not compelled to live in company housing and shop at company stores; such practices, widely deplored as exploitive, were banned in much of Illinois by the contracts demanded by the United Mine Workers union. Many of the workers at the McLean County Coal Company's mine in Bloomington lived in Stevensonville, a west-side neighborhood built for the company's miners and named after one of the owners.[23] In Pawnee many miners lived in company-owned houses on the west end of town, a neighborhood known as "the Patch."

In the mid-1800s such housing was rudimentary, little more than shacks. Not so the homes offered by the Standard Oil Company to employees of the two new coal mines on the edge of Carlinville in 1918. The company's Standard Addition consisted entirely of the same "Sears Modern" mail-order home-building kits purchased from Sears and Roebuck by at least seventy thousand middle-class buyers between 1908 and 1940. When the mines closed after only six years, the Standard Addition began to empty; after ten years only eight of the 156 houses were still occupied. Standard Oil got out of the house business by selling them off at a loss of ninety cents on the dollar. One hundred fifty-two of the houses still stand; locals boast that it is the largest single repository of Sears homes in the United States.

Keys Station on the Baltimore and Ohio Railroad, two miles east of Springfield, bore the name of Springfield banker Edward Keys, the mine owner who built it for his crews. In 1906 Keys developed a new kind of worker town. Rather than attract people to jobs, he would attract jobs to people. He laid out a three-hundred-acre subdivision on the edge of Springfield he called Harvard Park that provided space for recreation, work, and shopping as well as housing across the street from a popular park. This family-oriented workforce, Keys hoped, would entice companies to locate there. Just to make sure, Keys offered an Ohio farm implement maker three acres of land and a $15,000 bonus (paid for in part by the house lot sales stimulated by the factory opening) to move to Springfield, which it did, and this town within the town thrived.[24]

GOVERNMENT TOWNS

Selection as a government center was a plum worth climbing high into the tree to get. It meant visitors, which meant hotel and tavern and livery business. It meant jobs for lawyers and clerks, all of whom needed places to live, which meant new housing. Any town site within reasonable riding distance of a county's geographic center made a plausible seat. "Nearly every man or company that had a town-site," wrote one historian of Stark County, "had a map made to show that particular town as being the best situated for the county seat."[25]

The savvy town promoter had to work hard to distinguish his site as the true seat from so many pretenders. Postville was the original seat of Logan County and in 1840 built a wood-frame courthouse in which to do the county's business. (Lincoln frequently argued in its courtroom.) Eight years later, nearby Mount Pulaski helpfully suggested to county officials that their vital records were at risk from fire in Postville's tinderbox of a courthouse, and offered to erect a nice new fireproof brick courthouse to put them in; the officials agreed, the seat was moved to Mount Pulaski, and Postville became just another country town again.

The four speculators who founded Springfield in 1822 had in mind from the start to make it the permanent Sangamon County seat. On the river north of Springfield was Sangamo Town, whose sole owner had won election to the legislature on the promise that he would go to the state capital, Vandalia, and make his town the new county seat. As was the practice, five commissioners were appointed by the State of Illinois to decide the best spot and were lodged in Springfield at the tavern of hunter Andrew Elliott during their inspection tour. According to local lore, Elliott, acting at the behest of Springfield's founders, volunteered to guide the commissioners to Sangamo Town, which he did via a roundabout route that introduced the government agents to most of the neighborhood's bramble patches and creek crossings, then led them back by an even more trying route. The commissioners, warm and well-fed back at Elliott's tavern, concluded in favor of Springfield.[26]

County seat contenders used every weapon in the political arsenal against each other, even inventing one or two new ones. Allies of the Knox County seat of Knoxville, long under siege by Galesburg, had inserted in the new 1870 state constitution a clause stipulating that a proposal to move a county seat farther from the center of the county must be approved by three-fifths of the votes of the county, but if the new location is nearer the center of the county, as Knoxville was, a simple majority would do.

An especially baroque tale began when Cass County was created by the act of the General Assembly; the contest for the seat between Beardstown and Virginia featured vote fixing and midnight raids. (That story is told in chapter 9.) On a memorable night in 1895, the Fulton County courthouse in Lewistown was burned to the ground as the last act in a bitter county seat war between that town and Canton. The incident provided material for several of Edgar Lee Masters's poems, making it one of the few times county government has inspired readable verse.

If the prospect of winning a county seat could inspire such shenanigans, imagine the passions excited by becoming the state's capital city. In 1818 the brand-new General Assembly of the brand new State of Illinois had designated Vandalia as the state's temporary capital city, and there was little enthusiasm for renewing the town's lease when it expired. In 1818 Vandalia had been a southern Illinois town in a state whose population was mostly in southern Illinois; by the 1830s the state's population was mostly in middle Illinois. By 1834 the members of General Assembly were being pressured to follow the people and move state government to a more central location.

Most of the serious contenders—Jacksonville, Springfield, and Peoria—lay in mid-Illinois. In the expectation that the supporters for each would neutralize each other's votes, promoters proposed wholly new towns as compromise alternatives. One was to be built at the geographic center of the state, in Logan County. Another proposed town was Illiopolis, in eastern Sangamon County, whose name suggests the future that its promoters (including Governor Joseph Duncan) hoped for it. (Today's Illiopolis took root in a different spot.)

The political maneuverings were complex, with each faction pushing for the choice of a capital to be made by a commission or by popular referendum, according to which method favored the outcome it desired. Jacksonville offered its reputation as a civilized outpost, and Peoria lay at the inland transportation crossroads of the state; Springfield offered the state free land for a capitol square and $50,000 toward the cost of putting a capitol on it.

Editorialists in each contending town lambasted the claims of the others, warning that its competitors were unhealthful and inconvenient, that the local businesspeople were rogues, and the food indigestible. In this they were all correct to some extent, although only Jacksonville had the bad luck to suffer a cholera outbreak the year before the decision was made. The legislators decided in 1837. It took four ballots before Springfield could muster a majority, but win it did. Losing towns were quick to posit conspiracies to explain their failure, but Springfield proved that a town didn't need conspiracies if it had cash.

The capital proved cheap at the price, according to Simeon Francis, editor of Springfield's influential *Sangamo Journal.*

> The owner of real estate sees his property rapidly enhancing in value; the merchant anticipates a large accession to our population, and a correspondent additional sale for his goods; the mechanic already has more contracts offered him for building and improvement than he can execute; the farmer anticipates, in the growth of a large and important town, a market for the varied products of his farm; indeed, every class of our citizens look to the future with confidence that we trust, will not be disappointed.[27]

Sure enough, the town saw an immediate boom in population. One of these new citizens proved of special importance to the town's future. After adjournment of the session in Vandalia that saw Springfield named the capital, Abraham Lincoln, then a state legislator from New Salem, moved from that log village to Springfield and the wider opportunities for the practice of law and politics promised by its new status.

As Illinois boomed, state government boomed with it. The once huge 1840 statehouse on Springfield's square soon was bursting at the seams, and in 1867 legislators voted to build a bigger one. Without a usable capital building, Springfield no longer had an automatic claim to be the state's capital city. A new statehouse could have been built anywhere, and Peoria, Chicago, and Decatur were among the cities that tried to snatch the prize from Springfield. Macoupin County began construction of a new courthouse in 1867 that was grand enough to be a statehouse, and talk was that Carlinville interests hoped to see it used for just that purpose.

Springfield leaders were alert to the danger, however. They offered the state an attractive site for a new capitol in the form of a large block of land just west of downtown. (The tract had been originally purchased in the hope that Lincoln would be buried there, conveniently near the city's hotels and rail stations.) Sangamon County also offered to lower the cost of the project to the state's taxpayers by purchasing the 1840 state capitol for use as its courthouse—the first time that governmental body showed much interest in recycling. Springfield as a result won the state capital again and happily looked forward to decades during which its name would be cursed every time state government came up in conversation anywhere in Illinois.

Courthouses were not the only government prizes that towns lusted after. State-run custodial institutions, for example, had payrolls numbering in the hundreds and were coveted as much as any factory, which unfortunately they often resembled. Competition to be picked as a site for one was correspondingly fierce. Such prizes usually were awarded as regional politics dictated, and populous mid-Illinois got its share—the Illinois Soldiers' Orphans' Home in Normal (1869) for children orphaned by the Civil War, the boys reform school at Pontiac (1872) that became the Pontiac Correctional Center, the Illinois State Hospital for the Insane outside Peoria, and the Illinois Soldiers' and Sailors' Home in Quincy (1885) for veterans of the Mexican and Civil wars.

Educational institutions also were coveted. The siting in Jacksonville of the Illinois Asylum for the Education of the Deaf and Dumb (1839) had salved that town's disappointment at losing the state capital. The Illinois Industrial University, as the University of Illinois was originally known, was an even sweeter prize. Champaign-Urbana's success in being chosen the site for the new school led other towns to complain that the Twin Cities had lobbied unfairly, which in the context of Illinois politics is like complaining that a mugger is ill-mannered. If by "unfair" critics meant that Champaign-Urbana's bid was more generous than theirs, they were correct. Champaign County offered to donate more than eight hundred acres with a ready-to-use building on it in the form of the Urbana and Champaign Institute, a coeducational boarding school that stood in the open space between the two towns. (That is why the future University of Illinois's main campus is the hyphen in Champaign-Urbana.) The county also tossed in $400,000 in cash, $2,000 worth of shade and ornamental trees, and $50,000 worth of free shipping from the Illinois Central Railroad.

The Illinois State Fair began as an educational institution too. Travel in the mid-1800s was still inconvenient for rural residents, and the State of Illinois considerately sought to take its annual agricultural exposition to the people, staging it in twelve locations around the state between 1853 and 1893. By the end of the nineteenth century, railroads had made it so easy for farmers to get to the fair that the state no longer had to take the fair to the farmers. Bloomington, Decatur, Peoria, and Springfield vied for the chance to host a permanent fairgrounds. Each offered the state what amounted to a dowry, of which Springfield's was the richest—lots of free land fenced and piped, two years of free electric lighting, free water forever, plus $50,000 in cash. The new permanent fair thus produced at least one blue-ribbon sore loser. "The grass in the streets [of Springfield]," one Peoria newspaper writer sneered, "would make the farmers feel right at home."[28]

DEPARTING METROPOLISES

Nothing in the humanized landscape seems more permanent than a town, but hundreds of towns from the early Euro-American era no longer exist except in local records and lore.[29] Commercial towns, for example, died for want of commerce. As noted above, Sangamo Town on the Sangamon River was platted in 1823 and for a time was being promoted as the site for the new Sangamon County seat. When it failed to secure a future as a government center, Sangamo Town's only future was as a milling and service town, but it lost business to more energetic younger men at New Salem, eight miles away by water. The founders went bankrupt in 1844, milling at the site ceased by the early 1850s, and the site was eventually plowed and pastured, its exact location forgotten.[30]

Farm towns withered as rural populations shrank. Carl Van Doren and his brother Mark grew up in Hope, in west-central Vermilion County. Carl was to recall that as the 1900s dawned, Hope consisted of a church, a school, a blacksmith shop, two stores, and ten houses that were home to some fifty persons.[31] Well over a mile from any rail line, the town was doomed, and when Carl went back to visit in 1933 most of the houses were gone. Even the name had disappeared with the loss of the local post office. "Hope is a gray monument," he wrote. "Yet there a microcosm formed and dissolved, and there the essential story of an older America was compressed into three generations."[32]

Railroads probably killed as many towns as they helped create. One example of many is Frank McWhorter's New Philadelphia settlement in Pike County; its population peaked in 1865, when 170 people lived there, but the lack of a railroad connection killed it as a going concern, and today the site is farm fields.

Some towns facing extinction because a railroad did not come to them decided, as a Muhammed might do, to go the railroad. The Champaign County village of Homer grew up in the 1830s around a mill on the Salt Fork of the Vermilion River. When the Wabash Railroad laid track a mile or so south, an enterprising Homer businessman bought land and traded a lot in his new Homer for a lot in the old one, after which every building that could be moved was loaded atop a freight wagon and hauled to its new home.

House moving took literal form in the mid-1800s. The village of Bristol in Effingham County was bypassed when the Illinois Central went through about one mile to the northwest. The alert proprietors in 1852 laid out the new town of Mason along the new tracks, loaded Bristol's buildings onto "skid-poles" pulled by six yoke of cattle, and hauled them to the new town site. "There was no weeping, no sighing," wrote a commentator at the time, "for be it known that the citizens of Bristol, one and all, trudged along in the rear of their departing metropolis, like infatuated school-boys after a brass band, resolved to share alike in its prosperity or downfall."[33]

A few towns died only to rise again. Ramus was founded by Mormons in 1840 and renamed Macedonia in 1843. In 1845 its more than five hundred residents made it the third-largest town in Hancock County. It was largely abandoned after the Mormon exodus, in 1846. One of the Saints' erstwhile enemies in the press suggested that all Mormon place names be obliterated, the quicker to forget the painful episode. Scholar Susan Rugh explains that Macedonia, for example, began to call itself Webster. "Thus purged of all references to Mormons, the empty town . . . became habitable again."[34]

GRIDS AND SQUARES

As noted, each of the native peoples of mid-Illinois in successive eras built according to their own vernacular town-planning traditions, and their Euro-American successors were no different. Most French American villages in the Illinois Territory consisted of narrow individual house lots lining a road or a riverbank, behind each of which stretched "long lots" which the occupants farmed, behind which in turn lay an unfenced commons for grazing. The French-Indian trading villages at Peoria disdained the long lots as irrelevant to their economy.[35]

The first real metropolis in the Euro-American era was Nauvoo. Mormon leader Joseph Smith believed in cities, in part because proximity facilitated communalism of the sort on which Nauvoo's social order was based. In 1833 he borrowed from both the Old Testament and the New World (the latter in the form of the towns he had known in the eastern United States) to concoct a plan for his ideal "City of Zion." In some of its principal features, Smith's ideal city anticipated upscale subdivisions two centuries hence—houses in brick or stone set on deep landscaped lots with gardens in the back, with noisome land uses such as farms banished to the edge of town.

Smith's ideal city, however, would have been built on the imperial rather than the small-town scale. His plan called for a perfectly rectangular street grid that created square blocks that stretched six hundred feet on a side (twice as long as most city blocks) and covered ten acres each. (The statehouse grounds

Nauvoo panorama. A lithograph of a painting of abandoned Nauvoo, between 1848 and 1850. The size of the half-wrecked temple was exaggerated by the unknown artist, but the reality had been impressive enough. COURTESY LIBRARY OF CONGRESS, LC-USZ62–44132.

in Springfield cover only about nine acres.) These blocks were separated by streets that could have doubled as parade grounds, being 132 feet wide—twice as wide as the Mall that leads to Buckingham Palace in London, and a third again as wide as Pennsylvania Avenue in Washington, D.C. Smith might have concluded in the end that such extravagant public ways were an impractical use of precious real estate; when he laid out his actual City of Zion in Nauvoo, Smith made the streets closer to thirty feet in width and blocks less than four hundred feet on a side.

Many of the region's secular towns also had prophets of a sort in the persons of their businessmen-founders, but the god they served was profit. Virtually all mid-Illinois towns were alike in being laid out in rectilinear grids of easy-to-measure blocks that squeezed the maximum number of salable lots out of every acre of land. Reliable surveyors were more crucial to this work than town planners, and the good ones were respected and well paid. The work was especially appealing to the young and in-debt Abraham Lincoln; he trained himself, and during the town site craze in the 1830s laid out several mid-Illinois towns, including Petersburg and Bath.

Be their blocks square or rectangular, all promoters wanted a layout whose simplicity, clarity, and accuracy would forestall disputes over titles of the sort that bedeviled Pekin. When the site of Tazewell County's seat was surveyed and platted, it was done by the county surveyor who, lacking a proper surveyor's chain, did the job with a length of knotted string. The resulting confusion complicated local land titles for decades.[36]

When it came to providing for public uses such as marketplaces, courthouses, and parks, most town proprietors simply used templates they remembered from home. Some towns in mid-Illinois have squares on a Pennsylvania model, the "Philadelphia/Lancaster square," which is carved out of a street intersection by appropriating the corners of the adjoining four blocks; Monmouth, Jacksonville, Galesburg, and Shelbyville are among the region's towns whose business districts are graced with this elegant form. More common in the region is the square as perfected in Shelbyville, Tennessee, which is just an ordinary city block set aside for the purpose; Taylorville and Springfield opted for this layout.[37] Macomb's courthouse square will bring a tear to the eye of homesick Virginians, it being modeled on the layout pioneered in Harrisonburg, Virginia. Two adjacent downtown blocks are redrawn to form three smaller ones, with the result that a major east-west street intersects the courthouse block, creating an imposing view; it was laid out by McDonough County's first county clerk, a transplanted Kentuckian.

The towns-within-towns that are the college campuses at the heart of several Yankee towns in the region tend to resemble the centers of New England towns, with greensward commons flanked by chapels or important town buildings. Knox College, Monmouth College, Blackburn College, and Illinois College embody this style, as does the older parts of the University of Illinois in Urbana.

Indeed, one of the comeliest and best-planned towns in mid-Illinois is the University of Illinois's main campus. Such has been its growth that the Twin Cities of Champaign and Urbana came to seem misnamed. The urban center of Champaign County should be called the Tri-Cities, the third city being the University of Illinois. With total enrollments above forty thousand in recent years, the campus is, like most campuses, a world unto itself. Most sociologists would class the campus as an enclave on the order of a Chicago parish, not a city, but while the campus community is dependent for many ordinary services on the two cities that surround it, its size makes the university practically, if not officially, a sovereign power in its own right. For decades the U of I has been not merely the biggest employer in the county but also one whose payroll is ten times bigger than the next biggest employer. It has its own police force, its own urban planners, its own newspaper, its own power system, its own public transit system. It even can be said to have its own legislative delegation; so crucial is the success of the university to the success of its host cities that local legislators tend to vote as if they were representing it in Springfield as well as their districts.

TOWN REMAKERS

Town plats specified where squares and courthouses and, later, parks ought to be placed, but in most towns the siting of every other structure was decided by the dictates of an unregulated land market. Factories and mines blighted residential neighborhoods, train tracks dismembered neighborhoods and blocked streets. After World War I, businesspeople interested in healthier economies allied themselves with social reformers interested in healthier people; together they pushed for reforms in the ways cities were developed.

Two mid-Illinois cities hired the Chicago firm of American Park Builders to devise plans for a more ordered future city. The Decatur Association of Commerce in 1920 unveiled a comprehensive and ambitious blueprint for a new and improved "City Practical" in anticipation of growth that was expected to swell the city's population from roughly 45,000 people in 1920 to 150,000 or more over the next half century. Street bottlenecks would be straightened and automobile and rail traffic untangled. New parks would be built, private streetcar lines would be integrated, a new civic center would be built. Decatur's factory district had accreted along the Wabash Railroad's right of way in the center of town; the new plan would quarantine noxious enterprises in new, more remote factory districts.[38]

A similar plan for Springfield, published in 1923, was just as ambitious. (One of its ambitions, presumably, was to outdo Decatur.) Central to the scheme to make Springfield a capital city in fact as well as name were scenic drives and monumental boulevards linking a new multiline or "union" train station with Lincoln's home and tomb and the state capitol, a reliably clean public water supply, and improved sewage disposal. But while many improvements based on the plans were made in both Springfield (a new municipal reservoir) and Decatur (an elevated road over downtown rail yards), the Great Depression and war ensured that no work was done on the scale proposed. What little was realized took decades to build, and mid-Illinois lost its chance to become a showcase of progressive-era city planning.

THE UNMAKING OF THE MID-ILLINOIS TOWN

Since the 1920s or thereabouts, a new cycle of town unmaking began in mid-Illinois. Just as railroad and road bridges made river ferry stops obsolete, air-conditioning made summer resort towns along the Illinois River obsolete. Coal towns emptied as miners commuted to and from town in their cars just like clerks and counter help. Mid-Illinois farmers still live on isolated farmsteads as

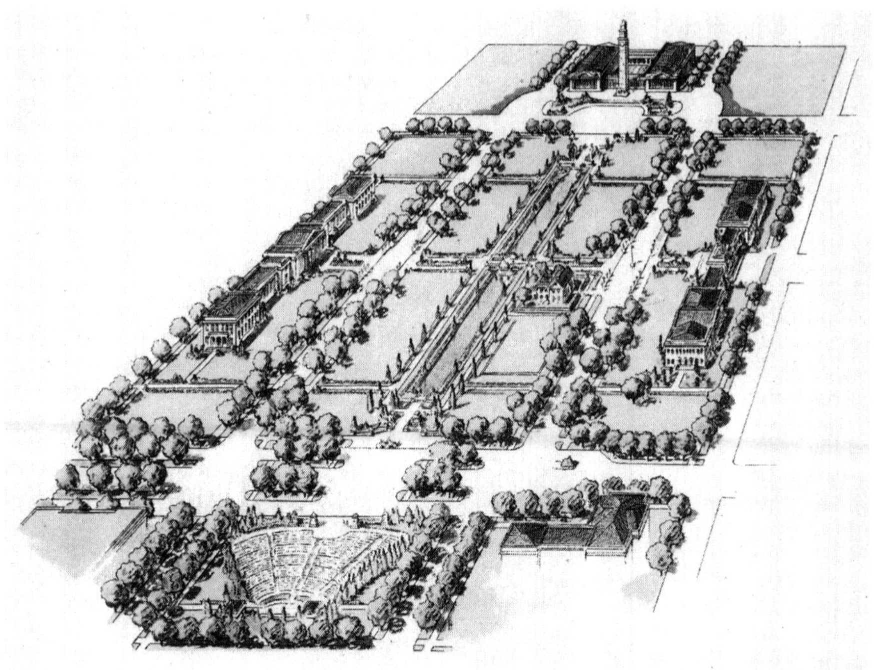

Proposed Lincoln home monument. History wins over hero worship. This 1920s proposal would have created for the Lincolns' home in Springfield "a setting to this modest little cottage befitting its importance" with an amphitheater and a reflecting pool flanked by public buildings. When the National Park Service took over the property in 1971 it undertook to re-create the house's original setting—a middle-class Springfield neighborhood of the 1850s. FROM *CITY PLAN OF THE CITY OF SPRINGFIELD, ILLINOIS*, BY MYRON HOWARD WEST, AMERICAN PARK BUILDERS, SPRINGFIELD ZONING AND PLAN COMMISSION (CHICAGO: MANZ CORPORATION, 1925), 4.

they have since the first scratch-and-poke agriculturalists squatted on government land in the 1820s. But scientific agriculture has come to mean peopleless agriculture, and the depopulation of the countryside that began about the time of the Civil War has continued unabated, sapping the populations of the small towns that once served the many farmers and their families.

Dozens, maybe hundreds, of small towns in the region have passed the point at which their populations can sustain themselves. They face again the dilemma described by Rebecca Burlend, who settled Pike County in the frontier era. Her new neighborhood, she wrote, "is very thinly populated . . . and on that account it is not the situation for shopkeepers." It is not the situation for local government either; as the twenty-first century began, more and more towns in the region found it hard to find people to serve on local government commissions and school boards and in volunteer fire departments.

In another paradox, the decline of farms and small towns in many cases has accelerated the urbanization of rural counties. Health care facilities and nursing homes that would have been impractical in very small towns cluster profitably in the larger ones. This concentration draws even more people in from the countryside, perpetuating a trend in which the smallest country towns lost people and business to their somewhat larger neighbors down the road. Pittsfield has always been the biggest town in modern Pike County, but while fewer than one in ten Pike Countians lived in the county seat in 1930, in 2010 the town was home to more than one in four of the county's people. Canton is another example. Since 1960 that Fulton County town has grown by nearly 7 percent while the county's population shriveled nearly 11 percent.

Many of the region's larger cities got that way thanks to a revolution in shipping—railroads—that dramatically dropped costs and made it possible to deliver goods manufactured in mid-Illinois to distant American markets. A similar revolution that began in the 1950s—containerization—made it possible to manufacture and ship goods to those American markets more cheaply than most mid-Illinois factories could. The resulting closures have spurred an exodus from the region's factory towns. In the forty years after the Civil War, Decatur's population grew more than fivefold, and between 1900 and 1980 the city nearly managed that feat again. Since then Decatur has been shrinking, losing nearly twenty thousand people by 2010. Danville peaked in 1970 with around forty-three thousand people and by 2010 had ten thousand fewer. Galesburg lost four thousand of its thirty-six thousand people in the same period, and Quincy was down 10 percent from its 1970 peak.

New ways to move people have also accelerated population shifts within the region. The availability of affordable automobiles (and roads fit to drive on) had promised, briefly, to revive moribund towns off the main rail lines. John Hallwas reports that when the state built Route 9 through Colchester, in 1925, the townspeople celebrated with a four-day Hard Road Opening and Fall Trading Festival complete with a "pavement dance."[39] Their glee owed to the expectation that shoppers from isolated farms and hamlets could now conveniently travel to the shops of Colchester. The new roads did indeed invigorate trade but not, ultimately, in Colchester. The new road made it just as easy for local shoppers to get to Macomb and Galesburg. Business in Colchester fell after it was connected to this wider world—a decline repeated in hundreds of mid-Illinois small towns whose once-captive buyers were liberated by the car.

Paradoxically, the automobile, having eviscerated so many isolated rural small towns, is saving many others that happen to lie within convenient driving distances of larger places offering jobs. Small-towners began driving into the cities every morning to work, and city people moved into small towns within commuting distance every evening to sleep. The more vigorous the local economy of these suburbanizing cities, the more energetically is settlement pushed out into the countryside. Its effects are especially plain around the mid-Illinois cities of Springfield, Bloomington-Normal, and Champaign-Urbana. Departing from the regional trend, these cities grew (albeit modestly) once they made a successful transition to more service-based economies based on health care, insurance, distribution, retailing, higher education, and government services.

Many a dying farm town now welcomes suburbanites as their great-grandparents welcomed settlers. These new pioneers arrive in SUVs rather than wagons, but they find in these once-dying towns the same attractions that appealed to their predecessors, mainly cheap land on which one could build a house and raise a family, only now the farmstead is a fenced-in backyard, the livestock pets, and the crop grass. In suburbanizing farm towns such as Sadorus and Savoy and many others, chances are good that the guy in the next booth at the diner talking about his new John Deere is describing not a combine harvester but a riding mower.

CHAPTER FIVE

"Well known repugnances": Antagonism and Accommodation in Mid-Illinois

> I felt we had four strikes against us: we lived in the south end of town, we were Catholic, we were miners, and we were foreigners.
> —member of a Moweaqua coal-mining family

In Springfield at the start of the twentieth century, the luckier among the city's orphaned African American children were adopted, in fact if not always in law, by local black families. The unlucky ones faced life on the streets, as the city's three orphanages shut their doors to children of color.

Eva Carroll Monroe thought that was wrong. In 1898 the not quite thirty-year-old Eva and her sister Olive Price Monroe bought a rickety house on Twelfth Street, four blocks from the Lincolns' old place, using as a down payment $125 that Eva had saved. There Monroe opened the Lincoln Colored Home, thought to have been the first orphanage for black children in Illinois, and installed herself as superintendent. Soon the home had more children to feed than Eva had money to feed them with. The African American Monroe found a benefactor in a wealthy white widow (and fellow club woman), who rescued Monroe from foreclosure, retired the mortgage, and arranged for a new house to be built on the site in 1904.

The death of her benefactor a year later left Monroe having to rely on donations and fund-raising in the black community to keep her charges clothed and fed. (The home later received modest subsidy from one of the new social service agencies that sprouted in Illinois cities during the Progressive Era.) So it went for twenty-nine years, as the house slowly fell apart. Monroe's home and her training were found to be substandard according to the stricter criteria of a later day, and her institution's state license was revoked in 1933. As one account had it, progressivism's success in protecting the professions from the

Eva Monroe. Born in Kewanee in 1868, Eva Carroll Monroe (*second from right, with three of her sisters*) was the founder and long-time superintendent of the Lincoln Colored Home, thought to have been the first orphanage for black children in Illinois. COURTESY OF THE SANGAMON VALLEY COLLECTION, LINCOLN LIBRARY.

untrained and incompetent meant that some of the most vulnerable children in Springfield were left unprotected from much worse.[1]

Springfield's historic sites commission today describes the house as "testament to the results of cooperation between the races in the early part of the previous century."[2] One could argue that the need for the home also was a testament to other, less admirable aspects of the relationship between the races in the early part of the previous century. The Fourteenth Amendment removed the color line from the Illinois statute books after the Civil War, but new, invisible lines were drawn on the maps—through neighborhoods, in workplaces, in theaters—to denote African Americans' place in mid-Illinois.

Mainstream mid-Illinois society was open-minded to the extent that prejudice had no prejudice. Migrant Others in every era were greeted with systematic social exclusion (with and without official sanction) maintained by means that ranged from shunning to terrorism. White Americans tried to force Illinois's remnant native population to live behind invisible lines on the land—lines only the white-skinned could see, and which they ignored or redrew when it was convenient for them to do so before they pushed the Indians outside the region altogether. The foreign-born, the Roman Catholic, the Jew tripped on such lines too, where they were drawn across the entrances to the region's parlors and clubs. Women had been constrained by lines drawn through the statute books, whose contents forbade them property ownership or equal guardianship of their own children. The mad and the slow-witted had no place in the wider world at all but were secreted at home or in poorhouses and jails.

As for white people, they were united only in their mutual denigration of people of color. Jacksonville in the 1850s, for example, was only one of many towns in the region where conflicting views among their citizens about religion, nativism, temperance, and slavery made political life not only turbulent but also downright dangerous. According to Don Harrison Doyle, there were "Southerners caning Yankees, vigilante mobs chasing abolitionists, Christians squabbling over the doctrine of infant baptism, police raids on Irish grog shops, violent demonstrations to protest the Civil War . . . a Hobbesian jungle of violent discord."[3] The description of Jacksonville as a jungle might be more vivid than accurate, but the potential for conflict there and in places like it across mid-Illinois was often real.

Such outbreaks as did occur were most common during periods of social upset. Disputes over the fur trade, over slaves, over ancient enmities set native peoples against each other with such vehemence that casualties were measured in villages, not just bodies. Turbulence came again, like an August thunderstorm, when Euro-American colonizers disturbed settled Indian ways; again during the couple of decades before 1812, when native peoples asserted themselves against the usurpations of the whites; and during the protracted emancipation of African Americans that began in 1870. White opposed white during the Civil War years and again during World War I; "native" opposed "ethnic" when both crowded into newly industrial cities. In each case, what was perceived, however improbably, as threats to the established order by outsiders led to communal violence in mid-Illinois. Even though sporadic and usually isolated in its effects, such violence is significant as evidence of the intensity if not the breadth of local feeling about such matters. Mid-Illinois's social landscape, then, is like its physical one in having a deceptively placid surface but shaped by the often violent clash of great forces on the global scale.

INDIAN WARS

Along a western bluff overlooking the Illinois River in Fulton County has been found evidence of a people of the Upper Midwest whose culture archeologists designated the Oneota. They were first in the valley around 1300 A.D., when the region was still occupied by peoples of the Mississippian culture, and traces of them disappeared a century and a half later. The coexistence of the two people was not, apparently, a peaceful one. Of nearly three hundred individuals buried at one Oneota site, the skeletons of fifty show evidence of violent death over a period of years. Twenty-six had had their heads cut off, probably to be kept as trophies; some of those whose heads were intact had been scalped. Arrows and stone axes and war clubs killed men, women, and children indiscriminately. One man in his thirties must have fought like a demon, succumbing in the end to four stone ax blows to the head, two arrows in the chest, two arrows through the back, and one embedded in the sternum. A child between two and three died from a blow to the head and was subsequently scalped. All the corpses were left lying where they fell, for the animals to have.

Because the history of the Illiniwek overlapped that of the Euro-Americans in Illinois, what happened to that Native American confederation is clearer, if no happier. As was noted in chapter 1, the Illiniwek nation once was a powerful alliance of five tribal groups, all cultural kin. It was they who met Jolliet and Marquette when the Jesuit missionary and the fur trader ventured into mid-Illinois in 1673. By then, however, the Illiniwek were a power in decline. The fur trade in the East had unsettled the continent. To secure pelts, the fearsome Iroquois moved west from their stronghold in the Northeast, pushing Great Lakes tribes, including the Illiniwek, ahead of them into Illinois and beginning (in 1655 or so) a series of murderous assaults on the Illiniwek.[4] The Iroquois were themselves finally pushed back east with the help of the French after 1667, but disease and the Iroquois had left the surviving Illiniwek too weak to repel new interlopers from the north who were politically more adept and militarily more formidable. Within a century of the Iroquois incursions, the Illiniwek were huddling behind the log walls of French fur-trading posts for protection.

Social relations among these interlopers were themselves complex and often violent during the century and a half before their own final expulsion from Illinois by Euro-Americans in the 1830s. There were constant clashes against each other, against the British with the French during the French and Indian War (1754–63), against the Americans with the British in the Revolutionary War, and later against American settlers.

From 1719 to 1730, for instance, the Mesquakie (or the Fox, as they were known to the French) fought the Illiniwek and the latter's French allies in a war that ended only after a siege of a fortified position near what is today the McLean County village of Saybrook. There, fourteen hundred French and Indian allies killed five hundred and captured three hundred (forty of whom were burned alive) of a Mesquakie force of nearly a thousand. (In proportion to population, this was carnage on the scale of Antietam or Shiloh, but the encounter is seldom remembered in histories of Illinois.) By 1733 fewer than one hundred Mesquakie remained alive.[5]

The French Canadians, like the British, had been interested in trade, which suited the Indians, however much the latter might have grumbled about its terms. The Americans, when they came, were interested in land, which did not suit the Indians at all. What white people called settlement was regarded by many Indian bands as occupation, and Indian resistance mounted when the newcomers made clear that they wanted it all, that they treated dishonestly, and that they would side with any white person against any Indian regardless of circumstance.

Incidents of aggression and retribution along the mid-Illinois frontier became common. James Gilham and his family lived on a remote farm in the future Logan County. While Gilham was away hunting in 1790, Kickapoo warriors kidnapped his wife, Ann, and three of her children, who were eventually ransomed by the husband.[6] A nineteenth-century historian of Fulton County mentions an episode from this period involving a resident of Dean's Settlement in the southeast part of the county. "One day when he was out in the woods hunting he came across one of his hogs that had just been killed in the woods. He told some of his neighbors he knew the Indians had killed his hog, and he was going to have his revenge. A day or two later a dead Indian was found propped up, sitting on the dead hog."[7]

A war of Native American resistance in the Ohio Country to the east of Illinois was ended by treaty in 1795. The agreement left the younger and determinedly anti-American leaders among them unhappy; to keep the peace, their elders encouraged them to move away from the white settlements into more sparsely settled territories to the west. Several of what Ann Durkin Keating calls "those troublesome young men" established villages in mid-Illinois, mainly along the Kankakee and Illinois Rivers.

The Indian communities already in Illinois were disturbed by this new presence among them. Among the Potawatomi, Gomo, one of the village leaders on the Illinois River, favored peace with the Americans; newcomer Main Poc and his followers, who lived not far away, ardently yearned to expel them. The Prairie Band of the Kickapoo were in favor of armed resistance; the head of the Vermilion Band, the prophet Kennekuk, preached accommodation. The debates among these leaders anticipated those among white people a generation later about ridding Illinois of slavery, or, a generation after that, about how to respond to other "invasions" of mid-Illinois by immigrants of southern and eastern Europeans, and, later, of Southern African Americans.

The Indians found allies in their fight against the Americans when the United States declared war on Britain in 1812. Territorial governor Ninian Edwards, eager for honors, organized attacks on the Native American allies of the British who were living around the future Peoria. In retaliation, Potawatomi warriors, traditional allies of the British, looted Ville de Maillet, now considered an "American" settlement.

Soon thereafter, Captain Thomas Craig arrived at Ville de Maillet with another troop of Illinois militia. They found the place occupied only by its elders and children. If some Indians hated the French because they now were putatively Americans, many Americans hated the French Canadians because they were only putatively French; the *métis* had Indian blood. (Many of the traders also had long ties of kinship and business with the British in Canada.[8]) Keating makes the point that to American militiamen, the French and métis traders were as much a part of the Indian country they sought to destroy as were the Indians themselves. When Craig's party was fired on, the outraged Americans burned to the ground the town's houses and barns and took forty-one men, women, and children as prisoners of war and transported them downriver where they abandoned them in freezing weather. In reality, the villagers had been kidnapped, despite most of them being American citizens.

The failed uprising in 1832 led by the Sauk war chief Black Hawk effectively ended Native American resistance in this part of the Midwest, and when the last of the Indians agreed to leave for new lands in the West, the final legal obstacle to white settlement was removed. The last actual obstacle to settlement was the Native Americans themselves. When the Potawatomi chief Menominee and his band at Twin Lakes, Indiana, refused to abide by the removal treaties, the State of Indiana sent militiamen to remove them. The result was a forced march across mid-Illinois in the autumn of 1838 that took some nine hundred people through Danville, Catlin (then known as Sandusky Point), Monticello, Decatur, Springfield, Jacksonville, Exeter, Naples, and finally Quincy. Some forty people died from fever or stress, many of them children, which is why the journey is known among the Potawatomi as the Trail of Death.

Such episodes have been presented variously as the extermination of vermin, as a sad but unavoidable side effect of civilization's march, as a test of competing economic systems. Seen from the perspective of the early twenty-first century, the expulsion of the native peoples from this part of Illinois looks more like the forced repatriations after World War II, the partition of the Indian subcontinent, the dismemberment of the former Yugoslavia—ethnic cleansing at its most ruthless.

ENEMIES WITHIN

The threat of insurrection rose again in the 1840s. The State of Illinois was but thirty years old. It had emerged from its frontier stage, but its institutions were still feeble, its official resources were limited, and the government in Springfield seemed a long way from most of its people in every sense. The possibility that the new state might fall victim to insurrection seems absurd today, but mid-Illinoisans were sufficiently convinced of it to take up arms against what they saw as a threat to the established order—the Mormon city of Nauvoo.

Many Latter-Day Saints were and remain inclined to see the Illinois experience as simply another instance of their victimization by religious bigotry, but the realities were anything but simple. John Hallwas has noted that the political thought prevalent in mid-Illinois's western counties sprang from a Jacksonian civic theology. Temporal and spiritual powers were seen to be fused in the common man, and the practice of popular sovereignty was understood as the best means to realize the nation's destiny, which many hoped to achieve in the new West.

The Mormons' theology, in contrast, fused temporal and spiritual power in their church and its priestly elite. Hallwas notes that the creed of prophet Joseph Smith was reactionary insofar as it looked back to the Puritan age rather than forward. Like Puritan leaders, Smith saw his followers as a morally superior people with a millennial mission to create a new society enjoying a covenanted relationship to God. "He asserted that the Mormons alone were the chosen people, not the American public," sums up Hallwas, "and that. . . . the nation would fulfill its divine destiny through the Saints."[9]

This was not a view likely to find favor among neighbors who believed just as fervently that it was through *them* that the nation would fulfill its divine destiny. If Mormons were convinced that the Gentiles of western Illinois threatened their religion, the Gentiles were just as sure that Nauvoo threatened their government. Critics of the Mormons, then and later, argued that the cause of the dispute was indeed ultimately political, not religious, and owed to the Mormons' attempt to establish for its faithful a separate state within the state for its faithful. "We believe they have the same rights as other religious bodies," wrote the editor of the Gentile newspaper in nearby Warsaw at the time. "But whenever they, as a people, step beyond the proper sphere of a religious denomination, and become a political body, as many of our citizens are beginning to apprehend will be the case, then this press stands pledged to take action against them."[10]

The new city-state would have troubled even a mature government, thanks to the privileged place occupied by Nauvoo and its citizens within the Illinois commonwealth. Since their arrival in 1839, the Mormons had voted as a bloc at the direction of Smith. Illinois was then evenly divided politically, and because bloc voting gave the Mormons enormous leverage in close statewide races, they were eagerly courted by both Whig and Democratic politicians. Smith sold his favor in Springfield in return for a unique state charter that allowed the town to operate effectively as a state within the state, having its own courts and its own militia (the Nauvoo Legion) entirely independent of the regular state militia and commanded solely by Mormon officers.

Smith did not shrink from exploiting these advantages. Attempts by Missouri authorities to extradite him to be tried in that state for various crimes (including plotting to murder a former governor) were frustrated by Smith's insistence that such charges be heard in Nauvoo, where his own municipal court quickly released him for want of evidence. When Smith's opponents in Nauvoo published a newspaper alleging that Smith misused money and courts and seduced women, Smith ordered the printing press smashed by his troops. Such incidents made wild rumors about Smith's plan to use the Nauvoo Legion to take over the state easy to believe.

When the printing press incident led to a charge of inciting a riot, Smith was ordered by Illinois governor Thomas Ford to face trial at Carthage. On June 27, 1844, fearful that the law might set him free again, some of the 150 or so armed men outside the Hancock County jail broke into the upstairs room where Smith was being confined. Smith was shot four times in the back as he ran for the window; he fell outside to the ground, fatally wounded. Thus was a martyr born and a controversy created.

Was ever there a mob that did not believe it acted for justice, to repair a breakdown in law and order? Smith's many enemies were convinced that the State of Illinois could not protect them from a Mormon Nauvoo that made and enforced its own laws; in such an extremity, they believed, mob law was better than no law at all. A breakdown in law and order in that part of mid-Illinois there clearly was. Governor Ford's promise to protect Smith and his companions from agitated locals proved beyond the state's ability to provide; the local militia company mustered to keep the peace was composed of anti-Mormon locals and offered no resistance to his murderers. The subsequent trial of Smith's killers ended in acquittals; neither juries of Nauvooites nor those of non-Mormons would convict anyone accused of violence against the other.

Alarmed, the legislature in Springfield repealed the Nauvoo charter, which left the city without a government and exposed it to both the depredations of its enemies and the arbitrary edicts of church leaders. After Smith's death, Mormons remained at Nauvoo for two years, a period of escalating threats, rumors, court fights, and the rushing to and fro of armed men. Mob violence erupted more than once in and around the city. Avoiding Nauvoo, which was defended by its own (superior) militia, the area's anti-Mormon irregulars turned on the isolated Mormon villages in the area. Mormon houses and barns were burned; Mormons were accused of retaliating by driving away cattle and stealing their opponents' crops from their fields.

Worse seemed possible. By the following June, an anti-Mormon force of about four hundred lay siege to Nauvoo, and by mid-July the local papers were reporting that an open state of war existed in the county. It was plain that the only solution to the violence was for the Mormons to leave Illinois. In February 1846, Brigham Young, who had taken over as head of the church after Smith's death, led four hundred families west across the frozen Mississippi in the first wave of an exodus that would eventually see the Saints reestablished in Utah. Nauvoo was largely empty by late summer when a "Battle of Nauvoo" broke out for several days. The city surrendered to a seven-hundred-man posse that guaranteed to protect the remaining Mormons until they could join their fellow citizens.

The Mormon War was, in military terms, not much of a war—a few skirmishes and one incident of cannon fire that mainly frightened the local cows. But it was clear that without the moderating effect of state officials, the potential for something like civil war had been real enough. The "old settlers," as the anti-Mormon faction in Hancock came to be known, saw themselves as defenders of the Constitution, public morality, and the American way of life. At a distance of some sixty years Theodore Pease rationalized the vigilantism of these western Illinoisans, stating, "The machinery of state government was then, it must be remembered, but a slight affair; and to enforce the will of public opinion, the resort to private war, though to be deplored, was inevitable."[11]

PREEMPTIVE COUNTERREVOLUTIONS

Marvin S. Hill argues in reply that the people of Hancock County had waged the same kind of "pre-emptive counter-revolution" to thwart a "revolution" led by prophet Smith that the Southern states would attempt fourteen years later when they faced a revolutionary threat to the Constitution, public morality, and the Southern way of life that was foretold by the national vote for Lincoln's Republican Party.[12]

Mid-Illinois's population had deep Southern roots, and Lincoln's war policies—in particular the imposition of conscription—were considered to be damnably seditious. What unionists defended as a prudent exercise of necessary wartime powers was seen by many Southern sympathizers as tyranny, and it seems likely that many more mid-Illinoisans in those years helped Union army deserters escape than helped runaway slaves.

Inevitably, opposition to what many saw as a Republican war took partisan political form. The line between being a dissenting Democrat and a disloyal American was too fine to see for many unionists. The Lincoln administration, in fear of having to fight insurrection behind its lines as well in front of them, cracked down. Mailing privileges were denied to the antiwar *Peoria Demokrat*. In August 1862 the publishers and editor of the *Democratic Standard* at Paris, the Edgar County seat, were arrested by the U.S. marshal and their paper shut down.[13] Military authorities in Missouri banned the *Quincy Herald* on grounds that it gave comfort to rebel sympathizers in that state. In December 1862 an attempt by the commander of the local army post to arrest the editor of the *Jerseyville Democratic Union* for disloyalty failed only because the editor fled town.[14] The pro-South *Bloomington Times* had its offices ransacked and their contents burned, and the press and equipment of its Kentuckian owners were tossed into the street by a mob that included such civic notables as Isaac Funk[15]; these scenes were repeated again in Paris after the publishers relocated to Edgar County.[16]

Southern sympathizers in Whistleville, the aforementioned settlement of Kentucky hill people on Big Creek in Macon County, were said to ride out by night to raid the countryside. Such incidents usually amounted to no more than barn burnings, but they terrified the area's unionist farmers. In June 1863, officers in Fulton County trying to enforce the draft were driven off by mobs; angry men in Mount Sterling and Peoria rioted on registration days. In Waverly a mass meeting protested registration and exhorted all freedom-loving citizens to resist the Lincoln tyranny.

In Coles County, local Democrats railed against what they called the military occupation of their county; local Copperheads in turn were subject to "[n]ame-calling and witch-hunting" and bullying by Union troops stationed in the area. (According to locals, the "favorite sport" of idle troops was forcing Democrats to their knees to take an oath of allegiance.[17]) Gunfire in 1864 between Southern sympathizers and Union soldiers on furlough in Charleston left nine men dead and twelve wounded, leading those so inclined to fear, briefly, a Copperhead uprising in the North.

Later analysis—more sober in every way than the Charleston antagonists had been—suggested that the cause was less national politics than local feuds. And there is much sense in the claim that the "revolution" faced by Charleston was no different from any faced by authorities every Saturday when bored, drunken young males gather to amuse themselves. But then, most revolutions begin with drunken mobs.

TREATED IN A SHACK

Slavery was a fact in Illinois for centuries. Native Americans enslaved women and children taken captive during their wars with other native peoples; indeed the economy of the Illiniwek had been substantially based on trading slaves with other tribes.[18] The French brought both native and African slaves with them to the Illinois territory during their brief colonial reign,[19] and American immigrants imported African slaves into mid-Illinois.

While slavery was tolerated in early mid-Illinois,[20] it was never universally endorsed. When it was proposed in 1824 that Illinoisans meet in convention to adopt a new, proslavery constitution, the men of the region said no, emphatically. In Morgan County the anticonventionists got 91 percent of the vote; in Sangamon County, 83 percent. Fulton County voted five for to sixty against; in Pike County the vote was 23 to 261.[21]

It would be an error to conclude that these majorities owed entirely to moral repugnance or a humanitarian concern for slavery's victims. Many of the region's Southern-born people voted against legalizing slavery not because they thought servitude immoral or inhumane but because they believed that their own physical labor would be demeaned in a slave-based economy as something fit only for slaves. Others simply despised African Americans. Down in the southeastern part of Montgomery County, the members of the Hurricane Church in November of 1819 agreed to send a letter to one Isaac Hill in Kentucky "to tell the new comers [*sic*] not to bring negroes. . . . This is good land favored by God and can make Christian living without the curse of black slavery. We are firm in this matter and ones beleevin in slaves will not be welcom and will be run out" (spelling in the original).[22] It was largely to forestall black immigration that the General Assembly in 1853 passed a series of odious "black laws" that gave the customs of racial discrimination the sanction of law.

Settlers who detested slavery as much as the slave were fewer but fervent in their belief. They tended to be found in the larger trading towns with sizeable Yankee and mid-Atlantic populations. In the more rural parts of mid-Illinois, antislavery agitators were isolated and often despised. An 1879 history of McLean County described the Congregationalists from Rhode Island and Massachusetts who made up the McLean County settlement of Mount Hope as "rank Abolitionists."[23] (Of the denominations then practicing in antebellum mid-Illinois, the Congregationalists stood most unified against slavery.) Widowed housekeeper Ann Dumville was a recent English immigrant whose vocal advocacy of an end to slavery in the 1840s so tested the tolerance of the Macoupin County Methodists with whom she worshipped that the congregation expelled her for a time. "She was an abolitionist," state church records, "and that was enough in their estimation to neutralize all her other excellences. For this she was turned out of the church."[24]

Indeed, the region's feeling against emancipation was probably not much less fervent than that against slavery, as Joseph O. King of Jacksonville recalled. "Although there was a New England settlement here, which in the main sympathized fully with the abolition movement, still the element of southern descent and feelings predominated, and the best and otherwise worthiest people of the town united in deeming us fanatics and revolutionists."[25]

While not the center of the state's antislavery activism, mid-Illinois had important abolitionist outposts. Illinois's first antislavery society was chartered in 1837 in Adams County. Compared with most towns, pre–Civil War Galesburg was a sanctuary for slaves and freemen; the town's founder, George Washington Gale, was indicted in 1843 for harboring escaped slaves, as were two Knox College trustees. (The charges were eventually dropped.) Also in 1843 the Putnam County Anti-Slavery Society resolved that despite the penal laws of Illinois, the "colored brethren" who were escaping were "peculiarly entitled to the sympathy, advice, assistance and comfort of the abolitionists."[26] Illinois College president Edward Beecher wrote the platform of the Illinois State Anti-Slavery Society, among its vice presidents were two college trustees, and Jacksonvillian Elihu Wolcott was chosen its first president; all four men would find themselves indicted by the local grand jury for harboring runaway slaves. William H. Herndon wrote, "My father, who was thoroughly pro-slavery in his ideas, believing that the college was too strongly permeated with the virus of Abolitionism, forced me to withdraw from the institution and return home."[27]

MIDWAY BETWEEN HELL AND FREEDOM

Illinois's territory straddles the South and the North, and the state thus beckoned escaping slaves looking for a route to refuge in Canada. A "main line" of the Underground Railroad's network of safe houses ran from Quincy to Princeton through the old Military Tract. In Fulton County the network linked houses in Bernadotte, Smithfield, Cuba, Canton, and Farmington to Galesburg via London Mills. The builder of the White House Inn in Quincy, Edward Everett, was said to have had secret rooms constructed to hide fugitive slaves. Another Quincy stop was a brick house four blocks from the river landings where lived Dr. Richard Eells. Eells was president of the Illinois Anti-Slavery Society and the antislavery Liberty Party's candidate for governor. His arrest and conviction in 1843 for harboring slaves ended up before the U.S. Supreme Court; the justices disappointed Eells supporters in not finding that the Fugitive Slave Law offended the Constitution.[28]

Whether they did so out of zeal for the abolitionist cause or Christian charity or simple human sympathy, at least one citizen in almost every town could be counted on to open his or her house to fugitives from a law thought to be cruel if not unjust. Accounts of fugitive escapes in the Springfield area mention the capital city plus Jerseyville, Jacksonville, Delavan, Chatham, Rochester, Beardstown, Carlinville, Berlin, Forrest City, and Waverly. The Luther Birge home in Farmington served as a central depot station in the Springfield area; outside Fiatt in Fulton County that role was performed by E. L. Boynton's house.

In the region's western counties, for example, such sanctuaries included the Pettyjohn and Burton houses at Bound Prairie in Hancock County, the houses of the Allison clan around Troublesome Creek and the Blazers on Camp Creek in McDonough County, and the Henry Dobbins place in Fulton County.[29] But while this town or that town is often referred to as a stop on the Underground Railroad, no mid-Illinois town of the times was welcoming to fugitives. As we have seen, even in somewhat abolitionist Jacksonville or Galesburg, people willing to act on their antislavery convictions were very much a minority.[30]

Most accounts stress the central role that white abolitionists played in this derring-do, and indeed white people had money, clothing to spare, and houses with helpfully large cellars and barns that made them very useful. Brave and decent such ministering angels were, but they faced few real risks. Successful prosecutions for aiding fugitives were rare, and while the identities of most sympathizers were known to their antiabolitionist neighbors, reprisals seldom amounted to more than intimidation and insult.

More recent scholarship suggests that most freedom-bound fugitives made their ways north by themselves or with help of local freedmen and freedwomen. African American William Donnegan claimed to have secreted scores of runaways at his house on Jefferson Street in Springfield. Other men of color in the capital known to have at least occasionally befriended fugitives were drayman Jamieson Jenkins and Rev. Henry Brown.[31] In the Jacksonville area, black conductors included Washington Price, Aaron Dyer, David Spencer, and Benjamin Henderson. Many, like Henderson, drove freight wagons, which they used to ferry runaways from one safe haven to another, often on bad country roads in all kinds of weather and usually in the dark, with armed slave catchers prowling the woods. Thrilling stuff to read about, but it must have been terrifying to experience; more than a few escapees were caught and returned.

SEPARATE AND UNEQUAL

Among the doors that were closed to African Americans in early mid-Illinois were those of schools. Until 1870 no state law required that black children be educated, and most towns did not volunteer to do the job. Even those few places in mid-Illinois that did offer schooling to their African American children in the 1860s (Decatur, Galesburg, Jacksonville, Peoria, Quincy, and Springfield) maintained separate facilities to protect white children from the presence of African American classmates.[32]

That these schools were not equal in quality to those open to white children probably does not need to be said. In 1854 the Quincy city council began to appropriate twenty-five dollars per quarter for a "colored school" conducted in a one-room hovel by a teacher who was paid a wage below what the female teachers in the white schools were earning. In 1858, Springfield taught its African American children in an outbuilding behind St. Paul's African Methodist Episcopal Church. There a single teacher had to cope with as many as sixty pupils in nine grade levels, for which heroism the teacher was paid nearly 25 percent less than his white colleagues; it was several years before the children had available to them well-equipped and staffed classrooms in a proper building. In Decatur the black school was in the basement of a black church; in Jacksonville and Peoria the circumstances were much the same. A public school for children of color was opened in Bloomington in 1860; the teacher, a woman who had been a missionary in Burma, must have found much that was familiar in her new situation.[33]

Public schools became focal points of feelings about race. In the 1870s black children attending the common school in the rural McLean County town of Dement had to endure white people expressing what were described as "well known repugnances" at their presence. Voters approved construction of a new, second school just for black students, but it was left unbuilt after opponents won a suit charging that such spending was a misappropriation of public funds.[34]

Knox College was unusual in welcoming students of color. In 1855 Hiram Revels, the man who became the first black U.S. senator, attended the Knox Academy, the college's preparatory school. Barnabas Root (born Fahma Yahny in Sierra Leone) was possibly the first black man to receive a college degree in Illinois when Knox awarded him one in 1870. More typical, alas, were the policies of the new Illinois Industrial University. Its charter, written in 1863, explicitly limited enrollment to white students; that language had to be abandoned after the Fourteenth Amendment was ratified in 1868, but the policy was not; the university did not admit an African American student until 1887, and none graduated until 1900.

A new Illinois constitution was adopted in 1870. Parroting the newly ratified Fifteenth Amendment to the U.S. Constitution, the state charter for the first time mandated public education for all Illinois children regardless of color. Integrationists faced a dilemma in making that ambition real, however. Because of the insults so many of their children endured, many African American parents in Illinois preferred that they not attend schools with white children.

Further, black parents did not have the influence over integrated schools that they had over segregated ones. Thus, while racial justice demanded integration, educational wisdom and local politics often suggested separate ones.

This awkward choice confronted Galesburg during the war years. As noted, Galesburg's reputation for racial tolerance had attracted to it escaped slaves who, because the Southern states prohibited teaching enslaved people to read and write, were often illiterate as adults. To spare these adult pupils the awkwardness of having to sit in classes with children, Galesburg's black leaders successfully petitioned the school board to establish a black-only school. In 1863 the Galesburg colored school opened, with children attending in the morning and adults in the afternoon. Thanks to this sensible accommodation, writes schools historian Robert L. McCaul, "segregated schooling for blacks came to exist in a community in which the ruling elite was atypically pro-black in sentiment."[35]

Beginning in 1857 a model or laboratory school to give would-be teachers "practical skill by actual service"[36] was operated in Bloomington by Illinois State Normal School under a contract between the university and the town. The school admitted black students and assigned black teacher-trainees to teach local white children.[37] When an illiterate thirty-five-year-old African American named George Brown applied for admission, Principal John Williston Cook assigned him to the classroom with children more than twenty years his junior. The teacher refused to admit him, and when the principal stood his ground some parents withdrew their children. The to-do caused laypeople to complain that the school encouraged miscegenation and—worse, in the eyes of many—wasted tax money educating race radicals. The town school board canceled its contract with the university and organized its own a system of separate black and white schools. The university, in one of those acts of institutional courage out of which social revolutions are always made, refused to abandon its race-blind policy.

Even though they were at odds with the state's new 1870 constitution, Illinois's black laws were not stricken from the books until 1885. Discrimination in the private realm, however, continued to flourish. Father Augustine Tolton, probably most accurately described as the first full-blooded African American priest in the United States, began his education in a Quincy parish school but left when parents of his classmates threatened to withdraw them; the Franciscans who ran St. Francis College (forerunner of today's Quincy University) also had to fend off protests. In the end, Tolton had to be prepared for his calling privately by area priests, because no seminary would accept him.[38]

The eighteen hundred workers of the Chicago and Alton Railroad repair shops in Bloomington were McLean County's largest industrial workforce.

The unions that represented them had polyglot memberships made up of white American, British, and European workers, but African Americans, who worked in the roundhouse and the scrap yard, were denied union membership. In Springfield from the 1880s to the early 1900s, black people of any class were almost entirely excluded from good-paying jobs on streetcars or in factories owing in no small part to resistance by most white-dominated labor unions.[39]

Coal mining did offer work for black men, albeit mainly jobs that were unappealing to most "white" men (a category from which also many miners of southern European origin were excluded). Leaders of the United Mine Workers of America reasoned that black miners welcomed inside the union would not be strikebreakers outside it, and indeed during a nasty strike in Virden in 1898 (described in more detail in chapter 11) black union miners from Springfield stood with their white brethren against the importation of black strikebreakers. As a result, Springfield in 1910 had five times the proportion of black men in its mines as Illinois as a whole.

THE JUSTICE OF THE ROPE

Even such modest success as African Americans enjoyed in mid-Illinois in the early part of the twentieth century sometimes excited murderous resentment. Illinois has the unhappy distinction of having hosted two of the ugliest race riots in U.S. history—at East St. Louis in 1917 and in Chicago in 1919. But mid-Illinois between 1893 and 1908 was the scene of preludes to those grim events. Less lethal in their extent than the later riots, the troubles were in one instance more far-reaching in their consequences and certainly more potent in their perverse symbolism.

In May 1893 a black man arrested on charges of having assaulted two local women was hauled from the Decatur jail by a white mob and hanged dead from a light pole at Water and Wood streets, within view of the county courthouse. The leaders of the mob were well known to locals, but two grand juries refused to indict them.[40] A year later, an African American porter in Decatur was arrested and charged with a similar crime, although this time a lynching was prevented by more than a hundred armed African American men who patrolled the streets of Decatur for three nights.[41] In July 1903 an African American man in the same situation in Danville excited six hundred white men to march down East Main Street toward the county jail where they encountered black men again bent on protecting one of their race. A black man fired a gun in self-defense, killing a white man in the mob, which dragged the gunman through the streets to the spot of their companion's death and

Antilynching cartoon. Cartoonist W. A. Rogers of *Harper's Weekly* joined the praise for public officials who asserted the law over mob rule in 1903 by preventing lynchings in Danville, Illinois, and Evansville, Indiana. *HARPER'S WEEKLY.* REPRODUCED WITH PERMISSION.

hanged him from a telephone pole. His corpse was later mutilated with bullets and burned. (No one was ever charged for his murder.) The mob was bent on doing the same to the prisoner whose arrest started the fray, but a heroic stand at the jail led by the Vermilion County sheriff saved the life of his prisoner.

In Springfield in mid-August 1908, the by-now familiar ingredients—booze, a hot summer, incendiary press accounts of a sexual assault of a white woman by a black man—combined in combustible amounts. Angry white men gathered outside the county jail in which the alleged assailant was held. Drunk and frustrated in their demands for the prisoner, the mob turned on Springfield's black community at large. Over the next two days, white rioters wrecked and looted the capital's black business district, set fire to whole blocks of African Americans' homes, and lynched two innocent black men, then indulged in the sorts of gruesome acts mobs usually find entertaining on such occasions, such as shooting the corpses.[42] Four white people also died and scores more were injured; it took the presence of several thousand state militia to bring calm to the city.

To injury was added insult. In February 1909 a crowd of nine thousand worthies gathered to celebrate the centennial of Abraham Lincoln's birth at the state arsenal by enduring speeches from William Jennings Bryan, among others. The city's African American citizens had not been invited. They had to mount their own memorial event, at a local church where speakers voiced their indignation at being barred from celebrating with the rest of the city the man to whom they believed they owed their freedom.

In a book originally titled *The Sociogenesis of a Race Riot*, Roberta Senechal de la Roche concluded that most of the theories usually offered in explanation of urban race riots in the United States are irrelevant or inadequate when applied to 1908 Springfield.[43] The more sophisticated among the capital's elites argued that the violence in Springfield expressed latent public outrage over black vice and the politicians who protected it—this in spite of the fact that no attacks were made on the white aldermen who were the agents and beneficiaries of corruption at city hall. The gambling halls and opium dens and whorehouses frequented by white men were untouched by the mobs, while many of the black businesses that were ravaged (such as barbershops) were eminently respectable by the standards of a town that was home to the General Assembly. Former Southerners were disproportionately scarce among the attackers. There had been no recent massive increase in black population, no "invasion" by families of color into previously all-white residential enclaves, no capture by black workers of jobs coveted by white people. Rather than seek out the criminal class, as apologists later claimed, the mobs sought as targets African Americans who were newly risen in social standing. As Jack S. Blocker put it, the significant contributory cause was black people getting "above their place."[44]

Sometimes the effect of events is a cause. The news from Springfield excited calls across the country for a revival of the old abolitionist spirit lest African Americans be subjugated again, this time by the slavery of terror. From a meeting of Northern activists in 1909 emerged the National Association for the Advancement of Colored People, which did much to effect a second emancipation for African Americans. If that outcome did not redeem Springfield in the eyes of history, it did in the eyes of its tourism promoters a century later.

Wreckage in the black belt on Springfield's east side after the outbreak of racial violence in August 1908. Acts of self-defense by African Americans turned the antiblack riots into a "race war," according to this postcard. The Illinois statehouse is in the distance. COURTESY BROOKENS LIBRARY, UNIVERSITY OF ILLINOIS AT SPRINGFIELD, ARCHIVES/SPECIAL COLLECTIONS, BOOTH-GRUNENDIKE COLLECTION.

"YOU HAD TO BE CAREFUL"

For two generations after 1908, de facto segregation in employment and schooling, housing, entertainment, and the professions was comprehensive across the region. Localities honored equality in their statutes but unapologetically enforced Jim Crow. Until well into the twentieth century Springfield's city government maintained a separate black fire department company, separate bathing beaches at its municipal lake, even a Colored Municipal Band. As late as the 1960s few Bloomington restaurants permitted black patrons to sit down and eat, and African American citizens were expected to sit in the "crows nest" in the movie theaters.[45] The same strictures applied in Decatur, where African Americans were discouraged from attending baseball games at Fans Field except when touring Negro league teams played.[46]

The region's state institutions of higher education did not set a higher standard of accommodation. In Normal, black students at Illinois State Normal University had to find housing with local black families, because no dorms were open to them.[47] Not until 1945 were African American women allowed to live in the dorms at the University of Illinois, and the school ended its policy of barring such women only under pressure and only on the condition that they room with other black women.[48]

Compliance with organized bigotry was enforced by the threat of violence. In a memoir, retired Peoria fire chief John Parker describes how he grew up in the 1940s in an integrated neighborhood on that city's near south side.

> You had to be careful traveling through the far north side or the far south side. North past Spring street was shaky. Past LeTourneaus and Hysters [factory grounds] was a no no. . . . We had to be careful frequenting the near bluff and the mansions of Moss Ave. or the Knolls. Only if you were a domestic could you traverse fairly freely with little concern of being accosted by neighborhood whites, gangs or even the Peoria Police Department.

It was not until the postwar years that the modern civil rights era began in mid-Illinois as in the rest of the nation, thanks to the legal tools created by the spate of meaningful national civil rights legislation beginning in 1964. In 1985 a federal lawsuit alleging that Springfield's at-large city council elections deprived African Americans of representation under the Voting Rights Act resulted in the city's commission form of government being overturned. Because enrollment was based on residence, de facto housing segregation made it possible for the local public schools to confine black kids to a few public grade schools, effectively creating segregated schools within a system that was open in concept.[49] A successful legal challenge in the 1970s desegregated Springfield schools in fact; the consent decree entered into by the parties to the case in 1974 was the first in the nation to remedy such violations by a voluntary program of attendance and staffing changes.

In most towns, discrimination that ceased to be a matter of public policy became a matter of private choice. As people of color moved into older neighborhoods, for instance, affluent white people retreated to their own same-color enclaves in new and usually costlier neighborhoods on the urban fringe; the all-white neighborhood school survived in Springfield, for example; only the neighborhood it served was now likely to be in a suburbanized former farm town nearby.

Peoria was typical of the region's larger cities. Because so many white residents left, Peoria's population declined by about five hundred during the 1990s even though nearly six thousand new black citizens had moved in. Not all of this shift should be attributed to racial anxieties among white residents. The white exodus from Peoria began before the onset of greater black in-migration in the 1970s, as working-class families fled, in part, higher real estate costs and inept city government. But later on, racial antagonism was probably the major, if not the only, force causing the city's white residents to exile themselves. Working-class white residents moved across the river to such places as East

Peoria or Pekin; the black population of the latter was less than 3 percent. Well-off white Peorians headed north and west, into posh new developments in places like Richwoods Township; Peoria Heights, an upscale suburb, was less than 6 percent black in 2010.

LOOKING FOR BRICKS TO HEAVE

Immigration from outside the United States was a cause of contention in mid-Illinois as early as the 1830s, when German and Swedish farmers and craftsmen and Irish laborers began making homes there. The Irish came to Illinois in the 1830s and 1840s because the state's ambitious program of railroad and canal building left it with more work for laborers than it had laborers. The employers of the Irish were usually Protestant Americans who felt little kinship with the newcomers. Workers sometimes were unpaid, and working conditions often were dreadful. (Some fifty Irish workers on the Illinois Central who apparently died of cholera in the 1850s are buried outside Bloomington in a mass grave marked by a Celtic cross.) Such conditions gave Irish laborers opportunities to express their practiced antipathy toward exploitation. The reaction took both impulsive forms, such as spontaneous riots, and organized forms, such as strikes and boycotts. Immigrant grievances over work matters planted the seed of labor unionism and thus established "union" and "immigrant" as synonyms in the minds of many Illinoisans.

The immigrant groups held disparate religious and political views; most Protestant Germans by midcentury had become committed to the Republicans' antislavery cause (as had the Scandinavians), while the Catholic Irish found a home with the proslavery Democrats. To the undiscerning majority, however, immigrants were all alike; they were clannish, they worshipped in the wrong church, they spoke the wrong language. The coming of the railroads to Galesburg beginning in 1850 brought Irish and Germans, who found the locals considerably less than welcoming. The feeling was reflected in the comment by a member of the school board that black children "would be better associates for our little children than the Irish and Dutch [*sic*] now attending the schools."[50]

Anti-German and anti-Swedish prejudice in mid-Illinois grew less virulent after the Civil War, in part because so many of the despised immigrants of the 1830s had, with their children, become the respected community leaders of the 1900s. Remembering the prejudices shown against Swedes in the Galesburg of his youth, Albert Britt observed, "When these aliens began to prove that they could be as good farmers as the native born and their children began to take prizes in school, all was well."[51] Britt's is perhaps a too-sunny view of a painful and protracted process of social adjustment. The Swedes' skills were probably just as often resented by the natives. "A stranger visiting Bishop Hill today, for the first time would be aware of its exotic origin with one glance at its architectures," wrote one history of that colony. "It is strikingly foreign with touches of craftsmanship by which the older countries mark the work of their hands." He added, "No such buildings were ever erected by Yankees or Hoosier settlers."[52]

Subsequent waves of immigrants attracted to the mid-Illinois mines and manufactories offered bigotry new chances to express itself. Of the Polish, Russian, Hungarian, Austrian, Italian, and Czech miners who came to work in Moweaqua, one historian of that Shelby County town wrote, "They were, sad to say, regarded with suspicion and mistrust by some of the residents. They spoke little English, they had many children and strange customs, and they labored like moles in the ground."[53]

The vocabulary with which Carl Sandburg came to understand the realities of life in a multicultural society in his native Galesburg in the 1880s and 1890s would send a modern liberal hurrying off to find a lawyer. "We believed that the sheenies on the quiet might be calling us 'snorkies' and calling the Irish 'micks' and that would be all right with us because that's what we were," Sandburg wrote. "But if they called us 'goddam snorkies' or 'goddam micks' then we would look for bricks to heave."[54]

By 1900 McLean County, the local German population (that is, native-born Germans plus second- and third-generation descendants) accounted for at least 30 percent of the total. German words and German ways were as everyday in that part of mid-Illinois as coffee with pie. Many thriving businesses were German-owned, as were some of the best farms. Local public schools had taught the German language since 1871, several churches held worship services in that language, and newspapers provided news in German.

The decision by the U.S. government to enter the European war against Germany in 1917 transformed such citizens from respected townspeople into feared enemies. The superpatriotic State Council of Defense of Illinois (slogan: "Get right or get out") was set up in 1917 to ferret out Americans suspected of disloyalty or, rather, of being possibly capable of disloyalty. Members of the McLean County chapter of the council included such social stalwarts as the Bloomington mayor, the president of the Association of Commerce, the presidents of the First National Bank of Normal and Illinois Wesleyan University, the county superintendent of schools, and a circuit court judge.[55]

Within weeks, the local council passed resolutions deeming as an act of disloyalty to the United States the printing in the German language of not only seditious material but also any paper or publication, the council apparently understanding German words to be a sort of secret code. In English words plainly meant to be menacing, the defense council also urged that the use of the German language in schools and churches be discontinued "in the best interests of American citizens of German birth or descent"; Bloomington public and parochial schools and a majority of the other county school districts and parochial schools cravenly obeyed. And patriots no doubt slept a little more soundly after the German American Bank was induced to change its name to the American State Bank.[56]

No physical violence was directed against German Americans, but there was intimidation enough. A crowd of several hundred residents from Colfax and the outlying countryside descended on Immanuel's Evangelical German Lutheran Church in Lawndale Township, demanding it end German-language services lest the church be burned. Similar threats were made in nearby Anchor. In Pekin some patriots threatened to burn down the house of the family of Everett Dirksen, a future U.S. senator from Illinois, because his mother displayed a picture of Kaiser Wilhelm on her wall.[57]

In September 1917, Joseph Hauptman, an ethnic German from Hungary who had grown up in the United States, tried to enlist in the armed services but was refused by the Bloomington recruiting officer because he spoke German. After Hauptman was able to enlist at Peoria by lying about his birthplace, he became, on June 6, 1918, the first Bloomington man killed in action.[58] In a tardy act of expiation, the Bloomington Post of World War Veterans, founded in 1920, was named the Hauptman, Morgan, Conley Post in honor of Hauptman and two other Bloomington men who died fighting Germans.

AMERICANIZATION ON ETHNIC TERMS

That social friction did not generate heat more often owed less to forbearance than to absence. Most sizeable ethnic populations equipped themselves with separate churches, taverns, and lodges, sometimes separate schools and even stores, often in parts of town made their own by countrymen seeking like neighbors. Scorned by outsiders (the Swedish quarter of Galesburg was dubbed by non-Swedes "Monkey Town"), such neighborhoods were to their inhabitants refuges from prejudice that satisfied the natural desire for social comfort felt by people trying to cope with strange languages and customs.

In time it became apparent that these foreigners were not so foreign as many feared. What sociologist Daniel Elazar notes about Illinois as a whole certainly applied to its midsection. New German arrivers, along with Scots, Scandinavians, and Jews, tended to supplement and reinforce cultures already established in mid-Illinois. "The [Germans], from the Calvinist tradition, behaved economically like Yankees," writes Elazar in *Cities of the Prairie*. "The Jews specialized in commerce, often replacing the Yankees who moved into industrial pursuits, to become the merchant princes, especially of Peoria, Champaign-Urbana, Springfield, [and] Decatur."[59] The Yankees' moralistic politics were reinforced by Jewish and North Sea immigrants who found it congenial. The individualist culture of the mid-Atlantic states found new allies among Eastern Europeans, Italians, and Irish, all of whom not only came to be admitted to the inner political circles of their new hometowns but also often dominated them.

By the late twentieth century, the region's residents with immigrant roots had long since become Americanized. Customs that once were provoking became widely accepted; indeed their ethnic origins were largely forgotten. The experience of Springfield's Trinity Evangelical Lutheran Church was repeated across the region. In 1844 newly arrived German Lutherans, having no church of their own, were invited to join an existing church founded by non-Germans, and for a decade Lutherans of all national backgrounds worshipped together. In 1854, Springfield's English- and German-speaking Lutherans divided amicably along linguistic lines, with the Germans founding the Deutsche Evangelische Lutherische Kirche, later renamed Trinity Lutheran. (Trinity was long known as "the Capitol Church" because it stands diagonally across the street from the Illinois statehouse.) The preservation of the old tongue during services was a comfort to early congregations who still felt themselves to be Germans in America. By 1860 enough worshippers had come to see themselves as German Americans that services gradually began to be introduced in English, although it was not until 1927 that the church's corporate name was rendered in English. Services in German continued for the elders, but in 1953, with fewer than twenty worshippers usually in the pews, regular German services were canceled.

THE OTHER SLAVE CLASS

Reading about mid-Illinois life in the early Euro-American era is a reminder that one class of slave was not emancipated in 1865—women.[60] It was not unusual for a man on the frontier to wear out two or three wives. "The male population may be pronounced unequivocally indolent" [while] "the females cannot be indolent if they would," observed Elizabeth Farnham about life in 1830s Tazewell County.[61] Analysis of female skeletal remains from the period in a family graveyard in mid-Illinois—thickened bones, worn joints—showed constant, heavy toil; even teeth were as worn from use as tools as the men's.[62]

However, it was probably not the rigors of field work and housekeeping that explain the high death rates among frontier women but those of constant childbearing and child rearing. In his account of the frontier-era Sugar Creek settlement in Sangamon County, John Mack Faragher found that nine of ten women living there in 1830 bore at least six children, and families of more than ten were common.[63] On the other side of Sangamon County was the farm of the Cross family. The matriarch, Margaret, bore a total of eleven children, which included three sets of twins. Roughly half of those babies died before they were five years old. Women born elsewhere before 1800 and who settled and bore most of their children in the settled places of Kentucky or Tennessee before coming to mid-Illinois died, on average, at age sixty-seven. Women born between 1800 and 1840, and who spent their childbearing years on the Illinois frontier, died, on average, at age fifty.[64]

Socially, life in an isolated frontier farmhouse meant loneliness and fear for a woman when her man was away, and sometimes when he was not. In her memoir of Montgomery County in the 1820s, Christiana Holmes Tillson gives a chilling portrait of one Brice Hanna, who made his young wife so miserable she clumsily tried to kill herself by jumping down a well. This kind of abuse and worse was not new to the region. Among the native peoples, Illiniwek women in particular led hard lives, bound as they were in polygamous marriages in which they were treated as virtual slaves, their sex sometimes used as currency with other males. These women's receptivity to Christian teachings can be attributed in part to the fact that Scriptures offered rationales against such abuse.

A better fate awaited those who took refuge in the house of a French trader, many of whom valued Native American women as wives.[65] These women knew how to grow and prepare food, of course, but they also were guides and herbal physicians. They brought to a marriage with a trader connections to an extended kinship network that was important in establishing and maintaining good relationships with distant trading partners in the Indian West.[66]

The Kickapoo women also occupied positions of standing. Indian trader Thomas Forsyth (later a government Indian agent) once observed that among the Kickapoo he knew around Peoria in the early 1800s everything belonged to the woman except her man's hunting and war implements.[67] Kickapoo women built and owned their own houses, for example, did not bear (or let live) more children than they could comfortably raise, and were free to divorce a lazy or a mean man. Most remarkably, explains Faragher, "Kickapoo women controlled the conditions and products of their own work and the distribution of food to the lineage," which gave them considerable authority within their band.

That kind of autonomy was denied Euro-American women, but at least they gradually ceased to be valued solely as drudges. New farming methods such as mechanization made possible improvements in crop production that in turn improved the lives of farm women. Farm surpluses could be sold for cash that allowed farm families to buy what the women once had to grow and make themselves.

Christiana Holmes Tillson was by birth and upbringing a New Englander of the sort too easily dismissed as merely proper. She came to Illinois in 1822 to live with her husband, who had ventured west three years earlier. Montgomery County by then had been conveniently cleansed of Native Americans. Eliza Farnham came west to Illinois in the spring of 1836 from upstate New York, eventually to wed and begin a family in the Tazewell County village of Tremont. Like Tillson, Farnham was no mere helpmate but one of those Eastern women who saw themselves as builders not merely of farms and families but of civilization—church builders, moral guardians, agents of uplift and culture.

Then and for the next two generations it was expected that they would exert this influence through the home. Major's Female College (in fact a college prep school), which operated in Bloomington briefly in the mid-1860s, was founded by a devout Disciple of Christ to ensure that the influence young mothers exerted on their children was Christian.[68] The trustees of the Illinois Industrial University in 1870 voted to permit the registration of women students. Not all of the eager applicants could have been pleased to discover what the university meant by education for women. As the new School of Domestic Science and Art explained,

> the house-keeper needs education as much as the house-builder, the nurse as well as the physician, the leaders of society as surely as the leaders of senates, the mother as much as the father, the woman as well as the man. . . . It is the aim of the School to give to earnest and capable young women an education, not lacking in refinement, but which shall fit them for their great duties and trusts, making them the equals of their educated husbands and associates, and enabling them to bring the aids of science and culture to the all important labors and vocations of womanhood.[69]

The vocations of manhood, alas, remained closed to women. Metamora's Mary Louisa Page, for example, was the first woman to earn a degree in architecture in North America when she graduated from the University of Illinois in 1879; she never practiced, however, but became a schoolteacher in Washington State.[70]

While women were gradually freed from toil, they were not freed from male notions of their roles, as was made all too clear by the case of Elizabeth Packard. In 1860 Packard, a mother of six and the wife of a Calvinist minister in the Kankakee County town of Manteno, was carried from her home and admitted to the Illinois Hospital for the Insane in Jacksonville. Her husband had concluded that she must be mad because she was disputing his Calvinist beliefs, which he held to be self-evidently true. State law then permitted a husband to commit his wife with the concurrence of the hospital's superintendent, as a result of which action Mrs. Packard was confined in Jacksonville for three years for having been impertinent. She was keenly aware of what had been done to her, and why. She was finally judged not insane, and the furor about the case led to Illinois's commitment law being changed for the better.

Post–Civil War industrialization had opened up new opportunities for women outside the home, but it exposed them to new dangers too. Young women working at the capital city's International Shoe Factory in the years just before World War I had to stand for ten hours a day, packing, inspecting, and sorting for five dollars a week.[71] Low piecework wages meant that many of International's employees were forced into prostitution to make ends meet. A series of hearings was held in Peoria, Springfield, and Chicago in 1913 by the special Illinois Senate committee investigating vice. "One [expert] blames bad housing, questionable dance halls, lack of education, of religious instruction, of ideals and so on down the long line of unfortunate and deplorable conditions," concluded the committee, "and, on analysis, they are traced back one by one, branches of the tree of poverty." Woman after woman recalled that her decision to sell herself for sex came after working in hotels or laundries for as little as three dollars a week with no prospect of advancement.

In spite of all the social barriers intended to prevent it, mid-Illinois at mid-century produced its share of remarkable women. Ohioan Mary Ann Bickerdyke was widowed and living in Galesburg when the Civil War erupted. Letters from solders about filthy conditions in the Union hospital in Cairo in far southern Illinois inspired Galesburgers to collect food, money, clothing, bandages, and medicine, which Bickerdyke volunteered to deliver. "[She] came down from the northern part of the State, with her chickens and cows," wrote one veteran of the home war. "Our own Central Illinois women bless her name, and were proud of her."[72]

Her errand done, Bickerdyke remained in Cairo unofficially, acting as nurse and organizer. General U. S. Grant, under whose command Cairo fell, eventually named her his chief of nursing. Imbued with the imperiousness of the convinced, Bickerdyke was indifferent to protocol and procedure, which made her a pain to many a commanding officer. Grateful enlisted men, however, affectionately called her "Mother Bickerdyke." She never returned to Galesburg, although her remains were sent home for burial; her memory endures there in the form of a statue on the lawn of the Knox County Courthouse.

Bickerdyke's career proved a sorry truth, that even the women who excelled in this period did so within the traditional social spheres of the female—teaching and nursing, principally. Those women who had an aptitude for business were able to use it only as partners or heirs to businesses founded by fathers or husbands. Peoria philanthropist Lydia Moss Bradley presided over the quadrupling of the value of the estate left her by her husband. Bradley in 1875 became the first female member of a national bank board in the United States when she helped lead the First National Bank of Peoria—possibly the only woman in Illinois to serve as director of a national bank at that early date, certainly one of a very few, which was reason enough for her induction into the National Women's Hall of Fame in 1998.

That opportunities for meaningful lives outside the home were limited might explain why so many women devoted themselves with zeal to the few that were open to them, such as improving clubs and charities. Some wives and daughters used their unprecedented freedom from work to attempt to remedy their own powerlessness through charitable and social reform. Women and their male legislative allies undertook to expand the public and private spheres of female action, law by law and issue by issue—the right of women to control their own earnings and property, to enjoy equal guardianship of children after divorce, to share in the estate of deceased husbands, and to practice law or medicine.

The General Assembly was not the only venue in which women asserted a claim to fuller lives. The Progressive Miners of America, or PMA, sprung up in Illinois as an alternative to John L. Lewis's hated United Mine Workers. The PMA was conceived as not only a new union but a new kind of union, a social movement as well as a narrowly focused labor organization. Women were given, and in some cases assertively took, leadership roles. Since the union's stronghold included much of mid-Illinois, the region's women made up a significant fraction of the estimated ten thousand women gathered in Springfield on January 25, 1933, to meet with Governor Henry Horner and demand state-funded unemployment compensation.

Chapter 9 will recall how Illinois women got the vote, and the role that mid-Illinois women played in that fight. Alas, the new dawn promised by empowered women never came. Female voters did not transform politics, in mid-Illinois or anywhere else. Women lived and worked in a wider world but mainly as a consequence of economic and social changes over which they had

PMA women. Women of the auxiliary of the Progressive Miners union, wearing their signature white dresses and headbands, march on the Illinois capitol on January 26, 1933, to demand state unemployment aid and to protest rough treatment of union protesters. COURTESY ABRAHAM LINCOLN PRESIDENTIAL LIBRARY AND MUSEUM.

little control; indeed, winning the vote was more an artifact of those changes than their cause. As the twentieth century progressed, women still were discriminated against in wages and advancement, and the latter-day feminism that emerged in the 1960s shifted its targets from statutory discrimination to social discrimination.

A conspicuous figure in that movement was Betty Friedan, author, founder, and first president (in 1966) of the National Organization for Women. Born Betty Goldstein in 1921 in Peoria, she was a bright child whose jeweler father insisted on "talking philosophy" to his daughter every evening after dinner. Friedan went to grade and high school in Peoria, as her mother had. She was an above-average student academically but found it "was not very useful to be too intelligent, for a girl, in Peoria when we were growing up."[73] She did realize her mother's ambition that she go away to Smith College, "where the brightest of the girls at the Peoria Country Club seemed to go."[74]

When Goldstein married a man named Friedan she faced the now-familiar dilemmas of the overeducated, understimulated upper-middle-class housewife, which she would later write about in *The Feminine Mystique*, her 1963 bestseller. The experience awakened her to the plight—lonesome, bored, wasted—of the women she called "the world's only discriminated against majority." That number included her own mother, who had attended what was to become Bradley University for two years and later became the women's page editor of the predecessor of today's *Peoria Journal-Star* newspaper. She loved the job but had to quit when she married; as her daughter put it, "Wives of businessmen did not work in towns like Peoria then, not even in the Depression."[75]

SO MANY LITTLE WARS, SO MANY HEROES

One by one, all of these once-excluded classes of citizen pressed for accommodation if not acceptance. Not all achieved it, but if the struggles of the different against the like did not leave mid-Illinois a fair and humane place, it left it fairer and more humane than it had been a century earlier. The physically handicapped have won accommodation in law and social arrangements, and many people once demeaned as the mildly retarded, instead of enduring barracks-like institutions, live in group homes and work in their communities; only the mentally ill remain threatening and strange. Women have won full rights in law if not always in practice; they have earned their place in the political realm as lawmakers and public administrators, and now often outnumber men in enrollment at colleges and universities that once shunned them.

Religion-based prejudice has become objectionable enough that it has been forced underground; slurs that once appeared on placards carried down Main Street by the Ku Klux Klan now are found mostly in graffiti or in anonymous comments sections on the Internet. Social discrimination against Jews, for example, has become rare enough that the biggest problem faced by the faithful is the loss of their numbers due to intermarriage with non-Jews. While the region's relatively few Muslims have replaced Roman Catholics as the bugbear of the region's xenophobes, Roman Catholics of European working-class backgrounds have so risen in business, the professions, and especially politics that they exemplify the American Way that they once were believed to threaten. One religious prejudice that remains nearly universally and unabashedly practiced is that against atheists. The Montgomery County Courthouse was for a time adorned by a sign, "The World Needs God," that occasioned a lawsuit by atheists in the 1990s; they successfully argued that believing in a god is one thing, but advertising that fact at public expense is another.

Mid-Illinois's newer immigrants are confronting, and overcoming, the same kinds of ethnic antagonisms that confronted the Irish, the Germans, the Poles and Lithuanians and Italians in the latter 1800s and early 1900s. Beardstown, once derided as a "foreign country" because of its many German residents, has become that again owing to an influx of Hispanic immigrants, most of them Mexican workers employed by a pork-processing plant that opened in 1987. If complaints about the newcomers are the same as those directed at Germans in the mid-1800s—they are clannish, they speak no English, they worship at the wrong church—the benefits of their presence are the same too, as they have enlivened what would otherwise be another moribund small town.

When the Beardstown High School football team took on the big-city favorites in a state tournament in 2014, the cocaptain rallied his teammates with a rousing talk as they headed into overtime, telling them, "Let's not win just for us but for the community."[76] Even if the football was soccer, and the cocaptain's last name was *Urquiza*, the words were in the best tradition of small-town high school sports and would have been cheered by most mid-Illinoisans in any accent.

CHAPTER SIX

"Making the world a little more Christian": The Salvation of Mid-Illinois

Democracy is the evangel of God, applied to civil affairs.
—Owen Lovejoy, to the Illinois House of Representatives, 1855

In Cass County, about five miles west of Virginia and just off what some still call the hard road to Springfield, stands the Shiloh Cumberland Presbyterian Church. It is a country church in the classic mold, nobly proportioned, with a graceful spire and the steep gables and pointed arches typical of the neo-Gothic style that was popular when it was built.

Shiloh Church was organized in 1827, which makes it ancient by mid-Illinois standards. In its nascent form it consisted of a few of the neighborhood's faithful joining in prayer in a home on Jersey Prairie of what was then Morgan County. Ten years after that first meeting, a member of the congregation built a log meeting house on donated land, and the twenty-nine members voted to attach their church to the Cumberland Presbyterian Church, thus building on two foundations at the same time. The founding elders and preacher were Kentuckians, and Cumberland Presbyterianism (so-called for the valley of the river of that name, which flows in part through the Bluegrass State) was one of many Kentucky seeds that sprouted in early mid-Illinois. To carry the word into the frontier the Cumberland Presbytery had begun ordaining ministers who were more passionate than learned, and around 1800 the practice inspired the mother church to dissolve the Cumberland Presbytery, leaving the dissidents to go alone. It was this brand of Presbyterianism—revivalist, conservative in doctrine, cussedly independent in spirit—that the Cass Countians chose to embrace, saying it "agrees with our views most in accordance with the Apostolic Mode."[1]

By 1857 the congregation's wealth began to match its piety, and members built nearby a proper wood-frame church made of mill-sawed white pine. That building was replaced after thirty-three years with a new church a little more than a mile away, in a location more convenient to the congregation. Lumber from the old church building was given to the man who had lent the congregation the money for the new one; he used it to build a double corn crib on his farm, which in rural mid-Illinois is very nearly a consecrated use itself.

The 1857 building is the one that can be seen today. Shiloh never got much bigger than a few dozen members, but over the years that number was enough to provide aid for foreign missionaries and aged ministers and for themselves a new organ, later a bell for the steeple, still later hot water and a full basement and stained-glass windows. They even built a manse, although it took years. "Too much could not be said for the loyal women of the church who shucked corn, stripped cane and did many other jobs to increase the fund," writes church historian Freda Kruse Leonhard, quite rightly.[2]

As the twentieth century began, a campaign was mounted to reconcile the Cumberland church to mainstream Presbyterianism. Some Cumberland congregations joined; the little church outside Virginia did not, even though the move was favored by one of its most respected elders. In such a tightly woven community, this disagreement was betrayal, and the wound reportedly took years to heal.

Car-bound commuters now whiz past the church to and from Springfield on the road that in 1827 carried wagons laden with grain or store goods shipped from Beardstown. What is interesting about Shiloh's story is that it is, in the context of mid-Illinois history, so uninteresting. There are hundreds of such churches like it in the region, most of them like Shiloh built and maintained, often against enormous odds, by ordinary people for whom the church community, not the civil community, was the center of their lives.

Pious accounts of the past tend to give too much credit for events in mid-Illinois to God, or rather to human faith in God. Most conventional histories tend to scant both. It is useful to recall that appeasing the spirits animated Native American works from pot making to mound building, that the first Euro-Americans to explore the region were missionaries in search of souls and not pelts, that many later Euro-American immigrants moved to mid-Illinois hoping to find either more freedom to exercise their beliefs or more scope for stopping others from exercising theirs, and that virtually all the region's early schools trained soldiers in sectarian wars. Whether newcomers saw the place as a God-given paradise (albeit one fashioned by a god that had an unaccountable liking for mosquitoes) or a godforsaken waste that awaited the healing touch of the pious to redeem it, gods and ideas about gods have been central to mid-Illinois's story.

PREHISTORIC INDIAN

To try to understand the spiritual life of the native inhabitants of mid-Illinois during the many centuries before the Euro-Americans arrived is to travel though a mental landscape that is not only unfamiliar but also strange, it being of a type once lived in by Europeans too but long since forgotten.

Twelve thousand years is a long time, but the basic aspects of prehistoric spirituality seem to have changed remarkably little over that span. The people worshipped no single god that lorded over creation, although they envisioned a great spirit as a sort of prime mover. Their cosmology was animistic, each of the things of this world being thought to be inhabited by its own spirit. Their totems were the creatures they knew from the streams and woods. Humans hoping to make their place safe in such a world needed therefore to master the arts of reading signs and codes from what would come to be called the natural world, thanking or pleading with the spirits as needed. The Native Americans encountered by the French in the 1670s, for example, are thought to have believed that the smoking of tobacco transformed it into a gift capable of propitiating the Great Spirit who gave it to them.[3]

Unchanging as the broad dimension of Native American belief might have been, the world of which it was a part nevertheless changed often and profoundly. Chill, damp forests gave way to dry grasslands, mastodon gave way to deer and bison, spruce woods gave way to oaks, and wild plants gave way to corn. As people relied more on cultivated plants, their society, ritual, and burial practices changed. As the anthropologists at the Illinois State Museum put it, "Their earlier world view that had been shaped by the nomadic existence of the hunt gradually changed to reflect a more settled village and gardening way of life. Older ritual symbols expressing the power of hunted animals were now combined with images of the earth's fertility."[4]

Much of what is known about the spirit world of the Indians comes from their graves, thanks to their tradition of interring the dead with objects from life. These burial rituals gradually became more elaborate, in some cases anticipating such modern practices as attempting to preserve the remains against decay and laying bodies to rest face up, as if sleeping. During the climax of the Middle Woodland period from 500 B.C. to 200 B.C., burial mounds with log-covered subfloor burial pits became typical across mid-Illinois. In 1884 workmen digging a new cellar for the house of farmer Elmer Ogden outside Havana caused the ground to collapse when the roof of such a pit under it gave way. The tomb had been built maybe two thousand years earlier, part of a mound that measured 175 by 200 feet. In it were found crematory basins laid out on a red-painted fiber mat and filled with burned ashes of many individuals (the decoration of graves with red ochre was by then a venerable tradition). The skeletal remains were of a man evidently of considerable social importance, since buried with him were necklaces of pearl, bone, and shell beads, copper implements, hundreds of canine teeth from grizzly bears, an unusual stone gorget, a twenty-five-pound nugget of lead, and a stone platform pipe whose tobacco bowl sat atop a sliver of carved stone

The late Robert L. Hall, a distinguished professor of anthropology at the University of Illinois at Chicago, once imagined in print how this tomb and others like it came to be. Members of a band who died while they were away on seasonal hunting trips or during winter when ground was frozen were "buried" on scaffolds or platforms in trees for a period of time until only bones remained. The skull and long bones of the arms and legs were retrieved, tied into a bundle small and light enough that it might be carried for a year or more. A sequence of rituals determined the time appropriate for reburial, and a rectangular pit was excavated into the hard clay center of a circular pit. "Into [this pit] the bundles were placed after a ceremony of mourning to dispatch the souls of the deceased along the spirit trail. Other bundles followed in later years, each covered with logs cut to fit. When the band abandoned the camp, the pit, the tombs, and the log vault were covered with a dome of earth."[5]

A belief in an afterlife has been inferred from other evidence. During the Woodland period, images of a menagerie of eagles, otters, ducks, and beaver were scratched, molded, or carved onto pots, jars, and pipes. Anthropologists speculate that these creatures were so represented because they could navigate between land and sky and between water and land, thus moving from one world to another as spirits were thought to do. Pipes, tools, weapons, adornments of stone and exotic shell, and specially made mortuary vessels of unknown function were placed in tombs. Increasingly sophisticated and exotic, such objects are generally assumed to have had significance not only in honoring the dead but also in enhancing their journeys through the next one.

The Mississippian period in mid-Illinois began about 900 A.D. and lasted until 550 years ago. Archaeologists believe Mississippian people divided their world into an upper world that is the realm of the life-giving sun, a middle world of the familiar earth, and a lower world that is the source of fertility. The Mississippians also are thought to have relied on rituals in which the spiritual powers embodied in human flesh and bones were returned to the cosmos from which these powers were derived, thus renewing the world. Some of the remains at Mississippian Cahokia are thought to be of humans slain as part of such rituals. Lawrence A. Conrad is among those who reject the notion that these dead might have been captives or casualties of war, seeing them instead as servants or kin sacrificed on the death of some powerful individual, perhaps to accompany him on his journey through the afterlife.[6] Robert Hall speculated that the remains might be evidence of an ancient Indian green corn ritual in which a surrogate of the corn goddess was slain each year on a platform formed by the bodies of four men who had been ritually roasted before their still-beating hearts were cut from them.

Dr. Timothy Pauketat, from the University of Illinois, is among those who believe that the influence of Cahokia over its hinterland, including Dickson Mounds and the rest of the valley of the lower Illinois River, was not exclusively economic or military but also religious and political (although influence then as now can be exerted by each or all.) Anthropologists wonder whether the social elite at Cahokia appropriated ancient symbols of fertility and world renewal from olden days, then re-created these earth mother figures in mica or quartz and distributed them to surrounding towns. The people of this hinterland, convinced by Cahokia's magnificence that its elite had access to power that they wanted to share, adopted their rituals.

The most conspicuous and most important Mississippian archeological site yet discovered in mid-Illinois is one such outpost, in today's Fulton County—Dickson Mounds and the towns and villages thought to be associated with it. At Dickson Mounds, Cahokia-like exotic trade goods, ceremonial mounds at the centers of stockaded plazas, and burial practices suggestive of new status differences among community members all appeared suddenly in the latter part of the eleventh century.[7]

And then the culture all but disappeared. Perhaps the old rites were seen to have failed when game disappeared in consequence of climate shifts, or floods rotted crops in the fields, or disease decimated villages. For reasons that probably will keep anthropologists debating for years, Cahokia's influence over its hinterland waned. It would be facile to describe the end of brief Mississippian flowering in mid-Illinois as a Native American Decline and Fall, but all along the Illinois River, towns were fortified, suggesting that rivalries had erupted between contending chiefs, as did burials from the period that show scalpings, malnutrition, and broken bones.[8] The Mississippians' hope for the renewal of their world proved vain.

"SOME SUPERSTITIONS"

Knowledge of the spiritual systems of later Native American peoples in mid-Illinois, better understood than those of their predecessors, is owed mainly to the diligence of French priests who carefully noted the rituals of the native peoples they encountered on their travels. Of the rituals themselves, the French thought very little. The details of the Indian belief system hardly mattered to Euro-American divines who were convinced that no system without the Christian god at its center could be called spiritual at all. Father Pierre-Gabriel Marest, a missionary among the Illiniwek peoples, wrote a colleague in 1712, "It would be difficult to say what is their religion. It consists entirely of some superstitions with which their credulity is amused."[9]

Those superstitions composed a comprehensive spiritual system that made both sense in and sense of their world of the duck and the deer, the corn and flood, childbirth and blood. At the heart was a powerful manitou, or spirit. The Illiniwek knew this deity as Kitchesmanetoa, the maker of all things, but they also honored other deities of the Upper World that maintained life and the earth's fertility. Elements of that system were shared by Indian peoples across the eastern third of the continent, and the beliefs persisted until that world was turned upside down by the arrival of Europeans.

Ignorance of this spiritual world led Euro-Americans to decry as barbaric Native American acts that often had noble ends. The warrior's practice of eating the heart of a fallen but valiant foe in the hope of nourishing his own courage should not have shocked priests whose sacraments included the ritual ingestion of their savior's body and blood. The death of a family member often sent the bereaved on the warpath, less for revenge than to obtain the spirit of a slain enemy to serve as a servant for the mourned kinsman while the latter was on

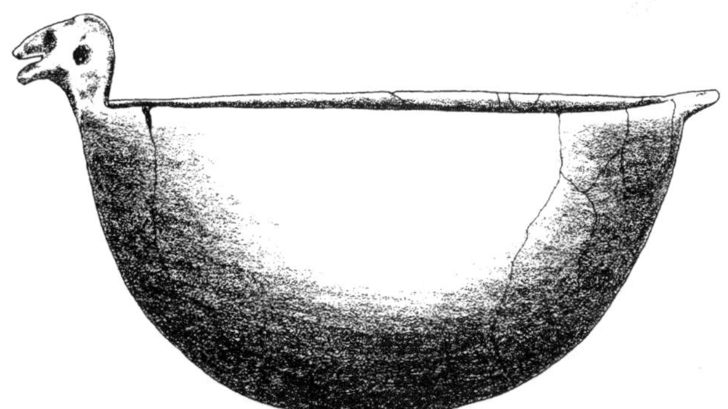

Mississippian effigy bowl found in a grave at Dickson Mounds, decorated with the head of what might be a crow. The significance of such decoration is not known. FROM *THE PREHISTORY OF DICKSON MOUNDS: THE DICKSON EXCAVATION*, BY ALAN D. HARN, 2ND ED. (SPRINGFIELD: ILLINOIS STATE MUSEUM, 1980), 107. COURTESY ILLINOIS STATE MUSEUM.

the spirit trail. Even thus accoutred, a spirit freed by death could not rest until someone had been adopted to replace its loss to the band. Because this spirit-substitute did not have to be a member of the deceased's tribe, war was waged to win captives for adoption; some of these unfortunates were Euro-Americans who were given the name of the deceased, whose spirit was thus freed.[10]

The cannier priests tried to replace the Indians' manitou with the Christian Almighty. Evidence suggests that often the Indians did not abandon their own faith as a response to Christian exhortations but merely augmented it with sympathetic borrowings from Christian fable and ritual. Among these borrowers was the Kickapoo chief known to us as Kennekuk, who led the Vermilion Band of Kickapoo and Potawatomi from the 1820s to 1852. His religion was an idiosyncratic synthesis of Protestant evangelism, Catholic ritual, and (at its heart) Kickapoo values and practices, which he thought essential for the Kickapoos' spiritual regeneration and, thus, their survival as a people.[11]

Nehemiah Matson of Bureau County was a diligent local historian who spent much time with the region's remnant native peoples. "The medals, crosses, and crucifixes which the Jesuits gave the warriors, pleased their fancy," he observed, "as they were fond of adorning their person with glittering trinkets." But Matson added that they also adorned their person with necklaces made of the dried fingers of those they had slain in battle.[12] Matson thus was skeptical of missionaries' claims of mass conversions. "Many were willing to be baptized every day in the week for a pint of whisky or a pound of tobacco," he wrote, but when the several missions up and down the Illinois River were abandoned, the natives quickly "relapsed into a renewed state of barbarism not at all in keeping with the teachings of the kindly disposed priests."[13]

Sincere converts there were made nonetheless, and it is not coincidence that most of them were among some of the dispossessed and despised peoples of the Illiniwek confederation. The men believed that the spirits that inhabited the white men's guns and iron must be powerful indeed, and the Illiniwek sensibly sought to propitiate them so they might end their wretchedness by success in war or in the hunt.[14] For their part, many of the women used Christian teachings on virtue to counter their husbands' taking of new wives or to justify their own resistance to sexual exploitation.[15]

All the native peoples of the region faced a crisis of belief as the 1800s unfolded, but not all these people were willing to pay even token respect to the Euro-Americans' god. Among the Illiniwek, the remnant Kaskaskia were eager converts, but the Peoria were not. The Kickapoo too were stubbornly insistent on their own beliefs.[16] The traditionalists among them blamed the outbreaks of strange diseases, the dearth of game, and the losses in war on their having turned away from traditional ways. They counseled that only by abandoning white people's clothes and tools and foods would the manitou make them strong again. Religion, long central to a shared native culture, became divisive. Indian villages of this period often sheltered people of different tribes—in Potawatomi villages along the Illinois, for instance, could be found Ottawa and Chippewa[17]—but seldom did converted Catholics dwell peacefully with native traditionalists.[18]

ECCLESIASTICAL WAR ON THE FRONTIER

In the opinion of many Euro-American learned divines, the religion of the frontier white people was scarcely less primitive than that of the Native Americans. The lack of religious fervor (as measured by strict Christian observance) among Euro-American tribes vexed observers back east, especially churchmen active in the ecclesiastical wars for converts. News that settlers hauled their produce to markets on the Christian Sabbath without qualm, for example, was alarming enough to send missionaries into this trackless wilderness.

Theodore Pease gave us this portrait of these early evangelists. "They had a strong contempt for college-bred ministers.... Men who had spent four years in rubbing their backs against the walls of a college were not the men to ride wretched roads week in and week out, swim their horses over creeks, and by address, by stratagem, or by force of superior muscle defeat the efforts of the rowdies to break up camp meetings."[19]

Eliza Farnham heard both circuit riders and resident clergy of the Methodist church in Tazewell County in the 1830s. "Before I had this experience I should have considered any true description ironical or libelous," she wrote. Their bellowing "renders it extremely difficult for the possessor of a cultivated ear to preserve both gravity and patience through one of their interminable harangues."[20]

Roving preachers hunted down converts like wolves hunted stray calves. No man showed more zest for the work than Peter Cartwright of Pleasant Plains. While virtue may be heroic, it is seldom regarded as romantic, but this Methodist circuit rider nonpareil made it appear so. He has been praised as the author of a classic of Americana (his *Autobiography*)[21] and was a stone in the boot of Abraham Lincoln for two decades. More than that, he was for this part of Illinois what Mike Fink was for the South or Bathhouse John Coughlin was for Chicago—an exemplar of an age, a fondly recalled hero whose life summed up virtues thought admirable but long vanished. Cartwright was typical of the best in his courage, his determination, his vigor, his honesty. He was also typical in his anti-intellectualism, his bigotry, and his unswerving belief in his own rectitude.[22]

Legendary Methodist circuit rider Peter Cartwright and his wife, Frances Gaines, in their old age, in an engraving from about 1866. Either of these formidable Pleasant Plains characters would have been a match for the devil in this world or the next. COURTESY LIBRARY OF CONGRESS, LC-USZ62–95736.

Cartwright, who died in 1872, outlived his era, but the mid-Illinois country preacher was not much changed by the 1890s, when Carl Van Doren heard one in his native village of Hope in Vermilion County. He took a more measured view of their deficiencies than did Farnham. "There is no discrepancy between [the congregation's] expectations and his abilities," Van Doren wrote in his memoirs, "and his position, therefore, becomes ridiculous only to better cultivated minds."[23] Even Farnham had felt obliged to acknowledge that while such men—and they were always men—were ignorant, even ludicrous in their discourses, "their presence and services are of great value to the communities among whom they minister."[24]

To the enthusiast, no practice is diligent enough, and many a preacher saw everywhere people lost in indifference to the Sabbath, ignorant of scripture, and lacking the fire of true belief. But there is no doubt that mid-Illinoisans wanted to be good, and that they believed that churches were the means to do so. Certainly they were eager to build churches. The *Peoria Register* in 1838 affirmed that every settler in the old Military Tract lived within ten or twelve miles of divine service on Sunday.[25] McDonough County proved the point: twenty-three Methodist Episcopal churches were formed in that county alone between 1833 and 1872.

Just as newcomers tended to build houses and barns like the ones they left behind, so did they seek to re-create on the desolate prairies the spiritual environment they had known back home. Southerners tended to be Baptist and Methodist, immigrants from New England and the mid-Atlantic seaboard imported their Presbyterian, Congregational, and Episcopal traditions, while the foreign-born (beginning with the Germans and Irish) added Lutheran and Catholic voices to the choir.

Old Presbyterian Church in Winchester, in Scott County, now demolished. Praised by the Illinois Historic Structures Survey as the finest Greek Revival church in any Illinois town of more than five hundred people, it showed what devoted small congregations could accomplish. COURTESY LIBRARY OF CONGRESS, HISTORIC AMERICAN BUILDINGS SURVEY, HABS ILL,86-WINCH,1-1.

For all the furious energy devoted to building, and filling, churches, it is not clear that religion kept many nineteenth-century mid-Illinoisans on the straight and narrow, unless "narrow" is construed intellectually. We might take as an indirect measure of the people's flagging spirit the number of times their religious spirit had to be revived. Revivalism swept across mid-Illinois repeatedly, almost as regularly as the prairie fires of old to which it was often likened. No savage's war dance exceeded in indecorum the frenzy that often accompanied those moved by the spirit at camp meetings and revivals. The "jerks" left people (according to one witness) in the throes of "twistings, bendings, strikings, kickings, and other violent motions of which the human frame is capable, together with occasional barking and other unusual sounds."[26]

On the other hand, we might with as much reason take as proof of the people's yearning for faith that they were open repeatedly to the hope of reviving it. Stephen Paxson, "the John the Baptist of the Illinois Sunday School Association," organized the first Sunday School Convention in Illinois at Winchester in 1846; a worldly fellow so fond of dance that he kept a fiddler on salary, Paxson found God at Sunday School and went on to set up fifteen hundred "Sabbath Schools" that enrolled seventy-one thousand children.

By the latter 1860s mid-Illinois was no longer a backwoods society but an emerging urban and industrial one, and maybe for that reason the old-time religion appealed all the more. Coles reports that Springfield in 1866 was the center of a "great awakening," with meetings at the state capitol and noon prayer meetings in the ward schoolhouses intended to excite an outpouring of the Holy Spirit upon the churches and people throughout the State. "All denominations made great gains during this bonanza year."[27]

The official rationale for the founding of the new Illinois Industrial University (IIU) in 1867 was utilitarian and democratic, but the founding generation of teachers and administrators shared a distinctly Christian personal vision that directed their work. In his interesting look at the early days of the future University of Illinois, Brett H. Smith observed that while nineteenth-century millennialist evangelical revivals frequently invigorated the piety of American private colleges, it was rare for a public university to advocate the transformation of society on religious grounds. The aim of the IIU leaders was to produce men of Christian culture able and willing to lend a helping hand in reversing the curse of Adam as found in Genesis 3:17–19. "Humankind, they believed, had toiled miserably for their sustenance since time immemorial. But now, by God's grace, the divinely ordained dignity of farming as covenantal co-laboring with God would be restored. . . . By putting their hands to the plow of agricultural education, they believed, the Lord would usher in nothing less than a 'Millennium of Labor.'"[28]

Both Illinois lawmakers and the state's farmers, it turned out, had other ideas about God and work and farming. The university's founders succeeded in their mission nonetheless, in a way. While the school quickly turned away from trying to elevate its farms to Edens, it did elevate its farmers to demigods able to marshal science to control plagues and engineer nature to their own specifications.

The revivalist era reached its peak, or arguably its nadir, with the performances of Billy Sunday, the baseball-playing, hokum-peddling "polygonal preacher" who could make hellfire entertaining and virtue fun, at least for a while.[29] Sunday brought his road show to Springfield in 1909 for six weeks of revival meetings and speeches. He was invited by the local Ministerial Association, whose members were convinced, as Springfield preachers had always been convinced, that their town was going to hell. Sunday staged his main meetings in specially built open-air "tabernacles," no other building being quite suited to the purpose. (Sunday's plans specified not only a stage, a choir, and seating for eight thousand but also a press box.) The Springfield version stood at First and Adams Streets, only one block from the Satan's den that was the Illinois statehouse.

Sunday offered a kind of Christian vaudeville, with jokes and music and sing-alongs. The centerpiece of each session was a sermon, by 1909 finely honed and audience-tested, selected from a repertoire with such titles as "The Devil's Boomerang," "Booze," and "When the Chickens Come Home to Roost." It

Billy Sunday. Evangelist Bill Sunday revives the sagging faith of Springfieldians in his specially built downtown tabernacle, 1909. How many people came for the salvation and how many for the show is impossible to say. COURTESY OF THE SANGAMON VALLEY COLLECTION, LINCOLN LIBRARY, SPRINGFIELD, ILLINOIS.

is doubtful whether the producers of any revival have ever admitted to having failed, but the backers of Sunday's Springfield revival claimed that well over half a million people crowded into the tabernacle,[30] impressive indeed at a time when the total population of the ten counties surrounding Springfield was less than half a million. The city was improved, certainly—its hotels and restaurants did good business, local churches got a good return on their investment in the form of new congregants, and a YWCA was founded—but saved Springfield certainly was not.

The religious life of the region was not left solely in the hands of glory shouters. Many of the leaders of mid-Illinois's sectarian colleges were scholars as well as churchmen. Most figure prominently only in church histories, but mid-Illinois also helped shape a religious figure of national note. As mentioned previously, Missouri-born Reinhold Niebuhr, arguably the most important American Protestant theologian of his era, grew up in Lincoln in the early part of the twentieth century, where his father was pastor at St. John's United Church of Christ Illinois, and was himself confirmed and ordained there. Abraham Lincoln's namesake city left a deeper mark on Niebuhr than he did on it; according to one biographer, Niebuhr found in the late president "an exemplar of [Niebuhr's] most profound theological views."[31]

SECTARIAN TENSIONS

The more fervent believers tended to see the Devil everywhere, of course, but seldom did he loom so large as when he took the form of a rival sect. Church building was a congregation's assertion of social and cultural identity, and intolerance of contrary views that could not be expressed in other ways found full expression in the churches of the period. Julian Sturtevant, an evangelist and Illinois College's first teacher, recalled the failure of initial efforts of the college's backers to obtain the needed legislative charter for a school whose founders were insistent Presbyterians. "The most prominent argument was the alleged discovery that Presbyterians were planning to gain undue influence in our politics, and were proposing to control the government of the state in the interest of Presbyterianism [even though] there were only a few hundred Presbyterians at that time in the entire state."[32]

However, nothing brought believers to the battlements more quickly than disputes within their own sects. Accounts of religious life of this and other parts of Illinois in the middle 1800s leave the impression that believers devoted half their time to reading the Bible and the other half to disputing what they had read, just as during the week they divided time between hoeing and milking. The devout population was overwhelmingly Protestant, and disputes about the fine points of doctrine or ecclesiastical jurisdiction led to feuds and factionalism. But doctrinal disputes per se did not completely explain the fissiparous nature of most congregations. The frequency with which new congregations were cleaved from old often seems to have had more to do with the social expectations that observance demanded. Many people came west looking for a very specific kind of freedom: to be left alone by bishops and theologians. They also resented the rule-making, busybody churches they knew back home that (to take the example of the Methodists, the Quakers, and others) resorted to public shaming of members thought guilty of ordinary human frailties. The spectacular rise in mid-Illinois of the Disciples of Christ, which disavowed doctrine of the usual sort, owed much to the desire of those left perplexed and peeved by demands of sectarian purists.

For some, church was a haven for differences that could not be comfortably expressed in a political, civic, or social setting. But while it was all those things, churchgoing was never only those things. A church also was a social center, for one thing; for another, observance marked a welcome respite from the week's hard work in factory or field or kitchen. And as Carl Van Doren explained, his family's old church at Hope was "a sober club for the encouragement of good behavior. While a few members were devout or dogmatic, most of them were easy-going in whatever faith they had. The motto painted in bold letters on the wall behind the pulpit, 'Christian Character the Test of Fellowship,' made up the whole creed. To be honest and decent in daily affairs was all that was required of any member, and that was required rather by the community than by the church alone."[33]

COMMUNITARIANISM AND GOOD BUSINESS

What any community required by way of the spiritual varied, of course, according to who was part of it. Certainly many a Yankee immigrant was convinced that a model existed for a better society in the form of his or her northeastern village. New Englanders and New Yorkers established on the prairie of mid-Illinois in the 1830s a half dozen colonies whose aim was to re-create that village. As Don Harrison Doyle notes, each was to be "a frontier version of the Puritan 'city upon a hill' . . . a homogeneous, stable, miniature society with its own church and school that embodied the community's collective values."[34]

Only one of these societies was a true colony in a legal sense. Most were land companies in which investors pooled resources for the purchase of land (usually government-owned, offered at a low $1.25 acre) that would then be sold to private buyers of farmland, the profit supporting the work of the community. Henry County attracted no fewer than five such settlements.[35] The Connecticut Association established Wethersfeld to promote "education and piety" in Illinois; shares in the proposed town were sold to New Englanders at $250 each, which gave the owner title to 160 acres of prairie, 20 acres of woodland, and a town lot. Andover, one of many land companies formed under the direction of Presbyterian minister Ithamar Pillsbury, was laid out in 1841 in the New England style. The LaGrange colony (later the town of Orion) traced its beginnings to Pittsfield, Massachusetts. The Geneseo colony was organized in its namesake New York county in 1835.[36]

Galesburg was born in 1835 when Presbyterian minister George Washington Gale circulated a prospectus among his parishioners in New York's Mohawk Valley, the "Burned Over District" where the fires of evangelical revivalism were said to have burned with special fierceness. Investors would get title to land and the right to send their children to a new college to be built on the site; the college would be supported by the sale of the rest of the land, whose value was assumed likely to appreciate as settlers built up the area. As Richard Lingeman noted in *Small Town America*, such projects had in common "communitarianism combined with good business"[37]—a very Yankee sort of approach.

The founders of Galesburg had a larger aim, however, which was to redeem not only Illinois but also the founders' own brand of Christianity. The new school, Knox Manual Labor College, would be open to people of color and to women willing to undergo a "thorough system of mental, moral and physical education" intended to prepare them to go forth and light the spiritual darkness in which Illinoisans then dwelt.

As town makers, these worthies proved to be excellent Christians, but only people blinded by the light could have so overestimated the market for community-sanctioned virtue in the mid-Illinois frontier. Town after town disappeared into the world each had tried to keep at bay. Wethersfield ended up being first outdeveloped and later absorbed by nearby Kewanee; the influence of Andover's Massachusetts Presbyterians was soon submerged by a tide of Swedish Lutherans.

Only Galesburg achieved something like its original purpose, and it made such a successful transition to a diverse, self-sustaining town that for a time in the latter 1800s it ranked with Illinois's larger cities. But while Galesburg thrived as a town, it too was not long a refuge for the pious in a wicked world. The arrival of newcomers not of the faith soon left growing Galesburg more socially liberal than the college, with the result that the town came to be seen, unusually, as a menace to the morals of the students in the eye of its conservative faculty and president. Also, as the civil community became more diverse, it no longer acted with unanimity on even small public questions. It became, like most Illinois cities, stratified by class and ethnic differences, its founding consensus about faith shattered into a dozen sects.

A perfect piety might be imposed on a new village in mid-Illinois but never on the more diverse townships or counties. Attempts to impose one's creeds on others were considered downright unneighborly by people jealous of their own freedom to worship what and how—indeed if—they chose. Earnest Elmo Calkins noted about early Galesburg that it "made itself obnoxious to its Knox County neighbors in such matters as Sunday observance, temperance and slavery, on all of which it took an extreme position."[38] The improved Lutherans of Bishop Hill, seeking to emulate Christ in every way, sent twelve apostles, in pairs, to convert to their creed a countryside that for some reason was not eager to be enlightened by them. One account of the Woodford County town of Eureka in the 1920s pointedly noted that Mennonites refused to join local grain marketing co-ops; further bad feeling owed to the refusal of local Amish and Mennonite property owners, who schooled their children at home, to approve taxes to build a public high school.[39] No wonder, as James Davis states, that because so few immigrants wanted such people as neighbors, the concentration of Yankee colonies in Henry County delayed settlement of the rest of the county.[40]

ROMISH PLOTS

On one point, at least, Protestants in early mid-Illinois spoke as one—their detestation of Roman Catholics. Strong anti-Catholic feeling lay behind the urge of Easterners to found schools to train the young in Protestant principles. To more effectively proselytize the frontier, the Methodists of the Illinois Annual Conference alone established seminaries-cum-academies in twenty-two Illinois towns between 1836 and 1856; fifteen of these were in mid-Illinois.[41] Most of the region's proper colleges likewise were built by Yankees to recruit and train missionaries to venture among the heathens—just like the region's vanished French Jesuit missionaries who braved so much to tell the Indians they were damned.[42]

Education of missionaries was one means to carry the evangelical message into the Wild West. So was the living example of pious, proper Christians of the right sort. To provide it, believers founded in the region such model communities as the aforementioned Wethersfeld and Andover. James Davis notes that the founders of the former hoped the new town would reap not only "temperance, justice, charity, and other moral characteristics" but also "a good crop of converted Catholics."[43]

Many Protestants of that era undertook such spiritual husbandry less to save Catholics than to save themselves. They believed that the "Romish plot" was intended to undermine the American republic in its then-western frontier, including Illinois, where the absence of a cohesive social order and proper religion—meaning established Protestant churches—had left it vulnerable.[44] Anti-Catholic anxieties swelled again as the twentieth century opened with an influx of Catholic immigrants from eastern and southern Europe. Recalling his Hope in the late 1890s, Carl Van Doren recalled that his Protestant neighbors in the late 1890s feared that the local Catholic Germans "would let the priest get them into the church, lock the door, and tell them how much money they must raise before they could go about their usual business."[45]

Bigots later mobilized under the banner of the Ku Klux Klan to combat this threat. In the mid-Illinois of the 1920s, this white supremacist secret society did not rail against African American and Jewish populations, which were so small that they posed no threat to local status quos. Rather than racial purity, it was mainstream Protestant values that the Klan marched to protect. Many a mainstream Protestant was certain that the Pope planned to take over the country in an armed revolution manned by the Knights of Columbus at the head of an army of recent Catholic immigrants. Education offered no protection against this virus; in Lexington in McLean County, Klan members included not only farm workers and laborers but also the mayor, large landowners, bank directors, doctors, and businessmen.[46]

Several large Klan gatherings were held in the Springfield area in the 1920s, most featuring parades, cross burnings, and secret rites. A Klan parade from the Illinois statehouse to the state fairgrounds in October 1924 presented banner-bearing floats urging the closure of Ellis Island and extolling the public, nonparochial school system as "good enough for us." A rally at Camp Lincoln in August 1926 culminated in the burning of an eighty-foot-tall cross, which organizers of course boasted was the "largest fiery cross ever built in Illinois."[47]

The anti-immigrant hysteria that the Klan sought to exploit was short-lived, but anti-Catholic prejudice proved durable. Writer J. F. Powers's experience as a Catholic in the Jacksonville of his boyhood between the world wars provided him with characters and a theme. In *Morte d'Urban*, Powers's National Book Award–winning novel of 1963, the priest-protagonist says of growing up in such a town, "If you were a Catholic boy you felt that it was their country, handed down to them by the Pilgrims, George Washington, and others, and that they were taking a risk in letting you live in it."[48]

In the two generations after Jews first arrived in substantial numbers in mid-Illinois, they too were both despised as poor immigrants and feared for their religion. In her analysis of the social causes for the two days of antiblack mob violence in Springfield in August 1908, Roberta Senechal noted that white people also had been targeted—Jewish businessmen. "Anti-Semitism has been under-appreciated as a motive for the rioting," she writes. One of the few arrestees brought to trial was a twenty-year-old Jewish fruit peddler from St. Louis named Abraham Raymer. As a foreign-born non-Christian with no roots in Springfield who harbored radical political sympathies, Senechal noted, Raymer was an atypical rioter but a perfect scapegoat. However, if the prosecutors counted on a jury's anti-Semitism to deliver a guilty verdict that might otherwise be hard to get, they were disappointed. Raymer was acquitted of murder and riot and was convicted only of stealing a militiaman's sword, results that suggest that racial solidarity in this case trumped religious bigotry.

Politics was more or less open to Jews, but social and business barriers were many and enduring. Springfield's major banks, for example, had no Jewish board members (one employed no Jew in any capacity) until the 1970s,[49] and Springfield-area country clubs barred Jews until declining membership forced them to open their doors to them in the 1970s. At the University of Illinois, Gentile fraternity houses sustained no-Jews policies until the middle of the twentieth century. Writing about the Peoria of the 1930s, Betty Friedan recalled in her autobiography, "Entering high school, the other girls and boys who lived on the West Bluff, which was the nice part of town then, were rushed for sororities and fraternities. No Jewish kids were ever invited to join those sororities or fraternities, which ran high school social life in Peoria."[50]

RELIGIOUS HYSTERIA

Mid-Illinois before the Civil War was a haven for refugees as well as redeemers. Native peoples of the eastern and northern woods had come here to escape the Iroquois, slaves came to escape bondage, poor white Southerners came to escape the slave economy, and Europeans came to escape poverty or political and religious repression. Among the last were the followers of Swedish dissident Erik Jansson, who came in the mid-1840s (described in chapter 8) and the Waldensians, members of a French Christian sect declared heretics by the Catholic Church in Europe, who in 1858 settled in Livingston County near Odell.[51]

To that list must be added the followers of the self-styled Mormon prophet Joseph Smith, who came here to escape Missouri. Like George Gale, Smith hailed from the Burned-Over District in western New York, center of the so-called Second Great Awakening of Christian revivalism. John Hallwas, one of the several scholars to devote fascinated attention to Mormonism in Illinois, explains.

> Mormonism . . . reflected a reactionary pattern of thought that arose among the New England clergy during the Revolutionary era: fear of moral degeneracy, demand for a republic of Christian virtue, and identification

Mormons' second temple, in Nauvoo, in Hancock County, from an 1890 lithograph. It is disputed whether the Mormons got closer to God than their neighbors, but the 165-foot temple certainly did. In its time it was the grandest building for religious observance in mid-Illinois, indeed the grandest building of any kind save perhaps the state capitol. In use for fewer than three weeks, the temple was vandalized by unbelievers, gutted by fire, and finally wrecked by winds. COURTESY LIBRARY OF CONGRESS, LC-DIG-PGA-03332.

of America with the millennial Kingdom of God. Smith absorbed that perspective too, but he asserted that the Mormons alone were the chosen people, not the American public, and that their development of a new social order, amid the apparent disorder of early nineteenth-century America, would hasten the Millennium.[52]

The Mormons became Illinoisans in 1839 only reluctantly, when five thousand Latter Day Saints landed at Quincy, having been expelled from Missouri by order of the governor and fleeing for their lives from vigilantes. Thus opened one of the most contentious chapters in Illinois history. Smith resettled his flock on land upstream from Quincy in Hancock County, in a town site called Commerce at the foot of a bluff overlooking the Mississippi. Smith renamed Commerce "Nauvoo," and it was to be the City of Zion, where Mormon faithful would gather to await the end of the world.

Like most waiting rooms, this one was uncomfortable. It was ill-drained, and the bluff top that offered safety from floods was inconveniently far from the river. Nonetheless, the Missouri refugees were quickly augmented by converts from the United States and England. Mormons also settled in the nearby countryside; in 1842, Hancock County had a Mormon population of sixteen thousand, with more living in the countryside nearby in Illinois and across the river in Iowa.

One such outpost was the community of Fountain Green, eleven miles outside Carthage on the road from Springfield to Nauvoo. An earlier influx of eighty Mormon families comprising more than five hundred individuals had overwhelmed the township's fifty original residents at the ballot box. The Mormon faction incorporated the settlement as a town that came to known as Macedonia. "On every front," writes Susan Sessions Rugh of Brigham Young University,

> the Mormons trespassed the bedrock values of the Fountain Green community, which were privately-held property, a free market, and local control of government. Mormons voted the way their leaders told them to, held property in common, created a separate economy, and practiced polygamy, a clear affront to agrarian patriarchy. To the farm families of Fountain Green, the behavior of the Mormons pushed the boundaries of religious toleration beyond the limit.[53]

Smith's promulgation of such controversial doctrines as plural marriage and baptism of the dead scandalized not only non-Mormons but even some within his own church. Dissent quickly matured into factionalism among the Saints; the leaders of the anti-Smith opposition, each an influential man in the church, published an anti-Smith manifesto in a local newspaper, the *Nauvoo Expositor*. Smith called out the local militia known as the Nauvoo Legion—in effect his palace guard—and ordered the city marshal to destroy the printing press on which the *Expositor* had been printed. It was the writ for Smith's arrest for this act, remember, that led to his arrest, which action culminated in Smith's murder at the hands of a mob at the Carthage jail on June 27, 1844, and the eventual expulsion of the Saints from Illinois, in 1846.

Historian Terry L. Givens asserts that Mormonism's heterodoxies posed a persistent and inimical threat to traditional Christianity, which excited something like religious hysteria in the Saints' enemies. (He adds that if Smith failed to respect the wall between church and state, so did many of his opponents, who mobilized local courts and militias in defense of Christian orthodoxy.) As Mormonism has become more respectable, or at least more successful, non-Mormon opinion has largely come around to Givens's view. In 2004 Illinois's lieutenant governor led a delegation to Utah to deliver a General Assembly resolution expressing sorrow for the state's role in what its authors described as early religious hate crimes committed against the Mormons.

After World War II, paranoid fantasies of subversion and revolution focused on new sets of exotic newcomers. Because they put loyalty to their creator above loyalty to the state, Jehovah's Witnesses refuse to salute the U.S. or any flag. Not sharing such principled fervor, many an anxious patriot in the 1940s ascribed the refusal to sinister motives. They contrived to convince themselves that members of the sect were in fact agents of the Nazi state bent on advancing in some undescribed way a planned invasion of the United States by Hitler's forces.

The Witnesses' traditional proselytizing forays into new communities were met by mob violence in forty-four states during 1940. One of them was Illinois. In June of that year, some one hundred Witnesses drove to Litchfield in Montgomery County from St. Louis to distribute literature house to house. The Witnesses' men were beaten in the streets by locals while police looked on; when women also were threatened, the county sheriff, whose chivalry apparently was more generous than his commitment to civil liberties, ordered sixty-four of the one hundred Witnesses taken to the jail for protection. A large American flag had been brought to the front of the jail; some of the male prisoners were forced by bystanders to salute or kiss the flag as they entered the jail, others were brought out of the jail to do so. Those who refused had their arms twisted until they were forced to their knees. Meanwhile twelve of the

Witnesses' cars were totally wrecked; the arrival of a company of state police from Springfield prevented worse, but the Witnesses had to be returned to St. Louis by bus.

INFIDELS

As the twentieth century neared, a remarkable if temporary change had come over public opinion in mid-Illinois and the rest of the country. People openly disputed not which god they ought to worship, or how, but whether one ought to worship any god at all. No one disputed more often, more publicly, or more gleefully than Robert G. Ingersoll. He was by birth a New Yorker, by profession an attorney, by religion an agnostic, by inclination a platform performer. He lived in Peoria for two decades of his early manhood, beginning in 1857. Ingersoll spoke regularly from Chautauqua platforms and in lecture halls on several topics, but is remembered mainly for his polemics on religion.

Nonbelievers of every ilk, accustomed then as now to being damned from the pulpit by righteous Christians, were delighted to hear Ingersoll damn the Christians right back, and do so with more wit and often more scholarship than the clergy. Thus did Ingersoll earn such nicknames as the "Great Church Disturber," "Pagan Bob," and the "Great Infidel." Interesting, then, that Ingersoll's father was a Presbyterian minister; the younger Ingersoll had managed to become a preacher like his father—a preacher of the gospel of science, but a preacher nonetheless.

Ingersoll in 1867 was appointed by Governor Richard Oglesby to be attorney general for a two-year term. Because construction on the present Illinois statehouse began when Ingersoll was in office, its cornerstone (more than eight feet long, four feet wide, and three feet thick) was inscribed with the names of Ingersoll and other senior state officials, as tradition dictated. The cornerstone there today, however, is bare of any inscription, and for years it was said around Springfield that ardent believers, offended by an agnostic being thus honored, surreptitiously removed the stone and buried it in a deep pit on the statehouse grounds.

Exactly how a stone that size might have been removed and buried and the scar of its entombment concealed was not explained; perhaps God helped. The *New York Times* in 1921 passed along the "news" that lightning struck the stone nearly every time a summer cloud passed over the Capitol, and that each bolt "seemed to aim itself" at the stone, with the result that over time Ingersoll's name was nearly erased.[54] Finally, a government agency report found in 1937 explained that the original stone had cracked badly and had been openly removed by state contractors some two years after it was laid. The original cornerstone was discovered beneath the east lawn of the statehouse in 1944, with Ingersoll's name intact, by workmen replacing some steps. It had been buried, not to save the state's soul but to save workmen having to haul it away.

Ingersoll might have been cheered for his apostasy, but lesser mortals were for decades subjected to more than merely social pressure to profess at least a ritual Christianity. The Illinois Supreme Court held, in 1885, that the University of Illinois could expel a student for refusing to attend religious services in the university chapel, a requirement that was long upheld in spite of the university's officially nonsectarian character. The student's general rights to freedom of worship, the court held, were circumscribed by his special status as a student subject to university regulations, to which he was assumed to have assented when he chose to enroll.

The desire to compel worship in officially nonsectarian schools never completely abated among some Christian believers. In 1940 the Champaign public schools gave fourth- through ninth-graders a choice of attending weekly classes in religious education (led in the school by clergy and lay churchmen) or attending "services or other activity at the church of their choice." Students not wishing to participate in any religious service would remain in school for a nonecclesiastical "study hour" to skirt the constitutional bar on government support of religions.

Champaign housewife Vashti Cromwell McCollum objected that the social pressure to conform faced by schoolchildren of that age meant that choosing whether to participate in these classes was not really voluntary. McCollum filed a legal challenge that ended up before the U.S. Supreme Court in 1948. *McCollum v. Board of Education* argued that such classes in effect established religions and thus violated the U.S. Constitution. The court found in her favor, setting a precedent that was long considered impregnable.[55]

A LITTLE MORE CHRISTIAN

The congregation of the region's Shiloh churches played their part (as Shiloh's historian put it in 1963) "in making the world a little more Christian." Thanks to them and many people like them, a great many churches and some fine small colleges were built, and a few charitable organizations founded where Christian kindness was institutionalized.

Whether religion proved on the whole to be a civilizing influence on mid-Illinois is too big a question for a small book like this one. Certainly mid-Illinoisans departed in no way from their fellows in other parts of the state in their indifference to the plight of unfortunates like the developmentally disabled and the mentally troubled and were just as niggardly when it came to spending to educate other people's children. As for "love thy neighbor," they were just as retrograde in their attitudes toward people who were not the same color or did not worship the same god as they were. But if the region was not better than it might have been thanks to religion, it's hard to see how it could have been too much worse without it.

CHAPTER SEVEN

The Urge to Improve: Educating Mid-Illinois

An oasis of intellectuality in a desert of fertility.

—President David Kinley, describing his University of Illinois

On a blustery October day in 1858, more than ten thousand people gathered at Knox College on the lawn of the building known as Old Main. They had come to hear Abraham Lincoln and Stephen A. Douglas debate freedom and the lack of it in the fifth of their soon-to-be-famous debates. To get the speakers out of the rain, the debate platform had been snuggled up next to the east side of the building. That placement required the participants to enter it from the inside, via a second-floor window; as he stepped onto the platform, Lincoln quipped, "At last I can say I've gone through college."[1]

Knox's opinion that Old Main thus is one of the most important pre–Civil War buildings in the Midwest can't exactly be called exaggerated. Of the buildings that hosted the Lincoln-Douglas debates, Old Main is the only one still standing, on which basis it was named a National Historic Landmark in 1961 and listed on the National Register of Historic Places in 1966. The chair in which Lincoln sat that day sits in Old Main's Alumni Room.

The last is an honor Lincoln would have appreciated. Lincoln, as every schoolchild used to know, was the quintessential self-taught man. His exploits as an eager learner—the reading by firelight, the famous treks to borrow books, the study sessions atop the store counter in New Salem—are part of his legend. It is hard to think of many other famous public people depicted by sculptors as they read, but in mid-Illinois there are several statues of Lincoln so occupied; typical is the roadside bronze just outside New Salem depicting a young Lincoln on horseback absorbed by a book in his hand.

Education also is near the heart of mid-Illinois's story. Lincoln schooled only himself, but some of his mid-Illinois compatriots help school the state. Jacksonvillian Governor Joseph Duncan was an early advocate of free schools. Jonathan Baldwin Turner, a professor at that town's Illinois College, was the father of the federal land grant university system. Newton Bateman, an IC alumnus, was the first superintendent of the public schools system of Illinois, indeed in many ways was its architect. The region also was the scene of important innovations in the education of the blind and the deaf, and it hosts sectarian colleges of national reputation and both Illinois's first public institution of higher education (today's Illinois State University) and its largest (the University of Illinois).

COMMON AS CORNCRIBS

Educated people there were aplenty in the mid-Illinois of the early nineteenth century, but they had brought their educations with them. Many of their less favored fellow citizens had to teach themselves and each other. One popular way to teach and be taught was the lecture lyceum. These member-run organizations sponsored lectures and other enlightening entertainments on topics ranging from politics and civics to natural history, science in all its branches (including such weedy offshoots as phrenology), technology, philosophy, and history. One scholar of the phenomenon called it "a huge, communal self-education project that linked small towns across the expanding United States."[2]

The first lyceum in Illinois was formed in Jacksonville sometime before 1832. Two years later, a group of Springfield's intellectual elite organized one there, plus a Young Men's Lyceum supported by younger and less formally accomplished men. The latter's purpose was described at the time as training a new generation of men in the oratorical and analytic skills necessary for leadership. One of that generation was a twenty-seven-year-old Lincoln, who in 1837 delivered a condemnation of mob violence titled "The Perpetuation of Our Political Institutions." The performance was not the last time that Lincoln, so long the learner, turned teacher. He later delivered lectures on discoveries and inventions in various sites in Illinois, including Bloomington and Illinois College in Jacksonville.[3]

The lyceums provided education by the elite for the elite (and would-be elite) in mid-Illinois. Education opportunities for the yeoman, the mechanic, the housemaid remained scarce. Stories about the young Lincoln show not only how eager he was for learning but how hard it was to obtain formal instruction in that place and time. What schools existed were private (usually religious in sponsorship and ambition) and charged fees. Illinois was the only state carved from the old Northwest Territory to adopt a constitution that did not even mention the provision of local common, or public, schools.[4] Its lawmakers resisted the idea of schools provided for and paid for by the public because so many of their constituents did. Most parents consented to giving their children enough schooling to read the Bible, but while parents accepted that some educatin' was necessary to get into the next world, they regarded it as little use in this one.

The State of Illinois, as parent to all local governments, was pleased to allow them to spend some money on schools, but few did. It took nearly fifty years for the concept of state-subsidized, locally managed and financed public schools to win legislative acceptance. In the meantime, learning languished. Poorly trained teachers taught poorly motivated students for as little as three months a year.

One of the better type of one-room country schools in mid-Illinois, in McLean County in 1917. Once too rare, such schools became too common as the twentieth century progressed and the region's rural areas emptied of people. COURTESY LIBRARY OF CONGRESS, LC-USZ62–50218

Livestock in many places was better provided for than learning, which had to be done in log houses, shanties, or temporary shacks; the average value of the twenty-one school buildings in Stark County, for example, was sixty-five dollars.

In 1855 the General Assembly finally imposed a modest state tax to support local schools. Within a decade, nearly two thousand school districts were organized and three thousand schoolhouses were built that together enrolled more than forty-four thousand children. The average school term now stretched to nearly seven months, and for the first time, prospective teachers had to pass examinations proving they knew something about all mandated subjects. The new system was embraced most warmly in Illinois's northern counties, but a few communities in mid-Illinois also proved to be zealots for education; among the first Illinois cities to open public high schools, for example, were Peoria (1856) and Canton (1860).

The drafters of the 1870 state constitution had hoped to give Illinois a charter appropriate to a modern state and thus enable Illinois to become one. At a stroke, the state's feeble early nineteenth-century provisions for public education were replaced by a commitment to providing "a thorough and efficient system of free schools, whereby all the children of this state may receive a good common school education."[5] Working this miracle was left to elected local school boards acting under the guidance of a state superintendent of public instruction.

Between roughly the Civil War and the Great Depression, when the region was at its most prosperous and populous, mid-Illinois towns built hundreds of schools. These were not the familiar one-room country schools of the previous generation but veritable temples of learning whose scale and architectural distinction often belied the modest size of the towns that built them. Typical of the first generation of these schools was the building known today as Pittsfield East School. Built of local brick and stone that had been floated down the Illinois River from Joliet and assembled to a design by the architect of the Executive Mansion in Springfield, it opened in 1866 as the East Ward School. Later versions included the handsome El Paso Township High School, built in the Woodford County town of that name in 1921 and paid for with taxes on 1,628 persons and, more significant, 168 sections of good mid-Illinois farmland.

The finest school buildings, of course, do little to advance a region's education level if children are not in them, and often they were not. According to state law of the time, no child could leave school to go to work without a school certificate that showed that the child was of age and could at least read and write. A survey of social conditions in Springfield in 1918 showed that approximately six hundred children between the ages of fourteen and sixteen

Springfield's Central High School. Opened in 1897, this glorious pile in the Romanesque Revival style, complete with six-story clock tower, occupied most of a city block. This was the kind of school building that prosperity and civic pride made common in cities and towns across mid-Illinois in that era. Within twenty years it was replaced because it was too small. COURTESY OF THE SANGAMON VALLEY COLLECTION, LINCOLN LIBRARY, SPRINGFIELD, ILLINOIS.

were leaving the local public and private schools of Springfield each year, but only about two hundred of them had the needed certificates.[6]

If the cities had problems getting kids to stay in school, the countryside soon had problems finding kids to attend them. A scattered rural people needed scattered rural schools, since schools had to be close enough to walk to. Most of the schools built in the early decades of the twentieth century had been built not in towns but in the countryside, where schools became nearly as common as corncribs. Even as the last of the new rural schools were being built, however, urbanization was beginning to sweep the mid-Illinois countryside clean of young families. The population of rural students in Illinois in 1919 was one-third of the number in 1900, even though the state's population overall had increased by more than a third.

By the 1940s, Illinois had more public school districts than any other state (twelve thousand plus), and most of them served its rural parts such as mid-Illinois, with the majority of those running one-room schools enrolling only a handful of students. The State of Illinois had made consolidation of these tiny districts feasible by finally providing roads capable of carrying motorized school buses to schools beyond walking distance of students; by the latter 1930s the state was helping to pay for busing itself. Even so, as late as 1945 McLean County (admittedly a very large one) still had more than two hundred one-room schools. Thus began a process that continues in the twenty-first century, as small rural school districts combine to build larger schools the equal of any in town, and yellow school buses are as familiar on the back roads of mid-Illinois as tractors and pickup trucks.

CENTERS OF PIOUS LEARNING

Opportunities for older students seeking formal instruction in the arts, letters, and science began to open up across the region by the latter 1830s. The legislature granted charters to 125 sectarian "academies" between 1818 and 1848. For decades these institutions were the only source of secondary education in the region, until public high schools began to open around 1860.[7]

The students were male for the most part, although most of the private academy charters awarded in mid-Illinois provided that girls should be educated as well (usually only "when sufficient money was at hand"[8]). Twenty-seven of these seminaries opened exclusively to girls in Illinois between 1830 and

Abandoned school. They built them; then they didn't come. Fewer farms mean fewer farm kids, so the abandoned country school has become a common sight across mid-Illinois. JACK L. BRADLEY COLLECTION, JB-P 559, BRADLEY UNIVERSITY LIBRARY, SPECIAL COLLECTIONS CENTER. REPRODUCED WITH PERMISSION.

1860, and quite a few were in the middle third of the state. The Jacksonville Female Academy, in operation from 1833 until it merged with Illinois College in 1903, was one of three female academies in Jacksonville; the others were the Methodist-run Illinois Conference Female Seminary (the future MacMurray College) and the Atheneum. No finishing schools, these—the curriculum was dauntingly and comprehensively intellectual. The chief difference in the course work between Illinois College and the female academies seems to have been that at Illinois College, Latin began in the freshman class with Livy, which assumed more skill on the part of the pupils, and that the boys also were taught Greek.[9]

When Eureka College, in the Woodford County town of that name, opened in 1855, it was the first college in Illinois and only the third in the nation to admit men and women on an equal basis. Monmouth College was one of the first institutions in the country to admit women from its inception, although in truth it did so in part to widen the pool of potential students. Nonetheless, many good deeds are done for dubious reasons, and Monmouth remained welcoming to women; Pi Beta Phi, the first national secret college society of women to be modeled after the Greek-letter fraternities of men, was founded there in 1867. Knox College was open to women, too, when not every institution of learning was. Knox students were precociously feminist and, as early as 1867, protested the college practice of teaching men and women in separate rooms. (The then-head of the school's Female Seminary, Lydia Howard, went on to become the first president of Wellesley College.)

Dozens of private denominational colleges—actual colleges, not prep schools—were planned in the 1830s, when both the region's population and its evangelical enthusiasm were rising. Among these centers of pious learning were such now-familiar names as Illinois College (1829), Knox College, (1837), Blackburn College (1837), and the short-lived Jubilee College (1839). Nearly as many others failed, being ill-managed or out-enrolled by other schools nearby; Aledo, Abingdon, Canton, Bushnell, and Springfield were among the towns that were able to call themselves college towns only briefly.

These schools were anything but playpens for idle youth. The founders of Galesburg's Knox College, for example, were not interested in producing gentlemen scholars. They had in mind instilling an especially robust sort of righteousness in the young. The system would not only open the minds of boys of all means but also strengthen their bodies to wrestle with heathen (that is, un-Presbyterian) beliefs in the rude place that was mid-Illinois. Impecunious students were required to perform three and a half hours of manual labor each day in exchange for tuition, books, and room and board.

Knox's founding traditions of social activism continued to inspire its students for decades. Samuel S. McClure helped found and edited the student newspaper, showing an inclination that manifested itself as an adult when he cofounded *McClure's Magazine* with two of his former classmates in 1892. Muckraking journalism was missionary work of a kind, and the muckraking that *McClure's* did made it a national force.[10]

Jacksonville's "Yale Band"—seven earnest young Christians from New England—came to Illinois to civilize the backward part of the world, to keep the already converted on the straight and narrow, and to train more of their kind to expand the work. They planned to establish a seminary of Presbyterianism in Jacksonville lest (as it was put in a circular requesting donations) the young country "grow up in ignorance and alienation."[11] Jacksonville listened to their plans with open ears; the Reverend J. M. Ellis, a Presbyterian missionary in Illinois since 1826, had long harbored a dream of opening a college there.

The result was Illinois College, which was founded in 1829. Its founders saw in the nascent school the seed of "a new and greater Yale."[12] Edward Beecher was its first president. (The first college building erected in Illinois, "Old Beecher," as Beecher Hall is sometimes called, was named for him.) Beecher retained close intellectual ties with New England, in part through his brother, Henry Ward Beecher, who preached and lectured at Illinois College. The Beechers' not-yet-famous sister, Harriet Beecher Stowe, visited occasionally.

That the college became only a new but lesser Yale was not, perhaps, a surprise. The financial panic of 1837, a calamity that stopped Illinois progress dead in its tracks for a decade or more on every front, set it back for years. Also, IC was too religious for some and not religious enough for others; it taught a dangerously loose kind of Presbyterianism that so aroused opponents within that church that the college founders were once formally accused of heresy. And the Illinois College campus was a hotbed of abolitionist agitation in the 1850s and 1860s, something outsiders found as alarming then as any antiwar demonstrations in the 1960s and 1970s were to the silent majority. However, while Illinois College might have been a poor Yale, it was an excellent Illinois College. Ralph Waldo Emerson, Mark Twain, and Horace Greeley were among the visitors and lecturers in the early years. Illinois College in 1835 granted the first bachelor's degree awarded in the state and in the 1840s offered the state's first academic instruction in medicine.

Illinois College was only one manifestation of what Theodore Pease described as the imperial dream of the Presbyterians and Congregationalists to conquer what was then called the West. In Carlinville in 1837, the Reverend Gideon Blackburn, a Presbyterian from the South, established a theological institution intended to train clergy to light the darkness in which he believed Illinoisans then dwelt. He purchased government land on behalf of eastern investors at two dollars an acre, setting aside fifty cents per acre to buy land for the college. The Blackburn Theological Seminary was thus endowed with seventeen thousand acres of fine farmland, which in Macoupin County is fine indeed.

The lord is said to help those who help themselves, and in 1912 a new president decided such a policy would be good for Blackburn College. He instituted a self-help plan like that initially installed at the old Knox Manual College. All students performed two and a half hours of manual work daily, running the offices and a farm that kept the student body nourished, and even constructing the school's buildings. Blackburn students still work for their degrees in every sense; the school is touted as one of only six nationally recognized "work colleges" in the United States.

Nearly forgotten today is Jubilee College, whose campus stood between Kickapoo and Brimfield in Peoria County. It was founded in 1839 by Philander Chase, the same Episcopal bishop who established Kenyon College fifteen years earlier in Ohio, when that state was at the same stage of development.[13] Chase's scheme was ambitious, even grandiose for the day. Jubilee College comprised a dozen or more structures on a thirty-five-hundred-acre tract, including a theological seminary, a college, a classical preparatory school for boys, and a seminary for girls, as well as small farming operations, a sawmill, and a gristmill. Freshmen studied Livy and Horace, Xenophon, Herodotus, Demosthenes, the Epistles of the New Testament, algebra, geometry, logarithms and trigonometry, classical antiquities, and ecclesiastical history. Such an ambitious course of study would have been dismissed as folderol by most Illinois Baptists, who believed that a minister needed only a Bible and a good horse. Mid-Illinois's Episcopalians proved too few to sustain it, and Jubilee College did not survive the death of the good bishop, who was thrown from his carriage in 1852.[14]

Prosperity and population growth pushed a second great wave of college building in Illinois that swelled in the latter 1840s and crested around 1860. That era saw the incorporation of two dozen new private, four-year, liberal arts colleges, several of which were in mid-Illinois. One was Monmouth College, established in 1853 by Scots-Irish Presbyterians. Galesburg's Lombard College had been founded in 1850 by the liberal Universalist Church. Officially nonsectarian, Lombard was where, as former student Carl Sandburg would put it, students would be free from the "creed drilling" of the hard-line church schools. Daughter Margaret Sandburg has noted that Lombard's spirit of intellectual and religious freedom was important to her father's development as a writer. But intellectual and religious freedom is never in vogue for very long in Illinois, and after years of struggles Lombard College merged with Knox College in 1930.

An outgrowth of the earlier Walnut Grove Academy, Eureka College was Christian Church (Disciples of Christ) in its religion, abolitionist in its politics, and improving in its instincts. Over the years the school hosted as lecturers such would-be improvers of the world as Abraham Lincoln, Susan B. Anthony, temperance reformer Frances Willard, Horace Mann, Christian Church cofounder Alexander Campbell, abolitionist congressman Owen Lovejoy, and Methodist evangelist Peter Cartwright.[15] Although one of mid-Illinois's smallest institutions of higher learning, Eureka produced a half-dozen grads who became governors or members of Congress. And one Eurekan—Ronald Reagan, class of 1932—became president of the United States. The young Reagan worked his way through school, played football, acted in school plays, and dabbled in economics and sociology.[16] (His degree, he would later joke, was more honorary than earned.[17])

Illinois Wesleyan University was another school founded to provide advanced training in godliness, in this case as understood by the Methodists. (Like most of Illinois's private colleges, it later turned secular to the extent it needed to, to stay solvent.) Illinois Wesleyan was a pioneer in making higher education available to all when it opened in 1850 at Main and Empire Streets in Bloomington. African American students were invited to attend in 1867, and women in 1870. Among its distinguished alumni—no college seems to be without them—is John Wesley Powell, soldier, explorer, geologist, and cofounder of the National Geographic Society.

Nineteenth-century Roman Catholics were quick to see the need to protect their young from the predations of Protestants. They built a refuge in the form of Quincy College. It began life in 1860 as St. Francis Solanus College, appropriately named after a Franciscan missionary to the Western Hemisphere. The school was subsequently known as Quincy College and Seminary and then Quincy College until it became Quincy University in 1993. Today the roughly one-thousand-student institution, which remains the only downstate Catholic university in Illinois, describes itself as liberal, Catholic, and Franciscan, though not necessarily in that order.

USEFUL ARTS AND SCIENCES

Like the region's first colleges, some of the mid-Illinois schools that opened in the latter 1800s were founded by missionaries, albeit of a new sort. Illinois by then was increasingly urban, industrial, and immigrant. To survive on this new and dangerous frontier, young people needed to be equipped with more than piety. To provide for them, the region received a new generation of public and private nonsectarian institutions devoted to the cultivation of the economic rather than the spiritual Illinoisan.

And who better to prescribe how the young should be prepared to thrive in this new Illinois than the self-made men and women who had themselves thrived? Lydia Moss Bradley had, with husband Tobias, become wealthy players in Peoria steamboating, distilling, banking, and real estate. Among her gifts to the city that made her rich was Bradley Park (the city's first public park) and Peoria's Home for Aged Women. Bradley believed that a modern education ought to furnish its students with "the means of living an independent, industrious and useful life by the aid of a practical knowledge of the useful arts and sciences"[18]—just the sort of educational opportunity she never had. Bradley had been raised to work, but like so many women of her generation—she was born in 1816—she had never been given skills beyond making lard and churning butter (which she did until a very old age).

In 1892 Bradley purchased a controlling interest in an Indiana school for watchmakers and moved it to Peoria. (Watchmaking was in that day a high-tech calling.) Bradley made plans to expand the training at her horological school to include not only other industrial arts and home economics but also instruction in the classical arts and sciences, as was being done at the new Lewis and Armour institutes in Chicago. The result was Bradley Polytechnic Institute, chartered in 1896, which offered instruction in biology, chemistry, English, German, French, Latin, Greek, history, mathematics, and physics, along with food work, sewing, manual arts, drawing, and of course watchmaking.[19] For years the whole enterprise was funded entirely by the widow Bradley, but it later stood on its own feet, becoming a four-year college offering bachelor's degrees in 1920 and a full university offering graduate programs in 1946, when it was renamed Bradley University.

In 1900 local businessman James Millikin challenged the citizens of Decatur and the leadership of the Cumberland Presbyterian Church to raise $100,000 to establish a new university in Decatur that would embrace the practical side of learning as well as the religious and classical. Obtaining a new university charter from lawmakers in Springfield proved tricky because of the opposition of already-established schools in the area, so businessman Millikin simply went out and bought what he could not persuade the legislature to give him—a charter belonging to Lincoln University in Lincoln. That school had been set up in 1865 by the Cumberland Presbyterian Church some thirty-five miles up the road in Logan County but had never thrived; Millikin in 1901 offered to give Lincoln University $50,000 for a new building if Lincoln would amend its charter to establish a cooperative arrangement between Lincoln and Millikin's new College and Industrial School in Decatur. The literary, classical, and godly side of education would be the province of Lincoln, and the practical arts that of Millikin's new school, with the two administered as the James Millikin University. Over time, the Millikin campus expanded its menu to include traditional academic offerings.[20]

SUMMER SESSIONS

Self-education had been a necessity in the 1830s and 1840s. Two generations later, self-education became a recreation. A system of summer school and correspondence school education was founded in 1874 at Chautauqua Lake, New York. Conceived as a summer school for Sunday-school teachers, the Chautauqua was quickly adapted to teaching all sorts of topics. Douglas Wilson of Knox College has noted that the Chautauqua movement owed its distinctive format to two earlier popular nineteenth-century institutions, the lecture lyceum and the religious camp meeting. Adding leisure to the formula made self-improvement palatable to Americans whose resistance to formal learning was as formidable then as it is now.[21]

Mid-Illinois had several Chautauqua grounds. In 1911 in Christian County, Pana built a thirty-five-hundred-seat pavilion on whose stage William Jennings Bryan, Billy Sunday, and Sergeant Alvin York held forth. The Chautauqua grounds at Clinton in DeWitt County were gradually improved with bridges and trails, a fine artificial lake outfitted with boathouse, bathhouse, and diving tower, and of course an auditorium. Sometimes more than three hundred families camped out there for the entire ten-day term of each summer's session; the grounds later made a dandy state park. Over in Shelby County, Shelbyville's Chautauqua hall was built in 1903. The building had a thirty-six-foot-square stage and a floor area of fifteen thousand square feet unobstructed by support posts, thanks to cunning engineering. As was true of most of the Chautauquas' summer homes, the walls were pierced by large doors that could be opened to cool it during sweltering nights.

In 1904 the Lincoln Chautauqua Association built an open-sided auditorium 160 feet in diameter that sat some forty-five hundred people. To today's eyes the auditorium looks like a parked flying saucer. A special streetcar line was laid to carry townspeople to and from the site. During assemblies, the grounds were equipped with a dining hall, feed yards for horses, and a garage for automobiles, even the site's own post office.

One of the most successful of all turn-of-the-century Chautauquas, the Old Salem Chautauqua, was staged a few miles south of Petersburg in Menard County. The fifty-four-acre grounds were less a summer campground than a resort for the many who flocked there for what organizers promised would be "wisdom, music and good cheer."[22] In addition to a five-thousand-seat auditorium, the grounds boasted a seventy-five-room hotel, a "Hall of Applied Christianity," bathhouse and pool, a quarter-mile-long cinder running track, tennis courts, baseball diamonds, croquet courts, basketball courts, a nine-hole golf course, rental boats, a fishing lake, and fields for quoits (a craze of that day). The Old Salem Chautauqua in its prime was thought to be the largest Chautauqua west of the Allegheny Mountains.[23]

Bible lessons were a staple at all Chautauquas, reflecting their origin, but the Chautauqua programs quickly came to resemble an intellectual vaudeville bill more than a Sunday school. Professors of every discipline spoke, but programs occasionally mixed classical music, opera, and plays. While some speakers took up topics such as economics and foreign policy that would empty a hall today, most lectures were short on education and long on exhortation. Former Jacksonvillian William J. Bryan—"the one American Poet who could sing outdoors,"[24] as admiring Springfield poet Vachel Lindsay once described him—was a regular on the Chautauqua circuit, which often brought him back to mid-Illinois.

Orators were entertainers of the higher sort, to whom people listened less to be instructed than to be dazzled or moved or amused or (a desire perhaps more common in those straitlaced times than today) outraged. Few on the Chautauqua circuit, or the lecture circuit generally, entertained more reliably than Robert Ingersoll, who is remembered mainly for his platform addresses on religion, though he spoke regularly on several topics. His audience was a middle class that in the 1870s was being liberated by science from smothering orthodoxies of all kinds, a class that briefly rushed to embrace new ideas with the same fervor that their descendants would show in the 1970s for new ideas about sex, drugs, race, and women's roles. One of Ingersoll's several biographers notes that some people who saw him in action in mid-Illinois courthouses likened him to Lincoln in eloquence.[25] Mark Twain—no mean platform performer himself—was a great admirer of Ingersoll; after hearing him in Chicago, Twain wrote to his wife, Livy Clemens, "Lord, what an organ is human speech when it is played by a master!"[26]

The Old Salem Chautauqua did not close until 1942, but most were out of business by the 1920s, undone by movies and radio. Their grounds continued to be popular as parks and playgrounds, but most of the old auditoria are gone.

Among the survivors in mid-Illinois are Lincoln's and the Taylorville Chautauqua Auditorium (1914) in Manners Park. The Chautauqua Auditorium in Shelbyville's Forest Park had outlived its original purpose by World War II and was used for storage until it was restored in the 1970s; it is reputed to be the largest building of its kind anywhere in the world.

INCONVENIENT CITIZENS

Jacksonville was the great downstate city that never was, but it managed to make itself into a great downstate town whose history is among the richest in the state. (The official historical marker on the major highways leading into town runs to 240 words—a veritable tome by historical marker standards.) A patch of mud in 1830, Jacksonville grew into what was considered a medium-size city of close to ten thousand people by 1870. However, its rapid growth up to the end of the Civil War proved wholly misleading, and in 2010 Jacksonville was home to fewer people than live in most Chicago neighborhoods.

In *The Social Order of a Frontier Community*, Don Harrison Doyle notes that the town lacked a river like Quincy's or Peoria's, and unlike Springfield and Bloomington it was off the beaten path between Chicago and St. Louis. In the end, Doyle notes, the city fathers chose to exploit what economists would call its one comparative advantage—education. By 1850 Jacksonville had made itself into a school town, much as other places became factory towns or railroad towns. Illinois College, like a weed in a field, had seeded other local institutions. The aforementioned Illinois Female Academy (known affectionately as the "Jail for Angels") was founded in 1846 by Methodist clergy, although it did not offer the baccalaureate degree until 1909.[27] (In 1931 the school adopted its current name, MacMurray College, in gratitude to a generous college trustee who funded its expansion.) Illinois College's name also pops up in the histories of Whipple Academy, the Young Ladies' Athenaeum, the Illinois Conservatory of Music, and the Jacksonville public school system (which in 1851 founded the state's first free public high school).

Jacksonville also was home to pioneering experimental schools for the education of people then still known as the deaf, the blind, and the retarded. The schools' presence owes to the educational mission of the town's Yankees, who believed that in a republic all people had a right to develop to the limits of their abilities. The Illinois Asylum for the Education of the Deaf and Dumb was established by the legislature in 1839 and was the State of Illinois's first such charitable institution. The inexperience of the institution makers showed, and the early years were hampered by underfunding and an unproven administrative setup that incited internecine power struggles. So low had the school's reputation fallen by 1855 that the job of superintendent was offered to anyone willing to fill it. Happily, that opened the field to newcomers with more talent and commitment than reputation, like twenty-four-year-old Phillip Gillette, a young minister who was employed at the Indiana School for the Deaf.

Gillette stayed for thirty-eight years, building the institution's foundations, its enrollment, and its reputation, making it into one of the foremost institutions of its kind in the country. Gillette had transformed the asylum into a school, which in 1867 was one of the first of its kind to introduce lip reading and speech therapy as an alternative to signing. The shift in approach allowed some nonhearing children to tackle a more conventional academic curriculum and enjoy a more conventional school experience, including playing (after 1923) in a musical band. By the mid-1950s, what had become in name as well as function the Illinois School for the Deaf was recognized as a school and not merely a custodial institution with an education program.[28]

The embryo of the Illinois School for the Blind was a small private school in Jacksonville begun by Joseph Bacon (himself without sight) in 1847. The General Assembly, which has seldom passed up a chance to discharge its obligations to its dependent citizens on the cheap, realized the economy of expanding an already-established institution, and Bacon's School was turned into a public institution in 1848. The larger ambition of the school's administrators was to turn dependent unsighted people into useful citizens independent of the public purse. Toward that end the Illinois School for the Blind tried to offer a high level of intellectual stimulation to its students, including a lecture series that brought the likes of Jane Addams, Edward Everett Hale, and Booker T. Washington to Jacksonville.

At first, sightless children were taught to read by using cumbersome raised letters. In 1892 Frank Haven Hall, the superintendent of what by then had become the Illinois Institution for the Blind, invented a portable typewriter capable of producing the easier-to-read combinations of embossed dots that are the alphabet of the Braille lettering system. The Hall Braille typewriter (also called a Braillewriter or Brailler) was the first successful machine of its type, and the basis for later models improved by others.[29]

Treatment and confinement, not education, was the object of the Illinois State Asylum and Hospital for the Insane, which opened outside Jacksonville in 1847. Children with developmental impairments were housed there with the insane, there being no place specifically for them; some children with limited mental capacities were placed at the Institution for the Deaf and Dumb for lack of anywhere better to send them. To provide properly for their needs,

Illinois Institution for the Education of Feeble-Minded Children, in Lincoln, around 1900. For years the asylum was an essentially self-sustaining community. Residents farmed nearby leased land, which was therapeutic both for them and for taxpayers. COURTESY LIBRARY OF CONGRESS, DETROIT PUBLISHING COMPANY PHOTOGRAPH COLLECTION, LC-DIG-DET-4A05244.

philanthropic Jacksonvillians opened an Experimental School for Idiots and Feeble-Minded Children. The General Assembly in 1865 appropriated money for a temporary school that would test a new idea of training such unfortunates for independence. At a minimum, the school hoped to teach retarded children to tend to their own needs and possibly even learn a marketable skill. The results were encouraging enough that the General Assembly in 1871 made the institution permanent.

The new school opened in the mansion of the late governor Joseph Duncan, generously provided by the governor's widow at a nominal fee. In 1875 the legislature proposed to fund a permanent home for the institution, on grounds big enough to house 250 people. Such a prize attracted competition from cities whose compassion for the afflicted had not previously been conspicuous but which coveted the state jobs that such a facility would bring with it. Eventually more than a dozen cities bid for the school. Most of them, including Jacksonville, were in mid-Illinois.

The winner was Lincoln, the most centrally located of the contenders. The new Illinois Institution for the Education of Feeble-Minded Children—later the Illinois Asylum for Feeble-Minded Children (in 1877), the Lincoln State School and Colony (in 1909), the Lincoln State School (in 1953), and the Lincoln Developmental Center (in 1975)—eventually occupied a sprawling complex of nearly one hundred acres, complete with a hospital, school, chapel, gymnasium, laundry, ice and cold storage plants, engine house, industrial buildings, workshops, and boys and girls residential cottages. But within a decade of its founding, the school's discouraged board of directors and superintendent were talking about the wisdom of establishing a custodial department for "people who could not profit from education but were in need of humane and intelligent care."[30]

As for the mentally ill, by the first quarter of the nineteenth century, medical thinkers had concluded that derangement was in fact an illness and not a symptom of sin or depravity. Asylums where such sufferers were humanely supervised were available to the wealthy, but the poor who suffered similar ills were banished to the local poorhouses, even jails—partly because of the absence of means, partly because of the absence of any notion that government support for such care was appropriate.

It was Massachusetts activist Dorothea Dix who brought new British ideas about the treatment of the insane to this country in the 1840s. She spent the next four decades pressing governments to improve the care of society's outcasts, from prisoners to the physically disabled and the mentally ill. Illinois's Dorothea Dix was Edward Mead, a professor at the short-lived Illinois College Medical School in Jacksonville. Inspired by Dix's work in the East, Mead made his own survey of the care of the mentally ill. He lectured about his findings in 1845 and reportedly wrote to seven hundred influential people to interest them in the establishment of a public hospital for the insane.

One of Mead's influentials persuaded Dix to come to Illinois to see for herself. In 1846 she visited jails and the old Morgan County poorhouse, where she found, among other abominations, "a violent insane man . . . confined in a shallow cellar, twelve feet square, with a trap door, under the smoke house, and who was without clothing and straw for his bed and was in a very filthy condition."[31] In all she found at least three hundred insane persons in the jails and almshouses of Morgan and neighboring counties alone.

The State of Illinois's new asylum in Jacksonville would have been strained to accommodate just those mid-Illinoisans who needed care, much less those in the rest of the state. The facility quickly became inadequate, and in 1895 the General Assembly voted money for a second, similar state institution, this one in Bartonville, just outside Peoria. Opened in 1902 as the Illinois Asylum for the Incurable Insane, it survived a succession of name changes, scandals, and therapeutic fashions until 1973.

Shackles, handcuffs, ball-and-chain manacles, and leather muffs, mitts, anklets, and wristlets used by county almshouses to restrain patients before they were delivered to happier fates at the new Illinois Asylum for the Incurable Insane at Bartonville. PHOTO COURTESY OF THE ALPHA PARK PUBLIC LIBRARY DISTRICT AND WESTERN ILLINOIS UNIVERSITY LIBRARIES.

The rise of Darwinism excited anxieties about the survival of the fittest even and perhaps especially in progressive, educated minds. The preferred solution to fears that people with developmental or mental handicaps—labeled by the directors of the Illinois State Institution for the Feeble-Minded as "the waste products of humanity"[32]—might corrupt the race was to isolate such contaminated genes from the rest of society. Thus did humane institutions that functioned as schools or rest homes end up being run in the "progressive" early twentieth century as warehouses for damaged goods.

Social philosophy was reinforced in Illinois by official parsimony, since the state government never had places enough for all the people who needed special services. To accommodate them, institutions such as those in Jacksonville, Lincoln, and Bartonville shifted their focus from rehabilitation and training to mere custodial care, which was cheaper. In the 1930s the Lincoln State School and Colony cared for some four thousand patients; by 1960 it was home to more than fifty-five hundred people. The Jacksonville State Hospital, which had expanded its duties to include treatment of the developmentally disabled, ultimately housed almost four thousand patients; at its peak in the 1950s, Bartonville's facility housed nearly three thousand.

Buildings became dilapidated and staff, hired for their patronage connections rather than their aptitudes, were ill-trained and poorly supervised. Eventually this warehousing of the incapable led to scandals that made the asylums' horrors too plain for even a complacent public to accept. Having become too costly to run and to awkward to defend, the big institutions in Jacksonville, Lincoln, and Peoria were doomed. Widespread misinstitutionalization led inevitably to calls for deinstitutionalization, a trend that began to sweep through Illinois's state establishments for the marginalized beginning in the 1970s. When it was announced in 1972 that what had become the Peoria State Hospital would close, its patient count had dropped to six hundred. By 2000 the Lincoln Developmental Center housed but four hundred people, many of them people with such severe emotional, mental, and physical conditions that they could not be cared for anywhere else. By the time what was then known as the Jacksonville Mental Health and Developmental Center closed in 2012, only a few dozen patients remained, bringing to an end not only these institutions but also the treatment philosophy that inspired them.

THE RISE OF PUBLIC HIGHER EDUCATION

If schoolhouses were few on mid-Illinois's frontier, qualified schoolteachers were fewer. Consider Mentor Graham, the New Salem schoolmaster who famously helped Lincoln with mathematics and lent him books on grammar. Graham will be forever known as (quoting the historical marker erected at his burial place in Menard County's Farmers Point Cemetery) the "Teacher of Abraham Lincoln." David Herbert Donald, like most modern Lincoln biographers, pooh-poohs this as flattery, arguing that Graham was only semiliterate. But the fact that Graham was regarded as educated by his neighbors suggests how low was the local standard.

The need for good teachers at any price was as dire in the 1850s as it had been in the 1830s. County examiners who tested teachers' knowledge under a new state teacher certification law were appalled to find that many of them could not answer questions that should not have troubled a twelve-year-old, assuming that the twelve-year-old had not been educated in an Illinois public school of the day. Expanding the common school system, as the state finally decided to do in the 1850s, would be pointless were there not good teachers to operate it. The State of Illinois thus undertook to teach teachers.

Mid-Illinois became home to the first of the state's "normal" schools set up to train tax-paid teachers. (The curious name reflects their mission to establish teaching standards or norms.) Belatedly inspired by Horace Mann's first state normal school in Massachusetts in 1839, Illinois authorized its own version in 1857. At that time there was already on the table in Springfield a proposal to establish a proper tax-paid university of the practical arts for the masses. The plan anticipated by some years the educational experiments of Bradley and Millikin, except that its emphasis on research in the emerging fields of natural sciences would prove important to Illinois's coal and agriculture industries.[33] By combining a university and a normal school into a single institution, the General Assembly also combined the votes of supporters of each. The result was not therefore the Illinois State Normal School but the Illinois State Normal University (ISNU), the first public institution of higher education in the state.

As usual, the choice of a site for the new school engendered a lively competition, to the delight of state lawmakers who saw towns bidding up the bribes each was willing to pay the state for the honor. Bloomington was chosen, even though Peoria's bid was the most generous.[34] Magnate Jesse Fell had been lobbying the General Assembly to put the school on land he donated in his new town of North Bloomington. (The spot was thus later incorporated as Normal, Illinois, earning the gratitude of punsters for decades to come.) As historian Henry B. Fuller put it in 1920, Fell "was desirous of founding at North Bloomington a town which should be characterized by sobriety, morality, good society, and all the other elements desirable for an educational center."[35] Normal did not permit the sale of liquor, and it banned the sale of cigarettes. Pool rooms and bowling alleys were as rare there as souks, and ISNU was free of social fraternities and sororities until the 1970s.[36]

Traditionally, men had taught school, but in the young Illinois the trades, even farming, paid better, so finding qualified men willing to do the work was hard. Women worked for less, and many parents would accept common schools that gave their children a mother's type of care. For decades, enrollment at the

A university in a box. "Old Main" was the first and for years the only building of what became Illinois State University, the oldest public institution of higher learning in Illinois. At its opening, the state's school superintendent described it as "an impregnable fortress, against which the wild waves of ignorance and tyranny might eternally beat in vain." Not quite eternally; Old Main was razed in 1958. COURTESY OF THE DR. JOANN RAYFIELD ARCHIVES AT ILLINOIS STATE UNIVERSITY.

normal university was mostly "indigent females," as they were referred to in 1833 by Jacksonville's Ladies Association for Educating Females.

To the disappointment of backers of the original state university plan, the official mission of the hybrid's school remained narrowly pedagogical. When ISNU opened, "higher education" was a relative term. As late the 1940s, teachers of elementary schools could be certified after a two-year junior-college-equivalent course, although ISNU soon devoted all its attention to preparing candidates for a single degree (a bachelor of science in education). What the new university did, it did well, however. It prepared so many students who went on to teach at or administer normal schools in other states that ISNU became known as "the Mother of Normals."[37]

Under the leadership of Governor John Peter Altgeld, the State of Illinois in the 1890s expanded its capacity to train teachers by opening three new normal schools. One was the Eastern Illinois State Normal School at Charleston, which opened in 1895. Another was the Western State Normal School, which opened in 1900 on the edge of Macomb. Each, like Illinois State, gradually enlarged its educational mission to encompass nonteaching majors, then added numerous doctoral programs as it evolved into a multipurpose university; thus was Eastern Illinois University and Western Illinois University born in 1957. In 1964 the first normal school finally became the proper university its founders envisioned with the birth of today's Illinois State University.

"LEARNING AND LABOR"

The publicly funded, general-purpose state university that ISNU's promoters hoped it would be opened in 1862, fifty-four miles down the road in Urbana. In the latter 1800s, rural workers rendered redundant by the industrialization of farming began migrating from farm to city in numbers that helped transform Illinois into an urban industrial state. The existing sectarian colleges were slow to expand on their traditional mission of training future clerics and professional men, so Illinois's state government undertook to do it. The new Illinois Industrial University (IIU) was in effect an early industrial retraining scheme intended to save idle hands from becoming a private disappointment and a public burden.

The idea of practical, publicly funded higher education for the masses had been promulgated by Jacksonville's Jonathan Baldwin Turner in an article in the *Prairie Farmer* in 1852. The concept was embodied in the Morrill Land Grant College bill, passed by Congress in 1862 and signed into law by Abraham Lincoln. The new act ordered that states be granted federal land, which would be sold to endow "industrial and agricultural" education. The land grant college would be not merely a public version of the private college but also a new kind of college. The Illinois version would offer a university-level education that had practical applications. (It revealed its intentions in 1870, when it became the first American university to offer shop instruction.) Its constituency would be not the elite's pampered sons, who continued to be fodder for private colleges, but the children of the upwardly mobile farm, factory, and shopkeeper classes. Fittingly, the university's motto, "Labor and Learning," was rendered in English instead of Latin.

The political forces arrayed against a new state-supported university had been formidable. By midcentury the established denominational colleges were so many and so successful that, as Arthur C. Cole would later phrase it, "many friends of education came to believe that the time when it was necessary for the state to foster a college had forever passed."[38] To the protests of proprietors of private schools were added those of critics who argued that higher education of any sort was wasted on the laboring classes. Illinois thus was the last of the original Northwest Territory states and among the last in the entire Midwest to found a land grant university.

What was to become the state's flagship public university came into being much like a new law does, being a compromise-filled expression of contradictory ambitions. For forty years, the reformers and social innovators who founded the IIU fought with education traditionalists and each other for the soul of the new institution. Some disputes focused on its industrial, others on the university aspect. Practical men, for example, thought the founding curriculum too traditional. (The General Assembly in Springfield in 1870 felt compelled to assign a legislative committee to investigate charges that too much time was being given to Greek and Latin.) Traditionalists found the course of study grimly utilitarian; the IIU would have none of the accoutrements of the traditional college—no school song, no school colors, no fraternities, and, most radical of all, no degrees.

The state's farmers in particular rejected instruction offered in their own craft as too intellectual, as they understood the term, and even much of the literate public agreed with them. "They take the young men out in the spring of the year and compel them to sit on the fence with kid gloves in their hands, umbrellas over their heads and fifteen cent cigars in their mouths, and there watch the men who are employed to do the work," sneered the *Hillsboro Journal*. "This is hard on the young gentlemen but they learn to farm, you know, and that is what the institution is for."[39]

The State of Illinois was attempting, in effect, to run two universities on one campus, and the squabbling over its mission meant that it ran neither of them well. Low enrollment throughout its first two decades justified legislators' starving it of funds it needed to expand. Survival demanded abandonment of the founders' brave new university in favor of something more recognizably collegiate. In 1877 student activists persuaded the General Assembly to allow the awarding of degrees. University colors were adopted in 1879, and a school song in 1880. In 1885 the name was changed to the University of Illinois to placate graduates concerned that their alma mater was widely perceived as a trade school. Such changes broadened the school's support, but enrollments did not surge until it permitted truly popular activities such as the fraternity and sorority system (in 1891) and organized athletics. It had taken thirty years, but as the twentieth century began the University of Illinois finally had a constituency in the General Assembly, among the public, and among the young.

And among farmers. The University of Illinois's main campus in Urbana has become to the farmer what Stanford University is to the computer programmer or MIT to the engineer. The grain farmer of the twenty-first century is more likely to be referred to in the farm press as a "producer" or a "grower," the term "farmer" being considered a bit backward to professionals eager to shed their reputation as hayseeds. These days he (and, increasingly, she) is as much engineer as husbandman. Hardly anything about the way farming is done in mid-Illinois is not engineered, from seeds and fertilizers to the fields and the machines used to work them, even—thanks to the ministrations of "food technologists"—the products made from them. The U of I even tried for years to engineer the weather, through experiments in cloud seeding. Indeed, the U of I as of the 1960s finally realized the dreams of its founders in the 1860s and become Illinois's industrial university—not by training its redundant farmers for new careers in industry but by helping turn farming itself into an industry.

The university's intellectual heft is considerable. Proud alumni are quick to remind visitors that nearly two dozen alumni or faculty won Nobel prizes. (One faculty member won two.) Critics retort that all but two of those Nobels were awarded for work in medicine, physics, or chemistry, and the medals confirm that the U of I is in fact a top polytechnic institute with a merely average liberal arts university attached to it. Nonetheless, for decades in the twentieth century, the university was the closest thing to Oz on the prairie. What marvels it offered to its neighbors!—state basketball tournaments in the Assembly Hall, homecoming weekends at Memorial Stadium, concerts. It was the symbol and agent of the region's rise, the biggest public employer outside Springfield, and, thanks to the occasional success of its varsity sports teams, the only reason after Lincoln that most of the world had even heard of mid-Illinois.

CHAPTER EIGHT

Realizing the Ideal: The Perfectionist Impulse in Mid-Illinois

In the building of utopian communities [Illinois] was a model of the national experience.
—Robert P. Sutton, "Experiments in Communitarianism"

What better place than a new state to begin not only a new life but also a new way of life? Historian Paul Elmen notes that many Europeans shared with many early settlers of America the archetypal notion of the flight from the wicked Egypt—read "Europe"—to the new Canaan, which flowed with milk and honey.[1] Those who know Illinois will smile at the notion that it might be anyone's New Canaan. Dreamers by the dozen (not to mention a swindler or two) nonetheless imagined it thus in the early 1800s. While these new utopians hoped to improve humans by improving the society they lived in, mid-Illinois also attracted social reformers who sought to improve society by improving the humans that lived in it. True believers in each approach were bound to be disappointed, but in trying they wrote some of the most interesting chapters in the history of mid-Illinois.

THE JANSONISTS OF BISHOP HILL

Swede Erik Janson[2] was the son of peasants. His education was the Bible, and he filled the space left by his lack of formal schooling in theology with visions of God. Janson preached, in effect, that anyone who wished hard enough to achieve angelic innocence could do so, by receiving the grace of God. Janson's sermons attracted followers who saw in him a second Christ. One Christ was enough for Sweden's state-backed Lutheran Church, however, which had him arrested more than once.

In 1846 Janson and some of his more ardent followers, most of them peasants of the province of Helsingland, fled Sweden for Illinois. The Jansonists traveled to Henry County and a spot on the bank of the Edwards River about twenty-five miles from Galesburg. There they set about building a new, more perfect community of believers, or rather, a community of more perfect believers.

The Jansonists gave their new town an English version of the name of where Janson was born—Bishop Hill. Just getting to the site tested the resolve of the faithful, many of whom had to walk, in those pre-railroad days, the 160 miles from Chicago. Bishop Hill was a colony in a literal sense, operating under a charter granted by the Illinois General Assembly. Property was owned by and held for the benefit of all, under the direction of seven trustees. About four hundred faithful joined Janson there at first, and before the commune dissolved in 1861, Bishop Hill for a time was home to more than one thousand people.

Like most later experimental communities in mid-Illinois, the Jansonist colony was run on vaguely communist principles (one historian precisely described the economy as "non-Marxist communal"[3]), although in this case the

Krans, *Harvest*. Bishop Hill artist Olof Krans committed to some two hundred canvases the everyday scenes he recollected from his boyhood in the old utopian colony, such as *Harvest*, from around 1875. Earnest Elmo Calkins described their method: "The fields were cultivated by small squads working in a sort of military formation, moving across the terrain and performing all operations in unison, . . . emphasizing in this humble way the cooperative principles of their undertaking." COURTESY OF BISHOP HILL STATE HISTORIC SITE, ILLINOIS HISTORIC PRESERVATION AGENCY.

principles were of scriptural origin. Like Christ and his disciples, the Bishop Hill settlers worked, ate, lodged, and worshipped together. They even died communally, as happened in the first frightful winter and again, in 1849, when cholera invaded the village and killed upwards of two hundred people. The colony's central building, whose design gave physical form to the share-and-share-alike ideal, was known as Big Brick. Two hundred feet long and forty-five feet wide, it had three floors and a basement that together housed a large dining hall and no fewer than ninety-six rooms; it was in effect the first apartment building in this part of the Midwest.

Janson died in 1850, shot through the heart in the county courthouse in nearby Cambridge; his murderer was a fellow Swede who had married Janson's cousin, apparently not happily. Janson's body reportedly lay in state without being embalmed, as members expected him to rise and walk again; after three days of warm weather, what rose from the bier was not the corpse, and he was quickly buried.

Janson did not rise again, but Bishop Hill did, if briefly. In fact, Bishop Hill might be regarded as more important (if less interesting) as a successful economic experiment than as an unsuccessful religious one. Ronald Nelson argues that the communal ethos proved a unique resource as the colonists strove after Janson's death to adapt to an evolving, not-quite-frontier economy. The colony's fields yielded, in addition to food, flax (for linen making), and broomcorn. Illinois was a dusty paradise, and the market for brooms was robust; one year the sale of brooms cleared $30,000, a handsome return for the time and place and one that, in the words of Janson's son, "raised the colony from a mere subsistence level to one of outright opulence."[4]

The Jansonists within a decade increased their land holdings more than eightfold and erected ten commercial and public buildings that would have left Chicagoans bragging. Its prosperity was trumpeted by colonists in letters home. ("The difference between the poor here and in Sweden is like between night and day."[5]) Such reports suggested that the citizens of Bishop Hill had found their promised land after all, and reports of their success are thought to have boosted Swedish immigration to the upper Mississippi Valley.[6]

Alas, like many a thriving family, the colony squabbled over money. The Bishop Hill trustees, who had recklessly speculated in railroad and bank shares and sold colony goods and services on credit, were undone by a national depression in 1857, and disenchanted colonists voted to disband the enterprise. For a century after that, Bishop Hill was just another mid-Illinois small town, much reduced in vigor until the town's rebirth as a real-life history theme park in the 1970s.

PHALANXES AND ICARIANS

The first French immigrants to mid-Illinois had contented themselves with preparing Native Americans for a better life in the next world, through the agency of Jesuit missions. Later French immigrants came west to prepare themselves for a better life in this world. Utopian theorist Charles Fourier had concocted a peculiar mix of communalism and free love as an alternative to the cruel and corrupt individualism of a capitalist society. As interpreted by his American disciple Albert Brisbane, Fourier's ideas inspired followers to found several colonies or "phalanxes" in nine U.S. states to turn his remedies into reality.

Fourierists believed that perfection lay not in the person but in the community. People could come to terms with their unruly natures not by purging themselves of "natural passions" but by (as Robert P. Sutton put it) "harmonizing conflicting human interests in a communal social structure"[7] under which the fruits of communal labor were distributed according to the shares each member held in the enterprise. The subscribers were solidly middle-class New Englanders whose confidence in conventional capitalism had been undermined by recurring economic depressions.[8] They thus found appealing alternatives based on common use (if not ownership) of resources, producers' cooperatives, and protective tariffs.

The first phalanx in Illinois was set up in Bureau County in 1843 but did not last a year. A second phalanx, established in 1845 in Fulton County, outdid its predecessor by failing almost immediately. The most successful of the Fourierist phalanxes in Illinois was the Sangamon Association, started in 1844 outside the farm village of Loami, some sixteen miles south of Springfield. The founding "associationists" comprised thirty-five adults and fifteen children whose numbers were augmented in 1846 by members of a similar group first formed in Ohio. Some members contributed land; others subscribed to stock. All agreed to live together in a 390-by-24-foot frame building, the precursor to a massive three-story central building called the Phalanstery that would have housed the 1,620 individuals expected in the mature community. (The Jansonists' Big Brick, noted Elmen, was very like the grand phalanstery planned by the Sangamon Association.[9]) Unlike the other Illinois phalanxes, this one managed to survive more than a few months before disenchantment spread, but by 1848 the experiment was finished, and the land returned to its original owners.

Etienne Cabet of Dijon was, among other things, a journalist, a lawyer, and a radical politician, none of which is the sort of vocation many think capable of prescribing the good society today. When French authorities convicted Cabet of treason he fled to England where he became acquainted with the work of

Robert Owen, the Welsh reformer whose New Harmony colony in Indiana had failed a few years before. Cabet drew up his own model for a new society that borrowed from Owen and Sir Thomas More's *Utopia*. His plans for a perfect society were appropriately expressed as fiction, in a novel titled *Voyage en Icarie* (1840), a sort of French *Looking Backward*. His Icarie was not only a fictional society but also a fantastic one, being an egalitarian community in which money, private property, crime, immorality, unemployment, and political corruption had no place.

Like the Fourierists, Cabet's disciples were idealistic members of the middle class made uneasy by capitalism as practiced in the early 1800s. Cabet and his followers immigrated to the United States and first tested his doctrine in 1848 in a settlement in Texas. Cabet established a second colony in mid-Illinois, at the old Mormon town of Nauvoo, renting buildings that had been abandoned when the Mormons fled to Utah territory three years before.

The Icarians, as the group's members were known, erected a few buildings of their own, the most famous being a school made of stone scavenged from the ruins of the Mormon Temple. As had happened in Texas, however, disputes rent the new project, and when Cabet was not reelected president in 1856, he and nearly two hundred followers left Nauvoo for East St. Louis, where he died not long after. The Icarian Colony back at Nauvoo carried on determinedly until 1860. Unlike the Mormon theocracy that had preceded it, the Icarian experiment was not so unconventional that it roused the bigoted to suppress it nor so successful that it roused the propertied to appropriate it. Thus it had virtually no impact on the subsequent history of Illinois beyond inspiring a good book.[10]

In the end, worldly failures doomed most of these perfectionist experiments. The Icarians, for example, wanted to build a community based on selfless brotherhood rather than private property or money. Uninterested in commerce or manufacturing, the group supported itself by a modest admission fee of one hundred dollars, the little money they made selling whiskey and flour to nearby towns, and the royalties from the sale of books by Cabet—about $25,000 in all. Predictably, the financial record for the years 1852 to 1855 indicate that the group's income never matched expenses.[11] Even had its members not been divided by internal disputes, Icarian Nauvoo had no future.

"HOOK AND EYE" AMISH

Occasionally, social or religious dissidents ventured to Illinois not to found a new world but to rebuild their old one. The Amish were originally of the Mennonite family of Swiss churches that practiced anabaptism (or rebaptism of adults). The practice was punishable by death in sixteenth- and seventeenth-century Europe, which was reason enough for Amish sects to immigrate to North America beginning in the 1700s. They founded communities in Pennsylvania, Indiana, Iowa, and Ohio, among other states, one of which was Illinois.

The serenity of the Amish way of life extolled by today's tourism ads never extended to doctrinal matters, and these sects were repeatedly riven by disputes that sowed the seeds of new and presumably more perfect communities. Amish dissidents started new settlements in 1835 in Bureau and Putnam Counties, in about 1850 near Chenoa, Gridley, and Meadows in McLean County, at El Paso in Woodford County, and at Cissna Park in Iroquois County. Small settlements also took root near Macomb in McDonough County and in Pike County.

In 1864 conservative Anabaptists settled near the Douglas County towns of Arcola, Arthur, and Tuscola. There, where scientific agriculture is the unofficial creed, grew a farm community that is resolutely if selectively antitechnology and in which the traditional crafts are not merely preserved but also practiced for gain. These so-called Old Order Amish (also known as "hook and eye" Amish, because their clothing is fastened with hooks and eyes of the sort in common use when the sect was founded) constitute the largest such community in Illinois.

In and around Arthur the visitor can glimpse the farm past that urban Illinoisans are so eager to admire and that mid-Illinois farmers have been so eager to leave behind. Members of this Amish community shun the use of telephones, electric lights, and cars. As a result the back roads are crowded not with pickups but with horse-drawn carriages. The Amish are a practical people, however, so if their creed forbids resort to electricity, they light shops with propane gas instead.

THE ROCKY PATH TO RIGHTEOUSNESS

For every visionary who sought to escape a wicked world in Euro-American mid-Illinois, there were dozens of others eager to engage that wickedness and change it. Christian missionaries believed that God and the Book—that is, their god and their book—would lead sinners to righteousness. Secular educationalists believed that learning would ennoble farming and allow rural populations to lift themselves out of brutish toil. Early feminists believed that admitting women to the voting booth would create a new polity, and temperance advocates were convinced that eliminating drink would allow the dissolute to be born again and communities to be restored to wholesomeness. Labor unions fought on the job, in the streets, and in the courts to remake capitalism into a fairer and more humane means of production. If these improving impulses were not quite strong enough to change the world, they did reshape the policy making, institution building, and town making of mid-Illinois during the century that ended with the repeal of Prohibition.

As towns grew into cities, the village drunk became the "Liquor Interest" and the local trollop became the brothel district. Vice ceased to be a personal foible and became a political problem. The solution many a larger town arrived at was to, in effect, segregate itself into two communities. One was upright and abstemious (at least in public) and a fit place for families, the other—well, the other was none of those things, being that part of town in which vice was contained, usually with unofficial official protection, to prevent its spreading into more respectable quarters.

One such abandoned community was Springfield's Levee district. At the dawn of the twentieth century, opportunities for vulgar misbehavior along Washington Street between Seventh and Tenth Streets were plentiful and convenient, there being no fewer than twenty-two saloons, a dozen backroom brothels, and unnumbered gambling parlors in the area. Many a Springfieldian who would never visit the Levee took a perverse sort of civic pride in it; crusading pamphleteer William Lloyd Clark might have damned the Levee for its "mass of dive saloons, pawn shops, questionable hotels, fourth rate lodging houses and assignation resorts, stenchful restaurants and brothels,"[12] but at least it was a source of distinction.

Liquor was widely thought to be the foremost agent of dissolution of the sort that blighted the Levee, because it weakened the resistance of even the virtuous to vice of other kinds. Liquor first manifested itself as a social problem in mid-Illinois during the French era. The sale of whiskey was a chronic problem at the trading posts at Peoria. The dispossessed remnants of the Illiniwek tribes there were sunk in drunkenness, and they reduced themselves to destitution by trading anything they had for the stuff. The liquor business was a constant source of friction between the government, which sought to curb it, and the locals who profited from it. As agent Thomas Forsyth complained about the situation to his superiors in Washington in 1824, "It appears to me that nearly all the settlers from the mouth of the river up to this place sells [*sic*] whiskey to Indians. . . . In a private conversation I had with Chamblee [Shabonee] an Ottowa Chief, he . . . said, Whiskey occasioned much trouble among all people, and hoped that the White people would not trade so much whiskey to Indians and then every thing would be peace and quietness."[13]

There was plenty of whiskey to sell in frontier Illinois. Distilling surplus corn into whiskey was common on farms, not only because whiskey was easier to ship than raw grain was but also because it fetched better prices. Whiskey was taken by farm families at meals (even, watered down, by the young), it was used as a medicine and a disinfectant, and it was a lubricant to social occasions from weddings to revivals to elections. A Warren County history tells how a bucket filled with whiskey was usually at hand near polling places. "It was customary in these days to have something to 'take' at all elections, and the 'take' was pretty generally indulged in by all."[14] Whiskey fueled the harvest of corn as well as the harvest of votes. David Rankin, who lived and farmed in Henderson County, recalled in a memoir, "In those days if you didn't have whiskey you couldn't get hands to harvest." The availability in 1849 of Cyrus McCormick's new reaper meant that Rankin could finally replace field hands who drank with a machine that did not. Wrote Rankin, "I have always said that McCormick made it possible for me to do my harvesting without liquor."[15]

It was debatable whether antebellum Illinois's hogs or its drunks did more damage when let loose; towns passed ineffectual ordinances against both. Christiana Holmes Tillson, a New Englander who settled in Montgomery County in 1822, described one of the first Illinoisans she met. "The landlord—a poor white man from the South—was a whiskey keg in the morning, and a keg of whiskey at night; stupid and gruff in the morning, by noon could talk politics and abuse the Yankees, and by sundown was brave for a fight."[16]

Agitation to end the evil, if evil it was, began in mid-Illinois as early as the 1830s. Drinking divided the people of mid-Illinois as deeply as did slavery, and pretty much along the same lines. "Yankees" tended to be against drink, ethnics and Southerners tended to be for it, and each against the other to that extent. Kentuckian Richard Oglesby, in the words of his biographer, honored bourbon as "the nectar of my native state"[17] and frequently ordered liquor by the barrel and champagne by the case both for his Elkhart home and for the executive mansion when he was governor.

The loudest condemnations of drink came from the pulpits, but the most compassionate came from organizations like the Washington Temperance Society. Another well-known Kentuckian, Abraham Lincoln, was a teetotaler, but when he took up the topic in a speech to the Washingtonians in Springfield in 1842, he preached against the preachers who damned dram drinkers as the authors of all the vice and misery and crime in the land. "When [drinkers] were told all this, and in this way," he said, "it is not wonderful that they were slow, *very slow*, to acknowledge the truth of such denunciations."[18]

Vigilantism was often tried when exhortation failed. Histories recount how a businessman in the 1830s who believed that a "little wine was good for the stomach's sake" put up a distillery in the town of Henderson. "It was burned and rebuilt, burned again, but not rebuilt again. Evidently there were some people here who did not believe in the above quotation."[19] Hepzibah Dumville recalled in a letter to her sister a similar incident from 1856 Jacksonville (spelling in the original).

> As you are a daughter or sis (as may be) of temperance you will laugh to hear of the procedings here. Week before last a paddy took it into his head to build a grog shop close to the second railroad crosing, which he did or began to do. He brought five barrels of the "good creation" oute to his establishment to begin operation, when lo! last Wednesday night a party of men in town disguised themselves went out the grog-shop caught the fellow and held him or tied him I dont know which, while they tore the building intirely down and cutting the timbers so that he could not make use of them again, and to crown the whole they drove in the heads of the barrels and let out the contents. . . . I assure you we have a rejoycing time in our neighborhood, in consequence of the distruction of the grog-shop.[20]

Drys usually resorted to less criminal means to discourage drink. During his four years as governor in the 1830s, Jacksonville's Joseph Duncan, a former Kentuckian, donated half his salary to support an Illinois temperance newspaper. John Neff Ebey, one of the region's pioneer commercial potters, made jugs for beverages in his Springfield shop but wouldn't sell them to saloon keepers.[21] Peoria, Knoxville, and Oquawka all had "temperance hotels"[22] for the teetotal traveler. Jesse Fell, the animating force behind the growth of North Bloomington (the future Normal) in 1857 burdened purchasers of lots in his new addition to the town with deed covenants banning the sale of alcohol on the properties. (In 1867 North Bloomington residents voted to make the prohibition universal by putting it in the statute books.)

Attempts in the legislature to impose statewide restrictions on the sale and consumption of liquor repeatedly failed, so regulation was left in local hands. The young Henry County—full of Yankee puritans and abstemious Swedes—is said to have never granted a license to operate a saloon. Monmouth became a town in 1831; it became a dry town in 1839. Slavery excited the special ire of Galesburgers, but they were so full of reforming zeal that they had plenty left over to ban booze in the town's first charter, and the sale of alcohol was not legal there until 1872. Most towns of any size, however, were obliged to find a kind of social equilibrium between local wets and drys. Drys who could not get the votes to impose a flat drinking ban, for example, accepted ordinances that limited saloons' open hours, while wets accepted slightly restrictive closing regulations to forestall calls for very restrictive ones.

Temperance parade. Crusaders from Church of the Nazarene in the Macoupin County town of Medora take part in a temperance parade in 1908 to protest the saloon's daily grind. COLLECTION OF LUC SANTE. REPRODUCED WITH PERMISSION.

In the twentieth and twenty-first centuries, leaders of the region's institutions of higher education would deplore the lack of sobriety and morality among college students, but the hope that the state's new generations might at least be sober if not wise burned bright in the mid-1800s. Among the ambitious Christians who shaped the character of the new Illinois Industrial University were Jacksonville's Jonathan Baldwin Turner and the university's first regent, John Milton Gregory. Both were temperance advocates, and they saw to it that the IIU forbade its students to drink when the school opened in 1868.[23]

The Civil War and its aftermath derailed the temperance movement for a time, but industrialization got it moving again after immigrants brought to mid-Illinois new thirsts and new attitudes toward drink. In the 1850s the taste for beer and whiskey among immigrant Germans and Irish had made temperance advocates out of Know-Nothings, who argued that them furriners would avoid a dry Illinois. The older farming towns that suddenly found themselves hosting factories and coal mines felt similarly under siege. According to one account, town worthies in Lincoln were appalled by the drinking of the several hundred Irish and Polish Catholic miners who worked the three local coal mines "and periodically let loose in Lincoln."[24]

Unacknowledged by most drys was the fact that drinking had some salutary social effects. The McDonough County mining town of Colchester in the 1870s and 1880s sustained four or five saloons. They had names like the Soldier's Home and the Miner's Arms, and they performed the same important social function performed by pubs in the British mining towns from which so many residents had come, as they offered a healing alternative to the fetid gloom of the mine tunnels.[25] Nonetheless, as John Hallwas put it in *The Bootlegger*, local temperance zealots regarded such places as "the source of all social evil, the devil's foothold in the community, and their struggle to stamp them out was a holy crusade."[26]

The 1872 Towns and Villages Act had given city councils the power to control intoxicating liquors, either by prohibiting their sale in certain districts or by licensing their sale under city regulation. Polite opinion in Galesburg favored regulation, but apparently the patrons of the White Elephant on Boone's Avenue—for years reputedly the biggest saloon in that part of Illinois—could vote as well as drink. In the mid-1800s, wet Galesburgers rejected licensing the sale of intoxicating liquors by a margin of 462 to 104.

In many a town, victory by any faction in a liquor referendum election was usually vulnerable to reversal in the next one. In 1885 all of McDonough County went officially dry, by forty votes, although the next year enough voters switched to overturn the ban, perhaps because Colchester's business had dried up along with the booze. Twice during the first decade of the twentieth century the Galesburg city council voted the town dry and twice the succeeding council voted it wet again.[27]

While the men gathered in the pubs, the wives and daughters of the men's bosses gathered in churches to plot the closure of these "poor man's clubs." By the early 1870s Colchester had a Ladies' Temperance Society and, in 1884, its own chapter of the Women's Christian Temperance Union. The liquor issue all but dominated the cultural life of the town. "There were temperance speakers, temperance debates, temperance plays, and temperance revivals," reports Hallwas. "Like the sound of a nagging spouse, the temperance crusader's voice was inescapable."[28]

Frustrated by their reliance on men to do the right thing on the saloon issue, many a disenfranchised mid-Illinois woman yearned for the vote so she could do it for herself. In 1891 the female citizens of Pittsfield petitioned the General Assembly for the right to vote in municipal elections "that we may no longer be subject to the control of besotted men and the vicious classes."[29] When, in 1913, Illinois women won the right to vote in nonconstitutional state elections, women in towns such as Galesburg promptly used it to ban local booze sales.

In the 1904 elections the Illinois chapter of the Anti-Saloon League concentrated its election resources on Peoria, the putative whiskey capital of the nation. The Illinois House was then organized into three-member districts, and voters if they chose could cast all three of their votes for a single candidate.

By encouraging supporters to concentrate their votes in this way, the league elected a Prohibition Party candidate in Peoria and defeated a pro-license incumbent and a saloonkeeper for the other district seats, even though drys were probably a minority among the local electorate. The victory over the liquor interest was only symbolic, but it suggested a trend.

In 1907 downstate temperance advocates joined Chicago area advocates in backing a bill to expand local governments' powers to ban liquor sales in their jurisdictions. By the time Illinois ratified the national Prohibition Amendment in 1919, fifty-five counties and 1,425 townships had already voted out the saloon under the terms of Illinois's 1907 local option law; among them were no fewer than fourteen mid-Illinois counties.[30]

Illinois helped ratify national prohibition in 1919, but feeling on the other side of the question could be measured in the millions of individual acts of civil disobedience committed in violation of the ban. Bootleggers such as Colchester's Kelly Wagle became local heroes, and ordinary citizens happily became criminals. Springfieldian William Menghini recalled life in the working class North End: "*My* parents continued to make wine just like they did all the time but for our own consumption. Many of the Italian families that we knew did the same thing. They wouldn't quit. I don't think they thought it was illegal, they just looked at it that it wasn't anybody's business."[31]

Back in the 1830s, Governor Joseph Duncan had campaigned to stop what he called the "dreadful ravages and baneful effects of intemperance."[32] The dreadful ravages and baneful effects of Prohibition would not become plain for another eighty years. They would include gang wars, the compromise of local government, the corruption of local law enforcement, and incidents such as a particularly nasty occurrence of alcohol poisoning in 1929 when twenty people died in Peoria and Knox Counties after drinking booze contaminated by wood alcohol.

"I WISHT I WAS IN PEORIA TONIGHT"

Urbanization and industrialization after the Civil War turned individual vices into lucrative recreations. Gambling and prostitution, like liquor, had been legal in the larger towns and cities of the region through the 1800s. They were tolerated even by those who disapproved, because such goings on were usually contained by custom if not law to particular parts of town, where they could be easily monitored by the police and easily avoided by everyone else.

Springfield's Levee district has been mentioned, but the special committee of the Illinois Senate investigating vice in 1913 found that nearly a dozen downstate cities including Peoria, Bloomington, Champaign, Danville, and

Pekin made some official effort to regulate houses of prostitution, mainly by segregating them in certain districts. (None actually tried to close them.) Quincy's riverfront bordellos at the foot of Oak Street were among the busiest on the Mississippi for fifty years after Appomattox. As many as fifty houses were open within a district whose boundaries were fixed by aldermen. In 1918 a reform faction pressed Quincy officials to shut them down. The criminalization of prostitution and the abolition of the red light district put an end to the controversy in Quincy but not to prostitution, which continued through the Prohibition era and into the 1940s. (A fourteen-year-old James Earl Ray, convicted assassin of Dr. Martin Luther King Jr., was caught stealing a customer's pants from Big Marie's brothel at Third and Vermont in Quincy in 1942.)

Gambling, in forms ranging from craps games in the alleys to slot machines in country clubs, was widely tolerated in many mid-Illinois cities, it being thought more benign in its effects compared with drink and paid sex. In Springfield during the administration of Governor Dwight Green, open gambling was on the table at the Lake Club, a posh nightclub popular with state legislators.[33] Even where it was illegal, gambling in nightclubs and social clubs was protected politically by elites who joined in the fun and closed their eyes to payoffs to local cops. Games offered in working-class taverns and brothels, in contrast, were shut down during cleanup campaigns in the first third of the twentieth century, the venues being judged unseemly for other reasons.

Crackdowns created new business opportunities for anyone willing to risk supplying popular services and products that were inconveniently illegal. Members of several southern and eastern European immigrant subcultures, having been kept from respectable trades by prejudice and language barriers, so diligently exploited those opportunities that they controlled vice industries in most mid-Illinois cities. This affiliation with vice put them at odds with old settlers, who added complaints about criminality to their unease about the newcomers' habits and religion—even though the buildings that housed vice operations often were owned by members of the upper-class and upper-middle-class Protestant ruling elite.

Enterprising immigrants were able to exploit their extended clan connections, and a business model of sorts existed in the brotherhood societies imported from the old country. Natives had clan connections too. The Shelton brothers for years dominated bootlegging out of their Williamson County stronghold until they were convicted of a 1925 mail carrier robbery and sent to prison. When Al Capone tried to muscle in on Peoria's gambling business, the local gambling king invited the Sheltons to act as his Swiss Guard on their release from prison. The Shelton brothers did more than protect Peoria rackets;

they began to run them. When the end of Prohibition eliminated bootlegging, gangs simply shifted to controlling newly legal liquor businesses such as taverns, which they used as one-stop shops to sell prostitution and gambling.

Peoria had always been a place where yokels could sneak away to kick up their heels. Carl Sandburg remembered of his hometown that everyone believed Galesburg was a decent, well-behaved city compared with Peoria. When a Galesburg man wanted a "bad woman" for the night, it was safer to go to Peoria, where brothels enjoyed official protection, than to try it in Galesburg, where police raids proved awkward for local respectables who got hauled in as clients. A popular song of 1926 by the musical comedy team of Billy Jones and Ernest Hare summed up the yearnings of every small town Midwesterner on a short leash: "I Wisht I Was in Peoria Tonight."

> Oh, how I wish I was in Peoria, Peoria tonight!
> Oh, how I miss the goils in Peoria, Peoria tonight!
> Oh, you can pick a morning Gloria (Yes, yes!)
> Right off the sidewalks of Peoria.
> Oh, how I wish I was in Peoria, Peoria tonight![34]

Local business leaders were indifferent to politics except insofar as it affected their profits, and they happily ceded authority over the political system to professional politicians in return for low taxes. One such politician was Peoria mayor E. N. Woodruff. Woodruff believed that vice was inevitable, and that the wise mayor learns to exploit it for the public good. Personally honest, Woodruff saw to it that money usually paid under the table to cops and city inspectors was paid openly, to the city. For example, a levy of twenty dollars per month was assessed on every slot machine in the city and the proceeds delivered to city hall, where it went into the city budget rather than someone's pocket.

Peoria was both damned and celebrated as one of the most wide-open towns in the Midwest under Woodruff's honestly crooked administration. During his eleven nonconsecutive terms between 1903 and 1946—twenty-four years in all—"Roaring Peoria" was host to not one but three red light districts, and gambling joints were as common downtown as fast food joints are today. The industry was impervious to churchmen, prudes, and editorialists, and it took the U.S. Army to shut it down. The city was a popular liberty town during World War II, being situated between two large military installations, Camp Ellis in Fulton County and Chanute Air Force Base in Rantoul, which at their peaks housed some sixty-five thousand soldiers. Federal authorities were appalled at the incidence of venereal disease among trainees in 1942 and threatened to close the city to servicemen unless it was cleaned up.[35] To keep servicemen healthy enough to be of service, federal authorities did what Peoria authorities would not do and cracked down. Even citizens not appalled at gambling and prostitution in their hometowns were appalled by the bad publicity the complaints caused. Those citizens included the owners of firms represented by the Association of Commerce (which spoke for such unignorable interests as the Caterpillar Company, the downtown banks, and the leading retailers), and in 1945 voters threw Ed Woodruff out of the mayor's office and put a reformer in.[36]

The press reports from Peoria are thought to have been partly responsible for launching a nationwide probe of major gambling syndicates in 1950 and 1951 by the U.S. Senate's Special Committee to Investigate Crime in Interstate Commerce, better known to avid newsreel viewers as the Kefauver Committee, after its chairman. Peoria's scandals also are thought to have had not a little to do with the success of Adlai Stevenson II when he ran for governor in 1948 on a clean-government ticket slated by the Democrats.

Stevenson was a descendant of Jesse Fell, and as Fell had worked tirelessly to make Stevenson's native Bloomington a town fit for people like Jesse Fell, Stevenson undertook to make Illinois a state fit for people like Adlai Stevenson. Stevenson's state police conducted raids across the state in 1950 and 1951, after which pinball and slot machines were arrayed for news photographers like a game hunter's trophies. In Macon County, seventy-one raids netted more than one hundred machines used in gambling. In Logan County, police confiscated seventy-six "one ball" pinball machines. In McLean County, candy stores, taverns, drugstores, pool rooms, roadside restaurants, and gasoline stations yielded more than one hundred nefarious gambling devices. Havana's days as a local gambling hub ended in a raid on October 31, 1953, when state officials shut down gambling operations in more than forty taverns.

Sociologist Daniel Elazar contrived a continuum on which to place Illinois's lesser cities in terms of their tolerance for vice. On the prudish end of the scale was Urbana, whose citizens had long had to cross the street into wicked Champaign for booze, sex, and games of chance. On the naughty end of the scale, with Peoria, was Springfield. For more than a century, Springfield was a town in which, as journalist Elise Morrow noted in the late 1940s, "tolerance of everything except excessive civic improvement has always been fundamental."[37] The capital was then notorious for the number of its saloons and brothels and the sumptuousness (for a town its size) of its nightspots. Its women were willing, its cops persuadable.

It was gambling, however, for which the town was best known. The state capital played host to a lot of out-of-towners, and just as an accommodating

Decatur slots. Illinois state police strike a blow for cleaner cities and duller taverns. In 1960, 129 slot machines were confiscated in raids in Lincoln, after which they were smashed by bulldozers before being set afire. Cash totaling $173.53 was first removed from the infernal devices for delivery to the Logan County treasurer. COURTESY *HERALD AND REVIEW*, DECATUR, ILLINOIS. REPRODUCED WITH PERMISSION.

party host accepts wine stains on the carpet, Springfield's leaders had long accepted vice—it was the price a state capital and tourist magnet pays for being hospitable. Gambling, from punchboards in mom-and-pop stores to slots in every tavern to card games in the clubs, would have been an open scandal were the locals capable of being scandalized. (In 1948 members of Springfield's country club argued against the removal of slot machines there on grounds that the resulting revenue loss would force hikes in their dues.) The people who organized the games paid a license fee, in effect, in the form of bribes to officials charged with enforcing the laws against them. A *St. Louis Post-Dispatch* exposé reported that Frank Zito, the head of Springfield's organized crime in the 1940s, was paying out $10,000 a week to city, county, and state officials.

GIVING GOVERNMENT BACK TO THE PEOPLE

As in Peoria, civic-minded businesspeople across the region (usually white, affluent, and educated, often Yankee in provenance and Protestant of belief) were tolerant of vice but narrow-minded about scandal and high "taxes" in the form of poor services and bribes imposed by corrupt city halls. Springfield for example had seen short-lived reform movements over nearly a century and a half, sparked by vote buying in the 1890s, graft in the 1900s, and organized gambling in the 1940s. Such organizations as Springfield's Jefferson-Lincoln Club and Good Government League wanted to rid city hall of the party hacks, grafters, and franchise seekers who infested it. They wanted to make government more efficient, more honest, more businesslike. They wanted, finally, to protect and preserve what they saw as the public interest against the private interests of party, machine, and money.

Unable to dislodge the boodlers from the ethnic wards, their solution was to eliminate the wards. Thus the fad for the commission form of municipal government, under which the ward system and its odious party hacks were replaced by a five-person commission chosen in nonpartisan at-large elections. The new system promised to be nonpartisan, cosmopolitan, efficient—everything municipal government then was not in most of the larger cities of the region.

Those mid-Illinoisans eager to change their local government structure not only voted for it; they (allied with local business and Chicago progressives) also successfully lobbied the General Assembly for the changes to the state Municipal Code in 1911 that would allow them to reform the system. The enthusiasm of Springfield's middle class owed to their conviction that corruption had something to do, in some never-quite-explained way, with the race riots that shocked the city in 1908; that city was quick to retire its aldermen for good by adopting commission government within months. Other cities where corruption had become a fiscal burden, a civic embarrassment, or both, like Champaign, Pekin, and Decatur, installed commission governments within a decade after its introduction.

Like most political reforms in Illinois, the commission reform changed local government but did not transform it. In most places the new way had been adopted by narrow margins provided mostly by a briefly mobilized middle class, and even their initial enthusiasm for the new system faded. Bloomington, 70 percent of whose voters endorsed the commission idea in 1914, abandoned it in 1922 to go back to the old alderman-and-ward system. Some major cities of mid-Illinois never did join the parade. Upright Urbana, which didn't feel the need for reform, was one. Anything-goes Peoria was another; it narrowly defeated adoption in a referendum because its influential businesspeople had long since made peace with (and profits from) the old aldermanic system.

Decatur and Champaign later opted to try another progressive-era remedy, the council-manager government. Under that scheme, legislation was left in the hands of a council elected by wards, but administrative duties were handled by a professional city manager. Even Peoria, smarting from the municipal scandals of the 1940s, went respectable with all the fervor of the recent repenter, becoming the first city in Illinois to approve a switch to efficiency-minded nonpartisanship. Among those voting for the changes were thought to be newly returned GIs who had been appalled to have learned in the barracks that their city's loose ways were the butt of rude comments by soldiers from across the country. Springfield, however, did not re-reform a city hall that had been reformed in 1911. Its commission government, while ostensibly nonpartisan, still left management (and its jobs) in the hands of politicians. As Elazar notes, "A highly political city, its articulate citizenry, reform-oriented or not, is not in the least interested in taking its city government 'out of politics.'"[38] Springfield's commission government would survive several attempts to undo it, only to finally fall under legal challenge as racially discriminatory in 1987.

Civic virtue would remain elusive in mid-Illinois. There are today no punch boards and slot machines in the back room but only because the State of Illinois offers a welter of legal games of chance. Prostitution driven from brothels has merely moved onto the World Wide Web and the streets (including those around the Lincoln Home National Historic Site in Springfield, which are conveniently empty of prying eyes at night; Lincoln would not dare walk at midnight these days, as Vachel Lindsay imagined him doing in his famous poem). The nation's war against drugs in mid-Illinois was no less fervent and no more effective than the war against booze had been, and recreational use of street drugs and prescription drugs were as popular among the middle classes as bootleg hooch was among their grandparents.

Looking back, these attempts to anticipate God's heaven on Earth through perfectionist experiment or politics appear naive, even comical. But if mid-Illinoisans have given up hope of perfecting the world, they are still animated by the possibility of perfecting their towns. The urge to retreat to the company of kindred souls survives in the suburbanizing impulse. Across the region, like-minded citizens continue not only to gather to create or perpetuate communities in which their particular notions of perfection might be realized but also to resort to ordinances and property restrictions to keep out the corrupting presence of nonbelievers. In some groups, members share a belief in the sanctity of private property and in the improving effects of education; others demand the strict control of alcohol or ban the corrupting influence of parties from local elections. Whether they are affluent suburbanites who were the heirs to progressivism or churchly small-towners, they created places as close to perfectionist communities as mid-Illinois is likely to ever produce.

CHAPTER NINE

Jiggery-pokery: Practical Politics in Mid-Illinois

> I was at Springfield several weeks during the sitting of the Legislature, and I suppose a more scaly set of one-horse thieves and low-lived political tricksters never assembled on earth.
>
> —Peoria politician and orator Robert G. Ingersoll

Beardstown in 1837 was Cass County's biggest and most bumptious town. Virginia was its most conveniently located one. Each wanted the prestige of being the county seat, or at least the business that went with that honor, and they wanted it badly enough to endure thirty-three years of legal wrangling and political high jinks undertaken (quoting from J. N. Gridley, a participant) "with the spirit that animated the Crusaders to recover the Holy Sepulchre."[1]

The conflict started when Beardstown, which had been named the seat at the county's founding, failed to comply with the legislature's requirement that it finance the needed county buildings. County commissioners in 1839 thus declared Beardstown's claim to the seat invalid and granted the right to Virginia. Beardstonians reacted by arranging in Springfield for a special election, which Beardstown won; this time the town built the required new brick courthouse, the one in which Lincoln's famous Almanac Trial would take place in 1858.

That settled the matter the way that Fort Sumter settled the dispute over secession. Election after election was held, and legislative act after legislative act was passed to undo each result. To win an 1857 referendum brought by Virginians, the people of Beardstown resorted to what Gridley called "unstinted frauds" that saw nearly two hundred more votes cast against removal from Beardstown than there were legal voters of the county. Another vote in 1867 found the sadder but wiser Virginians adopting the same tactics used by the Beardstonians a decade earlier, only worse. Nearly five thousand votes were cast; the entire legal electorate of the county was then, approximately, about sixteen hundred people.[2] As Gridley would later report, "The poll-books [showed] that all the poets and philosophers of ancient times, the signers of the Declaration of Independence, as well as a host of Union and Confederate heroes of the late war, had voted for Virginia."[3]

The matter was settled, again, in the winter of 1874–75 by a referendum that Virginia won by eight votes. But while the county seat was now legally in Virginia, the county's records remained physically in Beardstown—that is, until mounted Virginians made a midnight raid on the Beardstown courthouse, loaded everything in the county clerk's office into wagons, and hauled them to Virginia where they were kept under guard in the new courthouse, where they remain.[4] Thus were public questions settled in the commonwealth.

Illinois politics was not invented in mid-Illinois. That honor probably belongs to Kentucky or Tennessee. But mid-Illinoisans have practiced such politics for nearly two hundred years—long enough to get good at it. Mid-Illinois is where one president (Lincoln) matured, a second (Reagan) was educated, and two almost-presidents (Stephen A. Douglas and Adlai Stevenson) were either raised or came to maturity. Governors grew in the region like weeds in a field—fifteen, if one counts Quincy's John G. Wood, who as lieutenant governor served out the brief unexpired bit of his predecessor's term by commuting to Springfield. And five of the six state politicians thought deserving of memorialization in bronze on the east lawns of the statehouse in Springfield were mid-Illinois men—each a master of that storied genre of representative democracy known as the Illinois way.

CONVERGING STREAMS

In its frontier phase, mid-Illinois politics, especially at the local level, was elemental. Lincoln's youth reminds us that political influence was won by wrestling matches and free whiskey as well as speeches. Civic institutions were weak, personalities were strong, and interests compelling. John Shaw was a dark-complected New Yorker whom the Indians of early Pike County called Raccoon and the Americans called the Bashaw of Hamburg (after the village he owned) or the Black Prince of the Kingdom of Pike. Pike County then was still trapper and trader country, and Shaw gathered around him half-wild men who did not share the commitment to civic comity of the newer settlers. Being (as Christiana Holmes Tillson put it) "fond of rule,"[5] Shaw controlled elections by doctoring poll books and thus "earned every measure he desired."[6] Eventually he was run out of the county on a rail, or to be more precise, a steamboat.

The new country gradually rid itself of its Shaws, to the disappointment of historians eager to liven a tale. But while politics in the region grew less colorful it got more interesting. Illinois's modern political culture was analyzed by the political scientist Daniel Elazar in his influential 1970 book *Cities of the Prairie*. Each region of Illinois, like each part of mid-Illinois, was settled in different eras by different peoples. Each brought with them different economic priorities, social assumptions, and attitudes toward power that defined a distinct political subculture, which in turn underlay local partisan political affiliations.

Elazar identified well over a dozen such migration streams that met and mingled in mid-Illinois since the early 1800s, but he regarded three native (meaning Euro-American) streams as defining. One consisted of settlers who came from places like Kentucky and Tennessee as single families or in extended family groups. They imported such social and personal traits as loyalty to one's clan, caste, and church (as long as each was faithful to them in turn, as they saw it). These highly individualistic views (bolstered periodically by like-minded migrants from other places) also put the Southerners at odds with authority in the form of the bishop, the bank, or the boss. To them, the larger community and the democratic order by which it is governed is just another marketplace to be exploited to improve oneself socially and economically; patronage—the distribution of rewards among one's own, including reliable allies—was their preferred means of public administration, indeed the only one they recognized as legitimate. These individualists settled Springfield and Decatur and helped settle Urbana and Peoria, and the politics of those places reflect that heritage even today.[7]

Another of the important native migrations was that of the "Yankees," who came from New England by way of upper New York State (via the Erie Canal) and northern Pennsylvania and Ohio. Because they entered Illinois from Chicago, the Yankee stream settled first in northern Illinois and became dominant there, although Yankees also flowed into mid-Illinois via the Illinois River (many of them landing at Peoria) and the Illinois Central Railroad (which brought them to Champaign and other east-central counties).

These settlers of New England stock with Puritan roots were dedicated to civic virtue and individual redemption by means of hard work and uplift, and they formed communities organized to support both. They too emigrated in groups, but that group was less often the clan than the congregation. They were builders who believed the aim of politics was social betterment, not individual rewards (at least not rewards in this world). Elazar notes that the energy and determination of the Yankees often made them influential beyond their numbers, traits that many of their new neighbors were not moved to praise.

The early governors of Illinois tended to be Southern men, because most early Illinois voters were too; the arrival in mid-Illinois of the later immigrants from the East and Northeast changed that. Augustus French was born in New Hampshire and as a young lawyer settled in Edgar Courthouse (later renamed Paris). French, elected in 1846, was the first of twelve men with strong mid-Illinois connections who sat in the governor's chair in Springfield during the sixteen gubernatorial terms from before the Civil War to the start of the Great Depression.[8]

Mid-Illinois also was the western destination of migrants from the middle Atlantic states and their immediate western neighbors: New Jersey, New York, Pennsylvania, Maryland, Delaware, and Ohio. It was the mid-Atlantic culture's salient traits—Elazar lists commercial enterprise, commitments to ethnic and religious pluralism and yeoman agriculture, and a political order maintained by professional politicians—that most informed mid-Illinois public life. Like the Southerners, the mid-Atlantic migrants tended to enter politics out of self-interest, but they understood self-interest in broader terms than the Southerners did. Self-interest encompassed the interests of the communities of which those selves were parts, they believing that only healthy public institutions were capable of supporting the more ambitious forms of private enterprise. Lincoln's fellow Whigs, if not Lincoln himself, tended to be of this class.

Some version of this anthropological view of politics has informed most recent writing about Illinois politics, although not all writers accept Elazar's specific formulations. Richard J. Jensen, in his 1978 history of Illinois, preferred the terms "modernist" and "traditionalist." Terms in popular use—"insiders" versus good government types, or "goo-goos"—reflect the anthropologists' formulations reasonably accurately, if unknowingly.

The differences among these groups could be profound. The template against which the individualist patronage chief measures most political propositions, for example, is us versus them, that of the Yankee moralist is right versus wrong, that of the traditionalist is practical versus impractical. If the individualist saw society as a threat to his freedom, the communally minded reformer saw society as the reinforcer of it. And while the Yankees seasoned their politics with moral absolutism and evangelical fervor, Jensen notes, the mid-Atlantic migrants emphasized efficacy. "Their 'live and let live' attitude set a tolerant tone for the politics of central Illinois," Jensen wrote, "in contrast to the more rigid standards that prevailed in Yankee or Swedish settlements in the northern tier of counties."[9]

Such divergent principles engendered divergent municipal cultures. Springfield and Bloomington are like a rascal uncle and his scout leader nephew.

Champaign and Urbana stand across a street from each other but are a world apart politically. They developed distinct civic personalities too. Urbana was the county seat, upstart Champaign a railroad stop built twenty years later. Thanks at first to the railroad, Yankee-influenced Champaign has always affected a cosmopolitanism (or at least a willingness to experiment in the civic realm) that its elder twin disdained. Urbana has retained the same form of government, since the 1860s, but Champaign changed to the commission form in 1917, adopted council-manager government in 1959, had a referendum on aldermanic government which failed in 1968, and then modified the council-manager plan in 1972.[10]

The result across mid-Illinois was not a single blended political culture; instead, each group advanced its values in contexts where those values carried force. The moralistic Yankees tended to assert themselves when reform was on the agenda, then retreated to their churches and clubs. The day-to-day business of politics was thus left to the individualists whose tendency to exploit the system was braked by pressure from business-minded traditionalists who believed in efficient, low-cost government. What has been characterized variously as a struggle between good and evil, between private greed and the public welfare, politics in mid-Illinois is perhaps better understood as a diversity issue.

SWING DISTRICT

For a time, the rise of mid-Illinois's political men in state politics could be explained by demographics. From the 1840s until the rise of Chicago, the region was Illinois's most populous part. In 1850, six of Illinois's ten incorporated cities were in mid-Illinois, and the region as a whole was home to nearly 45 percent of the state's people[11]—good reasons why, in 1858, senatorial candidate Abraham Lincoln gave most of his campaign speeches in mid-Illinois, from Danville on the east to Carthage and Dallas City on the west.[12]

The corn latitudes were not only where the most votes were but also where the crucial votes were. For decades, Illinois was divided politically along regional lines on issues from banking and prohibition to slavery and the structure of local government. Sympathies in its northern latitudes were clearly with the Whigs and later the new Republican Party, and those in Illinois's southern third were strongly with the Democrats. In the 1860 presidential race, Lincoln won 70 percent of the vote in the northern counties and a mere 20 percent south of the old National Road; he carried the state by virtue of a thin margin in those counties of mid-Illinois where he was well known from his circuit-riding days.

The balance of party interests in the middle third of the state reflects its demographic mix. The region was what demographers call a mixing zone and what political analysts call a swing district. The western part of the region had been settled by Southern migrants for the most part; people in these counties remained loyal to the Jacksonian program, with its suspicion of commerce and progress, and marched under the flag of the Democrats. Mid-Illinois's eastern counties had been settled a generation later by pro-business mid-Atlantic immigrants and German farmers and craftsmen; those counties were just as fervently Republican because of that party's pro-business agenda. In the middle part of the region (centered roughly on Springfield) neither party dominated. Because mid-Illinois as a whole was a cross section of Illinois in its makeup and its partisan inclinations, any politician who appealed to this region always stood a good chance of doing well statewide.

THE REPUBLICAN ASCENDANCY IN MID-ILLINOIS

Abraham Lincoln rose from lower and ended up higher than his colleagues, but he was only one of a generation of remarkable mid-Illinois Republicans to emerge in that period. Richard Yates was a Whig congressman when he was elected Illinois governor during the Civil War. Yates spent most of his life in Jacksonville. He was a friend and classmate of William Jennings Bryan; both had attended Illinois College and as young men the two briefly considered forming a law partnership. Yates was genial, good-looking, and eloquent, although his postwar career in the U.S. Senate was blighted by drink. If the role of a war governor is to mobilize his state, Richard Yates was outstanding. Excited by Yates's oratory, Illinoisans signed up to fight in numbers that exceeded the state's quota for men again and again. (Historians have argued whether Yates helped save the Union or put more Illinois men in union cemeteries than needed to be there.) Like many of his Republican colleagues, Yates was impatient with what he saw as President Lincoln's dilatoriness over slavery. Writes Robert P. Howard, "More emotional than intellectual, he never comprehended the complexity of the president's wartime problems, one of which was him."[13]

Macon County gave the state only one governor—Decatur's Richard J. Oglesby—but it gave him three times. More memorable as an orator than as an administrator, Oglesby still managed to become the fourteenth, sixteenth, and twentieth governors of Illinois. (One term was aborted so he could go to Washington as U.S. senator for the term ending 1879.) Like so many of Illinois's early leaders, Oglesby was born in Kentucky, in 1824. An imperfectly educated farm boy, Oglesby enjoyed a lively young manhood, having fought in the Mexican War and taken part in the California gold rush. He worked variously as a farmer, rope maker, and carpenter while studying law in Springfield, after which he set up practice at Decatur. An accomplished solider in the Civil War, he returned to mid-Illinois and a career as a politician and country squire.

John M. Palmer was a two-time governor and U.S. senator, a description as inadequate as calling Lincoln solely a former congressman. Another Kentuckian, Palmer was a self-made man, having supported himself as a farmer, a

John M. Palmer. Abraham Lincoln was not mid-Illinois's only self-made man to rise to prominence. Palmer, of Carlinville and Springfield, began life as a schoolteacher, cooper, and clock salesman, and ended it as a principled politician, able general, resolute military governor of Kentucky, and presidential candidate. FROM *HISTORICAL ENCYCLOPEDIA OF ILLINOIS AND HISTORY OF SANGAMON COUNTY*, VOL. 2, PART 2, EDITED BY NEWTON BATEMAN AND PAUL SELBY (CHICAGO: MUNSELL PUBLISHING COMPANY, 1912), 640 FACING.

cooper, a schoolteacher, and a shoe salesman before working his way through college. Also like Lincoln, Palmer read law in his spare time; he practiced in Carlinville until 1866, when he and his large family decamped to Springfield, where he joined the firm of Milton Hay, one of the state's most prestigious.

An ardent abolitionist, Palmer left the Democrats for the new Republican Party, over whose founding convention in Bloomington he presided. A trusted colleague of Lincoln, Palmer entered the Union army as a colonel and left it a major general, after which the president appointed him military governor of his native Kentucky; there he used every weapon in the legal arsenal to extinguish the vestiges of slavery. Palmer's commitment to emancipation was personal as well as political. He pointedly withdrew his daughters from Springfield's exclusive all-white Bettie Stuart School for girls and enrolled them in the nearest public elementary school.[14]

Palmer changed parties more often than many of his colleagues changed their speeches. In his roughly sixty years in public life he was a Democrat, an Anti-Nebraska Democrat, a Republican, a Liberal Republican, a Democrat again, and finally a member of the splinter National Democratic Party. As governor he was open to progressive ideas (like other Liberal Republicans, for example, Palmer wanted to deliver the Republican Party from the boodlers who then controlled it) and sympathetic to the working class. As one historian put it, "There are not many men in our history who are more interesting or more important than this honest and intelligent humanitarian, who was for decades a key figure in the politics of a key state."[15]

Bloomington's David Davis was an attorney and judge and one of the state's biggest landlords—biggest in more than one sense, he being so physically large that no saddle horse, only a carriage, was strong enough to carry him while he traveled on the judicial circuit.[16] Davis was a Marylander by birth who had a good education in law before coming to mid-Illinois in the 1830s. He rode, or rather traveled, the circuit as a judge from 1848. "Not only did his Honor's ample girth and other physical proportions suggest a paterfamilias," wrote one early historian, "but his mental attitude toward the bar was at once domineering and fatherly, with the domineering element always prominent."[17]

Davis was one of the campaign advisers in the 1850s whose machinations secured Abraham Lincoln's presidential nomination in 1860; Davis was later named by Lincoln to the Supreme Court, where he demonstrated his independent streak by joining the majority in an important 1866 decision that undid Lincoln's policy of trying civilians outside the war zones in military courts. Elbert Hubbard, who grew up in the Bloomington area, told this story about a visit Davis made to the home of Hubbard's aunt and uncle.

Bloomington's David Davis, sometime between 1855 and 1865. Judge, landowner, and political insider, Davis is widely credited with having secured the 1860 Republican presidential nomination for Lincoln by his adroit politicking at the party convention. COURTESY LIBRARY OF CONGRESS, LC-DIG-CWPBH-02278.

After Judge Davis had gone, Aunt Hannah said, "You must always remember Judge Davis, for he is the man who made Abe Lincoln!"

And when I said, "Why, I thought God made Lincoln," they all laughed.

After a little pause my inquiring mind caused me to ask, "Who made Judge Davis?" And Uncle Elihu answered, "Abe Lincoln."[18]

Like John Palmer, Davis was more principled than partisan. Long a stalwart Whig, he helped organize the new Republican Party, was on a short list of potential presidential nominees in 1872 held by both Democrats and Liberal

Republicans, and in 1877 was chosen Illinois's U.S. senator by a coalition of Greenbackers and Democrats. While on the court his reputation for nonpartisan probity led to Davis being named to the commission appointed to settle the disputed 1876 presidential election.

"There was nothing dull or retiring about David Davis; he lived life to the full with zest and with strong prejudices," wrote Allison Dunham in 1961. "Activist though he was; prejudiced though he was; loyal though he was to friends who, by hindsight at least, did not deserve loyalty; David Davis both on the Court and off had the judicious attitude when a decision was necessary."[19] Allan Nevins fairly put him in "the second rank of eminence,"[20] but "to place him too far in the dusk of Lincoln's shadow," as Robert W. Johannsen put it, "is to deprive Davis of a greatness that is justifiably his own."[21]

The victory of the North in the Civil War had also been a victory for the Republican Party. In mid-Illinois as elsewhere, the party dominated for decades after Appomattox, not least because of the return to civilian life of voting veterans who remained steadfastly loyal to the political champion of their cause. A candidate did not have to do much more to be elected governor than to be a Republican, which was how John M. Hamilton (Marshall County), Joseph "Private Joe" Fifer (McLean County), and Richard Yates the younger (Morgan and Sangamon counties) found themselves in Springfield. Each was interesting in his own way (Hamilton, for instance earned a master's degree in the classics, the first Illinois governor to hold a graduate degree and long the only one to earn one in any field other than law), but each must be listed among the state's lesser chief executives.

The progressive era and the Great Depression ended the Republicans' long ascendancy in Springfield but briefly restored mid-Illinois to prominence. Adlai E. Stevenson II was delivered into a Bloomington Democratic dynasty by a mother who was heir to the fortune of town builder Jesse Fell. Stevenson lived in the Evergreen City until his teens. Perhaps "based in" is a more accurate term than "lived in"; his family took every opportunity to spend time away from the place. Biographer John Bartlow Martin believed that locals' rejection of the Stevensons as snobs (a rebuff that seems merited on the evidence) wounded the youthful Stevenson. For whatever reason, after acquiring the education of a gentleman of his class at Choate, Princeton, and Harvard Law, Stevenson never went back to live in Bloomington, choosing instead to make his home on Chicago's North Shore. That background made him suspect in both places to some extent and (as Donald Tingley put it) "denied him political acceptance by both the 'eastern establishment' and midwestern professional politicians."[22]

The Stevensons knew not only how to pronounce *noblesse oblige* but to live it. Adlai II's grandfather was a U.S vice president, his father an Illinois secretary of state under a reformist governor. His own impulse toward public service took him into politics, attracting the attention of a Democratic Party that needed a squeaky-clean candidate to help restore the party's reputation after a series of scandals. In 1948 Stevenson was slated by the bosses as the gubernatorial candidate and upset incumbent Republican Dwight Green in a landslide. In office he was antigambling and pro-roads, and made a good enough impression nationally to get himself nominated by the Democrats to run for president in 1952 and again in 1956.

While Stevenson never lived in mid-Illinois again after his governorship, he was generous about his debt to the place. In a speech in Bloomington during that 1948 campaign, Stevenson said that the city had taught him that "in quiet places, reason abounds"—a conclusion belied to some extent by the history of that particular place. He added, "My home town taught me that good government and good citizenship are one and the same, that good individuals make a good town and that nothing else does."[23] He might well have believed it.

UNCOMMON COMMON MEN

The U.S. Congress is not unlike mid-Illinois, insofar as both are places where people of diverse backgrounds and ambitions have to get along to get things done. Many of the mid-Illinoisans sent to Washington have therefore found it a congenial place, and a disproportionate number of them ended up helping to run it.

Joseph G. "Uncle Joe" Cannon was born in North Carolina in 1836 and raised in Indiana. Cannon moved in 1859 to Tuscola, in Douglas County, where he enjoyed success as a lawyer and prosecutor before settling in Danville and entering Republican politics. Cannon was politically conservative and personally uncouth (Teddy Roosevelt advised his daughter Alice not to place herself between Cannon and his spittoon), but that roughness was fine with his constituents. He served in the U.S. House of Representatives on and off for twenty terms between 1873 and 1923, four of which were spent as Speaker.

Cannon wielded the power of the Speaker's office with more than a firm hand, judging from how often such words as *tyrant* and *czar* are used to describe his rule. So secure did he feel in that post that he dared to openly mock his critics. "Behold Mr. Cannon, the Beelzebub of Congress!" he announced himself to an Elgin audience in 1909. "Gaze on this noble, manly form—me, Beelzebub—me, the Czar !"[24] Later generations of Washingtonians who did not suffer under his tenure tended to recall it for its longevity rather than its arrogance, and in 1962 the old House Office Building in Washington was renamed for Cannon.

Everett McKinley Dirksen was Pekin's gift to Congress and to the news camera. Beginning in 1933, "Ev" spent sixteen years in the U.S. House and another nineteen in the Senate. Like so many mid-Illinois politicians, he was from a family of modest means; he got to know his district delivering bread to the grocery-store customers of his German immigrant family's wholesale bakery. As the Senate minority leader in the Kennedy and Johnson years, Dirksen played a key role in the passage (and once, in the rejection) of landmark civil rights legislation.

Dirksen is probably more widely remembered for his oratory. In the 1940s he was voted Congress's most effective speaker—this in a day when most

U.S. senator Everett Dirksen in 1966 with petitions from citizens pushing for right-to-work laws. A statue of Dirksen installed at the statehouse in Springfield in 1977 depicts him with an oil can symbolizing his skill at lubricating the creaky machinery of Congress. ARTHUR E. SCOTT PHOTOGRAPH COLLECTION, GEORGE MASON UNIVERSITY LIBRARIES, SPECIAL COLLECTIONS AND ARCHIVES.

congressmen still knew how to talk and not just give speeches. Like Lincoln, Dirksen was a reader who drew on the Bible, although unlike Lincoln Dirksen actually spent time in a pulpit, as a substitute preacher. Also like Lincoln, Dirksen had more than a bit of the actor in him. (He loved theater and as a young man wrote profusely, and unsuccessfully, for the stage.) His performances were aided by a voice that inspired journalists to something like poetry. "Like the finest whiskey aged in fog,"[25] enthused one; "tonsils marinated in honey"[26] sang another. These are merely matters of style, however; in substance Dirksen was a doctrinaire Midwestern Republican.

Joe Cannon's longevity if not his celebrity was matched by Ford County's Leslie "Les" Arends. Running as a conservative Republican in 1934, Arends defeated an incumbent Democrat to win a U.S. House seat—the only GOP candidate in the entire country to pull off that feat that year. He went on to win nineteen more elections in a row, serving from 1935 to 1975, thirty of those years as GOP party whip, a tenure unmatched by either a Republican or a Democrat.

A Methodist farm boy, Arends was quintessentially mid-Illinoisan. He began his career in the Farm Bureau, which is to apprentice pols from rural Illinois what the Kiwanis Club was to its small-town kin. In Washington he showed himself to be a dogmatic Jeffersonian, preaching individualism and self-reliance, small government and isolationism. (Only Japan's aggression at Pearl Harbor reconciled him to the need to fight in World War II.) Arends found much to dislike in the New Deal, even more than many of his constituents did, but he never let principle interfere with politics, and he made sure that his district's farmers got their fair share of federal largesse.

Arends shared traits with the many mid-Illinois politicians who excelled in Washington leadership roles. He was congenial, trustworthy, and pragmatic, a team man and a skilled political operator. What he was not was philosophically adaptable. By the time he retired, he was seen even in his own party as an out-of-date mossback.[27]

Republican Robert H. Michel was born in Peoria, which he represented in Washington from 1957 until he retired in 1995. During the final fifteen years of that tenure Michel served as Republican Party leader in the House. Like Arends he was temperamentally fit for the role of party leader, but the political environment back home also prepared him for the role. Fittingly, Michel is recalled in Peoria by a bridge—the $40 million, four-lane Bob Michel Bridge that replaced an outmoded drawbridge linking Peoria and East Peoria.

Abraham Lincoln is only the most famous of the mid-Illinois politicians who saw in himself a president of the United States; others included Douglas, Palmer,

Bryan, Cannon, and Ronald Reagan.[28] Reagan was born in northern Illinois, but his four years in mid-Illinois as a member of the class of 1932 at Eureka College in Woodford County were formative. There Reagan delivered his first speech on public affairs (opposing too-strict economies insisted on by the college's president) and learned what little economics he knew. For years the school's leaders were ambivalent about their alum's politics, although they eventually reconciled themselves to the fund-raising potential of Eureka's connection to his celebrity.[29]

The roster of accomplished politicians from mid-Illinois is not limited to men who held high public and party office. Diplomacy is horse-trading politics of the higher sort, and one of the nation's more adept practitioners was John Hay, President Lincoln's personal secretary, who grew up in Warsaw in Hancock County, attended school in Pittsfield, and read law in Springfield; Hay later served as secretary of state under Presidents McKinley and Theodore Roosevelt. Springfield's Duncan McDonald, labor union organizer and social activist, in 1924 was nominated as the presidential candidate of the new Farmer-Labor Party under whose flag marched organized labor and the farm cooperative movement; the experience understandably disillusioned him and he retired to a quiet life as a Springfield bookseller.

Coal mine union politics made the General Assembly look like musical chairs. United Mine Workers of America president John L. Lewis began as a union organizer around 1909 in Panama in southern Montgomery County and later lived for years in Springfield. He decided early that he would rather work for miners above ground than work for a mine owner below it. As a UMWA official he was the very image of the cigar-chomping pol and ran a union political machine as formidable as any Chicago ever produced. He did it using most of the same techniques, from ballot stuffing to payroll padding. New immigrant miners tended to defer to the English-speaking Protestants like Lewis; in return for their loyalty and votes, union officials appointed the newcomers to union jobs they might never have won in contested elections—the same approach that the Irish used to dominate Chicago's ethnic wards.[30] He maintained his power by such means until he retired in 1960, after a new federal law removed his power to appoint union officers beholden to him.

"A MAN OF POPULAR ORIGIN"

If any mid-Illinois politician can be said to have been a product of the place, it is Abraham Lincoln. The nation recalls Lincoln as he appears seated in his famous memorial on the mall in the nation's capital; mid-Illinois recalls him on the stump. Mid-Illinois is where Lincoln learned politics, and indeed in his early career he deserved the name "Illinois politician." He was low and cunning when necessary, an enthusiastic horse trader in the General Assembly, and wise enough not to be someone everyone loves and sensible enough not to become someone people felt obliged to hate.

Lincoln the leader, Lincoln the statesman, Lincoln the thinker about government also were products of the political and social community of which he was a part. In his book, *Here I Have Lived*, Paul M. Angle explored the relationship between Lincoln and his home city. Angle summarized rhetorically the many ways that Springfield had been crucial to Lincoln's political development.

Lincoln in Pittsfield. Thanks to the camera, we can see Lincoln as mid-Illinoisans saw him. While on an 1858 campaign swing in Pittsfield, he posed for this portrait, a version of which hangs in the courthouse rotunda in Pike County. COURTESY LIBRARY OF CONGRESS, LC-USZ62–16377.

> Could Lincoln, for instance, have attained high standing at the bar if he had not resided at the one city in the state where the high courts sat? Could he have become a power in Illinois politics if the legislature and the courts had not drawn the political leaders to his home at regular and frequent intervals? Could he have learned to gauge the temper of the people as surely as he did learn to gauge it had he not been forced for years to evaluate the conflicting sentiments which these men were constantly reporting? Could he have attained to the mastery of political manoeuvre that was his had he not had years of association with venturesome and skillful politicians, both as friends and opponents? Could he have held to his faith in political democracy if he had not lived in a city where economic opportunity was a fact?[31]

Lincoln owed much to Springfield, then, but Springfield and Sangamon County did not feel it owed much to him. He was defeated when he ran for reelection to Congress in 1848. He might have won the great debates of 1858 on the platforms, but in the polling places Douglas Democrats in both Springfield and Sangamon County outvoted his supporters. In the presidential election of 1860, when he ran against two other candidates (including local favorite Douglas), Lincoln carried the city of Springfield by only 69 votes out of 2,752 cast; Lincoln lost Sangamon County as a whole by 42 votes. In 1864, running against Democrat John McClellan, Lincoln carried urban Springfield by an even slimmer margin of 10 votes and again lost rural Sangamon County by the not inconsiderable margin of 380 votes.

Contrary to myth, Lincoln was of the people and for the people—but never really like the people. While a son of toil, Lincoln was no Jacksonian. He eagerly sought to escape the hardships of pioneer agriculture (as a young man he had a reputation as a layabout) and advocated early attempts to apply mechanical and scientific knowledge to lighten its drudgery. He supported a state bank, promoted higher taxes to maintain state bond payments, and strongly advocated canals and railroads, all with an eye toward building a modern commercial economy of the sort that many of his cultural kin regarded as a suspect basis for a society.

Lincoln was mentored in law and politics and manners by the region's elite. His constituency, not surprisingly, included proportionately many more merchants and professionals, and fewer artisans and laborers, than in the electorate as a whole.[32] It was from the stratum of landowners and professional men that he drew many of the men who would figure prominently in his career. Indeed by the time Lincoln was being talked about as a candidate for major office he was one of them himself, an established attorney with a lucrative practice, leading the genteel life of the settled professional man. In a 2000 article, Allen C. Guelzo summarized how Lincoln had changed.

> Although the romantic legend of Lincoln as a lawyer offers us a vision of a community counselor . . . the bulk of Lincoln's law practice, not to mention its most profitable aspects, had moved by 1856 . . . to the service of precisely those agents of the markets which were most lethal to rural and local communities: the railroad corporations, the banks and insurance companies of Sangamon, McLean and Morgan counties, and even at least one St. Louis venture capital firm.[33]

His transformation was the fruit of a long-nurtured ambition. In the Jacksonville museum and archive of former mid-Illinois congressman Paul M. Findley is a mahogany sofa built for and used by Lincoln in his Springfield law offices. The sofa was purchased in 1837, just after Lincoln had moved to town on a borrowed horse with all his worldly belongings stuffed into two saddlebags. "Why, then," Erika Nunamaker asks, "did the man . . . buy such a monumental, expensive, and elegant a [*sic*] piece of furniture?"[34] We can speculate—everyone speculates about Lincoln's motives—that the sofa was a totem of the genteel life he had come to Springfield to make for himself.

Lincoln was a common man only in his youthful poverty, and hard work allowed him to bury that man. By the time he was being talked about as a presidential prospect, Lincoln's origins were forgotten by the larger public, if they were ever known. (The population turnover in mid-Illinois is those days was remarkably high; anyone living in the same town as long as five years qualified as rooted in the community.) The youthful Lincoln was resurrected in 1860 by his campaign advisers, who realized, in the words of Bloomingtonian Jesse Fell, that he needed to establish himself more strongly as "a man of popular origin" with whom the working people of the country would identify. Thus the Rail-splitter was born. Lincoln, who had striven his whole life to that point to overcome beginnings that he regarded as a cause for shame, for the rest of it had to endure seeing them offered up as reason for pride.

"THE ONLY DEMOCRAT IN TOWN"

Lincoln also was unusual in taking as his political hero Henry Clay. Thousands of mid-Illinoisans who came from Lincoln's background elevated Andrew Jackson to that rank. Thomas Carlin, a Greene County farmer who was elected Illinois governor in 1838, was a typical Jacksonian Democrat. Like Jackson,

Carlin was a creature of the new frontier, being an accomplished horseman, woodsman, and marksman. Alas, he was not an accomplished governor. Theodore Pease notes that Carlin, as he left office, "sent a farewell message to the General Assembly that is no more than a sigh of ''Tis a' a muddle.'"[35] Gubernatorial historian Robert Howard rates Carlin at or near the bottom of the roster of chief executives[36]; others describe him as honest but ignorant.

Jacksonvillian Joseph Duncan was a one-term governor whose career reflected the state's (which in effect meant mid-Illinois's) gradual disenchantment with Jacksonian policies. Duncan went to Washington in the 1830s a Democrat and returned a Whig, having seen Jacksonianism up close and deciding that he could not abide it. Concluding that a larger state role in the economy was appropriate, Duncan as governor inadvertently confirmed the wisdom of the Jacksonians' skepticism about central power by backing an ill-advised scheme to finance more new railroads and canals than the young state could afford.

While that internal improvements program was premature, Duncan's support for a modern transportation system was vindicated by history. The opening of Illinois to the railroads, for example, was a boon to the commercial agriculturalists of the region's eastern counties because it gave them an affordable means to ship their surpluses to urban East Coast markets or overseas. The many Jacksonians in the region's westernmost farming counties saw things differently. Local markets shrank when the railroads began to cross the Mississippi, because those trains carried into Illinois cheaper farm goods from the newly developing states farther west. Many western Illinoisans concluded that growth in the rest of the region was coming at their expense, and that their complaints were being ignored. Interregional resentment, once rooted, became impossible to eradicate; a century later, for example, a local journalist who believed his region had been slighted in the siting of state facilities and interstate highways facetiously dubbed the counties west of the Illinois River "Forgottonia," a nickname that caught on for a time.

The Jacksonian Democrats were a regional force in Illinois until the Southern culture that sustained them was overwhelmed in the 1850s by the very modernizing forces they railed against. Since then, the political party that has most consistently expressed the world views of most modern mid-Illinoisans—which is to say the heirs of the mid-Atlantic traditionalists—is that of the Republicans. Yankee communitarians also tended toward Republicanism, but traditionalists and communitarians populated two separate factions of the party. The Yankees embraced progressive Republicanism and were active in various clean-government reform movements at the state and local level. The traditionalists in contrast came to constitute the Republican Party's mainstream. They were pragmatists rather than ideologues who were more eager to advance material interests than any social agenda. Uneasy allies they might have been, but allies they usually were.

The Illinois Republican Party was organized in mid-Illinois (in Bloomington in 1856), and here patriotism of place has long been seen as indistinguishable from loyalty to the GOP. The region's prosperous farmers were conservative by personality if not principle. Each in effect being the proprietor of a small business, they found natural allies with their Main Street Republican counterparts. The Republicans' business-first ethos is personified in the family of George Mecherle, the farmer who founded the State Farm insurance companies. The Mecherles, explains George's biographer, "had been schooled from their earliest Illinois days in the traditions of Republicanism, and . . . saw peace and prosperity in the good, black McLean County soil."[37]

The Great Depression shook that faith. Wrote Carthage farmer Lewis Omer to a friend in 1932, "I believe that if the election were held tomorrow Roosevelt would carry Illinois by 500,000 votes. . . . The farmers are all in the state of mind of the farmer who had a cow drop a stillborn calf in the back pasture on a cold day last March. The farmer looked at the calf, then shook his fist and said, 'Well, damn Hoover anyway.'"[38]

But if hard times made some farmers doubt Republicans, good times found them damning Democrats again just like their grandfathers did. In 1948, when he was campaigning at the DeWitt County fair in Farmer City, Adlai Stevenson II recalled that farmers voted Democratic in the darkest days of the Depression. "But after Roosevelt and the Democrats had given you farmers a fair break with a parity price support, soil conservation, rural electrification, benefit payments, farm loans, the reciprocal trade agreements act and prices had gone up and up, you voted for the Republicans, who never gave you anything but Hoover's ill-fated Farm Board!" he reminded them. "I don't understand why people vote against their best friends."[39]

With the farmers among mid-Illinois's stalwart Republicans were many of the region's German immigrants. (The German-born parents of future U.S. senator Everett Dirksen, wanting them to be good Americans, named their three children in part after prominent members of the Republican Party.) They were artisans or prosperous farmers who would have inclined naturally toward Republicanism, even if many of them had not also shared the new party's antislavery views. Local Germans also were repulsed at the nativist bigotry that periodically came their way from that faction of the Democratic Party.

The Republican blend of agrarianism and commercialism—Main Street meets the farm—ruled the political and economic life of mid-Illinois in the century after the Civil War, just as it did that of the Midwest. All but one of the several Congressional leaders to hail from the region were Republicans, as were six of its seven governors. (Even Bloomingtonian Adlai E. Stevenson II, who was nominally a Democrat, held many views more in line with those of a progressive Republican of his father's day.) Outside the area's handful of largish cities, Republicans also dominated city hall and county politics. One among what the *Chicago Tribune* in 1932 called Illinois's "rural squires" was Galesburg's Omer N. Custer who ran a Republican political machine in that area from the mid-teens to the early 1940s.[40] Champaign-Urbana lawyer H. I. "Boss" Green was a perfect specimen of what political scientists have labeled the businessman-autocrat; he ruled both cities and their parent county from the mid-1920s to 1953.[41] While such leaders sometimes held minor public office, their power base was not the electorate but the oligarchy of businessmen and lawyers of which each was part.

Still, while Republican voters were as common as fence posts in the old Grand Prairie, small poor-land farmers in the western counties remained faithful to the Democratic Party through the Great Depression. Roman Catholic immigrants, beginning with the Irish in the 1830s, also tended toward the Democracy, often vociferously. Their political descendants were the blue-collar Democrat voters of manufacturing towns like Canton and Decatur and Galesburg who have leavened the region's Republicanism since the beginning of the industrial era in the 1850s. Farmers and agribusiness owners tended to back free trade, for example, while union members tended to be protectionists to the extent that their employers are vulnerable to foreign competition. Thanks to them, mid-Illinois's cities have long tended to vote less reliably Republican than do the small towns.

A COMPLETELY NONIDEOLOGICAL APPROACH

The Democratic and Republican parties today seem as eternal a presence in mid-Illinois as dirt in the streams. Episodes of political upheaval such as third-party movements have been rare in mid-Illinois—more on that below—and like the local thunderstorms such outbreaks were often furious but quickly spent. The sun, when it came out, still shone on a political landscape that was nonideological, pragmatic, bipartisan (rather than nonpartisan), and (depending on who does the defining) corrupt.

Any mid-Illinois politician combines at least three of those traits, in varying proportions. A casual attitude toward party ideology is perhaps the most common. The noted historian David Herbert Donald, after reading a biography of Joseph Cannon, was convinced that the twenty-termer from Danville never had an idea, perhaps because he never read anything except the *Congressional Record*. "The fact is that Cannonism did not represent thought at all, but a completely non-ideological approach to politics," says Donald. "His conservatism was not a matter of economics but of emotion. Instinctively he tried to restore the good old days when minimal government and a straight Republican ticket had made America, as the speaker tersely put it, 'a hell of a success.'"[42]

Similar in temperament was Shelby Moore Cullom, one of Illinois's most durable politicians. After earlier service as a state representative and a congressman, he was twice elected governor, leaving that office for what became a five-term, thirty-year career in the U.S. Senate. A Kentuckian by birth, Cullom grew up on a Tazewell County farm, then moved to Springfield, which was to be his home, with the District of Columbia, for the rest of his life. In Springfield he read law in the firm of one of Lincoln's former partners—a connection that Cullom never let anyone forget. Honorable and capable of bipartisanship, Cullom was known nationally in his day, but he is remembered, if at all, for having delivered the shortest nominating speech on record—seventy-nine words—in recommending Ulysses S. Grant for a second White House term.

Opinion is general that Cullom was neither a "brilliant disseminator of public policy"[43] nor an influential crafter of laws. Incapable of insights into the questions of the day, much less of tomorrow, he owed his durability to the fact that most of the people in the still-rural and small-town Illinois he presented understood as little of such things as he did. Needing to take a position on public questions, he simply followed the lead of smarter Republican leaders.

In mid-Illinois, the middle of the road saw a lot of traffic. Bloomington's Adlai Stevenson, vice president to President Grover Cleveland and grandfather to the 1952 and 1956 presidential candidate, took a convenient attitude toward doctrine, earning him the nickname "The Great Straddler."[44] Everett Dirksen managed to win the congressional district around Pekin in 1932 by the same number of votes as FDR carried it in the Democratic landslide that year. He pulled off that trick by posing as a Republican to Republican audiences and as a Democrat to Democratic ones; an unnamed newspaperman once said of him, "He delivered the best speech in favor of foreign aid and the best speech against foreign aid that I ever heard."[45]

Ideas do not vote, people do, and many mid-Illinois pols did not scruple about which people they were. Shenanigans at the ballot box are usually thought of as a defining Chicago tradition, but examples from mid-Illinois abound as well. In the closing months of Stephen A. Douglas's 1858 campaign for the U.S. Senate seat against Lincoln, for example, both Republican and

Politician Shelby Moore Cullom as rendered by Arthur Garfield Dove. Cullom's biographer, James W. Neilson, recalls that people could never be certain where Cullom stood on complicated issues, a trait that led the *Chicago Tribune* in 1895 to dub him "the tall, quaking ash of the Sangamon." COURTESY LIBRARY OF CONGRESS, LC-USZ62–67548.

pro-administration Democratic journals charged that the Douglas organization had prepared to colonize doubtful counties with "floating voters." Arthur Cole explains: "Evidence was submitted that Irish laborers drawn from Chicago, northern Illinois, Wisconsin, Indiana, and St. Louis were being shipped by the railroads, ostensibly as railroad hands, to such points as Mattoon, Champaign, Peoria, Carlinville, Bloomington, and Virginia."[46]

"THAT SMELL IN SPRINGFIELD"

If any hundred mid-Illinoisans were asked to summarize the signal trait of the state's politics, few would be likely to say "pragmatic" or "nonideological." The term that would come to the minds of most of them is "corrupt." Most members of the General Assembly for decades behaved like middle managers attending a convention. Tales of their high jinks during sessions—booze, women, and gambling mainly—however, were usually accepted as foible. What really made "Springfield" a dirty word were the auditors who stole money, the U.S. senators who bought their own appointments, and the office-holders who traded the public's resources for private profit and preferment.

Chicago might have produced the most theatrically crooked pols, but Springfield is, in the popular mind at least, just as bad. It is hard to look down on a building that is taller than the U.S. Capitol, but people in Illinois do it all the time when they visit the state capitol in Springfield. In the 1890s, reporter-reformer-writer Brand Whitlock drew on Springfield and the General Assembly for raw material for two influential novels and several short stories. "The ever-present theme of polities in Whitlock's stories almost always had the smell of decay and corruption about it," wrote one biographer, "and many stories were specifically about that smell in Springfield."[47]

Joel Matteson, a New Yorker who came to Springfield by way of Joliet in 1852 as a new governor, took advantage of the state's sloppy bookkeeping to get and spend nearly $400,000 of the public's money—an astonishingly large sum in that day. Matteson never admitted to the theft but agreed to indemnify the state for its losses. (As Robert P. Howard puts it, "In effect, he was willing to pay back the money he said he hadn't stolen."[48]) Some of that money went into the house Matteson built in Springfield that out-mansioned the Executive Mansion across the street; that house burned down when Matteson was out of office, as would Matteson, financially.

In the early days of the commonwealth, even honest elected officials indulged zestfully in conduct that people in later decades would decry as criminal. Lawmakers voted without qualm for public projects that would enhance their own holdings of land. Even the sainted Lincoln was not above this kind of thing. A proposed Beardstown and Sangamon Canal would allow commercial boat traffic to bypass the twisty bits of the lower Sangamon River and thus bring boom times to towns along the route. Legislator Lincoln voted for the incorporation of the canal company, after which citizen Lincoln bought forty-seven acres of land on the river at Huron, a paper town in today's Menard County a mile from the spot where the proposed canal would terminate. The canal was never dug, but Lincoln did better when he bought two town lots in Springfield in 1836, then happily voted eleven months later to move the state capital there; that decision drove up Springfield land values, as expected, and after just two months Lincoln sold one of his lots for three times what he had paid for it.

THE APPETITE FOR PORK

Enriching oneself by means of public office makes one a crook, even in Illinois, but enriching supporters or constituents has always made one a beloved politician, especially in Illinois. Maybe the Lincoln story that Springfieldians love the best recalls a bit of sharp business he did as a young and not-at-all naïve lawmaker. Lincoln was one of the famous Long Nine, the lanky nine-member Sangamon County legislative delegation in 1837, when the State of Illinois was deciding where to locate its planned new capital. For decades the assumption has been that Springfield won the prize thanks to its log-rolling legislators. A program of state-financed railroads and canals was then being talked about. As an unsuccessful candidate for the General Assembly in 1832, Lincoln had sensibly warned voters about the absurdly expensive infrastructure scheme, but in 1837 Lincoln and his colleagues were happy to trade their votes for a railroad here, a canal there, and grants of money to those who got neither in return for votes for Springfield as the capital. Their bargaining helped every corner of the state obtain something, which ballooned the cost from merely extravagant to ruinous.

There were rumors that more than votes had been traded. Morgan County's representative, Stephen A. Douglas, was appointed register of the land office at Springfield immediately after the vote. He was lambasted by local papers, who accused him of having traded a vote for Springfield against Jacksonville in return for the job. (It was the sort of thing that people were always saying about Douglas, mainly because he so often gave them reason to say it.) In this case the accusation of slick dealing is probably exaggerated. Springfield made a handsome enough bid for the prize to make its selection as capital city plausible. As for buying Douglas's vote with a job, the records show that Douglas voted for Jacksonville at each ballot to the end of the contest.[49]

The legend of the log-rolling Lincoln lives on, in part because it flatters so many mid-Illinoisans' notions of themselves as politically savvy. No matter that an important public issue was not decided on its merits, no matter that, as biographer Michael Burlingame has put it, the bargain crafted by Lincoln wound up benefiting Springfield at the expense of Illinois.[50] The Long Nine played the game and won the prize for the hometown, and that's what a good politician does.

To many Illinoisans, in fact, the smell that has wafted over Springfield ever since is not of corruption but of pork. "I can smell the meat a cookin'," said Paul Powell whenever there was a deal in prospect in the Illinois General Assembly. A politician who brings home pork in the form of jobs and contracts will be applauded by the same voters who condemn as rotten logrolling or patronage that benefits their neighbors. Uncle Joe Cannon is remembered fondly in Danville not because he opposed Woodrow Wilson but because in 1898 he arranged for a handsome branch of the National Home for Disabled Volunteer Soldiers to be built there, bringing with it jobs and contracts for able-bodied Danvillians. Among the several honorifics by which Cannon was known (some of them self-bestowed), such as "the Sage of Vermilion County" and "the Hayseed Member from Illinois," we must add "the Father of the Home."[51]

Joseph G. Cannon. "Uncle Joe" Cannon prepares to leave Congress for the last time in 1923. He served in the U.S. House of Representatives on and off for twenty terms beginning in 1873, four of which were spent as Speaker until the progressive faction in his own party ousted him in 1911. COURTESY LIBRARY OF CONGRESS, LC-DIG-DS-00663.

Jobs and contracts are the common currency of politics in mid-Illinois, as in the rest of the state. The trade in government jobs in the days before the progressive era was unapologetic. Public officials used appointments to government jobs to cement alliances, to reward allies, to advance bills. (When he was Springfield's postmaster in the 1850s, Isaac R. Diller complained to Douglas, who had appointed him, that the job was more trouble than it was worth, but he kept at it because "it gave me a position to help you and your friends."[52]) The first superintendent of the new state hospital for the insane in Jacksonville was a local member of the legislature, and he soon found himself in a dispute not over treatment of the patients but over how the supplies for the institution should be purchased. The superintendent insisted that everything possible should be bought in and around Jacksonville, while his trustees believed the proper practice was to requests bids from suppliers everywhere. Notes hospital historian Frank Norbury, "Those who are familiar with Illinois politics should not be surprised at this."[53] V. Y. Dallman, who used his *Illinois State Register* in Springfield to bang the drum for the Democrats, for years enjoyed a sinecure from that party as a collector of internal revenue, which led one reporter to dub him "Two-Jobs Dallman."[54]

The constant importuning of allies on behalf of favored candidates caused mid-Illinois politicians from Lincoln to Stevenson to complain that it distracted them from governing. Lewis Omer, writing about Depression-era Hancock County, voiced common sentiments. "Politics is a dirty game and I have yet to see the man in this country who can withstand the debasing effects of dealing and associating with [politicians]. I see men who are fine fellows get into the legislature and not a one of them can withstand the pressure of the machine for if they ignore it they get no 'gravy' and the constituency will not re-elect them."[55]

Paul M. Angle, who himself had no training as a librarian when he was hired as head of the Illinois State Historical Library in 1932, quickly learned how the system worked—and how to get around it. He would visit the bar of the Leland Hotel for several consecutive days until a party wheelhorse appeared.

> "Jiggs, two or three days ago they sent me over a guy for an assistant librarian who couldn't be the assistant librarian of a fire house. What am I going to do about him?"
>
> "Well, you know how it is, Paul. We've got to find jobs for some of these characters, even if they aren't any good."
>
> "Sure, I know, but why pick on me?"
>
> "OK, tell him to go back to the office, and we'll find something else for him."
>
> And then I would buy a drink. The problem had been solved.[56]

This state of affairs has been publicly deplored by many Illinoisans but is tolerated by most, at least until officials' reckless abuse of the privilege stirs that quiescent public to act. The usual solution in mid-Illinois as elsewhere is to change the official, not the system. For example, the mistreatment of patients in the big state institutions in Jacksonville, Lincoln, and Normal at the hands of staff who were untrained at best and criminally negligent at worst was a recurring scandal. Overcrowding aggravated by lack of funding was a factor, but easier to blame were the many caretakers who were patronage appointees. "From the politically appointed superintendent of the Soldiers' Orphans' Home to the merest probation officer or worker at the Lincoln Home for the Feebleminded," explains Joan Gittens, "partisan politics rather than commitment and training were the basis for selecting the staff who held children's lives in their hands."[57] Exposés usually led to the dismissal of administrators but no change to the underlying hiring system.

PROTEST AND PROGRESS

While the divvying up of spoils in the form of jobs has been the principal preoccupation of state and local politicians, even the professional politician was occasionally obliged to address policy matters. In 1870 eighty-eight delegates were chosen to draw up a new state constitution. Illinois was by then an urbanizing industrial state coping with new transportation technologies, new energy sources, new forms of industrial organization, and new citizens with new expectations of government, but its government was lumbered with political institutions designed for a frontier rural place. As had happened in the first years of the commonwealth, political parties, and factions within those parties, coalesced around the constitution-makers' basic questions—wet or dry? gold or silver? native or immigrant? regulation or laissez faire?

Farmers were among those who found that the ills of a new world needed new remedies. Disreputable firms sold farmers everything from fake seeds to lethal kerosene lamps. Farmers not only were sued for unknowingly violating patents on the farm equipment they bought but also were gouged by a barbed wire monopoly. The most pernicious weeds in farmers' fields were the warehouse companies, grain dealers, and railroads they depended on to store, sell, and ship their goods; many a farmer came to see such firms as a predatory cabal conspiring against them.

Frustrated in the courts and convinced that the mainstream parties no longer were reliable allies, farmers began to think about organizing themselves politically in self-defense. Between the dawn of the twentieth century and the beginning of World War I, farmers were not only one of the largest voting blocs but also one of least contented. They figured centrally in several of the political protest movements in that period, from the Grange and the National Farmers' Alliance to the Farmers' Mutual Benefit Association, the Southern Alliance, and the Patrons of Industry, and later the populist party.

Among the farmers' foremost champion was William Jennings Bryan—orator, lecturer, secretary of state, three-time presidential candidate. The Great Commoner is usually associated with Nebraska, but he was an Illinois man by birth and schooling. Born and raised in Salem in Marion County, one hundred miles south of Springfield, Bryan at fifteen was sent north to Jacksonville's Whipple Academy, the preparatory school for Illinois College. Bryan went on to graduate in 1881 from Illinois College, which honored him as valedictorian and class orator—the latter a rare case of a young person revealing in college what he would become in later life. He practiced law in Jacksonville in the 1880s before moving to Nebraska and a larger career.

The mature Bryan was a regular visitor to mid-Illinois as a campaigner and Chautauqua performer. Poet Vachel Lindsay was an impressionable teenager in 1896, when the great man came to Springfield during his first presidential campaign. Lindsay would recall in "Bryan, Bryan, Bryan, Bryan," that Springfield was "all one spreading wing of bunting, plumes, and sunshine."

> When Bryan came to Springfield, and Altgeld gave him greeting,
> Rochester was deserted, Divernon was deserted,
> Mechanicsburg, Riverton, Chickenbristle, Cotton Hill
> Empty: for all Sangamon drove to the meeting[58]

None of the agrarian parties managed to win a major office, much less win control over the new economy. Regulation did protect farmers against predators like the railroads, but the graver threat proved to come from other farmers. Mechanization, new higher-yielding hybrids, and the opening up of whole new Illinoises to the west meant that low prices resulting from chronic overproduction of grain sapped farm incomes. Disputes over what to do about these problems split the farm community in mid-Illinois as elsewhere. The reception in mid-Illinois given the New Deal Agricultural Adjustment Act (AAA) of 1938 was typical. The new program essentially paid farmers to store surpluses in bumper-crop years rather than selling them. Its most controversial provision set marketing quotas and levied heavy fines on farmers who sold more than their assigned share.

In the hog-and-cattle-producing counties of western Illinois, farmers didn't like being dictated to by other farmers any more than by bureaucrats who (many believed) probably were communists anyway. They were against the AAA and welfare, Washington and communism, and corn grown outside the Corn Belt. (Corn from Argentina was being used in Peoria distilleries, an especially galling development.) When the AAA became law, farmers in McDonough County who opposed it founded the Corn Belt Liberty League to oppose it and New Deal farm policy in general.

The Corn Belt Liberty League preferred cooperative farmer-directed efforts to control and market surpluses. From its office in Macomb, organizers spread word to other states, and within months league branches were set up in twenty-one Illinois counties—fourteen of them in mid-Illinois—and in four other states. This effort was to some extent a fight with not only Washington but with the more prosperous farmers of eastern and central Illinois; in congressional subcommittee hearings in Springfield in October 1937, farmers from McLean County, Springfield, Jacksonville, and Champaign spoke in favor of production and crop surplus control of the sort embodied in the AAA.

Within seven years, the Corn Belt Liberty League was legally dead. The full-time farmers who planted its seed could not tend it, and when war spending pushed up grain prices, interest in cooperative marketing evaporated.[59] The farmers revolt, while an interesting chapter in the history of mid-Illinois agriculture, was not an important one. The authors of *Agricultural Discontent in the Middle West, 1900–1939* noted that while Illinois farmers were hardly contented they were less discontented than their cousins in other states and they showed it by furnishing practically no leaders and originating none of the era's many farm movements.[60]

A WORKING-CLASS AGENDA

Beginning in the 1850s, factories and coal mines brought new citizens into most of the cities of mid-Illinois, and with them came new ideas about collective action on behalf of the working class. The region was still coal country in that period, and among the region's miners (especially those with British or continental roots) collectivist ideas were common. Leaders of the Illinois chapter of the United Mine Workers of America included socialists such as Braidwood's John H. Walker, Springfield's Duncan McDonald, and Macoupin County's Adolph Germer, a coal miner who served as national executive secretary of the Socialist Party of America from 1916 to 1919.[61] Under them, the Illinois UMWA was not only one of the largest but also one of the most radical chapters in the country.

Labor union members espousing pro-working-class policies occasionally appeared on the ballot in elections for local offices, but they seldom attracted support outside the brotherhood. In 1883, for example, the Knights of Labor put up a machinist from the C & A shops to be the mayor of Bloomington; he won only 22 percent of the vote in a three-way race. In 1911, however, candidates representing the Socialist Party were put up for city hall posts in Canton. Six hundred fifty of nine hundred trade unionists were thought to be members of the UMWA, and six compatriots were elected aldermen to the fourteen-member city council against divided opposition.

In office, Canton's new Socialist aldermen were socially liberal and fiscally conservative, but opponents branded them an antibusiness, even un-American, which was then a popular way to say "pro-tax" and "anti-temperance." The Canton establishment in February 1912 drew up a combined ticket to oust them, which the *Cuba Journal* greeted with disdain.

> Of all the unholy combinations of voters ever gotten together on the face of the earth, the one in Canton composed of Democrats, Republicans, Law and Order Leaguers, Wide Open Town Advocates, Preachers, Saloon Keepers, Church Members, Gamblers, Y.M.C.A.'s, Dive Keepers, Progressives, Mossbacks, Wets, Drys, Chiperfield-Snively crowd and Anti-Chiperfield-Snively, is the worst we ever heard of. Ordinarily these different factions would rather see the town go to the damnation bow wows than for any of the other factions to win. But when there is danger of the Socialists carrying the city, they all get together to fight them.[62]

The local Socialists gained a majority on the city council that year anyway, and might have elected a Socialist mayor in 1914 but for opposition from business and antisaloon women voters. However, in 1916 the makeshift anti-Socialist coalition was split over the issue of regulating booze, which allowed a Socialist candidate to take the mayor's chair with only 36 percent of the vote.

Canton's Socialists managed to pass a few progressive measures, such as hiring a physician to treat city workers injured on the job. But the Socialists were widely associated with German immigrants, and any hopes they had of effecting lasting change in local government were buried by the swelling tide of anti-German hysteria as World War I loomed. In 1918 Canton's Socialist mayor lost, and in 1919 the Socialists did not elect a single candidate for other offices.[63] The only lasting result of this dangerous experiment in the people's politics was a larger budget for public band concerts.

In the end, it was not politics but prosperity that kept socialists from ever again becoming a force in mid-Illinois affairs. War meant boom times in the factory and coal towns. Over time, wrote Daniel Elazar, those workers "came close to becoming an authentic proletariat at one time but, in the process of assimilating into American society . . . [acquired] the middle-class outlook of the society around them."[64] In 1923 in Bloomington, for example, railroad engineer Frank E. Shorthose defeated his Democrat mayoral opponent three to one, and of the twelve members of the new city council, eight were union men. (The labor turnout might have been higher than usual, thanks to a failed strike at the C & A shops.) A revolution hardly loomed, however; the workers had run as Republicans.

ONE MAN, ONE VOTE; ONE WOMAN, ONE VOTE

Revolution came to mid-Illinois, but it was not for working people. It took the form of the dramatic expansion of the franchise for African Americans, for women, and for Chicagoans, in 1870, 1919, and 1964, respectively. The effect was not the new social order that many hoped for, but it did achieve a new political order.

The Fifteenth Amendment to the U.S Constitution, which took effect in 1870, granted the right to vote in state and local elections to African Americans. Such a measure had never been politically plausible in antebellum Illinois and probably would not have passed for years after Appomattox. For decades the black vote was so reliably Republican that politicians could earn it by offering mere token rewards; in the Galesburg of Sandburg's youth, recalled the writer, "The Negro voters expected and were given two city jobs. There was always one Negro policeman in uniform. And a Negro drove the police patrol wagon."[65]

The generation of African Americans that came of age after 1865 pressed for more. Black Republicans in Quincy in the 1890s organized their own Republican club, hoping that by acting en bloc they could pry concessions from white party leadership. They wanted to see more black faces in polling places and at county and state party conventions as well as attention paid to civil rights issues such as job discrimination and antiblack violence.[66] Complaints at the Adams County party convention that sending an all-white delegation to the state convention would slight the black voters led to the selection of a single African American; that man in turn persuaded his white fellow delegates to appoint a colleague, the Reverend Jordan Chavis—Baptist church leader, first man of color to preach in the Illinois statehouse, and "an uncompromising, dyed-in-the wool stalwart Republican"[67]—to become the first African American from

Illinois to serve as an alternate delegate to the party's national convention. The advance was merely symbolic, but it opened a closed door by a crack.

While Emancipation had settled the issue of the black vote, the Civil War left unsettled a scarcely less controversial extension of the franchise. Giving women the vote was widely considered unnecessary at best, dangerous at worst. The Hepzibah Dumvilles of Macoupin County were legion in the 1850s; possessed of a lively mind that was interested in politics, Miss Dumville did not desire to vote, believing that it would be unwomanly.[68] Suffragists were many fewer, if no less certain in their opinions. The first documented speech urging women's suffrage in Illinois was made in 1855 by the editor of the local paper in the LaSalle County town of Earlville, A. J. Grover; that speech reputedly inspired Mrs. Susan Hoxie Richardson (a cousin of Susan B. Anthony) to organize Illinois' first women's suffrage society there.[69]

The rewriting of the outdated Illinois constitution in 1870 provided an opportunity to engrave in the state's fundamental law what many women had come to see as their own Emancipation Proclamation. A delegation of the newly formed Illinois Woman Suffrage Association traveled to Springfield in 1870 to present petitions to the Illinois Constitutional Convention calling for the vote for women. Soon afterward, convention delegates received almost an equal number of petitions against the issue, including one from 380 Peoria women who protested "having the ballot thrust upon them."[70] The men who went on to write the new state constitution ensured that it protected women from that burden, and by including a clause that rendered the document inviolate for twenty years seemed to have guaranteed that women would be voiceless in at least elections for state office for another generation.

Unable for the moment to win the war for the vote outright, Illinois suffragists turned instead to political raids on the enemy's poorly defended fortifications. They realized that the state constitution did not bar women from voting in elections not specifically called for by that charter, such as those to choose local officials, and pressed its allies in the legislature to allow it, office by office. Thus pressed, the General Assembly in 1891 authorized women to vote for members of local school boards and, later, University of Illinois trustees; Riverton elected a women president of its school board in 1894, and in 1911 two women were elected to the Springfield school board.[71]

Every advance was hard won. "Some men who had always believed in suffrage, were exceedingly kind, but no one regarded the matter as a serious legislative question which had the slightest possibility of becoming a law," recalled Grace Wilbur Trout. One of those kind men was progressive Republican state representative Homer Tice, from Greenview in Menard County.

"Mr. Homer Tice had charge of the suffrage bill in 1911 in the House, and he said that in consequence he became so unpopular that every other bill he introduced in the Legislature during that session, was also killed."[72]

Finally, in 1913, Governor Edward F. Dunne signed a bill making Illinois the first state east of the Mississippi River permitting women to vote for presidential electors and for all local offices not specifically named in the State of Illinois Constitution; the bill had been sponsored by Springfield Republican senator Hugh Magill.[73] Women thus had a say in choosing state representatives, members of Congress, and governors as well as various local offices, but it was not until 1919, when the General Assembly made Illinois the first state to ratify what became the Nineteenth Amendment to the U.S. Constitution that Illinois women achieved universal suffrage.

These new voters sent other women to Springfield as representatives. The first woman elected to the House, in 1922, was Pike County native Lottie Holman O'Neill, who had moved from Barry to Chicago to pursue a career; the first woman elected to the Illinois Senate—Florence Fifer Bohrer, in 1924—was a Bloomingtonian. The agendas of these new lawmakers tended toward the traditional domestic concerns. Bohrer's signature issues were child welfare, limits on dance halls, more state parks, and training and state licensing for midwives. O'Neill sponsored legislation limiting the workday for women in Illinois to eight hours; she also was an advocate for disabled children and for parks, as well as schools and civil rights.

It was at the local level that female voters made the biggest difference. As noted in chapter 8, women were instrumental in turning moderate demands for temperance into a not-at-all moderate demand for comprehensive prohibition of alcoholic drink. Whether their subsequent failure to save their towns or their homes from the foolishness of men is a fault of Illinois women or of Illinois politics is a question better left to other, braver authors.

REDRAWING THE LINES

If some male lawmakers feared that women voters might improve Illinois politics, others feared that the state's new immigrant voters would make it worse. While male immigrants could not be denied the franchise, they could be denied opportunities to use it. The 1870 constitution required that the boundaries of legislative districts be redrawn periodically to reflect population changes within the state. This rule had been dutifully followed after each of the four national censuses beginning in 1871. The influx into Chicago of immigrants from southern and eastern Europe left downstaters fearful of granting more seats in the General Assembly to politicians catering to what they regarded as this suspect class. The legislators, like the defenders of the Alamo faced by Santa Anna's army, held out for a half a century while lawmakers ignored their own constitution and suspended decennial redistricting. Mid-Illinois was one of the chief beneficiaries of this rotten system. Thanks to it, the region was long able to maintain a degree of political clout to which its population was no longer entitled. Twentieth-century Illinois remained an urban state in social and economic terms with a rural political culture until a series of U.S. Supreme Court decisions in the 1960s made such gerrymandering unconstitutional.

Mid-Illinois still produces political men and women of talent. (At the time of writing, Springfield's Richard Durbin, who has served in the U.S. Congress for twenty-four years, is a middle-of-the-road, middle-of-Illinois congressional politician of a very familiar type.) But in a political sense, "mid-Illinois" in the 2000s is metropolitan Chicago.

CHAPTER TEN

Rollover Territory: Getting from Here to There in Mid-Illinois

Low rate, swift as fate, never late, up-to-date
—Illinois Traction System slogan

Until well into the mid-1800s, mid-Illinois roads for much of the years were wet enough to bog down a wagon. This the locals expected. What annoyed them was that their roads were never wet enough to float a boat. Because the roads were so bad, commerce needed a river to move cargo. While shipping cargo by river in the region was possible, it was anything but efficient. Consider the intrepid trio of young Decatur men who resolved in 1831 to take goods to New Orleans to sell. The venture began with a canoe trip down the Sangamon River to Springfield, then a hike to the mouth of Spring Creek. There they spent two weeks chopping down several large trees, which then had to be rafted downstream to a sawmill on the Sangamon at Sangamo Town. From the resulting sawn boards the men built a flatboat eighty feet long and eighteen feet wide; it took them a month to do it.

The flatboat was loaded and set off down the Sangamon toward the Illinois River, but after only a few miles it ran aground, or rather it ran a-dam, being perched in shallow water atop a mill dam at New Salem. The craft took on water, so the cargo had to be removed and a hole drilled in the bow to drain the water, after which the hole was repaired and the flatboat eased over the dam and reloaded. The rest of the trip went smoothly enough, but it being not worth the trouble to pole or tow a flatboat upstream, the flatboat was dismantled and the lumber sold. The trip began in March, and the crew returned in July.

Apart from the fact that this particular flatboat had a future president of the United States on board, this trip was typical of the day and place. No wonder then that as politician and president, Abraham Lincoln championed better ways than roads to move things across mid-Illinois, from river improvements and canals to rail lines. No wonder, too, that mid-Illinois would be the place where many of those better ways would be tested.

THE RIVER FLEET

It would be hard to overstate how important mid-Illinois's rivers were to the area's development. As vital corridors by which goods, people, and information moved through the region when any other way was inconvenient, the rivers attracted trade and settlement. A map of mid-Illinois farms in the early 1800s would show most farms crowded near the Illinois and Mississippi rivers. In 1850, the only counties where more than 22.5 persons were settled per square mile remained those adjacent to the state's navigable rivers.[1] Quincy and Peoria became the region's earliest and largest city, respectively, because of their positions on big rivers.

The boats used on the waterways in pre-statehood Illinois made up as varied a fleet as today's motor vehicles. The bark canoes of Native Americans were handy for traveling but not for hauling. The French traders' pirogues were dugout versions of the canoe; propelled by oars, they could be as long as fifty feet and carry thirty barrels of molasses (which in those days was worth carrying). Unlike a pirogue, which could be only as big as the tree it was carved from, bateaux were constructed of planks and could be made big enough to carry fifteen tons. They were the river workhorses until the square-ended American-style flatboats that Lincoln knew pushed them ashore.

Steamboats were not much more than flatboats with engines. They appeared on the Mississippi River as early as 1811 or 1812, shuttling to and from St. Louis and Galena and, later, Alton, there then being no place in the mid-Illinois stretch of the river worth stopping at. Smaller boats capable of travel on the shallower Illinois River appeared in the late 1820s. Steam power enabled convenient travel upstream and down at speeds faster than those possible on river craft that had to be pushed, poled, or towed. Commercial men thus saw prosperity riding in the noisy contraptions, but some old settlers saw them as harbingers of doom. When the first steamboat to make it to Pekin arrived one night in 1827 "with boilers hissing and paddles thumping," it caused consternation. "The noise caused Hugh Barr to chase after it—rifle in hand and dog at his heels," recalled one local history. "And Jacob Tharp called his family from their beds to prepare for the end of the world."[2]

Steam-powered packet boats became the delivery trucks of the Illinois. Beardstown recorded 450 steamboat arrivals and departures in 1836; within a generation Peoria counted well over a thousand. Such craft did cause the end of one world. Affordable access to faraway markets sped the demise of pioneer-style subsistence agriculture in mid-Illinois. Farmers in those parts of the region closest to the Illinois River quickly took up commercial corn and livestock farming, while subsistence farming persisted for years in landlocked places.

The region's interior towns dreamed of the day when minor streams in that part of the region such as the Kaskaskia, the Sangamon, and the Vermilion also might be made navigable. Such rivers had sufficed to carry French fur traders, but because these waterways were shallow, narrow, and cluttered with fallen trees, none was navigable by cargo-carrying flatboats except when water was high. The shops of the many potters in Ripley, for example, sat on the La Moine River, which is no one's idea of a commercial waterway; moving their wares to cities such as St. Louis had to wait the coming of spring and high water.[3]

Still, a road of muddy water is better than road of watery mud, and promoters insisted that if these minor inland streams were cleaned up and straightened out, prosperity would follow as inevitably as mosquitoes after spring. Springfieldians certainly believed that about their Sangamon. The river traverses half of mid-Illinois from near the Indiana border to the Illinois. Its flow is fitful, its bed twisting and littered with snags and shallows. The young Lincoln's experience helping to maneuver his flatboat down the Sangamon qualified him in the spring of 1832 to help pilot a steamboat, the *Talisman*, up the Sangamon to Springfield. The expedition was arranged by a Springfield entrepreneur who had built a mill on the river. If steamer service could be established, not only Springfield's but also New Salem's merchants (among whom Lincoln hoped to be) would become rich. The little boat made it to Springfield, but while the town celebrated its new future the river fell. It might have been easier to drag the *Talisman* back to the Illinois on a sled than it proved to sail it down the Sangamon, and no such boat ever tried it again.

If a conservative can be said to be a liberal who has been mugged, a Whig was a Jacksonian who had tried to ship a cargo down the Sangamon. More than half of Lincoln's first speech when he began his campaign to be a state legislator in 1832 was devoted to the need for government action to facilitate steamboat travel there. In office, he argued that if nature's rivers were not up to the job, perhaps a man-made river would be. The freshman lawmaker proposed to incorporate a company to build a thirty-mile canal that would bypass one hundred miles of the twisting Sangamon upriver from Beardstown. Alas, a survey estimated that it would cost four times more to build such a canal than backers had been able to raise, and the project was abandoned.

Two canals that did get built helped transform the mid-Illinois economy, but they did not run through mid-Illinois. The Erie Canal linked New York City to the Great Lakes via the St. Lawrence, and the Illinois and Michigan Canal linked the Great Lakes to the Mississippi River via Chicago and the Des Plaines and Illinois rivers. When the canals opened, in 1825 and 1848, respectively, goods could be moved cheaply and expeditiously over water between New Orleans and the populous East via mid-Illinois. The region's farmers suddenly could sell more grain at higher prices than ever before, and in return they could buy a wider range of goods at affordable prices. The towns along the Illinois River boomed for a time; the valley's population more than doubled in the years after the I & M Canal opened, reaching half a million people by 1850.

The boats later brought amusement as well as cargoes to the river towns. Carrying pleasure seekers on day trips to picnic grounds and river resorts was a second career for many aging passenger and cargo craft. The South Side Social Club of Pekin hired the *Columbia* for a Fourth of July outing in 1918. Nearly five hundred persons boarded that evening, bound for Al Fresco Park, a popular Peoria amusement ground. The evening ended badly; on its return, while the passengers danced to an orchestra, the boat hit a submerged stump and sank in shallow water. The stress on the structure caused the ballroom ceiling to collapse, crushing or trapping many people below water as it sank; at least eighty-seven people died. The accident marked the end not only of the *Columbia* but of the excursion business on the Illinois, although steamboats outfitted for dining and dancing, some from as far away as New Orleans, docked at Illinois River towns into the 1930s.

ROADS TO PROSPERITY

The first Euro-Americans to arrive in mid-Illinois found it already crisscrossed by roads of a sort. They were Indian trails, many of which had first been cut into the prairie by the hooves of migrating bison herds. One such trail was the main north-south path across mid-Illinois. It became known as the Edwards Trace after territorial governor Ninian Edwards led a small expeditionary force over it to Peoria in 1763 to suppress a Kickapoo rising. The trace went north from Fort Russell (near present-day Edwardsville) to the site of the future Springfield, thence through the Sangamo Country toward Elkhart Grove and Fort Clark at Peoria. Like all Indian trails, the Edwards Trace kept to the high, dry ground, skirting dense timber and all but one sizeable stream. It became the wagon route, soon littered with farms and communities, used by most early settlers to reach the Sangamo country.

In his interesting survey of the history of the Edwards Trace, archeologist Robert Mazrim noted that evidence of the presence of native peoples during certain periods of prehistory has been found mainly in the major river valleys, leaving anthropologists to infer that the ancients were a river-dwelling people. They were puzzled, therefore, by a few artifacts discovered on the uplands in the middle of what appeared to be nowhere. Their location made more sense to Mazrim when he noticed that several of the prehistoric sites are along the Edwards Trace. "It is almost as if the Edwards' Trail corridor was the equivalent of a river channel, passing across the upland prairies, with these sites situated on either shore," he wrote.[4]

Gurdon Hubbard in 1824 was named new superintendent of the American Fur Company's trading posts. The company loaded trade goods onto horses for the trek south along a trail Hubbard had marked from Chicago to Vincennes, Indiana, through Momence, Watseka, and Hoopeston to Danville. Hubbard's trail became famous as the Vincennes Trace and in the 1830s was chosen as the route of Chicago-Vincennes Road. (Mileposts of the old road can still be seen here and there, such as near Chrisman in Edgar County.) Hubbard himself set up trading posts every forty to fifty miles along its entire length; the steady traffic in pack animals and wagons wore grooves in the land that were still plainly seen sixty years later.[5]

The farmers that followed the region's Hubbards had to move cargoes too. Where boats could not go, farmers and merchants shipped their goods by freight wagons they called prairie schooners. It was, however, anything but smooth sailing. To send grain to market in St. Louis, farmers on both sides of the Illinois River had to get their product to the river first, across muddy tracks and sloughs and unbridged creeks. (In wet weather, resourceful Monmothians mounted flatboats on wheels so they could float their goods across swollen stream crossings rather than unload and reload a wagon.[6]) Such treks could be ruinously expensive. In the 1840s, it cost Springfield-area farmers as much to ship wheat by wagon to Alton as they made selling it there, so they had to pay to first mill it into flour, because flour fetched a higher price.[7]

For a time in the mid-1800s, the high-tech solution to the problem of muddy and rutted roads was the plank road "paved" with two-by-six-inch wood planks. In 1850 a Canton businessman persuaded area merchants to subscribe to a scheme to lay one of these wooden turnpikes from Liverpool to Canton; twelve miles of planks were laid, with the costs recouped by tolls charged teamsters. Downriver, in Rushville, pork packing was a big industry before the Civil War; getting the product to the nearest river landing for shipment (in this case the town of Frederick) was impossible much of the year, so investors there opted to build a plank road between those points too.

The plank roads didn't last as long as the planks they were built from. In 1855, a plank road carrying freight over the sandy ground between Beardstown and Bluff Springs was unwisely made of cottonwood; the tree grew abundantly in the area and thus was cheap, but cottonwood planks curled in the hot sun, making for a very rough ride.[8] Competition gave investors even bumpier rides. The commercial death of plank roads became certain when, for example, a free road that was built near the Canton-Liverpool road took away much trade and travel from Liverpool; the planks from the toll road eventually were taken up and sold to repay investors some of the $3,000 per mile it had cost to build.

Less bulky goods that had a higher value, such as mail and people, could affordably be shipped by stagecoach. The region's coach roads were well made only by the low standards of the day. One ran along an old Indian trail from Peoria Lake to Galesburg, crossing the Spoon River at Maquon; Earnest Elmo Calkins in *They Broke the Prairie* recalls that the route was so crooked that one passenger concluded that it must have been laid out "by two men, two horses, a plow, and a jug of whisky."[9]

Poor roads inhibited travel for all purposes and thus accounts indirectly for the large number of counties in Illinois. Warren County was carved from Peoria County, for example, after locals complained to the legislature that traveling the more than fifty miles to the county seat in Peoria required that both the Spoon and Kickapoo rivers be crossed, which often was impossible because of flooding. The state's solution, there and elsewhere, was to create a new county and thus a new county seat with fewer miles of bad road between it and the citizens.

Paving mid-Illinois's roads was like reforming its sinners—neither ever stayed reformed for long. In 1875 the state department of agriculture issued a cookbook of good road-making techniques. (That this department proffered advice on roads is a reminder that rural roads were still considered a farm problem, not a transportation problem.) The report's authors concluded sunnily that roads "have only to be properly drained, graded and compacted" to be fit for travel, "except, as it may be, for a short season in the early winter and spring."[10]

DREAMS OF FUTURE GROWTH

Drainage tiles, along with better plows and cheap fencing, made farming on the mid-Illinois prairies possible, but it was a fourth invention, the steel rail, that made it reliably profitable. Railroad trains promised to be immune to mud and ice, as virtually all tracks built in the region were perched atop mini-levees of dirt and stone. By carrying farm goods quickly and cheaply in all months of the year, the railroads would give farmers cheap access to distant markets and transform subsistence farming in mid-Illinois into commercial agriculture.

As a result of the Internal Improvements Act passed by state lawmakers in 1837, mid-Illinois was chosen to be the site of the first commercial railroads built in Illinois. (Governor Joseph Duncan of Jacksonville, remember, was a railroad man, and his influence helped prevail over the lawmakers who wanted to see state money spent on canals and riverboats.) This granddaddy of all pork barrel bills was to have financed not only a rail line from Warsaw, on the Mississippi, to Peoria but also the Northern Cross Railroad, which would run (the term proved optimistic) across what was then the northern part of settled Illinois from Danville to Quincy via Springfield.[11]

Such schemes were overhyped and underfunded. The Warsaw-Peoria line was never built, and the Northern Cross—ill-financed, ill-built, and ill-run—probably should not have been built so soon. Beginning in 1837, twelve miles of track for the Northern Cross were laid from the Illinois River port of Meredosia east to Morgan City; expansion was delayed by the Panic of 1837, and it was not until 1842 that the line reached from Springfield west to Jacksonville.[12] The line never made money, and the State of Illinois auctioned it off in 1847, making back a nickel for every two dollars it had spent on it. (After several changes of name and ownership the Northern Cross eventually spanned Illinois's mid-section and, rebuilt, became the core of the Wabash Railroad system.[13])

The top speed of the line's single locomotive—the Rogers, made in New Jersey—was a bit more than six miles an hour under a good head of steam. (It was built without a cowcatcher, perhaps because it lacked the power to push a cow off the tracks.) The train rode on thin iron rails that sometimes snapped and curled up to spear the undercarriages of passing cars. When the Rogers wore out in 1844, there was no money for a new locomotive, and cars had to be hauled by mules. But while railroading in the 1830s proved to be immature as a technology, its backers turned out to be correct in their estimations of its potential as the solution to the state's overland transportation needs.

When more advanced rails and engines transformed railroading, railroading transformed mid-Illinois. Not every railroad crossroads town thrived, but every town that thrived did so because it was a railroad crossroads. Many north-south lines crossed at what was known as Danville Junction, bringing commerce to that town. Bloomington escaped its destiny as what the 1939 Federal Writers Project Illinois guide called a "sleepy and static county seat" when two railroad lines, the Illinois Central and the Chicago and Mississippi (later and better known as the Chicago and Alton) crossed tracks in the town in 1854.[14] (The Indianapolis, Bloomington, and Western and the ancestor of the Norfolk Southern later crossed near the town as well.) By the end of the decade, that town of about sixteen hundred people had become one of eight thousand. Five railroads crossed Decatur in 1894. The town was a major switching point for the giant Wabash system, and the line employed some seven hundred local workers.[15] Decatur functioned as a system hub in much the way that O'Hare International Airport functions today; its passenger depot sold more tickets than any other on the system, including Chicago and St. Louis.

These early railroads did not just better serve existing freight and passenger traffic. They also helped create new traffic by bringing invigorating commerce to places that had wobbled on the weak legs of local trade. When boosters urged Warren County to donate $50,000 toward building the Chicago, Burlington, and Quincy line through that county's seat, opponents scoffed that the annual agricultural production of the county would not fill even one train and the stagecoaches that then served Monmouth were never more than half full. Adversaries failed to consider that the stagecoaches were half-empty not because Monmothians did not wish to travel but because they didn't wish to travel on stagecoaches. When the C B & Q finally came to Monmouth it set off an economic boom.

Having a rail link at first gave a town a useful advantage over its neighbors; once every town's commerce shifted to rails, not having a railroad link was a fatal disadvantage. To secure the blessings of connectedness, town promoters offered railroad companies free rights-of-way or depot sites, bought chunks of stock, and in some cases even promised to subsidize operating costs—a preview of the incentive wars fought by Illinois governments in the latter part of the twentieth century over new and relocating factories.[16] Bushnell was founded in 1854 as a stop on the old Northern Cross Railroad but never thrived; when the Rockford, Rock Island, and St. Louis Railroad announced plans in the 1860s to extend its line west past Beardstown into the old Military Tract, Bushnell's forward-looking citizens bid to have the new line laid there. Deciding that one railroad was not enough, in 1867 they also subscribed to stock in the Toledo, Peoria, and Warsaw railroad, then abuilding, to insure its tracks ran through the town too. An irrepressible booster put it this way in 1885: "As the sound of the locomotive's whistle could be heard in the distance . . . dreams of future growth and greatness pervaded the minds of all."[17] By then, alas, the region had more railroads than its railroads had business. Grow Bushnell did, however—to 2,316 people by 1880.

ITS Illiopolis. Steel rails on a dirt street, electric trolley met by a horse-drawn wagon—the twentieth century meets the nineteenth as the Illinois Traction System's eastbound car 221 makes a station stop at the Illiopolis depot in 1907. ITS PHOTO, DALE JENKINS COLLECTION.

In 1854 Schuyler County subscribed $75,000 toward the cost of building the Peoria and Hannibal Railroad, and in 1856 "did the hospitable act of welcoming all comers" and voted the same amount to support local construction of a new Rock Island and Alton line as well. As a result, taxpayers found themselves paying more in interest on railroad bonds than they did to run county government. Quincy likewise went calamitously into debt making bad bets on new rail lines.[18]

The costs of being bypassed by a rail line usually justified the risks. In 1858 the Peoria and Oquawka Railroad planned to run tracks through the Iroquois County town of Middleport, which balked at the customary tribute in the form of free land for a depot. Go-getting owners of land about a mile southeast of town were more cooperative, so the tracks were laid there, through the newly invented town of South Middleport. The upstart's name was changed in 1865 to Watseka, which eventually absorbed its laggard rival.[19]

Albert Britt, in *An America That Was,* tells Oquawka's sad tale. It began in the 1850s when promoters started talking about building a new line from Illinois across Iowa to Omaha and beyond. Locals believed Oquawka's selection to be inevitable, it being the only logical point for the line to cross the Mississippi going west, and local voters defeated a measure that would have allowed the county to subscribe to $50,000 worth of stock in the line. Alas, the company's owners bypassed the ungrateful Oquawkans and crossed the Mississippi at Burlington, twenty miles to the south. Robert P. Sutton in 1990 documented the subsequent collapse of the bypassed town, whose adult population declined from 88 percent of Henderson County residents in 1860 to only 40 percent ten years later. "Oquawka," concluded Sutton, "was, figuratively, the moon that never rose."[20]

At first, new rail lines expanded the existing commercial advantages of the region's river towns by providing a more efficient means to move river-borne goods to and from the hinterland. Railroad companies had quickly laid track from Chicago to the busy Mississippi port at Quincy, which by 1870 had passed Peoria to become the second-largest city in Illinois, with more than twenty-four thousand residents. But for rail companies to serve the booming West—the new West that is, the frontier having moved from Illinois to beyond the Mississippi—they needed to bridge the Big Muddy, which the Chicago, Burlington, and Quincy Railroad did at Quincy in 1868. "Quincy, as its new bridge demonstrated, was no longer the last point on the line, the city on the edge of the Mississippi," writes Thomas J. Brown. "It was becoming merely a point in the middle of the United States instead of the central national crossroads that its residents had envisioned."[21] By the mid-1870s, new bridges had the same effect on river termini such as Pekin, Beardstown, Meredosia, and Naples.

Peoria proved different. The Illinois River was reliably navigable by larger craft only as far upstream as the city, where sandbars blocked the way at low water. Peoria thus became a "break-in-bulk point" where the larger boats that worked the wider lower Illinois off-loaded cargoes onto smaller boats capable of navigating the treacherous upper Illinois. Because it was already a major steamboat entrepôt, Peoria became a rail center as well, extending its reach well beyond the river in all directions. For years Peoria was the fourth-largest regional hub in the U.S. rail system, and the cars of no fewer than fifteen railroads rumbled into and out of the city, many of them converging on a riverfront crowded with railroad bridges, depots, roundhouses, switching yards, and passenger stations. Thanks to the steel roads, Peoria's commercial focus was reoriented from north-south to east-west, to new markets in the new West.

Quincy's fate offers an instructive contrast. Quincy had always had close commercial ties to St. Louis, and to some extent Quincy rose as St. Louis rose. Unfortunately for Quincy, the growth of St. Louis itself was curtailed, its commercial hinterland being the farming South. Chicago's great commercial empire was the industrial Northeast, and as a Chicago outpost Peoria after

1870 overtook Quincy to become mid-Illinois's largest city and a nationally known manufacturer, while Quincy became known as a great old river town.

EVERY HAMLET A CINCINNATI

Many new rail lines were built before markets for them were proven, in the hope of creating those markets. Usually that plan worked, as in the case of Monmouth, but sometimes it did not. However ill expansion sometimes served investors, the furious competition among lines for business kept shipping rates to farmers gratifying low—too low in fact for all of the railroads to survive. Some lines went out of business, many more were bought up by stronger competitors who were thus free to set rates to please shareholders rather than customers.[22] After hailing the railroads as saviors, many a farmer thus began damning them as they were used to damning droughts or Democrats.

Rate fixing was the most common complaint. The main thrust of the state constitution adopted in 1848 had been to constrain the power of state government to intervene in the economy. The 1870 state constitution for the first time gave government a role in limiting the new power of monopolistic capital, indeed had been adopted in part to give government that power. Frustrated farmers pushed legislators to establish the Railroad and Warehouse Commission in 1871, a precursor to the Illinois Commerce Commission that was empowered to regulate rates and practices of railroads, warehouses, and grain elevators.[23]

A mid-Illinois man, Bloomington lawyer Ruben M. Benjamin—Harvard-trained and passed into the bar by Abraham Lincoln—was instrumental in providing the arguments that animated state policy in this area. The Chicago and Alton Railroad charged a higher rate to move lumber 110 miles from Chicago to the McLean County town of Lexington (a route on which it held a monopoly) than it did to move it 126 miles between Chicago and Bloomington (a route on which it faced competition). Benjamin in 1872 sued the C & A in a case that went to the U.S. Supreme Court. The high court issued a complicated ruling affirming states' right to regulate the rates of railroads and (by implication) other companies, which made it a ruling of national importance.[24]

Passing a law to regulate business practice was one thing; actually regulating business practice was quite another. The State of Illinois set up a rudimentary system to set fair rates for moving both passenger and freight, but the enforcement powers granted by the legislature were weak and the railroads simply ignored them. The companies routinely charged more for tickets than the maximum fare stipulated in the state law, so farmers boarding trains on their way to farm conventions sometimes offered to pay only the "legal fare." At Rantoul, conductors uncoupled an entire car of protestors and left them on a siding; McLean County farmers formed a club and rose en masse so they could repulse conductor's attempts to bully them.[25] Cases challenging such cavalier behavior inevitably were rejected by Illinois state court judges whose pockets, complained *Prairie Farmer* magazine, were "filled with free railroad passes."[26]

Rising rail rates stirred farmers to look anew at an old shipping method. Transporting bulky cargo like grain by river was cheaper than rail shipping, but only if it could be done on craft larger than flatboats. Unfortunately, nature left the Illinois River too shallow to accommodate deeper-draft barges along much of its length through mid-Illinois. Farmers and grain dealers pressed lawmakers in both Springfield and Washington to do what nature had not and turn the Illinois into a modern all-season commercial artery.

Before 1872 the Illinois River near Henry in Marshall County ("Best Town in Illinois by a Dam Site") was low enough to be forded. That year a dam was built to back up the Illinois's flow and create a deeper pool. That dam and its accompanying lock was at the time the largest such facility on the continent, and it made that stretch of the Illinois deep enough to carry smallish barges even in dry seasons. After this remodeling of the river, the cost of moving freight through mid-Illinois between Chicago and St. Louis and intermediate points dropped to only three-fifths what it cost to haul by rail, and the region's farmers and food processors thrived.

In response, railroads lowered their rates and invested in higher-quality handling facilities, thus winning back a lot of that trade. A steady fall in the number of barge tows set off another round of river improvements. Bigger barges meant lower shipping costs, and in the 1890s, the U.S. Army Corps of Engineers began to remodel the river to accommodate them. The Corps built two more locks and dams, at Versailles and Kampsville, so boats needing seven feet of water could move unimpeded from Chicago to Grafton. In the 1920s the State of Illinois would deepen yet again what had ceased to be merely a river and become the Illinois Waterway, with new and larger locks and dams replacing the old ones.[27]

"DEE-PO" DAYS

Moving people as well as goods, railroads transformed the region's social life as much as it its economic one. Six passenger trains a day rumbled through little Rushville, for example, making it possible to buy a ticket there to go anywhere in the United States. Perhaps more useful to Rushvillians was a new freedom to travel within the region. As would happen in the 1950s and 1960s with interstate highways, local residents were delighted to exploit for local travel a transport system built for interstate trade. The Illinois Central's network of branches functioned as a Central Illinois Railroad. The Sidney-Champaign branch of the Wabash for years shuttled passengers to and from the University of Illinois, pushing cars one way and pulling them on the return trip, as there was no turntable on which the locomotive might be turned around.[28] The Chicago, Burlington, and Quincy Railroad ran local passenger trains between Quincy and Keokuk; Buda and Rushville; Concord, Jacksonville, and Herrin; Davenport, Rock Island, and Sterling; Streator and Walnut; Galesburg and West Havana; Quincy and Burlington; the "Q" thus figured in the memories of uncounted holiday jaunts and visits to grandma. The B & O did not advertise it, but one of their branch lines stopped at fairyland. That, anyway, was how Madeline Babcock and her young friends recalled the shops and the bustling streets they encountered when they alighted from their train on visits from Rochester to downtown Springfield in 1900. Wrote Babcock, "I wouldn't have been surprised to see a window display of gauze wings, tiny glass slippers and wands tipped with dewdrops."[29]

Rail historian Cary Clive Burford notes that for most towns in Illinois the "dee-po" was as much a locus of community as the public square, Main Street, and the old bank corner. "The day's events were tuned to 'train time,'" he wrote in 1958. The arrival of the 4:38 on Sunday afternoons in Burford's home town of Farmer City, in Piatt County, was a gala event. "The area in front of the depot was filled with buggies, surreys and carriages, and there would be well over a hundred greeters in attendance."[30]

Trains crowded with people were no less likely to wreck than freights, and such wrecks were occasionally calamitous. At about one in the morning on August 10, 1887, not long after it had pulled out of the station at Chatsworth in Livingston County, a fifteen-car excursion train on the Toledo, Peoria, and Western carrying seven hundred passengers to Niagara Falls piled into the side of a creek after a bridge collapsed. "All the railway horrors in the history of this country were surpassed," wailed an early report by the *Chicago Times* correspondent on the scene.[31] Early fears that hundreds had died proved exaggerated, but the reality was bad enough—more than eighty died and at least 169 and possibly as many as 362 were injured, many grievously.

Chatsworth wreck. A postcard view by L. L. Booth shows the aftermath of the Great Chatsworth Train Wreck, when a Niagara-bound excursion train crashed into a Livingston County culvert at midnight, August 10, 1887, killing more than eighty travelers. COURTESY OF KNOX COLLEGE LIBRARY SPECIAL COLLECTIONS AND ARCHIVES.

THE TRACTION

Even the region's tangle of mainline branches did not serve all the transportation needs of its farms and small towns. Station stops were far apart, relatively few trains ran per day, and tickets were costly in the years after the Civil War. An alternative was a precursor to today's light rail transit, the streetcar-like electric trains known as interurbans. One firm offering such service, the Illinois Traction System, or ITS, became the largest interurban network in the Midwest. Known as "the Road of Good Service" to its marketers and simply as "the Traction" to many of its customers, this system was the creation of William B. McKinley, a Petersburg native turned Champaign banker and politician.

Beginning with a streetcar line in Danville in 1901, McKinley gradually extended his interurban network west across mid-Illinois toward its eventual terminus in St. Louis by acquiring and linking smaller local systems. Managed as a single system, these lines offered more frequent passenger service than did the main lines and served the many towns that the main lines bypassed.[32] (In its latter years, the line had forty-eight stations or stops on the thirty-seven-mile run between Bloomington and Peoria, most of them "flag" stops where passengers could flag down a passing train.[33]) As early as 1911, the ITS ran a daily schedule of 165 trains. In addition to passengers, the 644-mile rail network handled freight, including coal, gravel, and grain. The system was large enough that it had its own power company, Illinois Power and Light, to supply electricity to the lines, and it built its own bridge across the Mississippi at St. Louis, the handsome McKinley Bridge, which still stands.

Not many railroads can be plausibly described as a "friend and neighbor,"[34] but many thought of the ITS that way. People rode it to get to work, to take eggs to a neighbor, to go to church or shopping. Mark Van Doren and his brothers used to trundle back and forth visiting relatives in Hope, Urbana, and Potomac the way Chicago kids of that day took streetcars to the lake or the ballpark.[35]

The automobile and truck did to the local railroads of mid-Illinois what the railroads did to the steamboats and stagecoaches. As traffic began to shift to rubber wheels, the region's rail system shriveled until it consisted of only a handful of main lines and a few of the branch lines of the sort that once ran to every sizeable factory and mill. Typical was the fate of "the Dolly," which ran on the Q's tracks for more than eighty years between Burlington, Iowa, and Galesburg via Oquawka, Aledo, and Galva. Nicknamed for Dolly Varden, the then-popular American entertainer, the Dolly was at first a proper train, complete with separate mail, baggage, and express cars, a smoking car, and a ladies' car. As fewer people rode, it gradually shrank to a "doodlebug" consisting of a single self-propelled car separated into compartments for mail, baggage, and passengers.[36] The last run of the Dolly was made in 1952. The new "hard" or paved road connecting Urbana and Paxton ran essentially parallel to the tracks of the planned Urbana-to-Kankakee interurban line whose first leg opened in 1924. The interurban ended up being built only as far north as Paxton, the rest of the route being abandoned when riders began deserting the rail cars for private automobiles.[37]

One big advantage of the interurbans had been that they entered Main Street on local trolley tracks and thus could deliver passengers directly to each town's business and shopping center. (From the west, interurban cars came into Bloomington via Market Street, for example, looping through downtown and the warehouse district.) But when the region's Main Streets became increasingly crowded with cars beginning in the 1920s, the interurbans' lack of a dedicated right of way meant their cars got stuck in traffic, leaving conductors to get out and play traffic cop.[38] In the 1930s the ITS began relinquishing many of its city street trolleys and by the end of the decade had reorganized itself as the Illinois Terminal Railroad, which hauled mainly freight rather than people.

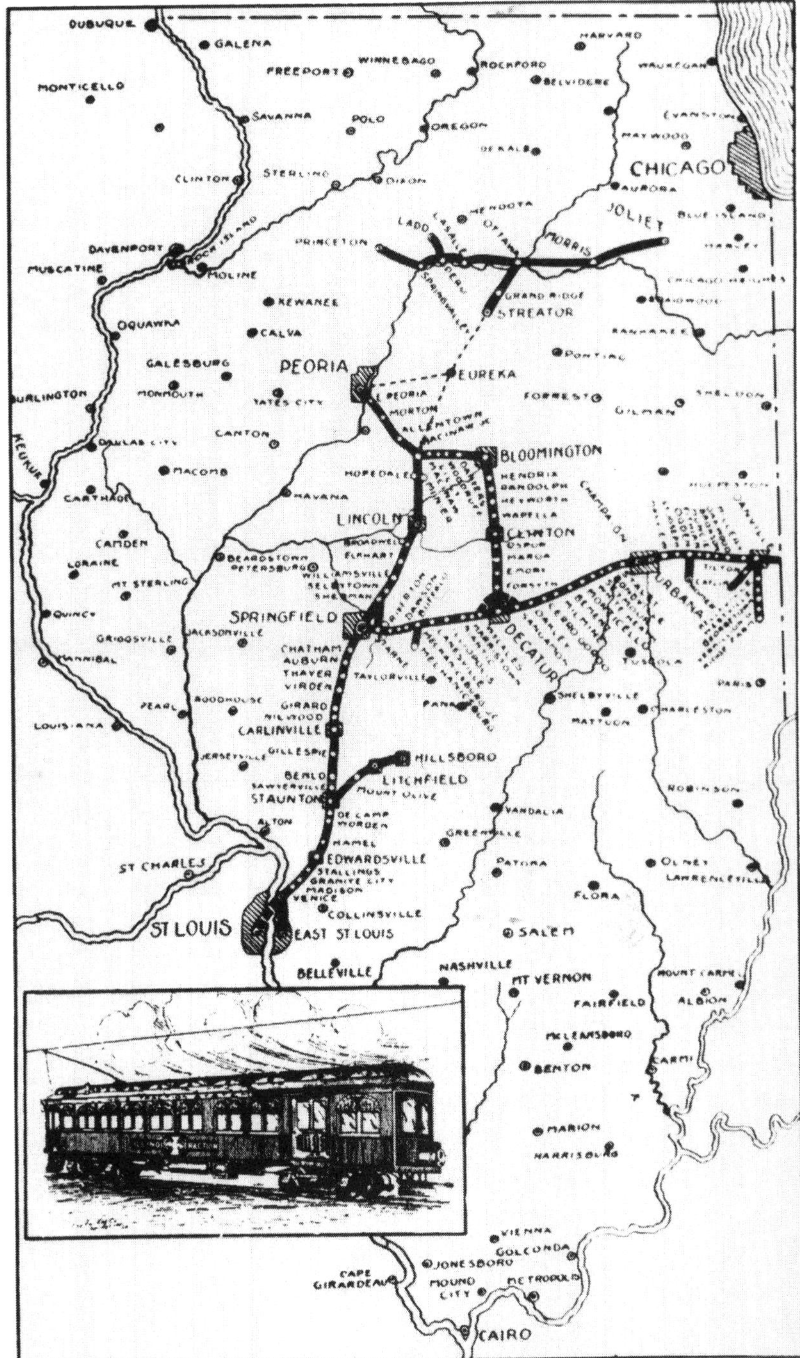

ITS map. "Travel is perfection" on the trains of the McKinley Illinois Traction System. The Road of Good Service served mid-Illinois until the 1950s. COURTESY OF THE MCLEAN COUNTY MUSEUM OF HISTORY.

GOOD ROADS TO THE MOTHER ROAD

While mid-Illinois was an early adopter of steam-powered train technology, the region lagged in providing for the gasoline-powered motor vehicle. Such contraptions needed reliable all-season roadways, which mid-Illinois governments proved reluctant to build. Roads were a local responsibility, to be built and repaired by townships. In most parts of mid-Illinois, the principal landowners (and thus taxpayers) in the townships were farmers, and they were no less eloquent than their brothers in other parts of the state in damning the state of the roads in one breath and cursing the cost of better ones in the next.

The paving of streets in the region's cities went more quickly. Politically potent commercial interests understood that paving meant profits, and towns' urban concentrations of taxable property could support higher spending. Streets paved with crushed rock or planks or wood blocks proved unable to stand up to traffic, so city engineers turned to dirt roads of a very advanced sort—pavements of clay that had been first fired into bricks. Building bricks were too soft, however; the only bricks capable of standing up to iron- and steel-covered wagon wheels were machine-made blocks of ground shale baked at high industrial temperatures.[39]

Laid down in 1877, the pavement of Bloomington's Center Street at the courthouse square was the first such in Illinois and a model for what came to be known as the "Bloomington System." Local brick maker Napoleon Bonaparte Heafer put sand atop a four-inch base of coal cinders, and on that base a layer of bricks laid flat, more sand atop that, and then a second layer of bricks set on edge. Brick streets became ubiquitous across the region, but they offer noisy, bone-rattling rides and are hard to repair. Rushville, Taylorville, Springfield, and Jacksonville are only a few of the mid-Illinois towns where brick streets survive, but nowhere do they remain in wide use. (Bloomington today has only three and a half miles of brick streets out of 320 miles of streets in the city.[40]) As survivors of a past era, the brick streets that are left are protected by ordinance in Champaign and Urbana; Bloomington adopted a brick street strategic plan to ensure their preservation.

In 1893 bricks were used to pave a highway near Monmouth, and they were still being used as late as 1932, when was built a stretch of Illinois Route 4 between Chatham and Auburn in Sangamon County that is listed in the National Register of Historic Places. But bricking proved much too expensive a way to pave highways. Out in the country, exceptionally good local roads existed only in a few places where exceptionally bad road conditions had spurred exceptional local efforts to fix them. Because of its boggy terrain, the old Grand Prairie

Road grading. Making roads in mid-Illinois was not much different from plowing a field until the 1920s. This tractor and road grader were made by Peoria's Avery Power Machinery Company. PEORIA HISTORICAL SOCIETY/BRADLEY UNIVERSITY LIBRARY. REPRODUCED WITH PERMISSION.

was the center of the downstate "good roads movement" in the latter part of the nineteenth century. The authors of the aforementioned 1875 state Department of Agriculture guide to road building offered as models the townships of Chabanse, Ashkum, and Douglas, which had learned to cope with being in what they described as "one of the worst natural localities for roads in the state."[41]

But even the best dirt road was still a dirt road. Through a series of acts beginning in 1913, the state legislature gradually took from township officials the job of financing, building, and maintaining "hard roads," which relieved farmers of their responsibilities and the General Assembly of its reputation for parsimony. Lobbying by the good roads coalition was persuasive enough that voters approved the sale of $60 million in bonds in 1918 to build a statewide system of properly engineered concrete highways. The appropriation proved inadequate to keep the concrete pouring, so Governor Len Small recommended a further $100 million bond issue in 1924. Damned as pork spending at the time, the bond issue nonetheless allowed Small to claim credit for having built, in just six years, what was for a time one of the finest road systems in the world, comprising some nine thousand miles of primary highways.

To ensure that the taxpayers' money was well spent, the State of Illinois in 1920 created its own outdoor lab to find the materials best suited to Illinois's pavement-unfriendly weather. Different materials were installed on a two-and-a-half-mile test road in western Sangamon County near Bates to see how they stood up to wear. A local man who worked on the road as a youth would recall that his neighbors thought that building a road and then driving trucks back and forth on it to wear it out "seemed to be the most foolish thing."[42]

The dispersal of industry into the countryside that began in the railroad era intensified in the highway era, since the wider reach of roads put more developable sites within reach. As for pleasure travel, heretofore a cross-country motor trip through the region had taken pioneer pluck, but that changed—eventually. In the summer of 1923, Quincy dentist Raymond J. Padberg took his wife and their two daughters on a ten-day motor trip. On their way home they drove happily on the new hard road west through Niantic, Illiopolis, and Buffalo only to learn that the pavers had stopped at Riverton. Mrs. Padberg's diary tells what happened next.

> We saw the mud stretching before us and knew we had seven miles to go. Ray put on the chains and we went into it.... About ten cars were mired but with the help of an accommodating farmer we were able to creep past them. We had chains so could go ahead and make ruts for his car to follow, his wife driving and he walking beside us and leaning against our car to keep it from slipping into the ditch....[43]

The sight of people pausing on their travels through mid-Illinois to photograph bits of abandoned paving might be thought merely to confirm the region's lack of scenery, but usually it just means that one is somewhere along Route 66. This federal highway, built between 1926 and 1938, was the fabled cross-country route whose stretch from Chicago to St. Louis took it through the heart of mid-Illinois. The highway's nicknames—the Mother Road, Main Street of America—suggest something of its nostalgic appeal to the generation that was the first to grow up on the open roads of America.

New ways of cross-country traveling inspired new ways of eating and sleeping. Dixie Truckers Home, which opened in McLean in the late 1920s, was one of the nation's first twenty-four-hour truck stops. Up the road in Bloomington, in 1934, there opened the first Steak 'n' Shake, a pioneer drive-in restaurant chain. At the Ariston Cafe in Litchfield, travelers could eat dinner served on white table linens, which was like pumping gas while wearing a tux.

The state of the art when it opened, the two-lane Route 66 was quickly rendered outmoded by the explosion of auto traffic. As early as the 1930s, planners were arguing for a four-lane superhighway to supersede what was already an overburdened stretch of the original road between Chicago and St. Louis. That more capacious Route 66 was eventually built, in stages. The Chicago-Joliet leg of this proto-interstate was the first to be upgraded; it was followed, in 1937, by a five-mile strip between Springfield and Sherman.

No part of Route 66 survives in Illinois as a highway, but parts of the original pavement are still in use as small-town main streets or interstate frontage roads. In McLean County, old Route 66 runs along the west side of I-55 for just over four miles between the Dixie truck stop and Funks Grove, rejoining I-55 after another four miles near the town of Shirley. Logan County is home to what may be the longest remaining segment of historic Route 66, which parallels I-55 on the west on its way through the communities of Atlanta, Lawndale, Lincoln, Broadwell, and Elkhart.

Route 66 draws the tourists, but the region's interstate highways now draw the traffic. (Five interstate highways crisscross mid-Illinois.) It is perhaps not a coincidence that the three mid-Illinois cities that have best weathered the deindustrialization of the region's economy that began in the 1970s are each at the intersection of east-west and north-south interstates—Champaign-Urbana (57, 72, and 74), Springfield (55 and 72), and Bloomington-Normal (55 and 74).

The new public highway system replaced the old private rail system for everyday transport. Private-sector intraregional passenger rail service is extinct; only long-haul freight traffic thrives, in the form of trains that are longer and heavier than anything the drivers of the Northern Cross's Rogers locomotive could have imagined. In most places streetcars have not rumbled and rattled down the streets since the 1930s. As for the interurban Illinois Traction System, ridership declines that began in the 1930s were interrupted, briefly, in the 1940s, when wartime rationing made driving difficult. The massive Sangamon Ordnance Plant, the ammunition factory that the War Department built on some twenty thousand acres of farmland outside Illiopolis, would have been unfeasible had not the interurban been available to ferry thousands of workers in and out of the site each day from Springfield, Decatur, and the towns in between. In the same way, Chanute Field near Rantoul kept the fare boxes of the Kankakee and Urbana Traction cars filled from the start of World War I until the end of its successor. Its hopes thus buoyed, the Illinois Terminal Railroad invested millions in new passenger equipment, but the end of the war in effect meant the end of the interurban era. The passenger part of the system shut down in 1956.

Here and there the ghosts of the region's old transportation infrastructure survive to tantalize memory, like Route 66's orphaned pavements. Being closed in the countryside are bridges that carried farm wagons over creeks but are now too narrow and rickety to support modern farm machinery. Typical is the bridge that since 1901 has carried Bolivia Road from near Lanesville in Sangamon County south across the Sangamon River to the hamlet of Bolivia in Christian County; one of only two bridges in Illinois using a Parker truss, a version of a design invented in 1844 by Thomas and Caleb Pratt, it is deemed officially Historic by Illinois and federal officials who decide such things. But the State of Illinois has little enough money to operate bridges as bridges, and none at all to save one as a memorial, so the Bolivia Road bridge would seem to be doomed, someday to be forgotten, like the era that built it.

CHAPTER ELEVEN

Growing Factories: Mid-Illinois's Industrial Heyday

Factories spring up on ground that has coal as subsoil.

—*Atlas Map of Peoria County, Illinois*, 1873

The native peoples of mid-Illinois were not its only inhabitants to leave behind earthen mounds that mystify later travelers. Two huge mounds, visible from old U.S. 51 (now I-39) north of Minonk in Woodford County, were too regular in form and too purple in color to be natural, but to the eye innocent of the region's history they appear too large to be manmade. They are anything but majestic mountains, but geology guide Raymond Wiggers once confessed that when he was in an impish mood he would describe them to tourists as remnants of the "Illinois Volcanic Field."[1]

These volcanoes did in fact come from deep in the earth. They were made of waste rock known as slag or gob ("garbage off bituminous") that decades ago was piled near the mouths of underground coal mines. Unsightly and useless they might be, but many older people cherish their local gob piles as reminders of times when the town had jobs and their young people stayed put. The Marshall County town of Wenona used to welcome visitors with signs that included an image of its gob pile with other icons of the Midwestern small town—the water tower, the grain elevator, and the church steeple.

To everyone else, gob piles are useful reminders of mid-Illinois's industrial past. For a century after the Civil War, coal made mid-Illinois as well suited to building factories as nature had suited it to growing corn. Situated close to new markets in the West and to old capital in the East, this part of the state had coal mines, it had railroads, it had inventors. Mid-Illinois firms were the first or the biggest or the best in a dozen industries, and for a time smokestacks rivaled grain silos for domination of the horizon.

SHIPPING CORN IN A BARREL

The biggest business enterprises in the pre–Civil War years processed surplus grain into products that could be more easily shipped and sold. One such product was meat. Pork and beef could be sold to hungry cities at a higher price than could the corn that went into making it. As noted, the mid-Illinois cattle industry exported a great deal of corn on the hoof, but the mid-Illinois traffic in hogs was lively too. Some twenty thousand hogs went to their doom in St. Louis by steamboat from Quincy in 1847 alone; a few years later annual hog shipments there had risen to seventy thousand animals.

As the young Lincoln learned while herding hogs onto a flatboat in 1831, they are easier to ship in barrels than on the hoof. Happily, every river town counted at least one merchant who would buy slaughtered or "dressed" hogs in the fall, pack them in salt, and store them in warehouses until spring made the rivers navigable, after which the goods would be shipped to St. Louis, New Orleans, or Cincinnati for sale.[2] (Slaughtering could be done only in winter, since the only refrigeration available to keep flesh fresh was that supplied by nature.) Hog shipping points in the region thus tended to become pork packing points as well. Rushville, Peoria, Pekin, Beardstown, and Meredosia, on the Illinois, and Oquawka and Quincy, on the Mississippi, drew business from miles around.

While packing and shipping customers' pork had been done in Canton since the 1830s, the first "pork house" did not open there until the 1850s. About a dozen firms entered the trade, and at its peak in mid-decade nearly thirty thousand hogs a year were processed in the Fulton County town.[3] The Chicago, Burlington, and Quincy Railroad came to Canton in 1862. Railroads enabled local farmers to ship live hogs to faraway cities such as Chicago, where bigger packing houses offered them better prices. By 1865 not a single hog was packed in Canton, a fate that eventually befell all the river packing towns in the region.

A hog's ability to convert raw corn into pork makes the animal something of a genius, but humans have performed their own miracles in transforming corn into shippable, sellable products. One doesn't usually think of refining corn the way one might refine petroleum, but a kernel of the stuff is a complex creation crammed with useful starches, proteins, and sugars from which clever machines could create a grocer's shelf of products. Corn refining began in the United States around the time of the Civil War, when a process to extract starch from corn was perfected, to the relief of the commercial laundry industry. In 1866 the industry's wizards learned how to extract first dextrose (a form of sugar) from the starch and then anhydrous sugar, in 1882; in 1889 millers learned how to recover the oil in the germ of the kernel. At the turn of the twentieth century, the Kidder Corn Milling Plant in Paris in Edgar County processed area corn into hominy, corn flour, brewers' supplies, and corn flakes. Here the practices of the frugal mid-Illinois farmer of that era were reimagined on the industrial scale, as the factory not only squeezed several finished products from raw corn but also burned the cobs to power the machinery and packed the husks into bales and sold them as stock food.

Corn processing firms, who by then also realized the potential value of fiber and protein even in the leftover bits they had been throwing out, perfected ways to convert these nutrients into valuable animal feeds. Allied Mills, Incorporated, catered to the appetites of hungry Westerners, specifically the region's cattle, hogs, and poultry. (Chickens everywhere have reason to be grateful to the firm, as it was in a Bartonville lab where scientists determined the vitamin D and manganese requirements needed to make healthier birds.) Its Wayne Feeds were so popular by 1920 that Allied built in Bartonville an eleven-story plant, the largest feed mill in the world at that time.

Mid-Illinois firms were among the nation's masters of this industrial alchemy. Set in the middle both of the world's most deliriously productive corn country and of a huge and hungry nation, Decatur was perfectly situated to become a national grain processor. Augustus Eugene Staley the man was earning a living selling food starch in Baltimore, but he realized there was more money in making the product and bought a factory in Decatur in 1906. A. E. Staley the company grew to be one of the largest processors of corn in the United States and the purveyor of such popular products as Staley Pancake and Waffle Syrup, Sta-Puf fabric softener, and Sta-Flo liquid starch.

Staley was unconventional, forward-looking, and paternalistic, the perfect industrial baron of his day. (Among the amenities he provided for his workers were opportunities for organized sport; the footballing Chicago Bears got their start in 1918 as the Decatur Staleys, a factory team.) The founder's biographer recalls how farm folk used to drive to Decatur in buggies and just sit and look at Staley's dazzling fourteen-story headquarters; built in 1930 of Indiana limestone and kept lit at night as a beacon, the "Castle in the Cornfields" was rivaled in scale in mid-Illinois only by the statehouse in Springfield and the occasional tornado funnel.[4]

Decatur's grain-processing factories made an impression, too. Most locals have always regarded the smell of cooking grain just as Houstonians regard the stinging pollution from that city's petrochemical plants, that is, as the sweet smell of prosperity. Writer David Foster Wallace grew up in Champaign County and recalled of his youthful visits to Decatur for tennis tournaments

Staley Works. The first commercially successful U.S. soybean-crushing company, the A. E. Staley Company is also the oldest soybean crusher in business today, and is still an acknowledged leader in the industry. Its Decatur works dominates downtown. COURTESY *DECATUR HERALD AND REVIEW*. REPRODUCED WITH PERMISSION.

that the air was "so awash in the stink of roasting corn that kids would play with bandannas tied over their mouths and noses."[5]

Decatur advertises itself to the world not as the Corn Capital of the World but as the Soybean Capital of the World, being to soybean crushing what Detroit was to auto assembly and Chicago to meatpacking. Local businesses bear such names as WSOY (an AM radio station) and Soy Capital Bank. When the A. E. Staley Company announced in 1922 that it would begin processing beans at its new Decatur plant, area farmers that year planted more than five times more acres in beans than they ever had done. And they kept planting. The opportunities in catering to Staley's appetite for beans were as much a factor as soils, climate, and terrain—and a stiff tariff against imported soy oil—in explaining farmers' rapid conversion of newly redundant feed crop acreage to soybean cultivation, and why a field of hay or oats is as rare in this part of mid-Illinois as a socialist at a Farm Bureau picnic.

Following Staley's lead, other firms opened soybean-processing plants. The first, though short-lived, plant to use the now-standard solvent extraction method was built in 1923 at Monticello by the Piatt County Cooperative Soy Bean Company (also known as the Monticello Grain Company). In the 1920s the American Milling Company of Peoria began crushing beans. Eugene D. Funk Sr., scion of the Funk Brothers Seed Company family, opened a plant in 1924 in Bloomington; a second Funk plant in Taylorville, sold to Allied Mills during the Depression, became an industry leader in production techniques.[6]

In most smaller mid-Illinois towns, industry for decades remained closely tied to the farmers who were both their customers and the source of many raw materials. Rushville in Schuyler County was typical of the industrializing rural town of the 1880s. A woolen mill and a knitting factory processed local fibers into higher-value goods that were sold to distant buyers.[7] Other local firms made farm necessities in the form of field tile and wagons, and processed farm products at two flour mills, a grain elevator, and a tannery. In Paris, the Merkle-Wiley Broom Company made brooms from sorghum grown in and around Edgar County, beginning in 1879. While it is uncertain whether the firm's factory at the corner of West End Avenue and Broom Street was the largest broom manufacturer in the world during the early part of the twentieth century, as locals claimed, there is no question it was the largest in Paris, producing thousands of brooms per day at its peak.[8]

Seemingly innumerable makers of farm implements added their clang and clatter to the factory districts of sizeable mid-Illinois towns. Many of them made machines to their owners' designs. Robert Culton developed what he

Allied Mills plant in Taylorville, 1956. After harvesting the beans from the field comes harvesting the oil from the beans, methods of which plant manager I. C. Bradley helped perfect. MERCURY STUDIO COLLECTION. COURTESY OF THE SANGAMON VALLEY COLLECTION, LINCOLN LIBRARY, SPRINGFIELD, ILLINOIS.

called the Diamond Plow (named for the shape of its plowshare, which is the business end of a plow) and began building them in a Canton shop in 1840. He was joined there by blacksmith William Parlin, a Massachusetts native who was said to have arrived in Fulton County with three hammers, a leather apron, and twenty-five cents in his pocket. A partnership ensued in 1846 that manufactured a number of clever machines to designs drawn up by Parlin—stalk cutters, disc plows, and double-plows, or listers. By 1852 the Parlin and Orendorff Company was an established firm whose factory hammered out more than one hundred different sizes and styles of plows plus cultivators, sulky plows, stalk cutters, harrows, and road scrapers.

Parlin's tinkering spirit was alive everywhere in mid-Illinois. In 1851 Galesburger George Brown assembled the first horse-drawn corn planter, with which two men and a team could plant an amazing sixteen to twenty acres of corn in a day. Robert Hanneman Avery was a Galesburger too. Born in 1840, he got his formal education in local schools and at the Knox Academy, but he got his mechanical education from his inventor granduncle and later at George Brown's corn planter manufactory. Captured and imprisoned during the Civil War, Avery used his time to invent an improved seed drill. After the war he went back to farming but spent his winters tinkering in a Galesburg machine shop on a new-fangled riding cultivator. When he went into the farm implement business himself, he made it big selling a new spiral corn stalk cutter and the Avery thresher before becoming rich selling steam tractors.

Working out of a small shop in Rochester, near Springfield, in 1851, brothers Archibald and Marshall Sattley made farm machinery well enough to expand to a plant in Taylorville in 1858 and then to a four-block complex in Springfield, where the company thrived until the 1950s after being bought up by national firms.[9] In a shed on a rented farm in Tazewell County, Peter Sommer invented and made woven steel wire fence for farm use.[10] A small factory was built in 1890 in Tremont, the nearest town, but the fence—"horse high, pig tight and bull strong"—proved so popular that larger quarters were needed. Sommer moved his works to Peoria in 1895, then to nearby Bartonville in 1901. By 1905 the company, Keystone Steel and Wire Company, had enough business to support its own wire mill, and by World War I it was making its own steel.

JUGTOWNS

The topsoils of mid-Illinois underlie its biggest industry in every sense, but the sticky subsoil clays that were a curse to the plow were a gift to the region's potters. Most of these artisans were farmers who made pottery on the side, converting into jugs and bowls known as redware the deposits of brick clay that happened to be on their land. Such objects were fairly crude but good enough to attract local buyers.

Once local clays necessary to produce the finer ceramics known as stoneware were discovered, potting began on a more commercial scale all over western and west-central Illinois. So extensive was the pottery business in Ripley in Brown County that it became known as Jug Town. On the Fourth of July 1859, a local potter set what was thought to be a world's record by single-handedly turning out 636 one-gallon jugs in eleven and a half hours. "Jug Town was alive with patriotism," recalled a local historian, "and not until a late hour of the night could anything like quiet be thought of."[11]

Illinois was soon second only to Ohio among U.S. states in pottery output, and much of the product came out of mid-Illinois. White Hall was dubbed by one local historian "the town clean dirt made famous."[12] August Pierce built the first shop there and turned its first jug in 1863. Other firms imitated him; A. D. Ruckel's White Hall Pottery Works in the 1890s was shipping three hundred railway cars full of pottery annually.[13]

The kitchen was not the only place where one might find mid-Illinois ceramics. For a time, field drain tile manufactories were probably more common in mid-Illinois than public libraries. In White Hall the first shop to make drain tile opened in 1865.[14] Big works opened at Harristown and Maroa in Macon County, and in the south Macon County town of Blue Mound alone, two plants turned out sixty-one miles of tiles per year. The 1887 McLean County business directory listed fifteen tile works outside Bloomington. Terra-cotta tiles were even used to make barns, which enjoyed a vogue in the early twentieth century, they being maintenance-free, dry, and rat-proof. (One survives on the grounds of the Prairieland Heritage Museum in South Jacksonville.)

While plants in Galesburg also made jugs and crocks (Carl Sandburg would recall his brief experience as a "ball pounder" in such a shop), that town's fame, in pottery terms, owed to paving bricks. Founded in 1890 on Galesburg's East Side, the Purington brick works by 1895 had become the world's largest manufacturer of paving and building bricks. To call Purington's paver a brick is to flatter all other bricks. Measuring four inches by four inches by eight inches, it was a bread loaf of vitrified clay. Purington bricks were used in such exotic locales as Bombay, Paris, and Chicago, and these days admirers share news of remnant Purington streets or alleys like birders alerting each other to a rare warbler.

Making ceramics was transformed during the latter half of the nineteenth century from a family-operated craft to a mechanized industry under corporate control. By the early part of the twentieth century, several of the larger, more productive factories in western mid-Illinois—Monmouth Pottery and Weir Pottery in Monmouth, Macomb Stoneware and Macomb Pottery in Macomb, and D. Culbertson Stoneware in White Hall—plus firms in nearby Iowa and Missouri were consolidated and did business as the Western Stoneware Company. This "Macomb model" characterized production in Illinois from about 1880 until the Great Depression, when many of the large firms succumbed to economic and consumer pressures and closed their doors. So did the smaller ones; by the 1930s no trace remained of the more than twenty-five potteries once operated in and around Ripley.[15]

Swimming against this grim tide was the Abingdon Sanitary Manufacturing Company, which made the Knox County town of Abingdon famous, in ceramic collecting circles at least. Founded in 1908, the firm in 1928 began making vitreous china plumbing fixtures, including the first colored one (an advance for civilization for which the firm has not received nearly the fame it deserves). To stay in business during the Depression, Abingdon in 1934 broadened its line to include artware made of the same vitreous china as its plumbing fixtures; these pieces nicely complemented the home decorating styles of the 1940s and ended up being sold nationwide in fine department stores. Between 1934 and 1950, over 6 million pieces were produced in a thousand designs and nearly 150 colors. Turning mid-Illinois dirt into corn was not nearly so neat a trick.

Another way to make money from mid-Illinois dirt. The Macomb Sewer Pipe Company was one of the many firms that converted the clays of the region's western counties into drain tile, sewer pipe, and household ceramic wares. JACOBSON NORTON COLLECTION, NEGATIVE 209. COURTESY OF WESTERN ILLINOIS UNIVERSITY LIBRARIES, ARCHIVES AND SPECIAL COLLECTIONS.

PANIC, PEE WEE, AND THE HOODOO OLD SHAFT

Were it not for the sixteenth president's fame, mid-Illinois might have become known as the Land of Coal rather than the Land of Lincoln. The repeated rising and sinking of the swampy primeval coastline that occupied this part of the future Illinois left behind some forty identifiable seams of coal that spread beneath whole counties. (The various seams were named by Illinois's state geology office for the place where each had been discovered, and many of those places were in mid-Illinois. The Colchester, or number 2, coal, being the second such seam as counted from the surface, was identified near that town; the number 5 coal was known as the Sangamon.) Burning the past in boilers powered Illinois's transition to a modern industrial economy and sustained a mining boom that made mid-Illinois for decades the major coal region of one of the nation's major coal-producing states.

Mining before the Civil War was limited to the harvesting of "crop coal" where erosion left seams exposed at the surface. (The Christian County town of Pana was originally known as the Stone Coal (as distinct from charcoal) Precinct because of an outcropping of coal along Coal Creek.) For years, official coal production from such "coal banks" was measured in bushels, not tons. "Coal miner" did not yet exist as an occupational specialty; most deposits were worked by the farmer whose land they happened to be on, or by small-time entrepreneurs backed by local capitalists. Harvesting surface deposits yielded only small amounts of coal, but then demand was small. Production in the whole of Sangamon County in 1840 was estimated to be only thirty-three hundred tons, but that was enough to supply the blacksmiths and small iron works that used it in forges and (beginning in the 1850s) the Springfield Gas Light Company, which used it as the raw material for the manufacture of illuminating gas.

Where thicker coal seams were exposed at the surface, miners tunneled into them horizontally rather than nibbling at their face. At one time twenty-five or thirty small mining operations dotted the miniature valley known as Argyle Hollow in McDonough County north of Colchester. Coal also was dug in Mercer County near Viola and in Stark County east of Toulon. The young Edward Scripps, the future newspaper magnate, helped his father dig from a vein of soft coal that ran along Willow Creek on the family's Schuyler County farm near Rushville, selling the surplus in town. Such operations were common.

As demand from coal users went up, the coal diggers went down, into crudely dug underground mines. Dozens of towns in the region recount tales like this one from Sangamon County: In 1858 well diggers at work on Springfield's east side bit into coal some two hundred feet down and passed through as many

Coal dog. Mine ponies, the usual beast of burden in nineteenth- and early twentieth-century coal mines in mid-Illinois, were too large for primitive "dog holes" dug into shallow seams. A state mine official in 1903 found that the mines in McDonough County employed thirty-one dogs like the mastiff shown here. FROM THE ILLINOIS DEPARTMENT OF MINES AND MINERALS *1903 ANNUAL COAL REPORT*. COURTESY OF THE ILLINOIS STATE LIBRARY.

as four more veins before hitting bedrock at eleven hundred feet. But no seam was judged thick enough to risk the construction of a full-scale mining facility. Coal prices picked up in the 1860s as steam engines began eating the stuff by the ton, and that made even thinnish seams of deep-lying coal commercially tempting, and a shaft to recover coal at 237 feet opened in 1867 south of town, the first of many in the area.

Every town of any ambition hoped to find cheap supplies of coal nearby. The discovery in 1889 of a seven-foot-thick seam that lay 540 feet below the Shelby County town of Moweaqua culminated a search paid for by what amounted to crowd funding in the form of donations from interested citizens ranging from one to one hundred dollars. The editors of the *Moweaqua Call* greeted the news by practically jumping up and down in print. "We Howl a Whoop!," they wrote. "Yea Verily! We Yip a Yawp! We'll Paint the Town Red!"[16]

By 1880 or so, mid-Illinois coal counties were among the state's production leaders, and they remained so for years. Either Macoupin or Sangamon county led in production thirteen of the years between 1886 and 1905. By 1893 twenty-one mines were being worked within Sangamon County's borders, producing 3 million tons of coal per year that was shipped by rail to (mostly) Chicago and St. Louis. The year 1893, in fact, marked the opening of a decade during which Sangamon County ranked as the most important coal county in the nation's most important coal state. In time, all but the central core of the capital city would be undercut by a maze of coal tunnels.

In 1910 Macoupin County had twenty-two mines employing nearly five thousand men; to this day Gillespie-area businesspeople fancy themselves the Coal Country Chamber of Commerce. The Peoria-area towns of Dunfermline, Bryant, Fiatt, St. David, Elmwood, and Farmington made their livings working such pits as the Panic, the Pee Wee, the Hoodoo Old Shaft, and the Big Creek. The poetry of those names has been largely forgotten already, but verse of another kind proved a more durable legacy: among the dead memorialized by poet Edgar Lee Masters in *Spoon River Anthology* was coal miner Gabriel Buissono, killed in a roof fall.

Deep mining posed dangers above ground too. The State of Illinois built a massive hospital for the insane in Bartonville in the 1890s, but it had to be abandoned because it sat atop abandoned mine diggings that rendered it unsafe. (One history of the hospital says it was torn down because it offered the wrong therapeutic environment; such an extravagant gesture on behalf of good medical practice is so out of character with state government as to not be credible.) In the 1940s, airport runways in that area developed dangerous cracks thanks to the Mohn Mine in Bartonville, which had operated since 1919; the Greater Peoria Airport Authority purchased the remaining mineral rights to the property and shut the mine down in 1952 to stop future undercutting.

Deep mining was inherently inefficient, in part because for every ton of coal removed, a ton had to be left in place to support the mine roof. Happily, several thick coal seams in parts of mid-Illinois bent near enough to the surface that they could be exposed by stripping away the thin soils, or overburden, that covered them. Such was the case in Vermilion County, which was why the first strip mining in Illinois is reckoned to have taken place there, at Grape Creek near Danville, in 1866.

Strip-mining is cheaper than deep mining and harvests all the coal at a site. Such work was done largely by hand until the 1870s, when a local mine owner named Kelly thought to use horse-drawn scrapers.[17] This idea proved to be only one of the important innovations in strip-mining technology to debut in mid-Illinois. Shovels adapted from machines built for earthmoving of all kinds were introduced and tested by strippers in and around Danville, like the steam-powered dredge that Consolidated Coal Company hired from an Indiana drainage contractor and beached without a hull on its land.[18] Fulton County, especially its eastern half, was another place whose rich coal deposits inspired some of the nation's earliest large-scale surface mining operations.

The first large crawler shovel for coal stripping was installed at Cuba in 1925 at the United Electric Coal Company mine.[19] Outside Canton, the forty feet of overburden at a pit belonging to Central States Collieries was worked by a steam shovel with a bucket forty-eight feet wide. The Fulton County poorhouse was shut down in 1953 after compelling poor people to work for welfare became temporarily out of vogue; the poorhouse was torn down by the United Electric Coal Company, which had bought it to get at the coal that lay under it, making Fulton County's one of the rare poorhouses to turn a profit.

"A WHOLE SHIPLOAD OF BELGIUMS"

The emergence of a coal industry in mid-Illinois broadened not only its economic foundation but also its demographics. Many of the more exotic surnames in the telephone books in the region's rural parts trace their origins to the coal era. As was noted in chapter 1, the mines were magnets for foreigners, and in the early years, able and willing immigrants were a godsend to owners like J. S. Morin, owner of the Kirkland mine northwest of Tilton in Vermilion County, who found he had to import "a whole shipload of Belgiums [*sic*]"[20] to operate his new mine.

The population of the Macoupin County mining town of Benld (an acronym based on the founder's name and pronounced "ben-*eld*") was largely Italian, but the town counted Russians, Croatians, Serbians, Bohemians, Ukrainians, Hungarians, Letts, Greeks, Lithuanians, Slovaks, Swedes, and Germans among its citizens. (Nearby Gillespie had a lot of Scots, which livened the soccer contests between the two towns.[21]) Most of the miners around Benld had left their families elsewhere. A town filled with unattached younger men is a ripe market for rowdier amusements. In its early days more than forty taverns operated in Benld to serve a population of only around five thousand people. The Benld Coliseum had the biggest dance floor (ten thousand square feet) between Chicago and St. Louis and featured the orchestras of Tommy Dorsey, Duke Ellington, Kay Kyser, Count Basie, and most of the other well-known big bands of the day.[22]

Mining with machines did not require the skill of the old ways, but it still demanded courage. While most mid-Illinois underground mines had solid roofs, thanks to geology, they presented miners with every other danger that comes underground, from explosions and poison gas to fire, flooding, and crushing coal cars. Most fatal mine accidents took only one or two lives at a time, but not always. In 1932 an explosion of gas at the Moweaqua Coal Company's mine killed every one of the fifty-four men in the mine at the time.

The Wilmington Coal Mining and Manufacturing Company's mine in the Grundy County coal hamlet of Diamond stood on marshy land that had no natural drainage. In 1883 the weight of that year's melting snow, ice, and heavy rains pushed water down through subsoils into the mine tunnels and flooded them. Seventy-four miners died; forty-six remain buried there.

Among the dead at the Diamond were boys. Boys as young as ten or eleven were employed everywhere underground. In 1872 the General Assembly banned boys fourteen or younger from jobs underground, but such work was by then a tradition in coal communities; a group of miners in McDonough County petitioned the legislature to modify the law, stating they were "unable to see any good reason why they should be prohibited from employing their sons at their business which did not apply as well to all other vocations in life."[23]

CAPITAL VERSUS LABOR, THE STATE VERSUS LABOR, LABOR VERSUS LABOR

The large number of mines in Illinois spread profits pretty thin in most years. Survival demanded that operators squeeze the most output possible from a mine or a field at the lowest cost. That meant using machines. Mechanization saved many a mine, but such innovations sowed the seeds for the eventual demise of the industry. The undercutting machine, for example, could do the work of six men, but to recover the costs of owning and using them, companies had to run such machines all the time. The resulting overproduction led to gluts.

The owners made less money when prices were low, but the miners often made none. Mine owners responded to price drops due to seasonal lags in demand or surges in supply by reducing payroll, either by laying off men or cutting wages or both. As a result of such stoppages, miners and their families often went without food for days, were usually behind with the rent, and were often in debt to local stores.[24] A Sangamon County miner in 1914 was paid from 57 cents to $1.27 a ton for coal, depending on the nature of the seam being worked. At these rates a miner working steadily could bring in some two thousand dollars in a year, but few miners did work steadily; many of Sangamon County's more than three thousand miners were idle more than a third of the year and so earned less than six hundred dollars annually.

In 1914 a research team from the Russell Sage Foundation undertook a study of industrial conditions in the capital city. Among other findings, the Sage team noted that irregularity of employment is greater among coal miners in Springfield than in any other important occupation group. "To the miner and his family the very irregular work . . . is a serious matter." Indeed. Layoffs meant the loss of more than a third of the breadwinner's working time. "A large proportion of the miners," the report concluded, "are, therefore, idle while rent and insurance bills pile up and groceries and meat are secured on credit. The effect, incidentally, of these frequent periods of idleness on the order and security of family life and on any hopeful plan for the future must necessarily be detrimental."[25]

The only weapon miners had against layoffs was the strike, such as happened at the mine in Minonk in 1894; the walkout led to riots over wages and working conditions that prompted the governor to call in troops to keep order. A company struck by miners in one pit could simply shift production to other mines whose miners were grateful for the work. That changed with the pioneering national coal contract that the United Mine Workers of America (UMWA) negotiated in 1898, which set pay and other standards for all mines. Partly for that reason, the contract was opposed even after its signing by some mining companies who believed they could not profit under its terms.

Two of the most committed of these antiunion companies had operations in Macoupin and Christian Counties—the Chicago-Virden Coal Company (then the largest single producer of coal in the state) in Virden and the Pana Coal Company in Pana. The mine owners locked out UMWA miners through the early months of 1898. In August both companies resolved to import 180 nonunion African American workers from Alabama. The Pana company managed to sneak the train carrying the strikebreakers and their families into Pana and to house them behind a stockade near the struck mines. The Chicago-Virden Company planned to do the same at their properties, and hired fifty men from Chicago and St. Louis—"guards" in company accounts, "professional gunfighters" or worse in miner lore—and armed them with rifles to protect the train carrying the scab workers.

News of the train's impending arrival in Virden spurred miners from Gillespie, Benld, Staunton, and particularly Mount Olive to head for Virden bearing weapons ranging from pitchforks to shotguns. (Some observers counted a thousand of them, others twice that many.) Governor John Tanner quickly sent the militia into the area with orders to prevent violence. It was not unusual for Illinois governors to send in troops in such situations. What was unusual in Virden was that Tanner did so to protect the workers' right to strike; his predecessors typically had used the public's resources to protect mine owners' property or the sanctity of contract. Tanner was a law-and-order Republican, but by the dawn of the twentieth century it was the capitalists who were seen as disorderly, and Tanner's decision to thwart the owners by ordering troops to prevent the strikebreakers from leaving the train won wide support.

A stalemate developed with the train stopped beside the company's "fort." Shots were fired that set off a furious ten-minute gun battle in which five guards, some thirty miners, and several strikebreakers were wounded and four guards and seven miners were killed. An outraged Tanner asserted that the miner had the same right to fight for his property, that property being his labor, as the mine owner did to protect his property, adding, "These mine owners have so far forgotten their duty to society as to bring about this blot upon the fair name of our state;" Fred W. Lukens, manager of the Chicago-Virden Coal Company, retorted, "The blood of every man shed here is on the governor's head."[26]

No one was ever convicted of crimes committed during the battle of Virden. As for the strikebreakers, when their train moved on to Springfield it was met by a crowd so hostile that authorities feared for the safety of the people aboard and held them there, virtual prisoners. Later the passengers were taken to St. Louis and abandoned. Other African American strikebreakers bound for other mines were intercepted across the region and forced off the trains. By the middle of November the Chicago-Virden Coal Company accepted defeat and reopened its mine under the jurisdiction of the UMWA.

Relations between capital and labor were not much more settled in the region's railroad towns. The Great Strike of 1877—the first national strike in the United States and the first major strike against the railroad industry—halted rail traffic at Bloomington, Peoria, Decatur, and other railroad junctions throughout the state; strikers in those towns were joined by miners; the Illinois state militia put down disturbances in Peoria, Galesburg, Decatur, and LaSalle, among other cities.[27] In 1894, Decatur railroad workers were among thousands throughout Illinois who walked out during the Pullman strike that year,[28] one of the seventeen times militia were called out to prevent or contain strike-related violence in mid-Illinois between August 1877 and November 1904.[29]

The owner of Illinois Traction's streetcar system in Bloomington and Normal, William B. McKinley, was resolutely antiunion. His company had broken a six-month strike by the twin cities' workers in 1904. In 1917 workers struck again after McKinley's local superintendent refused to collectively negotiate with a workforce frustrated over long workdays and low pay. The company hired thugs to prevent workers from vandalizing company property or intimidating their replacements. As was usually the case in that period, the company was backed by local courts, the press, and elected officials.

A public boycott of the Illinois Traction System was called by workers. The local union council brought to town "Mother" Mary Harris Jones—union organizer, child-labor protester, and general hell-raiser—to rally the faithful. According to one account, the only surviving words of her speech were "Go out and get

"The First Strike Vote," probably published in the *Washington (D.C.) Star* in 1943. On August 4, 1943, the workers in the Allis-Chalmers plant in Springfield voted to strike in spite of the recent passage of a wartime federal antistrike bill. The plant made artillery tractors, bulldozers, self-propelled guns, and troop carriers. Cartoonist Clifford K. Berryman clearly disapproved. COURTESY LIBRARY OF CONGRESS, CLIFFORD BERRYMAN COLLECTION, LC-USZ62–92950.

'em!," which the workers did. They roughed up a conductor and a company detective on a streetcar outside the union hall, chased down and kicked and stoned the car's motorman, then broke the windows of the railway's powerhouse and headquarters and ransacked a second streetcar. Six people were injured during the melee. The National Guard marched into town after the mayor called them; that action spurred workers in the Bloomington shops of the Chicago and Alton Railroad to march too. McKinley backed down and recognized the right of men to organize only in the face of a looming general strike, resulting in a first-ever contract with streetcar workers that called for a wage increase of about thirty-five cents a day and a reduction in the workday—a rare victory for workers.[30]

"AND THE MINERS WAGES WENT TO HELL"

When time came in 1932 to negotiate a new four-year contract for the Illinois coal industry, UMWA national president John L. Lewis insisted to his members that they would have to accept cost-cutting machinery in UMWA mines even at the cost of jobs; if they did not, owners would simply open new mines in other states without the union. The owners, who had already won wage reductions in the 1928 contract in Illinois from $7.50 to $6.10 a day, proposed a further reduction in the basic daily wage scale to five dollars a day, to which union negotiators agreed.

Five dollars a day, when few men worked more than a few days a month, was too much for the members, or rather too little, and they rejected the proposed contract by a vote of more than two to one. A second vote was held. All evidence suggested that the contract proposal was again roundly rejected, but before the votes could be counted, the ballots were stolen on the street in downtown Springfield. Lewis himself a few days later announced that the disappearance of the ballots constituted an emergency under union laws, and he ordered the miners back to work under the new terms.

The contract dispute convinced many mid-Illinois miners that not only the UMWA contract but also the union's leadership was illegitimate, a view expressed in this bit of doggerel about the UMWA leadership:

> John L. Lewis blew the whistle;
> John H. Walker rang the bell;
> Fox Hughes stole the ballots,
> And the miners wages went to hell.[31]

The more militant anti-Lewis members convened in September 1932 in Gillespie's old Colonial Theater and resolved to form a new union, which they called the Progressive Miners of America, or PMA. Within two months the upstart union had signed up seventeen thousand members. The PMA members fancied themselves strikers against an illegitimate contract, the UMWA saw them as turncoats; the PMA castigated the UMWA as a bunch of thugs and crooks, the UMWA railed against the PMA as communists and saboteurs. Besides the two factions of the old UMWA, the antagonists included security guards, the Peabody Coal Company, the railroad that hauled Peabody's coal, local police and sheriff's officers, and any locals such as publishers or merchants foolish enough to declare their allegiance. Labor writer Louis Adamic compared the contested coal field that straddled the Sangamon and Christian county line to Yugoslavia, and indeed the dispute must have seemed to many outsiders as indecipherable as a Balkan war.

The potential for trouble was everywhere. Everyone was armed—miners, National Guardsmen, state troopers, deputies, hired guards, local police. Violence was inevitable. Over the next couple of years the area saw sniping, car bombings, murders on deserted back roads. In a typical incident from 1933, seven hundred miners at the Peerless mine near the state fairgrounds in Springfield were routed by troops with tear gas and bayonets after ten UMWA members had been wounded. The state police at one point memorably described the situation around the capital as "quiet except for a few scattered bombings."[32]

At news of an outbreak of fighting, people from the towns around Springfield drove out to the scene in their buggies and Model Ts to watch, as Washingtonians had gathered to watch the first battle of Manassas outside the nation's capital. Residents in the coal towns were ordered by troops to stay off their porches lest they attract fire, and when negotiations conducted by Governor Henry Horner failed, he banned mass picketing and ordered the disarming not only of union members and "special deputies" (in fact, vigilantes) but also ordinary citizens in Christian County.

As the fighting dragged on into 1935, assaults on corporate property became more common. Railroads that hauled UMWA-dug coal were singled out for bombing attacks. In the two years between 1933 and 1935 there were eleven bombings and six attempted bombings of mines, trains, trestles, and tracks in the Springfield area in spite of armed sentries and floodlights installed to protect them. Hardest hit was the Chicago and Illinois Midland Railroad, which hauled coal dug from four Peabody mines in Christian County along the "Midland Track" between Taylorville and Auburn. The bombings eventually added up to more than two hundred, the dead around three dozen, the number of wounded unknown. Eventually forty-one PMA members were indicted on federal charges of conspiracy to disrupt interstate commerce and impede mail delivery by committing twenty-three bombings and six attempted bombings of railroad property between December 1932 and August 1935. The jury took only three hours to find thirty-six of the defendants guilty as charged, a verdict that in effect sentenced the PMA to death as a serious alternative to Lewis's UMWA.

The rival unions fought over not only the future of mine labor in mid-Illinois but also its past. The only union-owned cemetery in the nation lies in Macoupin County, within spitting distance of the Mount Olive town line on North Lake Street. For years it was anything but a place of rest. Among its headstones are those of the four Mount Olive miners killed at the Virden riot in 1898. They first had been buried in the town cemetery, where for the first half of the twentieth century miners gathered every year to commemorate the day they died. Several thousand came to these ceremonies most years, and once a reported thirty thousand people marched in parade out to the cemetery.[33]

The donor of the land used for the Mount Olive city cemetery objected to these demonstrations. The bodies could not be moved to the nearby Immanuel Lutheran Cemetery because the churchmen regarded the dead strikers as murderers. Adolph Germer, then a coal miner in Mount Olive and not yet a well-known socialist leader, suggested to members of the UMWA local that they purchase their own burial ground. The union bought one acre for this purpose in 1899, the Union Miners Cemetery was laid out, and the bodies of the four shunned men were reinterred there.

Mother Jones had asked that on her death she be buried near "her boys" in Mount Olive, which she was, in 1930. Leaders of the PMA wanted to build a memorial to Jones at her gravesite, but the cemetery was still owned by the UMWA, whose national president, John L. Lewis, she despised. PMA leaders had to challenge the UMWA in court for permission to build the memorial, which they won. (The Progressives eventually took over the cemetery, which in 1972 was added to the National Register of Historic Places.) It took years, but by 1936 enough money had been raised to buy a bronze and Minnesota pink granite memorial featuring a bas-relief of Mother Jones at its center. At the dedication on Miners Day in October 1936, fifty thousand people came to Mount Olive to march in a parade, hear tributes to Mother Jones, and cheer denunciations of John L. Lewis and his "fascist" UMWA. Thereafter, the annual gathering in Mount Olive became known as Mother Jones Day.

Had they realized the need for it, Mother Jones's boys might have added a monument to the region's coal industry. Much mid-Illinois coal had been sold to make illuminating gas, to power steam locomotives, and to heat homes, but by the time the Mother Jones monument was dedicated, those markets were already being lost to natural gas, electricity, and diesel oil. Sangamon County, once the leader among mid-Illinois coal counties, lost its position as leader among Illinois coal counties to new deep mines in southern Illinois during the 1920s; by 1930 Sangamon stood fourth in coal production, by 1940 it slipped to ninth, and by 1952, when the county's last coal mine closed, Sangamon was no longer a significant producer. For a time, busy mines in Montgomery County helped push Witt's population to five thousand; in 2010 Witt's population was nine hundred. (One of the big mine operators in Macoupin and Montgomery Counties, for example, was the Superior Coal Company, a subsidiary firm set up by the Chicago and Northwestern Railroad to supply its locomotives, which eventually stopped using coal.) Benld was incorporated as a coal-mining village in 1900 and as a coal-mining city in 1930, when the population exceeded three thousand, but eighty years later that Macoupin County town had only half that many residents.

RAIL CONNECTIONS

Railroads not only served industry; they also were an industry themselves. In Montgomery County, the economy of early Litchfield was based on the workshops that the Terre Haute and Alton Railroad opened to service and repair its equipment. The Chicago and Alton (C & A) opened its shops in Bloomington. "Shops" is an inadequate term for a factory complex that included a roundhouse, locomotive repair shop, foundry, paint shop, wheel and axle shop, powerhouse, offices, and rail yards. The first of George Pullman's famous sleeping cars rolled out of the Bloomington shops in 1857; that firm's first dining car, the Delmonico, followed a decade later. The C & A Shops was the city's largest employer for approximately fifty years. At its busiest, the more than forty-acre complex on the west side of town employed more than twenty-five hundred in a city with fewer than seventeen thousand residents.[34]

In Galesburg, the Chicago Burlington Quincy Railroad—the Q—built a switchyard that had 210 miles of track, which Galesburgers liked to think was more than at any other switchyard in the world.[35] Because it was a division point on the line where many trains ended their runs, many train employees made their homes in Galesburg; at one point Galesburg counted twenty-four hundred Q employees living in it, and for years the national headquarters of the Brotherhood of Railroad Trainmen was there.

For a generation after its founding in 1829, Decatur was indistinguishable from a hundred other mid-Illinois villages—until 1854, to be exact, when trains from a revivified Northern Cross Railroad first pulled into town. That line, which later became part of the Norfolk and Western system, was joined by the Illinois Central (IC) and Wabash railroads in 1854 and 1869, respectively. Decatur for a time was the main stop on the IC between Chicago and St. Louis; when the Wabash shops were moved to Decatur in 1884, the city became the hub of all that railroad's operations as well. The Wabash shops attracted skilled metal workers, and in time companies there that supplied parts for the railroads branched into the manufacture of other metal products, such as residential plumbing equipment, and they helped sustain a manufacturing boom in Decatur that lasted until the Great Depression.

All mid-Illinois cities shifted from making things for the region's farmers to making things for markets farther afield. In 1860, mid-Illinois produced more

Wabash Railroad's locomotive repair shop in Decatur in 1927. Crews could service more than one hundred engines a day using a crane capable of hoisting two hundred tons; the facility also built locomotives and freight cars. COURTESY *DECATUR HERALD AND REVIEW*. REPRODUCED WITH PERMISSION.

factory goods than did Chicago, and while Chicago pulled ahead by 1870,[36] that was because manufacturing in the Windy City exploded, not because manufacturing in mid-Illinois declined. Indeed, growth in the industrial sector fueled growth in size and wealth in virtually every city in the region. Quincy's factories turned out plows, stoves, organs, corn planters, and steam engines. In the mid-1870s, Quincy's E. M. Miller Carriage Company was producing fifteen hundred carriages per year, some fine enough to attract buyers abroad. (Locals never weary of telling tourists that Czar Alexander II was riding in an E. M. Miller carriage when he was killed by a bomb blast in 1881. Whether the carriage survived is unclear.)

Canton sat on the Burlington Northern Railroad's main line between Minneapolis and St. Louis, and the Toledo, Peoria, and Western offered direct connections with fourteen other railroads that allowed east-west cargoes to bypass crowded railroad terminals such as Chicago and St. Louis. That put Canton at the center of at least one world—cigar making. The town reigned for years, improbably, as the maker of more stogies than any other city in the Midwest. Buyers bought tobacco in Havana and had it shipped back to Fulton County, where it was rolled by hand into smokes that sold under many names, including Beam-Dean Little Havana, and Duke of Bouillon. Between eighteen and twenty factories operated in Canton in the 1890s, producing approximately twenty million cigars annually, mostly the popular five- and ten-cent varieties. All of Canton's cigar factories were out of business by the 1920s, however, undone by changes in smoking habits and by automation.

By the late 1940s, products as varied as bricks, candy, butter, textiles, hardware, paper boxes, and mining machinery were marked "Made in Danville." Much of the early University of Illinois was built with bricks from Danville's yards; this fact inspired Carl Sandburg to the ode "Danville Yes. . . ." in which is sung the praises of the city that sold enough bricks to make a wall three feet high around the circumference of the earth.

THE DOWNSTATE CHICAGO

Peoria epitomizes mid-Illinois's industrial golden age. In its early days the city was the northernmost commercial outpost of a Southern trading region centered in St. Louis and New Orleans. After the Erie Canal opened, Peoria became the westernmost outpost of an Eastern trading region centered in New York, and when the railroads were built (the first one rolled into town in 1855) Peoria became (with Chicago) an eastern terminus of a Western trading region.[37] Its position at this crucial rail nexus gave local manufacturers access to most of a continent, helped trigger a boom that began in the 1880s and lasted until the Great Depression, and made the city the center of a mini-megalopolis.

Local legend has it that in its prime, Peoria shipped no fewer than nine hundred separate products that bore the words "Made in Peoria"—from farm machines and barbed wire to nails, barrels, booze, and building equipment. Making things in Peoria made it one of the fifty largest cities in the country by the beginning of the twentieth century. Sociologist Daniel Elazar noted that in spite of the sniggers directed at it around the country as an uncitified city, Peoria acquired "a certain cosmopolitan tone unusual in cities of its size because of its far-flung industrial and commercial operations," at least compared with its companion cities in mid-Illinois.[38]

Englishman Graham Hutton, writing in the 1940s, observed that the Illinois River at Peoria is wider than the Danube at Budapest. That's the only way Peoria and Pekin of that day were likely to be thought superior to the old cities of Buda and Pest, but in every other way Peoria's natural advantages were admirable. As it grew, Peoria itself became an advantage. Its early industries created conditions in which others might also thrive. Thus Peoria became not only mid-Illinois's first city but also Illinois' second city, the downstate Chicago.

Peoria's liquor industry, for example, was a symphony of synergies. The city was blessed by convenient supplies of water—not the muddy Illinois River but clean ground water stored up in buried sands that fill that part of the Illinois

River valley. And it had Germans who knew how to make whiskey and beer. However, Peoria would never have become a whiskey town had it not also been a cattle town and a grain town. When the city's grain mills overbought raw materials, they could conveniently off-load that grain on local distillers. In turn, the leftovers from the distilling process, known in the trade as slop or feed mash, was a ready-made cattle feed. Peoria stills soon were producing enough of the stuff to keep twenty-eight thousand animals fat and, temporarily, happy. Indeed, the Peoria Union Stockyards, which became one of the largest stockyards in the country, was founded in 1874 not by a cattle man but by a distiller named Thomas Neill.

Animal pens sprawled over thirty to thirty-five acres of land at the foot of South Street. The yards once welcomed more than eleven thousand hogs in one day. (Few city people have seen that many hogs in one place, and most who did rued the day.) The yards attracted slaughterhouses; in the early twentieth century lambs in the tens of thousands were slaughtered in Peoria for markets in New York and New England.[39] The Peoria operation continued to do good business through the 1970s by buying and selling animals rather than killing and packing them, and managed to survive into the 1990s.

From the opening of the first brewery in 1843 until the industry hit its peak just after World War I, twenty-four breweries and seventy-three distilleries did business in Peoria. (The number varied because of mergers and takeovers.) During the height of the industry, no other place on earth produced so much bourbon and rye, and only three cities made more malt liquors.[40] Joseph Greenhut's Great Western Distillery for a time was known as the largest in the world. The title was later claimed by Hiram Walker and Sons, who purchased the facility in 1933 and there made Hiram Walker's Ten High Bourbon, which made Peoria a familiar name to tipplers who were thirstier than they were rich.

After building mansions for themselves along Peoria's High Street and Moss Avenue, Peoria's booze barons proceeded to try to make a mansion of Peoria. Their gifts paid for parks, churches, and schools such as Bradley University, endowed by the wife of early whiskey king Tobias Bradley.[41] Much of that wealth, however, was not entirely well earned. Visitors might have found it a grimy factory town, but to federal tax collectors Peoria looked like the goose that laid golden eggs; more money flowed from Peoria into the U.S. Treasury in the form of the federal excise tax on distilled spirits than from any other revenue district in the United States.

Free enterprise is, however, never more innovative than when its practitioners are devising ways to escape the effects of free enterprise. Sometime around 1870, certain of those federal tax collectors conspired with distillers

Clarke's Rye. Whiskey men of Maryland, Kentucky, and Pennsylvania bow to Miss Peoria. The flagship brand of the Clarke Brothers and Company distillery on Grove Street in Peoria was Clarke's Pure Rye, the popularity of which helped make plausible Clarke's boast that it was the "largest whiskey distillery in the world." Peoria did not specialize in premium whiskies, as this advertisement makes plain. COURTESY PEORIA HISTORICAL SOCIETY/BRADLEY UNIVERSITY LIBRARY. REPRODUCED WITH PERMISSION.

to leave off the books an agreed percentage of what they brewed; in return, the distiller kicked back to the agent roughly half the money the distillery thus saved in taxes. More than three hundred people (distillers and government employees) were eventually arrested for their involvement in what became known as the Whiskey Ring.

Thwarted in their attempts to cheat the government, the distillers sought next to cheat their customers. The Distillers and Cattle Feeders Trust (later the Distilling and Cattle Feeding Company) was a sort of OPEC of booze. The trust was organized in 1887 to limit U.S. production of whiskey so as to avoid price-ruining overproduction. It did so by offering stock in the trust to distillery owners (who often were bullied into accepting) in exchange for control of their companies, which (usually) were shut down. The companies that joined in the trust changed over time, but at no time were fewer than half of the member distillers based in Peoria. The "whiskey trust" was busted by Theodore Roosevelt at the turn of the century; its illegal manipulations of supply and demand added another item to the indictment of alcohol that led to Prohibition.

It is not whiskey and beer but bulldozers and other farming and earth-moving equipment that Peoria is known for today. The aforementioned Avery Company, the farm implement maker, eventually branched out to make steam-powered traction devices for use on farms. These miniature locomotives helped pull agriculture, and Avery, into a bright new future. Robert Hanneman Avery's firm operated out of Galesburg until 1882, but the need for better rail access to markets spurred it to set up shop in Peoria. Avery's biggest tractors came too late to do the original Illinois prairie farmers any good, but sod busting was still big business farther west, and there Averys were common sights. His machines could pull massive plows capable of breaking through roots as thick as a man's thumb; the *American Thresherman* marveled when an Avery at the 1906 Iowa State Fair pulled a ten-bottom plow across a field "where the ground was as hard as some men's conscience."[42]

In 1912 the Avery Company plant covered more than twenty-seven acres known as Averyville, on the riverfront south of today's McClugage Bridge. At its height, Avery called itself the largest tractor company in the world and employed twenty-six hundred men making products that sold in many U.S. farm states and a dozen countries. Calamity struck in 1924, however, when the firm went broke along with so many of its customers in the post–World War I farm depression, although smaller successor firms struggled along until World War II.[43]

While Peoria would remain downstate's Chicago, it never rivaled Illinois's Chicago. Management failures or bad luck kept local firms the little fish that bigger fish ate, as Hiram Walker and Sons had eaten the Great Western Distillery. The city became a prosperous branch operation for expanding firms owned elsewhere that made products invented elsewhere. Typical was Pabst Blue Ribbon beer. The brand was a Milwaukee invention, but Pabst in 1934 expanded production by opening a new brewery in Peoria Heights.

In 1935 a California maker of earth-moving equipment, R. G. LeTourneau, Incorporated, bucked a trend and looked east for its future. LeTourneau's "Tournapulls" could move twenty-seven tons of dirt at seventeen miles per

Peoria-made Avery undermounted steam traction engine breaking sod with a gang plow in Manitoba around 1910. Peoria sold many of the tools needed to build the postfrontier West. Avery's line offered farmers a power source for cutting brush and silage, plowing, seeding, shelling, sawing, hauling grain, grading roads, and moving houses. COURTESY MUSSER PUBLIC LIBRARY, OSCAR GROSSHEIM COLLECTION, MUSCATINE, IOWA.

hour. That made them perfect machines to anyone who has to build roads or airfields in a hurry, which the U.S. armed forces did during World War II. LeTourneau bought the recently shuttered Avery Company plant in 1941 and there produced thousands of Tournapull scrapers, bulldozers, rooters, and rollers for the military.

In 1910 the California-based Holt Manufacturing Company also bought a factory in Peoria, this one an empty farm implement and steam traction engine facility. Caterpillar Tractor Company had been formed in 1925 when Holt merged with another firm and relocated its headquarters to the East Peoria plant in 1930. Hauling artillery through mud was no challenge for machines designed to pull plows through fields, and World War I saw the company refocus on construction equipment. Its machines found eager buyers in this country and abroad as the global economy recovered from war.

Peoria no longer is Cat—the firm has plants around the world—but Cat for decades was Peoria. Musician Dan Fogelberg summed it up in the 1960s like this: "I mean in Peoria you either end up working at Caterpillar or at Hiram-Walker, you know? Or Pabst Blue Ribbon. That's all there is, you know? You're either chasing your beer with whisky or chasing your whisky with beer in Peoria. That's about it. And making tractors all day."[44] Fifty years later Pabst was closed, and Caterpillar's workforce—still larger than the other nine largest employers combined—was increasingly a headquarters operation that housed not metal bashers but designers, technicians, engineers, managers, and marketers. In Peoria's eight-thousand-acre riverfront, efforts were undertaken to convert hundreds of relic warehouses and industrial buildings into residential lofts, shops, offices, and pubs—a factory district for Peoria's new knowledge economy.

FERRIS WHEELS AND SELF-OILERS

Farming was not the only realm that excited the ingenuity of clever mid-Illinoisans. Jacksonville was home, briefly, to two of the nation's most famous men, as Stephen A. Douglas and William Jennings Bryan began their law practices there in 1834 and 1883, respectively. But in some circles Jacksonville is better known as the home of the Eli Bridge Company, the country's oldest maker of Ferris wheels. The wheels are portable versions of the ride devised by Galesburg's George W. G. Ferris for the Columbian Exposition in Chicago in 1893, and Eli unveiled its first version in 1900 in Jacksonville's Central Park. In recognition of the company's part in putting Jacksonville on the map businesswise, the town's chamber of commerce includes an Eli wheel in its logo.

Peoria has given the world two inventors of note. Frenchman Octave Chanute, one of aviation's many fathers, was born in 1832 and grew up in the United States. He lived in Peoria from 1856 until 1864, and wed there. A civil engineer by training, Chanute worked for the Chicago and Alton Railroad, among other of the region's lines; the Peoria and Oquawka Railroad hired him to design the first railroad bridge to cross the Illinois River at Peoria. Chanute began a new career in his sixties, experimenting with gliders. His wing design—essentially a bridge truss in the shape of an airfoil—became the standard for biplanes. Chanute Air Force Base, which operated outside the Champaign County town of Rantoul from 1917 to 1993, was named in his honor.

Charles Duryea, the inventor and automobile manufacturer, was born in 1861, near Canton. After his graduation in 1882 from the Gittings Seminary at La Harpe in Hancock County, he entered the bicycle trade, launching his own business at Peoria. By 1891 he had drawn up plans for a carriage propelled by a gasoline engine, which he built and tested in 1893 with his brother Frank in

Massachusetts, where the Duryea bicycle was manufactured—the first successful American automobile. Unfortunately for Peoria, his attempts, with various partners, to turn that city into a car-making center failed.

Springfield for decades was better known for builders than for bureaucrats. The Illinois Watch Company in 1878 marketed the first open-face pocket watch movement ever made in the United States; it later specialized in timepieces that met the exacting demands of the railroader, which made the company famous wherever trains ran in this country. Local machinist Albert Ide in 1884 took out the first of a dozen patents on his "Ideal" high-speed automatic high-speed self-oiling steam engine; the Ideal proved to be a perfect beast to do the heavy lifting in a day when electricity was produced with on-site generators at public buildings, streetcar lines, and large hotel and office buildings here and abroad. The John W. Hobbs Corporation, which manufactured automotive accessories in Springfield beginning in 1938, produced the first electronically wound clock for cars.

Electricity inspired invention of a different kind in the brain of Ludwig Gutmann, a German engineer based in Peoria who already had several patents for meters that could measure electricity usage. He was looking for a firm to make his newest one, an induction watt-hour meter, when he met Jacob Bunn Jr., a vice president of Springfield's Illinois Watch Company, who was looking for new ways to make money. With Bunn's money, Gutmann's prototype was refined into a usable product, and Bunn and colleagues set up the Sangamo Electric Company in 1899 to make and market it. The Sangamo plant kept the north end of town humming from 1899 to 1978.

Ira Weaver was an Iowa farm boy who learned his craft by tinkering with his neighbors' worn-out mowers, reapers, and seed drills. He came to Springfield as chief designer at Sattley Manufacturing Company. On his own time, Weaver developed a chuck for high-speed drills (on such small miracles of engineering do the fates of industrial nations swing) and opened a shop with his brother in 1910 to make it. Weaver Manufacturing became the country's largest manufacturer of all sorts of cunning machines for the automobile shop, from jacks to wheel aligners. Most of them were Weaver's own designs; he racked up a hundred patents in his name.

What is today the National Center for Agricultural Utilization Research near Peoria's Bradley University opened in the 1930s as the Northern Regional Research Center. One of four regional labs set up by the U.S. Department of Agriculture (USDA), the Northern Lab was charged, among other things, to find ways to expand markets for agricultural commodities by transforming them into new food and industrial products. The staff there played important parts in, among other achievements, developing soybeans from a plant that nourished soil to one that nourished people (including mid-Illinois farmers.)

Learning how to grow a very different kind of crop made the Peoria USDA lab famous. In 1943, as the invasion of Europe loomed, the U.S. military's stock of penicillin was woefully inadequate. Then-current methods of making the drug were inefficient and slow, and federal officials eager to boost production turned to the Peoria lab. Scientists there discovered that growing penicillium mold in a slurry-like by-product of the wet corn-milling process increased production tenfold, making commercial production possible. Having found a better medium, researchers went on to find a better bug. The lab's interest in new molds was well known locally, and in 1943 a keen-eyed shopper showed up with a moldy cantaloupe she found in a shop. On it was growing a strain of penicillium that produced fifty times more of the drug than any strain then known. Dr. Dorothy I. Fennell of the Peoria staff isolated this miracle mold and helped perfect ways to mass-produce it.[45]

The Peoria researchers were proof that by the 1940s the lonely inventor in his shed had himself been reinvented. Today's Ferrises and Ides and Chanutes and Browns and Gutmanns and Weavers are likely to be salaried professionals working in company labs. Since the latter 1800s, industrial innovation has been increasingly institutionalized in the laboratories of large industrial firms. At Caterpillar's massive research and engineering campus in Mossville near Peoria, modern tinkerers are perfecting heavy earth-moving machines that drive themselves around a field and emit no pollution. Such astonishing machines resemble George Brown's horse-drawn corn planter about as much as a butterfly resembles a garden slug, but they have the same ancestors.

THE CAPITALIST NEXT DOOR

A successful business is itself a machine of sorts, and the region produced clever inventors of all types of firms. New Jerseyan Jacob Bunn came to Illinois in 1836 and explored opportunities in Springfield, Beardstown, and Naples before settling for good in the new capital in 1840. He and his younger brother John W. singly or together founded, invested in, or ran firms that mined coal, manufactured shoes, made watches and (as noted) electricity meters, ran streetcars, published newspapers, and produced electricity and gas for lighting. James Millikin arrived in mid-Illinois from Pennsylvania in 1850. He settled for good in Decatur in 1856, where the arrival of the railroad two years before had opened up tempting commercial possibilities. Millikin made money grazing beef cattle on rented land, the profit from which he used to buy up government land, and later used the capital thus acquired to enter banking. His bank for a time was the largest such institution in Illinois outside Chicago. Over fifty years Millikin money was behind imposing downtown buildings, an iron works, and a coal mine, and he founded the college (now university) that bears his name.

The firms such men invested in tended to be locally owned and managed. They would dominate their hometowns' finance and retailing sectors until the second half of the twentieth century. By then, most big mid-Illinois firms suffered from ills common to those in all mature industrial states of the eastern third of the United States. They were lumbered with older workforces, sclerotic management, and creaky infrastructure. The region suffered too from geographic factors unique to it; its location in the middle of the middle of the country, which left it extremely well situated to exploit markets in a national economy, put it at a disadvantage in an increasingly international one.

In 1919 the Canton works of Parlin and Orendorff became a part of the International Harvester Company in the same way that a frog becomes part of a garter snake. From the late 1930s the International Harvester plant at East Elm Street and 2nd Avenue—heir to the old Parlin and Orendorff works—employed as many as two thousand people making more than fourteen hundred types of plows, harrows, discs, and other tools of the husbandman's trade. But in the 1970s workers' wage demands precipitated a 170-day walkout that set a record as the longest-running strike in United Auto Workers history. International Harvester ended up closing the troubled plant in 1983. (The empty nineteen-acre facility was destroyed fourteen years later by a fire thought to be the result of arson; the complex was so large that it took four days for it to burn.) By the late 1990s, Canton listed not one manufacturer among its big employers.

What happened in Canton happened across the region. Peoria's big distilleries and brewers were all gone by the 1980s; the Pabst brewery in Peoria Heights closed at a cost of one thousand jobs in 1982, the same year that the maker of fuel ethanol, which had purchased the Hiram Walker distillery, closed that iconic riverfront plant. Of the Peoria area's top fifteen employers in 2012, only two were manufacturers. The Eureka vacuum cleaner plant in Bloomington, the Borg-Warner and Maytag plants in Galesburg, the Sangamo Electric, Allis-Chalmers, Pillsbury, and Hobbs plants in Springfield—all closed. The still-viable firms were bought out by foreign competitors; Decatur's A. E Staley, the century-old Bloomington candy maker now known as Kathryn Beich, Incorporated, and Bloomington's pioneer hybridizer Funk Brothers Seed Company were taken over by British or Swiss firms.

Apart from a rudimentary hospitality trade and a thriving business in lawsuits involving contract disputes and roving hogs, the service economy during

Lincoln's day hardly existed. Yet in the space of a single lifetime, beginning roughly slowly after the Civil War and accelerating through the twentieth century, services (chiefly government services, insurance, public higher education, and medical care) became the way most mid-Illinoisans made their livings.

Nine of the ten largest employers in Bloomington-Normal, for example, are in service industries. What heavy equipment is to Peoria, insurance is to Bloomington-Normal. Founded in 1925 to provide insurance to farmers, the twin cities' Country Companies is Illinois's third-largest auto and home insurer, with some two thousand employees at its Bloomington headquarters in 2014. State Farm was founded in 1922 by tractor salesman and farmer George Mecherle, who believed that insurance companies cheated farmers on auto insurance by basing rates on the high incidence of accidents racked up by city drivers. Mecherle suggested county Farm Bureau staff become authorized agents and sell State Farm insurance on a commission basis. Mecherle got the customers he needed, and the state Farm Bureaus got the cash they needed to keep their organizations viable.[46] Today State Farm employs more than ten times the workforce that its host cities' largest manufacturing firm does, which is why visitors must be forgiven for not realizing (as one local columnist put it) that when locals use the phrase "the Farm" they are probably talking claims instead of cows.

Epilogue

By 1950 or so, mid-Illinois was a settled place in every sense. The prairie was long plowed, the land drained, and the roads built. The region had survived, with only a few scars, a series of wrenching transformations as it moved from Indian country to Euro-American frontier to industrial heartland to colonial outpost of a global service economy. Mad social experiments such as Prohibition had been tried and abandoned, as had, apparently, the very idea of social experiments. After the Civil War, the Democratic and Republican parties had seen off all challengers to their proprietorship of the apparatus of government, and instead of arguing about how to build a modern state government, politicians in Springfield after 1950 increasingly squabbled over how to pay for one. The small town died in the countryside but was reborn on the fringe of cities, where social life remained comfortably familiar in its essence, however much it changed its focus; small-town sports rallies, with their bonfires and pep rallies and parades, recall the nineteenth-century political campaigns that in many ways satisfied the same social needs.

The arrival and assimilation of a succession of new peoples had briefly disordered politics and social life in their turn, but reordered it always became. After the labor union wars of the 1930s, no serious outbreak of communal violence occurred anywhere in mid-Illinois for eighty years. Social conflicts that once were settled in the street were now resolved by Congress and the General Assembly via elaborate legal procedures to decide civil rights disputes. Debates over worship and the proper relation of secular and sacred tended to be conducted in the courts, if never quite settled there. And the exploitative impulse of capital has been chastened by government regulation.

The result was a mid-Illinois that by many measures was dull, complacent, cautious, and bland. Things continued to change, of course, but instead of being different they were mostly just new. Mid-Illinois's farms produce more of this and less of that than they used to, but flatboats loaded with the products of that good land still float down the Illinois River seeking better prices, even if those flatboats are now grain barges, each of which carries thousands of tons of grain heading to Japan. The farm machines kept getting bigger and more sophisticated, enabling one farmer to manage and cultivate ever more land; the rural population in consequence keeps getting smaller, but those trends began around the Civil War and by now are as accepted as spring rains and occasional droughts—it's just the way things are. Nobody much cuts down trees for firewood anymore and the land no longer gives up much coal, but farm fields are still mined for energy, in the form of fuel ethanol made from corn rather than hay and oats. And the rail corridors that ushered in a new era of economic development by opening the region to interpersonal communication are doing the same thing again as fiber optic cables are buried in the old interurban rights-of-way.

As for the economy, the gradual shift in the region's economic base from manufacturing and food processing to services is merely the newest in a long line of such transformations. In two hundred years, the region abandoned subsistence farming for commercial agriculture, artisans' shops gave way to mechanized production in ever-larger factories, markets that were local became regional, national, then global, and a resource base that first counted only plants, soils, and coals now includes information. This is not history repeating itself so much as it is asserting itself in new guises.

Some things have changed, however, and they are important. For at least a century after 1830, mid-Illinois's position in the middle of everywhere left it well situated to exploit old markets to the east and new markets to the west, and to receive invigorating flows of people from all directions. These days, being in the middle of the continent puts the region well away from today's new opportunities, which lie on the nation's coasts if not beyond the nation's ocean shores. Even within Illinois, the region can seem a backwater. In 1870, Quincy was the second-largest city in Illinois, with more than twenty-four thousand residents. The Gem City continued to grow, its population not peaking until 1970, but like every other city in the region it had grown much less vigorously than Chicago and its satellite cities and suburbs. In 2010, Quincy was only the forty-first most populous Illinois city, smaller than twenty-eight cities and towns in the Chicago metropolitan area.

Quincy fell unusually far from eminence, but it was not unique in falling. Peoria was the third-most-populous city in the state as late as 1960; in 2010 it was the seventh. Bloomington-Normal, Champaign-Urbana, and Springfield were doing better, but even Springfield slipped from fourth to sixth in population rank in that period, in spite of having grown by more than half in those fifty years. The geographic center of Illinois remains in mid-Illinois (in the Logan County village of Chestnut), but the economic, social, and political centers of Illinois these days have shifted well to the northeast.

Some of mid-Illinois's immigrants came to escape their pasts, the Irish being driven to Illinois by hunger and religious persecution, the Germans by political repression, southern and eastern Europeans and Southern African Americans by poverty. Most of the rest, going back to the Kickapoo, wanted to improve the life they had, or might have had back home, if home had more freedom or more land or better land or fewer people or, in some cases, fewer sheriffs. In all cases, it was the future in which these transformations would occur, and it was the future that for more than a century preoccupied the region at the personal and political level after mid-Illinois began to develop in earnest.

Today it is the past that beckons. After more than three hundred years, Euro-American history has a history in mid-Illinois. In many towns, the past—that is, the local consciousness of its past—began when the first generation of residents began to die as the 1800s waned. Every town's history then still resided largely in the memories of the "old settlers," as they usually were known. (A wonderful photograph taken at the Old Settlers picnic in Decatur's Fairview Park in 1937 shows us five of these heroes, aged ninety-one to ninety-six; their erect postures and stern visages make them look every bit the kind of people who could make a city out of nothing.[1]) Old settlers societies were formed to provide a venue for the sharing of those memories, which eventually were recorded, often in the form of the subscription histories or "mug books" that were popular around the dawn of the twentieth century.

Local history in such works often took the form of stories, anecdotes, and fables. Their sometimes suspect accuracy mattered little. The point of collecting them was to celebrate the town or county and the people who made it—and, not coincidentally, to affirm the status that this class had on local society in an era in which newcomers were asserting their own claims. More recent centennial and sesquicentennial celebrations of nation, state, and town had much the same purpose, often taking the form of a kind of retrospective boosterism, in which the booster extols what a great place the town used to be.

Civic affirmation took different forms during the Great Depression. In those dark days, celebrating the heroes who made the town was thought to be one way to inoculate the young against the foreign *isms* of the moment by instilling in them local pride, if not in what their ancestors had done then in the country that made it possible for them to do it. Instruction rather than inoculation is the aim of more recent projects to convey the past to new generations. Nauvoo and Bishop Hill, for example, maintain what amounts to antiques collections on the civic scale, the motive being religious affirmation in the first case and ethnic affirmation in the second.

Today's mid-Illinoisans find themselves tourists in the foreign land of the past. The mid-nineteenth-century farm is as exotic to mid-Illinois fourth-graders as an Indian village or a French trading post. Several "history farms" and agricultural museums in the region cater to their curiosity. Time has also rendered romantic many structures built in the 1800s. When Progress threatened them, several mid-Illinois towns moved the buildings out of harm's way onto parklike grounds to create a "history village." These zoos of rare and exotic historical creatures are sometimes managed by the local historical society, sometimes by new groups usually organized to rescue endangered period buildings. It was an 1847 log cabin, for example, that inspired the formation of the Pana Pioneer Heritage Guild in 1981, which went on to create the Stone Coal Log Cabin Village on the Pana Tri-County Fairgrounds where four log buildings from the early Illinois era are displayed. The Christian County Historical Society Museum features an 1820 log house, the 1839 Christian County courthouse (where Lincoln argued cases), the one-room Buckeye Schoolhouse from 1856, and the Old Owaneco Depot. At the Macon County Historical Society Museum one can see the courthouse where Abraham Lincoln practiced in the 1830s, a log house, a one-room school, a circa-1880 railroad depot, a smithy, and a print shop. Some visitors doubtless leave such places having learned only that nineteenth-century mid-Illinois was surprisingly like a theme park, but to the people who have done so much to create and maintain such sites, these relics are icons of local identity.

As such ersatz villages go, the rebuilt New Salem is special. Publishing magnate William Randolph Hearst had an abiding personal interest in Lincoln. He bought the New Salem site in 1906, then conveyed it in trust to the Old Salem Chautauqua Association, which in turn conveyed it to the State of Illinois in 1919 with the intention of seeing it reconstructed as a memorial to Lincoln's early years in Illinois. How much the reconstruction looks like the village Lincoln knew is difficult to say. The research that guided the reconstruction of the town and its buildings by the Civilian Conservation Corps in the 1930s was fastidious by the standards of the day, but the only indisputably authentic elements of the new New Salem were a few pieces of original furniture donated by descendants of Lincoln's old neighbors, and the shell of the Onstot cooper shop.

While it would be very hard to re-create old New Salem as an environment, it would be even harder to re-create it as an experience. The twenty-first-century tourist tends to see the hearth as a fireplace, not a cookstove, and the oxcart as a theme park ride, not a truck. The modern version of the village is lacking the dirt, the pestilential insects, the stink of smoke and dung that must have permeated the original. Even with more faithful attention to such detail, the visitors would still be mere spectators. The village would be a more accurate sort of museum diorama but still a diorama.

The same dilemmas confront managers of the Lincolns' house in Springfield. It and the late president's tomb in Springfield's Oak Ridge Cemetery are the two most significant historic sites not only in mid-Illinois but also in the nation. The house sits on a partially restored nineteenth-century residential block that is the centerpiece of the four-block Lincoln Home National Historic Site, administered by the National Park Service, which took over the house and site in the 1970s. The changes since were fairly summed up by travel writer Jan Morris as "sanitized for the tourists by the guardian nannies of the national Park Service."[2] Certainly there was much about 1850s Springfield that a responsible agency would not want to re-create, such as slippery and uneven wooden sidewalks, but for visitors to experience the street as the Lincolns did, they would need at least to smell the sting of coal smoke in the air and the stink of hogs in the streets and see a few unpainted fences, some unmowed lawns, and clothes hanging on wash lines.

MASCOTS

As well as being a source of information and local pride, mid-Illinois history also is a source of borrowed identities. The term "Illini" as applied to the students and athletes of the University of Illinois's Urbana campus dates from the 1870s. The nickname, which seems to have been coined by students, was never quite officially adopted by the school. The real Illini (that is, the Illiniwek)—who delighted in the torture of captured enemies, sold wives and daughters for trinkets, traded in slaves, and gambled and drank their way into poverty—left much to be desired as models for youthful endeavor.

Not that the Indian motifs that enliven the school's songs and symbols are very specifically Illiniwek. The song "Illinois Loyalty" contains the refrain, "Chehee, Cheha, Cheha-ha-ha/Go Illini Go"—an exhortation of uncertain meaning, whatever its power to excite business majors in touch with their inner warriors. The most famous of these appropriations was the buckskin-clad Chief Illiniwek, who performed a war dance at halftimes of certain athletic contests beginning in 1926. The Chief was not derided as politically incorrect until the 1970s, but the character was anthropologically dubious from the start; while the Illiniwek were originally Algonquian people of the eastern forest, the Chief's costume, hair, and dance were that of a Plains Indian. The real Illiniwek were a hybrid people who had adopted some lifeways of the Plains peoples with whom they traded, but the Chief's performance was probably no more authentic than the hoedown in Rodgers and Hammerstein's *Oklahoma!*.

In spite of the controversy over the Chief's propriety, the university board of trustees for years refused to abandon what most alumni (especially most sports alumni) still regarded affectionately as a totem of their own college history. Resisting to the last, the trustees did not send Chief Illiniwek to his well-earned retirement until 2007, but the Chief and his dance continued to be performed at nonofficial university events.

Abraham Lincoln is another historical figure to have been dragooned as a mascot to inspire team efforts against competitors, specifically contests to win tourists' dollars. The State of Illinois has officially called itself the Land of Lincoln since 1955. Lincoln has long adorned the Springfield city seal, and unofficial uses of his image are ubiquitous. (There are enough bronze Lincolns on the streets of mid-Illinois to earn the region another representative in the General Assembly were they counted as citizens by census takers.)

It is not always clear whether Springfield is proud to be associated with Lincoln because he was a great and good man who inspired people or because he was a famous one who inspires sales. (In the 1960s Springfield mayor Nelson Howarth liked to remind people that a tourist is worth five hundred bushels of corn and is lots easier to shuck.) Making Lincoln, the ultimate Dead White Male, into an advertising icon is a challenge that area officials have undertaken with more verve than taste. In the 1990s Lincoln was given a spiked haircut for a new series of promotions; in 2008 the logo of the Abraham Lincoln Tourism Bureau of Logan County depicted Lincoln tipping his top hat as he drove U.S. Route 66 in a red convertible. Such hard sells have generated the inevitable backlash; one Springfield antiquarian bookstore has done a nice business for years selling T-shirts bearing his portrait and the caption, "They'd have to shoot me to get me back to Springfield."

GHOSTS

For most mid-Illinoisans most of the time, the real history of the region has been not a matter of pride or self-identification or curiosity but indifference. Uncountable numbers of Native American village and camp sites and graves have been destroyed by farmers or by looters, but several generations of Euro-Americans in mid-Illinois were not much more careful about preserving the artifacts of their own era. The "Log City" was the temporary abode of the families who built Galesburg in the 1830s. Earnest Elmo Calkins noted caustically that the town's trustees sold the site of Log City to a man who tore it down and built a brickyard on it, paying for it with bricks used to build the earliest Knox College building—which also has been torn down.[3] "If Log City had been likewise preserved [like New Salem] it would be a historic monument of which any city might be proud," Calkins lamented in the 1930s. "But the Galesburgers had no sentiment, no sense of the historic significance of what they did, and no emotion but religion."[4]

The construction of a mill was always a landmark event in a town's development, but save for a foundation or a crumbling dam here and there, the region is bare of any trace of them. Eighteen commercial potteries employed more than two hundred workers in the town of Ripley; by the 1930s, they were not just closed but gone. The top works of hundreds of coal mines have disappeared; even evidence of strip mining is fading as former pits are converted into parks and lakes. Some mining gob piles have been mined themselves, for construction material; the larger of Minonk's two piles was hauled away and used as fill when Interstate 39 was built nearby.[5]

In 1942 the wartime U.S. government bought nearly eighteen thousand acres of Fulton County, including the town of Bernadotte, to build the massive Camp Ellis, for army training. This instant city had more than two thousand buildings, its own landing field, road network, and water system; at its peak, it housed forty thousand military and civilian personnel as well as (later on) five thousand prisoners of war. Within ten years Camp Ellis not only had been closed but also had been practically eradicated from the landscape. The camp's buildings were either demolished or sold, many camp roads were reclaimed as farm fields, and by the mid-1990s all that was left was an old concrete water tower and a few brick chimneys.[6] The sprawling ordnance factories in eastern Sangamon County that employed two thousand people suffered the same fate, surviving only as a few blastproof bunkers in cornfields.

It is sometimes alleged (more often merely assumed) that Springfield's decades-long recent silence about the race riots that wracked that city in 1908 was a willful forgetting prompted by shame. But there was no cover-up in the capital city; there was never any need for one. As the generation that had lived through the riots died off, the community's memories simply began to fade, like a billboard too long in the weather. Springfield by the 1960s was ignorant of the events of 1908, to be sure, but no more ignorant than it was about the origins of the city's ongoing experiment in municipal socialism or the inter-union violence that sparked gun battles between miner factions in the streets of the capital in the 1930s.

There is what is forgotten, and there is what is merely overlooked. Lincoln's law career in mid-Illinois was the most important part of the life that is most important to Springfield. Nonetheless, in the 1980s staff of what was then known as the Lincoln Legals project combed courthouses and libraries and discovered ninety-seven thousand documents pertaining to more than four hundred cases by Lincoln and his partners that collectors and historians had never thought to (or bothered to) look for; the finds made possible major scholarly advances not only in Lincoln studies but also in the history of mid-Illinois and the Midwest.

The mid-Illinois landscape is peopled with spirits of these forgotten people and places and things, from mute Indian mounds and unexplained turns in country roads to the shells of houses in the middle of cornfields. Old interurban and streetcar tracks still run through many a Main Street, buried beneath newer paving; where streets are worn, the rails sometimes are exposed, like the bones sticking out of a grave. The old Route 66 crossed a creek valley that was flooded to create Lake Springfield in the late 1930s; when the water is low enough, the old pavement reappears like a ghost.

The most evocative of these relics is a two-hundred-foot-long remnant of the historic Edwards Trace. That former Indian trail runs along a ridge in what since the 1930s has been public parkland on the shore of Lake Springfield. At that spot survives an indentation in the earth that is six feet wide at the base and in places as much as two feet deep. Like an Anglo-Saxon *hol weg*, the path was grooved into the earth over centuries by the passage of hooves and wheels and tramping feet of people plodding from their own past into the future.[7]

NOTES

INDEX

NOTES

IN THE MIDDLE OF EVERYWHERE: AN INTRODUCTION TO MID-ILLINOIS

1. Edgar Lee Masters, *The Sangamon* (New York: Farrar and Rinehart, 1942), 20. Douglas, it must be remembered, was happiest when telling his audience whatever they wanted to hear. Speaking to a hometown crowd back in Vermont, Douglas said, "Here I learned to love liberty. . . . Liberty loves the mountains." Robert Walter Johannsen, *Stephen A. Douglas* (Urbana: University of Illinois Press, 1973), 4.

2. Robert Michael Morrisey, *Empire by Collaboration: Indians, Colonists, and Governments in Colonial Illinois Country* (Philadelphia: University of Pennsylvania Press, 2015), 5.

3. Douglas K. Meyer, *Making the Heartland Quilt: A Geographical History of Settlement and Migration in Early-Nineteenth-Century Illinois* (Carbondale: Southern Illinois University Press, 2000), 289.

4. Springfield Survey Committee (Springfield, Ill.), *Springfield Survey* (New York: Russell Sage Foundation, 1920), 30.

5. John Hay to Nora Perry, Springfield, May 20, 1859, John Hay Papers, Brown University, cited in Michael Burlingame, *Abraham Lincoln: A Life* (Baltimore: Johns Hopkins University Press, 2008), 412.

6. Meyer, *Making the Heartland Quilt*, 295.

7. Springfield Survey Committee, *Springfield Survey*, 30.

8. To the extent that today's mid-Illinoisans identify with any region, that region tends to be downstate, mid-Illinoisans sharing with the rest of Illinois outside Chicago a reflexive animus toward the Gomorrah of the Great Lakes.

1. A CLASSIC MIXING ZONE: THE PEOPLING OF MID-ILLINOIS

1. Robert F. Mazrim, "Recent Research at the Old French Village of Peoria," *Illinois Heritage*, Winter 2003, 12–15.

2. John Walthall, Kenneth Farnsworth, and Thomas E. Emerson, "Constructing [on] the Past," *Common Ground* 2 (1997), https://www.nps.gov/archeology/cg/vol2_num1/constructing.htm.

3. Kenneth B. Farnsworth and Thomas E. Emerson, "The Macoupin Creek Figure Pipe and Its Archaeological Context: Evidence for Late Woodland–Mississippian Interaction beyond the Northern Border of Cahokian Settlement," *Midcontinental Journal of Archaeology* 14 (1989): 18–37.

4. *History of Logan County, Illinois, Together with Sketches of Its Cities, Villages, and Towns, . . .* (Chicago: Inter-State Publishing, 1886), 18.

5. The remnants of at least nine bluff-top burial tumuli from 200 B.C. to 1000 A.D. were thus protected by the city in the late 1880s and today are being restored.

6. Rockwell Mound is not unique of its type in Illinois but is nearly unique in never having been plowed or plundered; today it is preserved as a park (complete with hilltop pavilion) by the City of Havana.

7. *History of McDonough County, Illinois, Together with Sketches of the Towns, Villages and Townships, . . .* (Springfield, Ill.: Continental Historical Company, 1885), 695.

8. "Woodland Archeological Sites," Illinois State Museum website, accessed Oct. 27, 2014, http://www.museum.state.il.us/muslink/nat_amer/pre/htmls/w_sites.html. During the middle Woodland period (200 B.C. to 500 A.D.) Native Americans of the Hopewell cultural tradition in mid-Illinois were linked by trade in metals, rare stones, and shells to their cultural kin in the Rockies, the Upper Midwest, the Carolinas, and the Gulf of Mexico. (The town of Hopewell, Illinois, is in Marshall County.)

9. There was a sister site to Cahokia where St. Louis now stands. It was possibly almost as big.

10. Robert L. Hall, *An Archaeology of the Soul: North American Indian Belief and Ritual* (Urbana: University of Illinois Press, 1997), 141.

11. The origin and exact pronunciation of this name and its variant are unknown. Michael McCafferty, "Illinois Voices: Observations on the Miami Illinois Language," in *Protohistory at the Grand Village of the Kaskaskia: The Illinois Country on the Eve of Colony* (Urbana: Illinois State Archaeological Survey, 2015), 122.

12. "Native Americans," Illinois State Museum website, accessed April 11, 2006, http://www.museum.state.il.us/muslink/nat_amer.

13. Lottie E. Jones, *History of Vermilion County, Illinois* (Chicago: Pioneer Publishing, 1911), 19–20.

14. Jones, *History of Vermilion County*, 19.

15. The student of the Native American interregnum in mid-Illinois would be wise to not attempt to construct its history from these names. The town of Pontiac in Livingston County, for example, indisputably owes its name to the Ottawa chief of that name but not because he came anywhere near the place; it was given that name by homesick white settlers from Pontiac, Michigan.

16. Dr. Peter J. Couri Jr., "The First European Settlement in Illinois," Peoria Historical Society website, accessed Oct. 27, 2014, http://www.peoriahistoricalsociety.org/!/History-Of-Peoria/First-European-Settlement-In-Ill.

17. Ann Durkin Keating, *Rising Up from Indian Country: The Battle of Fort Dearborn and the Birth of Chicago* (Chicago: University of Chicago Press, 2012), 180.

18. Ernest E. East, "Lincoln and the Peoria French Claims," *Journal of the Illinois State Historical Society* 42 (1949): 41–56.

19. John C. Hudson, *Making the Corn Belt: A Geographical History of Middle-Western Agriculture* (Bloomington: Indiana University Press, 1994), 93–95.

20. Floyd Dell, *Homecoming: An Autobiography* (New York: Farrar and Rinehart, 1933), 3.

21. Douglas K. Meyer, *Making the Heartland Quilt: A Geographical History of Settlement and Migration in Early-Nineteenth-Century Illinois* (Carbondale: Southern Illinois University Press, 2000), 289.

22. Eliza W. Farnham, *Life in Prairie Land* (Urbana: University of Illinois Press, 1988), 38–39.

23. James Harvey Young and I. M. Wetmore, "Land Hunting in 1836," *Journal of the Illinois State Historical Society* 45 (1952): 241–51.

24. Theodore Calvin Pease, *The Frontier State, 1818–1848* (Springfield: Illinois Centennial Commission, 1919), 440.

25. Dr. E. Duis, *The Good Old Times in McLean County, Illinois* (Bloomington, Ill.: Leader Publishing and Printing House, 1874).

26. John E. Hallwas, introduction to *Spoon River Anthology*, by Edgar Lee Masters (Urbana: University of Illinois Press, 1992), 4.

27. Arthur C. Cole, *The Era of the Civil War, 1848–1870* (Springfield: Illinois Centennial Commission, 1919), 21.

28. Meyer, *Heartland Quilt*, 281.

29. "Iroquois County Places," Illinois GenWeb Project, accessed Oct. 27, 2014, http://iroquois.illinoisgenweb.org/places.htm.

30. Federal Writers' Project, *Illinois: A Descriptive and Historical Guide* (Springfield: State of Illinois, 1939), 422.

31. Bill Kemp, "Welsh Farmers One of Area's Unheralded Immigrant Groups," *Pantagraph*, Dec. 12, 2010, accessed Oct. 27, 2014, http://www.pantagraph.com.

32. Robert W. Frizzell, "Reticent Germans: The East Frisians of Illinois," *Illinois Historical Journal* 85 (1992), 166.

33. Albert Britt, *An America That Was: What Life Was Like on an Illinois Farm Seventy Years Ago* (Barre, Mass.: Barre Publishers, 1964), 57.

34. Earnest Elmo Calkins, *They Broke the Prairie* (Urbana: University of Illinois Press, 1989), 6–7.

35. "The John Wood Mansion," Historical Society of Quincy and Adams County, accessed June 8, 2016, http://hsqac.org/tours-events/the-john-wood-mansion/.

36. Shelby M. Harrison and Springfield Survey Committee (Springfield, Ill.), *Springfield Survey* (New York: Russell Sage Foundation, 1920), 3: 22.

37. Amy Zahl Gottlieb, "British Coal Miners: A Demographic Study of Braidwood and Streator," *Journal of the Illinois State Historical Society* 72 (1979), 187.

38. Joseph Corcoran, "Historical Sketch," in "McLean County Coal Company," McLean County Museum of History website, 2008, accessed Oct. 31, 2014, http://mchistory.org/old/find/mcleancountycoalcompany.html.

39. David Dechenne, "Recipe for Violence: War Attitudes, the Black Hundred Riot, and Superpatriotism in an Illinois Coalfield, 1917–1918," *Illinois Historical Journal* 85 (1992): 221–38.

40. Victor Hicken, "Mine Union Radicalism in Macoupin and Montgomery Counties, IL," Illinois Labor History Society website, accessed Oct. 27, 2014, http://www.illinoislaborhistory.org.

41. Richard Wightman Fox, *Reinhold Niebuhr: A Biography* (New York: Pantheon Books, 1985), 6.

42. Frank J. Fonsino, "Everett McKinley Dirksen: The Roots of an American Statesman," *Journal of the Illinois State Historical Society* 76 (1983): 17–34.

43. Frizzell, "Reticent Germans," 174.

44. Frizzell, "Reticent Germans," 166.

45. James E. Davis, *Frontier Illinois* (Bloomington: Indiana University Press, 2000), 416; Daniel J. Elazar, *Cities of the Prairie: The Metropolitan Frontier and American Politics* (New York: Basic Books, 1970), 222.

46. Sylvestre C. Watkins Sr., "Some of Early Illinois' Free Negroes," *Journal of the Illinois State Historical Society* 56 (1963): 495–507.

47. It could not have been; the Illinois Town Incorporation Law of 1830 stipulated that only white men could incorporate a town. A different Illinois town, Brooklyn, in Madison County, was officially incorporated by African Americans in 1873 under a revised law.

48. Earnest Elmo Calkins reported that black Galesburgers "were not supposed to live north of Main Street or east of Cedar Street, but there was no legal restraint." He called this "a gentleman's agreement." Calkins, *They Broke the Prairie*, 6.

49. A. Martin Byers, *From Cahokia to Larson to Moundville: Death, World Renewal, and the Sacred in the Mississippian Social World of the Late Prehistoric Eastern Woodlands*, Newfound Press, DOI: 10.7290/V76Q1V59.

50. Robert Michael Morrissey, *Empire by Collaboration: Indians, Colonists, and Governments in Colonial Illinois Country* (Philadelphia: University of Pennsylvania Press, 2015), 11–38.

51. Hudson, *Making the Corn Belt*, 5–6.

2. EDEN DESPOILED: NATURE'S ECONOMY IN MID-ILLINOIS

1. Rebecca Burlend, *A True Picture of Emigration* (Chicago: Lakeside Press, R. R. Donnelley and Sons, 1936), 86.

2. Clarence P. McClelland, "Jacob Strawn and John T. Alexander: Central Illinois Stockmen," *Journal of the Illinois State Historical Society* 34 (1941): 177–208.

3. Samuel Augustus Mitchell, *Illinois 1837: A Sketch Descriptive of the Situation, Boundaries, etc.* (Philadelphia: Grigg and Elliot, 1837), vi–vii.

4. A. Cameron Grant, ed., "Letters from a Cass County Farmer," by Archibald Campbell, *Journal of the Illinois State Historical Society* 64 (1971): 327–36.

5. Porter McKeever, *Adlai Stevenson: His Life and Legacy* (New York: Morrow, 1989), 18–19.

6. Paul Mowrer, "The Seasons," in *Prairie Child: A Poem of Illinois* (Wauwatosa, Wis.: n. pub., 1959).

7. John Carroll Power, *History of the Early Settlers of Sangamon County, Illinois* (Springfield, Ill.: Edwin A. Wilson and Company, 1876), 571.

8. See Arthur Weldon Watterson, *Economy and Land Use Patterns in McLean County, Illinois*," Department of Geography Research Paper 17 (Chicago: University of Chicago, 1950).

9. Archibald Campbell, "Illinois Commentary: Letters from a Cass County Farmer," *Journal of the Illinois State Historical Society* 64 (1971): 327–36.

10. Paul Wallace Gates, "Frontier Landlords and Pioneer Tenants," *Journal of the Illinois State Historical Society* 38 (1945): 143–206.

11. Robert Michael Morrissey, *Empire by Collaboration: Indians, Colonists, and Governments in Colonial Illinois Country* (Philadelphia: University of Pennsylvania Press, 2015), 63.

12. Hermon B. Fagley, "Blackman at Illinois Salt Lick, 1819," RootsWeb, accessed October 12, 2011, http://archiver.rootsweb.ancestry.com.

13. Frank H. Bradley, "Geology of Vermilion County," in *Geological Survey of Illinois* (Springfield, Ill.: State Geologist, State Journal Steam Press, 1870), 4: 263.

14. Jack Moore Williams, *History of Vermilion County, Illinois* (Topeka, Kans.: Historical Publishing, 1930), 92–97.

15. Edmund Flagg, "The Far West," in *Early Western Travels, 1748–1846* (Cleveland: Arthur H. Clark Company, 1906), 26: 127.

16. Oscar B. Hamilton, ed., *History of Jersey County, Illinois* (Chicago: Munsell Publishing, 1919), 622.

17. Frederick Koeper, *Illinois Architecture: From Territorial Times to the Present* (Chicago: University of Chicago Press, 1968), 184.

18. Allison Carll White, "Monuments to Their Skill: Urbana-Champaign Carpenters, Contractors, and Builders, 1850–1900," *Illinois Historical Journal* 85 (1992): 37–46.

19. Rodney O. Davis, foreword to *French and Indians of the Illinois River*, by Nehemiah Matson (Carbondale: Southern Illinois University Press, 2001).

20. "People and the River," in "Illinois River Timeline, 1673 to the Present," Illinois State Museum, accessed April 16, 2016, http://www.museum.state.il.us/exhibits/changes/pdfs/Illinois_river_timeline.pdf.

21. These creatures were and remain marvelously prolific. In the early twentieth century one Meredosia dealer shipped thirty-four thousand muskrat pelts to London in one year and one hundred thousand to St. Louis the following year.

22. Gillum Ferguson, *Illinois in the War of 1812* (Urbana: University of Illinois Press, 2012), 24.

23. Jacques Marquette, *The Mississippi Voyage of Jolliet and Marquette, 1673* (Doc. no. AJ-051, Wisconsin Historical Society Digital Library and Archive, 2003), 257, http://www.americanjourneys.org/pdf/AJ-051.pdf.

24. Flagg, "Far West," 125.

25. John Thompson, *Wetlands Drainage, River Modification, and Sectoral Conflict in the Lower Illinois Valley, 1890–1930* (Carbondale: Southern Illinois University Press, 2002), 168.

26. Thompson, *Wetlands Drainage*, 178.

27. Howard Edlen, "History of the Pearl Button Business in Meredosia, Illinois," Illinois State Museum, accessed Dec. 14, 2013, http://www.museum.state.il.us/RiverWeb/harvesting/harvest/mussels/industry/hedlen.html.

28. Cheryl Claassen, "Washboards, Pigtoes, and Muckets: Historic Musseling in the Mississippi Watershed," *Historical Archaeology* 28 (1994): 1–145; Davi Warden-Michl, "Pearl Button Industry Threat to Mussel Beds of the Mississippi," BQC (Before Quad Cities) website, https://bqc.wikispaces.com/Pearl+Button+Industry+Threat+to+Mussel+Beds+of+the+Mississippi. The buttons business kept food on the table of Meredosians longer than in most musseling towns. The Wilbur E. Boyd Button Factory, the last independent pearl button factory in the United States, held on until 1948, but only by processing shells harvested in other places.

29. Cited by Harriet Bell Carlander, "A History of Fish and Fishing in the Upper Mississippi River" (Mississippi River Conservation Committee, 1954), at

Native Fish Lab website, Marsh and Associates LLC, http://www.nativefishlab.net/library/textpdf/17391.pdf.

30. Howard Edlen, "Fishing Industry in Meredosia," Illinois State Museum, accessed Oct. 30, 2014, http://www.museum.state.il.us/RiverWeb/harvesting/harvest/fish/industry/hedlen.html.

31. Quoted in Nancy Nixon, "Bootlegging in Illinois," *Illinois Country Living*, April 2001, 11.

32. Thompson, *Wetlands Drainage*, 177.

33. *A Century of Biological Research*, Illinois Natural History Survey Bulletin, vol. 27, article 2 (Urbana: State of Illinois, 1958), 132.

34. Thompson, *Wetlands Drainage*, 196.

35. Lawrence Beaumont Stringer, *History of Logan County, Illinois: A Record of Its Settlement, Organization, . . .* (Chicago: Pioneer Publishing Company, 1911), 16.

36. Federal Writers' Project, *Illinois: A Historical and Descriptive Guide* (Springfield: State of Illinois, 1939), 423.

3. "WONDOROUS PLANT": THE INDUSTRIALIZATION OF NATURE IN MID-ILLINOIS

1. Roy V. Scott, review of *Fields of Rich Toil: The Development of the University of Illinois College of Agriculture*, by Richard Gordon Moores, *Agricultural History* 46 (1972): 339–40.

2. "Champaign County, Illinois: Early Weather and Other Dangers," excerpted from *History of Champaign County, Illinois, with Illustrations, 1878*, submitted by Celia G. Snyder, Champaign County IL GenWeb Project, http://champaign.illinoisgenweb.org/history/weather.html.

3. Harold Sinclair, *American Years* (New York: Literary Guild of America, 1938), 9.

4. Carl Van Doren, *Three Worlds* (New York: Harper, 1936), 26.

5. Paul Wallace Gates, *The Illinois Central Railroad and Its Colonization Work* (Cambridge: Harvard University Press, 1934), 176.

6. Virgil Vogel, *Indian Place Names in Illinois* (Springfield: Illinois State Historical Society, 1963), 149.

7. Robert W. Frizzell, "Reticent Germans: The East Frisians of Illinois," *Illinois Historical Journal* 85 (1992): 161–74.

8. Margaret B. Bogue, *Patterns from the Sod: Land Use and Tenure in the Grand Prairie, 1850–1900* (Springfield: Illinois State Historical Library, 1959).

9. Hugh Prince, *Wetlands of the American Midwest: A Historical Geography of Changing Attitudes* (Chicago: University of Chicago Press, 1997), 190.

10. Quoted in James E. Herget, "Taming the Environment: The Drainage District in Illinois," *Journal of the Illinois State Historical Society* 71 (1978): 107–18.

11. John Thompson, *Wetlands Drainage, River Modification, and Sectoral Conflict in the Lower Illinois Valley, 1890–1930* (Carbondale: Southern Illinois University Press, 2002), 196.

12. John Mack Faragher, *Sugar Creek: Life on the Illinois Prairie* (New Haven: Yale University Press, 1986), 6.

13. Frank Webster Farley, "History of the Beef Cattle Industry in Illinois" (bachelor's thesis, University of Illinois, 1915), 36.

14. Farley, "History of the Beef Cattle Industry," 36.

15. Clarence P. McClelland, "Jacob Strawn and John T. Alexander: Central Illinois Stockmen," Journal of the Illinois State Historical Society 34 (1941), 191.

16. *Historical Encyclopedia of Illinois and History of Morgan County* (Chicago: Munsell Publishing, 1906), 954.

17. L. M. Glover, *Discourse Occasioned by the Death of Jacob Strawn, the Great American Farmer* (Jacksonville, Ill.: Franklin Printing Office, 1865), 5.

18. "A Great Farmer's Maxims," *Pacific Rural Press*, vol. 2, no. 12, September 1871, 179.

19. Thomas D. Isern, review of *Feedlot Empire: Beef Cattle Feeding in Illinois and Iowa, 1840–1900*, by James W. Whitaker, and *Agriculture in the Great Plains, 1876–1936*, by Thomas R. Wessel, *Journal of the Illinois State Historical Society* 71 (1978): 233–34.

20. "Mr. Lincoln's Friends," Lincoln Institute, accessed August 17, 2012, http://www.mrlincolnandfriends.org.

21. Paul W[allace] Gates, "Cattle Kings in the Prairies," *Mississippi Valley Historical Review* 35 (1948), 392.

22. Undated newspaper excerpt, accessed Oct. 27, 2014, http://genealogyandfamilyhistory.yuku.com/topic/1330/Newspaper-Articles-Highlighting-Michael-L-Sullivants-Lif.

23. Robert P. Howard, *Illinois: A History of the Prairie State* (Grand Rapids, Mich.: William B. Eerdmans Publishing, 1972), 266.

24. *New York Times*, February 3, 1879.

25. Gates, "Frontier Landlords and Pioneer Tenants," 154.

26. Gates, "Frontier Landlords and Pioneer Tenants," 155.

27. Gates, "Frontier Landlords and Pioneer Tenants," 189–90.

28. *History of Logan County, Illinois* (Chicago: Inter-state Publishing Co., 1886), 368.

29. *History of Logan County, Illinois*, 367.

30. Ernest Ludlow Bogart and Charles Manfred Thompson, *The Industrial State, 1870–1893* (Springfield, Ill.: Illinois Centennial Commission, 1920), 221.

31. U.S. Census Office, *Productions of Agriculture, 1880* (Washington, D.C., 1883), 3: 28–101, cited by Hugh Prince, *Wetlands of the American Midwest: A Historical Geography of Changing Attitudes* (Chicago: University of Chicago Press, 1997), 199.

32. Allen C. Guelzo, "Come-Outers and Community Men: Abraham Lincoln and the Idea of Community in Nineteenth-Century America," *Journal of the Abraham Lincoln Association* 21 (2000): 1–29.

33. Jeremy Atack, "The Evolution of Regional Economic Differences within Illinois, 1818–1950," in *Diversity, Conflict, and State Politics: Regionalism in Illinois*, edited by Peter Nardulli (Urbana: University of Illinois Press, 1989), 61–94.

34. Jane Martin Johns and Howard C Schaub, *Personal recollections of early Decatur, Abraham Lincoln, Richard J. Oglesby and the Civil War* (Decatur, Ill.: Decatur chapter Daughters of the American Revolution, 1912), 125–26.

35. One of them was corn king Michael L. Sullivant. It was said that he could ride in a direct course fifteen miles through his own cornfields in the Scioto valley of Ohio, but he moved west to the Grand Prairie of mid-Illinois, which was "suited to his notions of farming on a magnificent scale." Undated newspaper excerpt, accessed Oct. 29, 2014, http://genealogyandfamilyhistory.yuku.com/topic/1330/Newspaper-Articles-Highlighting-Michael-L-Sullivants-Lif.

36. Fred Kohlmeyer, "Illinois Agriculture in Retrospect," in *Illinois: Its History and Legacy*, edited by Roger D. Bridges and Rodney O. Davis (St. Louis: River City Publishers, 1984), 1.

37. U.S. Census Office, "Productions of Agriculture," 1870 (Washington, D.C., 1874).

38. Jerome L. Rodnitzky, "Farm and Gown: The University of Illinois and the Farmer, 1904–1918," *Journal of the Illinois State Historical Society* 72 (1979): 13–20.

39. Rodnitzky, "Farm and Gown," 16.

40. F. Garvin Davenport, "Natural Scientists and the Farmers of Illinois, 1865–1900," *Journal of the Illinois State Historical Society* 51 (1958), 360.

41. Bogart, *Industrial State*, 236.

42. Thomas D. Isern, review of *The Business of Breeding: Hybrid Corn in Illinois, 1890–1940*, by Deborah Fitzgerald, *American Historical Review* 96 (1991), 1622.

43. Funk's Research Acres was "a mecca for agronomists and plant breeders from all over the world." Paul Weatherwax, review of *Seed, Soil and Science: The Story of Eugene D. Funk*, by Helen M. Cavanagh, *Indiana Magazine of History* 57: 175–76.

44. Frank Richard Hall, "An Illinois Village, 1873 and 1923," *Journal of the Illinois State Historical Society* 20 (1927): 370–410; Steve Tarter, *Peoria Journal Star*, Oct. 25, 2011.

45. JBG, "Correspondence from the First State Fair," *Journal of the Illinois State Historical Society* 43 (1950): 62–67.

46. Donald F. Tingley, *The Structuring of a State: Illinois, 1899 to 1928* (Urbana: University of Illinois Press, 1980), 46–47.

47. "Pana, Illinois, City of Roses, Centennial, 1856–1956, July 1–4" (Pana, Ill.: Pana News-Palladium, 1956), accessed Oct. 28, 2014, https://archive.org/details/panaillinoiscityoopana.

48. Eliza W. Farnham, *Life in Prairie Land* (Urbana: University of Illinois Press, 1988), 92.

49. JBG, "Correspondence from the First State Fair," 64.

50. *The Combined History of Schuyler and Brown Counties, Illinois, 1882* (Philadelphia: W. R. Brink and Company, 1882), 234.

51. Oscar B. Hamilton, *History of Jersey County, Illinois* (Chicago: Munsell Publishing, 1919), 487.

52. Mentor Graham to William H. Herndon (interview), Petersburg, Illinois, May 29, 1865, Douglas L. Wilson and Rodney O. Davis, eds., *Herndon's Informants*, 9, cited by Michael Burlingame, *Abraham Lincoln: A Life*, vol. 1 (Baltimore: Johns Hopkins University Press, 2008).

53. Carl Sandburg, *Always the Young Strangers* (New York: Harcourt, Brace, 1953).

4. TOWN MANIA: THE URBAN FRONTIER OF MID-ILLINOIS

1. Lawrence B. Stringer, "The Lincoln Town," unpublished essay, no. 11, Stringer Papers, Abraham Lincoln Presidential Library, Springfield, cited by Michael Burlingame, *Abraham Lincoln: A Life* (Baltimore: Johns Hopkins University Press, 2008), 1: 518.

2. The Grand Village of the Kickapoo was occupied until 1813, when the U.S Army burned it down in retribution for its inhabitants' refusal to abide by the peace after the War of 1812. Though the site has been listed on the National Register of Historic Places since 1982, publication of its exact location is restricted by the National Register due to fear of vandalism and looting.

3. Judith A. Franke, *French Peoria and the Illinois Country, 1673–1846* (Springfield: Illinois State Museum, 1995).

4. *Stark County Illinois and Its People: A Record of Settlement, Organization, Progress, and Achievement*, vol. 1, ed. J. Knox Hall (Chicago: Pioneer Publishing Company, 1916).

5. Fred Gustorf, "Frontier Perils Told by an Early Illinois Visitor," *Journal of the Illinois State Historical Society* 55 (1962): 255–70.

6. Joseph Duncan died poor after his lands were sold off at dirt-cheap prices to settle a debt resulting not from speculation but from signing a note for a crooked son-in-law.

7. Thomas J. Brown, "The Age of Ambition in Quincy, Illinois," *Journal of the Illinois State Historical Society* 75 (1982): 242–62.

8. Robert P. Sutton, "Illinois River Towns: Economic Units or Melting Pots," *Western Illinois Regional Studies* 13 (1990), 23.

9. Frances Milton Irene Morehouse, *The Life of Jesse W. Fell* (Urbana: University of Illinois, 1916).

10. Loring C. Merwin, "McLean County's Newspapers: Particularly the Pantagraph," *Journal of the Illinois State Historical Society* 51 (1958), 10.

11. James E. Davis, *Frontier Illinois* (Bloomington: Indiana University Press, 2000), 236.

12. Juliet E. K. Walker, "Entrepreneurial Ventures in the Origin of Nineteenth-Century Agricultural Towns: Pike County, 1823–1880," *Illinois Historical Journal* 78 (1985), 60.

13. Robert F. Mazrim, *The Sangamo Frontier: History and Archaeology in the Shadow of Lincoln* (Chicago: University of Chicago Press, 2008), 64–69.

14. Walker, "Entrepreneurial Ventures." That dynamic still shapes mid-Illinois towns; only today it is interstate highway exchanges on the urban fringe that beget new settlements.

15. Rev. P. C. Croll, "Thomas Beard, the Pioneer and Founder of Beardstown, Illinois," *Papers in Illinois History and Transactions for the Year* (Springfield: Illinois State Historical Society, 1917), 218.

16. A. W. French, "Early Reminiscences," *Transactions of the Illinois State Historical Society* (Springfield: Illinois State Historical Society, 1901), 61.

17. Robert P. Howard, *A New Eden: The Pioneer Era in Sangamon County* (Springfield, Ill.: Sangamon County Historical Society, 1974), 21.

18. Croll, "Thomas Beard," 209.

19. Paul Wallace Gates, *The Illinois Central Railroad and Its Colonization Work* (Cambridge: Harvard University Press, 1934), 236; *History of Christian County, Illinois* (Philadelphia: Brink, McDonough., 1880), 185.

20. "Pana, Illinois, City of Roses, Centennial, 1856–1956, July 1–4" (Pana, Ill.: Pana News-Palladium, 1956), 5, accessed Oct. 28, 2014, https://archive.org/details/panaillinoiscityoopana.

21. Dannel A. McCollum, "Champaign: The Creation of a City of Champaign," City of Champaign website, accessed Oct. 28, 2014, http://ci.champaign.il.us/about-champaign/history/creation-of-champaign/.

22. H. W. Beckwith, *History of Iroquois County, Together with Historic Notes on the Northwest* (Chicago: H. H. Hill and Company, 1880), 232.

23. Bill Kemp, "West-Side Coal Company Town Once Home to Swedes," *Pantagraph*, Oct. 20, 2014, accessed Oct. 26, 2014, http://www.pantagraph.com.

24. Tara McClellan Andrew, "Spirit of Progress," *Illinois Times*, Sept. 24, 2008, accessed April 14, 2016, http://illinoistimes.com/mobile/articles/articleView/id:5306.

25. J. Knox Hall, ed., *Stark County Illinois and Its People* (Chicago: Pioneer Publishing, 1916), 111.

26. Howard, *New Eden*.

27. Paul M. Angle, *Here I Have Lived: A History of Lincoln's Springfield, 1821–1865* (Chicago: Abraham Lincoln Bookshop, 1971), 57–58.

28. "Illinois State Fair: The Early Years," *Cook-Witter Report* 17 (2002), 2.

29. Typical of the best of the local catalogs of such lost towns is this installment in Howard Dyson's "Old Times in Schuyler" series in the *Rushville Times* in 1918: "Town Sites Long Forgotten," *Rushville Times*, accessed Oct. 31, 2014, http://schuyler.illinoisgenweb.org/OldTimesInSchuyler/OTIStownsites.html. Dyson found records of ten such town sites in this, one of the smallest counties in mid-Illinois.

30. Mazrim, *Sangamo Frontier*, 227–46.

31. Carl Van Doren, *Three Worlds* (New York: Harper, 1936), 2.

32. Doren, *Three Worlds*, 22.

33. *History of Effingham County, Illinois*, ed. William Henry Perrin (Chicago: O. L. Baskin and Company, 1883), 195.

34. Susan Sessions Rugh, *Our Common Country: Family Farming, Culture, and Community in the Nineteenth-Century Midwest* (Bloomington: Indiana University Press, 2001), 52. See also "Conflict in the Countryside: The Mormon Settlement at Macedonia, Illinois," Article 12, *BYU Studies* 32 (1992), http://scholarsarchive.byu.edu/byusq/vol32/iss1/12.

35. Robert F. Mazrim, *At Home in the Illinois Country: French Colonial Domestic Site Archaeology in the Midwest, 1730–1800* (Urbana: Illinois State Archaeological Survey, 2011).

36. Fred W. Soady Jr., "'In These Waste Places': Pekin, Illinois, 1824–1849," *Journal of the Illinois State Historical Society* 57 (1964), 157.

37. Michael P. Conzen, "The Non-Pennsylvania Town: Diffusion of Urban Plan Forms in the American West," *Geographical Review* 96 (2006): 183–211.

38. Myron Howard West, *The Decatur Plan* (Decatur, Ill.: Association of Commerce, 1920), 69.

39. John E. Hallwas, *The Bootlegger: A Story of Small-Town America* (Urbana: University of Illinois Press, 1999), 216–17.

5. "WELL KNOWN REPUGNANCES": ANTAGONISM AND ACCOMMODATION IN MID-ILLINOIS

1. Wanda A. Hendricks, "Child Welfare and Black Female Agency in Springfield: Eva Monroe and the Lincoln Colored Home," *Journal of Illinois History* 3 (2000), 103–4.

2. "Lincoln Colored Home," Historic Sites Commission of Springfield, Illinois, accessed May 12, 2012, http://historiccommissions.springfield.il.us/LincolnColoredHome.asp.

3. Don Harrison Doyle, *The Social Order of a Frontier Community: Jacksonville, Illinois, 1825–70* (Urbana: University of Illinois Press, 1978), 10–11.

4. Among the Illiniwek phrases recorded in the dictionaries and phrase books compiled by several French priests of the period is "how to scare children into behaving by mentioning the Iroquois." Michael McCafferty, "Illinois Voices: Observations on the Miami-Illinois Language," in Robert Mazrim et al., *Protohistory at the Grand Village of the Kaskaskia: The Illinois Country on the Eve of Colony*, Studies in Archaeology, no. 10 (Urbana: Illinois State Archaeological Survey, University of Illinois, 2015), 119.

5. Lenville J. Stelle, "History and Archaeology: New Evidence of the 1730 Mesquakie (Renard, Fox) Fort" (Champaign, Ill.: Parkland College, 1992).

6. Randall Parrish, *Historic Illinois: The Romance of the Earlier Days* (Chicago: A. C. McClurg and Company, 1905), 34–35. In 1815 Congress granted Ann Gilham a section of land—it was Indian land in fact if not title—in compensation for the hardship she endured.

7. Harvey Lee Ross, *The Early Pioneers and Pioneer Events of the State of Illinois* (Chicago: Eastman Brothers, 1899), 57.

8. Ann Durkin Keating, *Rising Up from Indian Country: The Battle of Fort Dearborn and the Birth of Chicago* (Chicago: University of Chicago Press, 2012), 24.

9. John E. Hallwas, "Mormon Nauvoo from a Non-Mormon Perspective," *Journal of Mormon History* 16 (1990), 54.

10. Quoted in Thomas Gregg, *History of Hancock County, Illinois: Together with an Outline, . . .* (Hancock County, Ill.: Brookhaven Press, 1880), 1: 275.

11. Theodore Calvin Pease, *The Frontier State, 1818–1848* (Chicago: A. C. McClurg Company, 1922), 362.

12. Marvin S. Hill, "Carthage Conspiracy Reconsidered: A Second Look at the Murder of Joseph and Hyrum Smith," *Journal of the Illinois State Historical Society* 97 (2004): 107–34.

13. "Disloyalty in Illinois," *Illinois State Journal*, Springfield, August 11, 1862.

14. "Military Arrest in Jerseyville, Ill.," *Missouri Democrat*, December 10, 1862.

15. Loring C. Merwin, "McLean County's Newspapers: Particularly the Pantagraph," *Journal of the Illinois State Historical Society* 51 (1958), 23.

16. Bill Kemp, "Mob Destroyed Bloomington's Pro-South Newspaper in 1862," accessed Oct. 29, 2014, http://www.pantagraph.com.

17. Charles H. Coleman and Paul H. Spence, "The Charleston Riot, March 28, 1864," *Journal of the Illinois State Historical Society* 33 (1940), 15; Robert D. Sampson, "'Pretty Damned Warm Times': The 1864 Charleston Riot and 'The Inalienable Right of Revolution,'" *Illinois Historical Journal* 89 (1996): 99–116.

18. Robert Michael Morrissey, *Empire by Collaboration: Indians, Colonists, and Governments in Colonial Illinois Country* (Philadelphia: University of Pennsylvania Press, 2015), 32–39.

19. Michael J. Sherfy, review of *Stealing Indian Women: Native Slavery in the Illinois Country*, by Carl J. Ekberg (Urbana: University of Illinois Press, 2007), in *Ohio History* 116 (2009): 136–37.

20. Not until 1845 did slavery officially disappear in Illinois, after new, Yankee-influenced state judges ruled slavery unconstitutional in any form.

21. James E. Davis, *Frontier Illinois* (Bloomington: Indiana University Press, 2000), 167. See also *Confronting Slavery: Edward Coles and the Rise of Antislavery Politics in Nineteenth-Century America*, by Suzanne Cooper Guasco (DeKalb: Northern Illinois University Press, 2013).

22. Walter R. Sanders, "The Negro in Montgomery County, Illinois," *Illinois State Genealogical Society Quarterly* 10 (1978): 1–3.

23. *The History of McLean County, Illinois: Portraits of Early Settlers and Prominent Men . . .* (Chicago: William Le Baron, Jr., and Company, 1879), 581.

24. Cited in *Women, Work, and Worship in Lincoln's Country: The Dumville Family Letters,* edited by Anne M. Heinz and John P. Heinz (Urbana: University of Illinois Press, 2016), 18.

25. Charles M. Eames, *Historic Morgan and Classic Jacksonville* (Jacksonville: *Daily Journal,* 1885), 136.

26. Larry Gara, "The Underground Railroad in Illinois," *Journal of the Illinois State Historical Society* 56 (1963), 513.

27. Quoted in Charles H. Rammelkamp, "Illinois College and the Anti-slavery Movement in Illinois," *Transactions of the Illinois State Historical Society* (Springfield, Ill.: Illinois State Journal Company, 1909), 4.

28. The judge in the original case was Stephen A. Douglas. The National Parks Service has declared Dr. Eells's home at 415 Jersey Street in Quincy to be one of the country's forty-two most important Underground Railroad sites.

29. D. N. Blazer, "The History of the Underground Railroad of McDonough County, Illinois," *Journal of the Illinois State Historical Society* 15 (1923), 581.

30. Emancipation turned many people who had been fence-sitters into fervent emancipationists. Jacksonville's Timothy Chamberlain would recall that "a good many persons now claim to have been avowed abolitionists certainly were not very outspoken then." Eames, *Historic Morgan*, 141.

31. These men all had a connection with Abraham Lincoln. He was a customer of Donnegan, a shoemaker; Jenkins was a neighbor; and Brown labored for the Lincolns and led Lincoln's horse in his Springfield funeral procession.

32. Robert L. McCaul, *The Black Struggle for Public Schooling in Nineteenth-Century Illinois* (1987; repr., Carbondale: Southern Illinois University Press, 2009), 51–53.

33. McCaul, *Black Struggle,* 51–53.

34. Bill Kemp, "Chase v. Stephenson Step toward Ending School Segregation," *Pantagraph*, March 3, 2013, accessed Oct. 28, 2014, http://www.pantagraph.com.

35. McCaul, *Black Struggle,* 50.

36. *Semi-centennial History of the Illinois State Normal University, 1857–1907* (Normal: Illinois State Normal University, 1907), 77.

37. Helen E. Marshall, *Grandest of Enterprises: Illinois State Normal University, 1857–1957* (Normal: Illinois State Normal University, 1956), 355.

38. "Father Augustus Tolton," Diocese of Springfield in Illinois website, accessed Dec. 17, 2016, http://www.dio.org/tolton/about-father-tolton/the-tolton-family.html. After his ordination in Rome in 1886, Tolton returned to Quincy to celebrate his first public mass, at St. Boniface Church. He became pastor of St. Joseph Church in Quincy before leaving for Chicago, where he remained until he died in 1897; he had asked to be buried at Quincy's St. Peter's Cemetery.

39. Roberta Senechal, *The Sociogenesis of a Race Riot: Springfield, Illinois, in 1908* (Urbana: University of Illinois Press, 1990), 64.

40. Sundiata Keita Cha-jua, "'Join Hands and Hearts with Law and Order': The 1893 Lynching of Samuel J. Bush and the Response of Decatur's African American Community," *Illinois Historical Journal* 83 (1990): 187–200.

41. Jack S. Blocker, *A Little More Freedom: African Americans Enter the Urban Midwest, 1860–1930* (Columbus: Ohio State University Press, 2008), 128.

42. One of the victims was the aforementioned William Donnegan, then eighty-four.

43. The book was reprinted under the title *In Lincoln's Shadow: The 1908 Race Riot in Springfield, Illinois* (Carbondale: Southern Illinois University Press, 2008).

44. Blocker, *A Little More Freedom*, 130–31.

45. Mildred Pratt, "Turning Points in African American History in Bloomington-Normal, Illinois," *Illinois History Teacher* 7 (1999), 31.

46. Stephen Chicoine, "One Glorious Season: How Baseball Helped to Integrate Decatur, Illinois," *Journal of the Illinois State Historical Society* 96 (2003): 80–97.

47. Pratt, "Turning Points," 31.

48. Joy Ann Williamson, "The Snail-like Progress of Racial Desegregation at the University of Illinois," *Journal of Blacks in Higher Education* 42 (2003–4): 116–20.

49. Roger D. Bridges, "Blacks in a White Society," in *Illinois: Its History and Legacy,* edited by Roger D. Bridges and Rodney O. Davis (St. Louis: River City Publishers, 1984).

50. Quoted in McCaul, *Black Struggle,* 49.

51. Albert Britt, *An America That Was: What Life Was Like on an Illinois Farm Seventy Years Ago* (Barre, Mass.: Barre Publishers, 1964), 57.

52. Theodore J. Anderson, "100 Years: A History of Bishop Hill, Illinois," published by the author, ca. 1946, 5.

53. Betty Shaw, "The Coal Mine," at "Mining More in Moweaqua, 1889–1940," accessed Feb. 4, 2014, http://www.miningmoreinmoweaqua.com/pdf/chap6.pdf.

54. Carl Sandburg, *Always the Young Strangers* (New York: Harcourt, Brace, and Company, 1953), 286–87.

55. Bill Steinbacher-Kemp, "Pictures from Our Past," *Pantagraph,* June 2, 2007, accessed Oct 28, 2014, http://www.pantagraph.com.

56. Tina Stewart Brakebill, "'German Days' to '100 Percent Americanism': McLean County, Illinois, 1913–1918; German Americans, World War One, and One Community's Reaction," *Journal of the Illinois State Historical Society* 95 (2002): 148–71.

57. Frank J. Fonsino, "Everett McKinley Dirksen: The Roots of an American Statesman," *Journal of the Illinois State Historical Society* 76 (1983): 17–34. As a mature politician, Dirksen exploited a similar hysteria against "Reds." Scott Lucas, Democratic whip and Senate majority leader under Harry Truman, was born near Chandlerville, schooled at Illinois Wesleyan University in Bloomington, and practiced law in Havana before taking up politics. Lucas enjoyed the support of both liberal and conservative members of the Democratic Party as a Senate officer, but Dirksen branded him without cause as "soft on Communism" in their election campaign of 1950, and Dirksen went to Washington in Lucas's place.

58. Brakebill, "'German Days' to '100 percent Americanism.'"

59. Daniel J. Elazar, *Cities of the Prairie: The Metropolitan Frontier and American Politics* (New York: Basic Books, 1970), 222.

60. "At the outbreak of war the abstract question was abandoned while the 'gentler sex' turned its energies into constructive work in the cause of the union;

and after years of hard toil in the fields, in shops, in hospitals, and in relief work, the women felt that they had indeed earned a claim to consideration in the civil life of the state equal to that of the liberated Negro." Arthur C. Cole, *The Era of the Civil War, 1848–1870* (Springfield: Illinois Centennial Commission, 1919), 427.

61. Eliza W. Farnham, *Life in Prairie Land* (Urbana: University of Illinois Press, 1988), 219.

62. Clark Spencer Larsen, *Skeletons in Our Closet: Revealing Our Past through Bioarchaeology* (Princeton, N.J.: Princeton University Press, 2000), 207–8.

63. John Mack Faragher, *Sugar Creek: Life on the Illinois Prairie* (New Haven: Yale University Press, 1986), 118.

64. Larsen, *Skeletons in Our Closet*, 207.

65. Morrissey, *Empire by Collaboration*, 64–78.

66. Keating, *Rising Up from Indian Country*, 24.

67. Faragher, *Sugar Creek*, 115.

68. Bill Kemp, "Major's Female College Was an Early Bloomington School for Young Women," *Pantagraph,* March 25, 2012, accessed July 7, 2013, http://www.pantagraph.com.

69. Quoted in Kalev Leetaru, "Woman at the University," UIHistories Project, accessed Oct. 18, 2014, http://uihistories.library.illinois.edu.

70. "The Illinois School of Architecture: A History of Firsts," Illinois School of Architecture website, accessed Oct. 14, 2014, http://www.arch.illinois.edu/welcome/history-school.

71. Shelby M. Harrison and Springfield Survey Committee (Springfield, Ill.), *Springfield Survey* (New York: Russell Sage Foundation, 1920), 3:130.

72. Eva Munson Smith, "Sangamon County Illinois Ladies' Soldiers Aid Society, 1861–1865," *Transactions of the Illinois State Historical Society for the Year 1912* (Springfield: Illinois State Journal Company, State Printers, 1914), 200.

73. Betty Friedan, *Life So Far: A Memoir* (New York: Simon and Schuster, 2006), 25.

74. Friedan, *Life So Far*, 17.

75. Friedan, *Life So Far*, 17.

76. "Diverse Beardstown Soccer Team Pulls Together," *State Journal-Register,* September 9, 2014.

6. "MAKING THE WORLD A LITTLE MORE CHRISTIAN": THE SALVATION OF MID-ILLINOIS

1. Freda Kruse Leonhard, "History of Shiloh Cumberland Presbyterian Church," Oct. 1963, accessed Oct. 14, 2014, http://genealogytrails.com/ill/cass/Shiloh_church.htm.

2. Leonhard, "History of Shiloh Cumberland Presbyterian Church." The Shiloh women were hardly alone in this. "Much of the work that was essential to the organization and maintenance of the church," write Anne M. Heinz and John P. Heinz about the region's Methodists, "was done by uncompensated women." *Women, Work, and Worship in Lincoln's Country: The Dumville Family Letters,* edited by Anne M. Heinz and John P. Heinz (Urbana: University of Illinois Press, 2016), 35.

3. It has been speculated that shamans might have smoked tobacco in quantity to achieve a trancelike state in which they could communicate with the spirits directly.

4. "Native Americans," MuseumLink Illinois, Illinois State Museum website, last modified Feb. 6, 2002, accessed Jan. 22, 2014, http://www.museum.state.il.us/muslink/nat_amer/index.html.

5. Robert L. Hall, *An Archaeology of the Soul: North American Indian Belief and Ritual* (Urbana: University of Illinois Press, 1997), 25.

6. Lawrence A. Conrad, "The Middle Mississippian Cultures of the Central Illinois Valley," in Thomas E. Emerson and R. Barry Lewis, eds., *Cahokia and the Hinterlands: Middle Mississippian Cultures of the Midwest* (Urbana: University of Illinois Press, 2000), 130.

7. Biloine W. Young and Melvin Leo Fowler, *Cahokia: The Great Native American Metropolis* (Urbana: University of Illinois Press, 2000), 272.

8. Young and Fowler, *Cahokia,* 302. There is strong evidence that climate or environmental change was at least a factor in Cahokia's rise and fall.

9. Marest to Father Barthélemi Germon, 1712, quoted in John G. Shea, *Discovery and Exploration of the Mississippi Valley* (New York City: Redfield, 1852), 26.

10. Hall, *Archaeology of the Soul,* 33.

11. Lee Irwin, "Freedom, Law, and Prophecy: A Brief History of Native American Religious Resistance," *Native American Spirituality: A Critical Reader,* edited by Lee Irwin (Lincoln: University of Nebraska Press, 2000), 39.

12. Nehemiah Matson, *French and Indians of the Illinois River* (Carbondale: Southern Illinois University Press, 2001), 118–19.

13. Charles J. Martin, ed., *Historical Encyclopedia of Illinois and History of Cass County* (Chicago: Munsell Publishing Company, 1915), 2: 746.

14. Christopher Bilodeau, "'They Honor Our Lord among Themselves in Their Own Way': Colonial Christianity and the Illinois Indians," *American Indian Quarterly* 25 (2001): 352–77.

15. Robert Michael Morrissey, *Empire by Collaboration: Indians, Colonists, and Governments in Colonial Illinois Country* (Philadelphia: University of Pennsylvania Press, 2015), 75–78.

16. Mary R. McCorvie and Mark J. Wagner, introduction to "Contested Lands: The War of 1812 in Illinois," *Illinois Antiquity* 47 (2012).

17. R. David Edmunds, "The Illinois River Potawatomi in the War of 1812," *Journal of the Illinois State Historical Society* 62 (1969): 341–62.

18. Susan Sleeper-Smith, *Indian Women and French Men: Rethinking Cultural Encounter in the Western Great Lakes* (Amherst: University of Massachusetts Press, 2001), 89.

19. Theodore Calvin Pease, *The Frontier State, 1818–1848* (Chicago: A. C. McClurg Company, 1922), 24–25. The Methodists, for example, believed that God chose preachers and that "God never called an unprepared man." Leonhard, *Women, Work, and Worship*, 35.

20. Eliza W. Farnham, *Life in Prairie Land* (Urbana: University of Illinois Press, 1988), 220–21.

21. Robert Bray, *Peter Cartwright: Legendary Frontier Preacher* (Urbana: University of Illinois Press, 2005), ix.

22. John Hallwas, *A Reader's Guide to Illinois Literature,* edited by Robert Bray (Springfield: Illinois Secretary of State, 1985), 5. See also Robert Bray, *Peter Cartwright: Legendary Frontier Preacher.* About Cartwright's backwoods bildungsroman, one reader at the time wrote, "We could not expect a polished production from an unpolished source. Nevertheless, . . . it is *rather* amusing as well as instructive." Leonhard, *Women, Work, and Worship*, 77.

23. Carl Van Doren, *An Illinois Boyhood* (New York: Viking Press, 1939), 223.

24. Farnham, *Life in Prairie Land*, 223.

25. Pease, *Frontier State*, 426.

26. Quoted in Arthur C. Cole, *The Era of the Civil War, 1848–1870* (Springfield: Illinois Centennial Commission, 1919), 251–52.

27. Cole, *Era of the Civil War*, 424.

28. Brett H. Smith, "Reversing the Curse: Agricultural Millennialism at the Illinois Industrial University," *Church History* 73 (2004): 759–91.

29. "Rev. W. A. Sunday Meetings at Springfield, Illinois, Souvenir. March–April, 1909" (Bloomington, Ill.: C. U. Williams, Publisher, 1909), 2.

30. "Rev. W. A. Sunday Meetings at Springfield," 55.

31. Scott R. Erwin, *The Theological Vision of Reinhold Niebuhr's "The Irony of American History": "In the Battle and Above It"* (Oxford: Oxford University Press, 2013), 5–6.

32. *Julian M. Sturtevant: An Autobiography,* edited by J. M. Sturtevant Jr. (New York: Flemming H. Revell Company, 1896), 178.

33. Van Doren, *Illinois Boyhood*, 9.

34. Don Harrison Doyle, *The Social Order of a Frontier Community: Jacksonville, Illinois, 1825–70* (Urbana: University of Illinois Press, 1978), 29.

35. *The History of Henry County Illinois* (Chicago: H. F. Kett and Company, 1877), 137ff.

36. *Atlas of Henry Co. and the State of Illinois* (Chicago: Warner and Beers Publishers, 1875).

37. Richard Lingeman, *Small Town America: A Narrative History, 1620–the Present* (New York: Putnam, 1980), 73.

38. Earnest Elmo Calkins, *They Broke the Prairie* (Urbana: University of Illinois Press, 1989), 229.

39. Frank Richard Hall, "An Illinois Village, 1873 and 1923," *Journal of the Illinois State Historical Society* 20 (1927): 370–410.

40. James E. Davis, *Frontier Illinois* (Bloomington: Indiana University Press, 2000), 266.

41. The academies were in Quincy, Danville, Wyoming, Georgetown, Springfield, Griggsville, Bloomington, Urbana, Shelbyville, Peoria, Abingdon, Aurora, Fulton, Henry, and Onarga.

42. F. Garvin Davenport, "The Pioneers of Monmouth College," *Journal of the Illinois State Historical Society* 46 (1953): 45–59.

43. Davis, *Frontier Illinois*, 266.

44. Doyle, *Social Order of a Frontier Community*, 27.

45. Carl Van Doren, *Three Worlds* (New York: Harper, 1936), 3.

46. Terri Clemens, "Kluxing in Korn Kountry: The 1920s Ku Klux Klan in Central Illinois," master's thesis, Illinois State University, 2005.

47. "Ku Klux Klan, 1920s," Sangamon Link: History of Sangamon County, Illinois, March 5, 2014, accessed July 12, 2015, http://sangamoncountyhistory.org/wp/?p=4339.

48. J. F. Powers, *Morte D'Urban* (New York: New York Review Books, 2000), 75.

49. Morris Myers memoir, Oral History Collection, Archives/Special Collections, Norris L Brookens Library, University of Illinois Springfield, 20–21.

50. Betty Friedan, *Life So Far: A Memoir* (New York: Simon and Schuster, 2006), 24.

51. Arthur C. Cole, *The Era of the Civil War, 1848–1870* (Springfield: Illinois Centennial Commission, 1919), 18. "The Waldenses are very poor in this world's goods," reported one Springfield newspaper, "although exceedingly rich in Christian virtues." *Illinois State Journal*, April 3, 1858, 3.

52. John E. Hallwas, "Mormon Nauvoo from a Non-Mormon Perspective," in *A Reader's Guide to Illinois Literature*, edited by Robert Bray (Springfield: Illinois Secretary of State, 1985)53–69.

53. Susan Sessions Rugh, *Our Common Country: Family Farming, Culture, and Community in the Nineteenth-Century Midwest* (Bloomington: Indiana University Press, 2001), 31.

54. *New York Times*, Jan. 24, 1921.

55. Dannel A. McCollum, "Origins of the 'Champaign System': Prelude to the McCollum Case, 1945–1948," *Journal of the Illinois State Historical Society* 75 (1982): 137–47.

7. THE URGE TO IMPROVE: EDUCATING MID-ILLINOIS

1. Fergus M. Bordewich, "How Lincoln Bested Douglas in Their Famous Debates," *Smithsonian Magazine*, Sept. 2008, accessed Oct. 30, 2014, http://www.smithsonianmag.com/history/how-lincoln-bested-douglas-in-their-famous-debates-7558180/?all.

2. Stewart Winger, "High Priests of Nature: The Origins of Illinois State Normal 'University' in the Antebellum Lyceum," *Journal of the Illinois State Historical Society* 101 (2008), 129.

3. Winger, "High Priests of Nature," 133.

4. Robert P. Howard, *Illinois: A History of the Prairie State* (Grand Rapids, Mich.: William B. Eerdmans Publishing, 1972), 175.

5. Ill. Constitution of 1870, article VIII, 34.

6. Shelby M. Harrison, *Social Conditions in an American City: A Summary of the Findings of the Springfield Survey* (New York: Russell Sage Foundation, 1920), 41–42.

7. And for some time thereafter. Edgar Lee Masters attended Knox College's prep academy for only one year, from 1889 to 1890, but it made an impression; three Knox professors appear as characters in his *Spoon River Anthology*.

8. Clarence P. McClelland, "The Education of Females in Early Illinois," *Journal of the Illinois State Historical Society* 36 (1943), 389.

9. McClelland, "Education of Females in Early Illinois," 404.

10. William Eaton, review of *Missionaries and Muckrakers: The First Hundred Years of Knox College* by Hermann R. Muelder, *Illinois Historical Journal* 78 (1985): 143–44. *McClure's* also published such writers as Rudyard Kipling, Robert Louis Stevenson, Jack London, Lincoln Steffens, and Willa Cather, but it is as a scourge of monopolists such as Standard Oil Company and U.S. Steel that the magazine is usually remembered.

11. Cited by Don Harrison Doyle, *The Social Order of a Frontier Community: Jacksonville, Illinois, 1825–70* (Urbana: University of Illinois Press, 1978), 26.

12. Theodore Calvin Pease, *The Frontier State, 1818–1848* (Chicago: A. C. McClurg Company, 1922), 436–37.

13. Virginius H. Chase, "Jubilee College and Its Founder," *Journal of the Illinois State Historical Society* 40 (1947): 154–67.

14. "A Brief Biography of Philander Chase," The Papers of Philander Chase, accessed Oct. 30, 2014, http://www2.kenyon.edu/Khistory/chase/biography/biography.htm.

15. "Eureka College at 160," Eureka College website, accessed June 12, 2016, http://www.eureka.edu/160/blog/articles/january-4/.

16. "Ronald Reagan," White House website, accessed Oct. 30, 2014, http://www.whitehouse.gov/about/presidents/ronaldreagan.

17. "Address at Commencement Exercises at Eureka College, Eureka, Illinois, May 9, 1982," Ronald Reagan Presidential Library, accessed Dec. 17, 2016, https://reaganlibrary.archives.gov/archives/speeches/1982/50982a.htm.

18. "About Bradley: History," Bradley University website, accessed Dec. 12, 2013, http://www.bradley.edu/about/history/.

19. *Bradley Polytechnic Institute: The First Decade, 1897–1907* (Peoria: Bradley University, 1908), 124.

20. Jason A. Butterick, "A Brief History of Millikin University," Millikin University website, accessed Nov. 7, 2014, https://www.millikin.edu/staley/about-library/university-archives/mu-history. Lincoln University today does business as Lincoln College, independent of both Millikin and the Presbyterians. True to its founder's promise, Millikin was never terribly sectarian, although daily chapel services and convocations were required until 1970.

21. Douglas L. Wilson, "Chautauqua: Old and New," *Illinois Issues* 16 (1991), 23.

22. "Excerpt from the 1904 Old Salem Chautauqua Program," Old Salem Chautauqua website, history page, accessed June 5, 2016, http://oldsalemillinois.com/oldsalem/history/.

23. Katharine Aird Miller and Raymond H. Montgomery, *A Chautauqua to Remember: The Story of Old Salem* (Petersburg, Ill.: Silent River Press, 1987), cited in Wilson, "Chautauqua: Old and New," 21.

24. Vachel Lindsay, "Bryan, Bryan, Bryan, Bryan," *The Poetry of Vachel Lindsay: Complete and with Lindsay's Drawings*, vol. 1 (Peoria, Ill.: Spoon River Poetry Press, 1984), 343.

25. C. H. Cramer, *Royal Bob: The Life of Robert G. Ingersoll* (Indianapolis: Bobbs-Merrill, 1952), 64–65.

26. Mark Twain to Livy Clemens, Chicago, Nov. 14, 1879, Mark Twain Letters, accessed March, 3, 2012, http://www.marktwainletters.com.

27. Paolo E. Coletta, "'Won, 1880: One, 1884': The Courtship of William Jennings Bryan and Mary Elizabeth Baird," *Journal of the Illinois State Historical Society* 50 (1957), 231.

28. Joan Gittens, *Poor Relations: The Children of the State of Illinois, 1818–1990* (Urbana: University of Illinois Press, 1994), 164.

29. Walter B. Hendrickson, "The Three Lives of Frank H. Hall," *Journal of the Illinois State Historical Society* 49 (1956): 271–93.

30. Gittens, *Poor Relations*, 176.

31. Frank B. Norbury, "Dorothea Dix and the Founding of Illinois' First Mental Hospital," *Journal of the Illinois State Historical Society* 92 (1999), 19.

32. Gittens, *Poor Relations*, 181.

33. Winger, "High Priests of Nature," 127–62.

34. Helen E. Marshall, "The Town and the Gown," *Journal of the Illinois State Historical Society* 50 (1957): 144–45.

35. Henry B. Fuller, "Developments of Arts and Letters," in *The Industrial State, 1870–1893*, by Ernest Ludlow Bogart and Charles Manfred Thompson (Springfield: Illinois Centennial Commission, 1920), 190.

36. Richard G. Browne, review of *Grandest of Enterprises: Illinois State Normal University, 1857–1957*, by Helen E. Marshall, *Journal of the Illinois State Historical Society* 50 (1957): 204–6.

37. Browne, review of Marshall, 204–6.

38. Arthur C. Cole, *The Era of the Civil War, 1848–1870* (Springfield: Illinois Centennial Commission, 1919), 236.

39. Quoted in Brett H. Smith, "Reversing the Curse: Agricultural Millennialism at the Illinois Industrial University," *Church History* 73 (2004), 788.

8. REALIZING THE IDEAL: THE PERFECTIONIST IMPULSE IN MID-ILLINOIS

1. Paul Elmen, *Wheat Flour Messiah: Eric Jansson of Bishop Hill* (Carbondale: Southern Illinois University Press, 1976), 108–9.

2. He was born Erik Jansson but changed the spelling of his name to "Janson" on arrival in the United States.

3. Gunnar Benson, review of *Bishop Hill: Svensk Koloni Pa Prairien / Bishop Hill, Illinois: A Utopia on the Prairie*, by Olov Isaksson and Sören Hallgren, *Journal of the Illinois State Historical Society* 63 (1970): 214–16.

4. Ronald E. Nelson, "Bishop Hill: Swedish Development of the Western Illinois Frontier," *Western Illinois Regional Studies* 1 (1978), 115.

5. Lilly Setterdahl, "Emigrant Letters by Bishop Hill Colonists," *Western Illinois Regional Studies* 1 (1978), 152.

6. Nelson, "Bishop Hill," 109.

7. Robert P. Sutton, "Experiments in Communitarianism," in *Illinois: Its History and Legacy*, edited by Roger D. Bridges and Rodney O. Davis (St. Louis: River City Publishers, 1984), 67.

8. Kelley A. Boston, *Utopian Socialism in Sangamon County* (Springfield, Ill.: Sangamon County Historical Society, 2006).

9. Elmen, *Wheat Flour Messiah*, 125–26.

10. That book is Robert Sutton's *Les Icariens: The Utopian Dream in Europe and America* (Urbana: University of Illinois Press, 1994).

11. Robert P. Sutton, "Experiments in Communitarianism," 62.

12. William Lloyd Clark, "Hell at Midnight in Springfield, or A Burning History of the Sin and Shame of the Capital City of Illinois," 5th ed. (Milan, Ill.: n. pub., 1924), 5.

13. James W. Covington, "The Indian Liquor Trade at Peoria: 1824," *Journal of the Illinois State Historical Society* 46 (1953): 142–50.

14. *The Past and Present of Warren Co., Illinois* (Chicago: H. F. Kett and Company, 1877), 111.

15. David Rankin, *David Rankin, Farmer: Modern Agricultural Methods Contrasted with Primitive Agricultural Methods by the Life History of a Plain Farmer* (Tarkio, Mo.: 1909), 24.

16. Christiana Holmes Tillson, *A Woman's Story of Pioneer Illinois* (Carbondale: Southern Illinois University Press, 1995), 47.

17. Mark A. Plummer, *Lincoln's Rail Splitter: Governor Richard J. Oglesby* (Urbana: University of Illinois Press, 2001), 28.

18. Abraham Lincoln, "An Address, Delivered before the Springfield Washington Temperance Society, on the 22d February, 1842," in *The Collected Works of Abraham Lincoln*, edited by Roy P. Basler (New Brunswick, N.J.: Rutgers University Press, 1953–55), 1: 273.

19. *Portrait and Biographical Album of Knox County* (Chicago: Biographical Publishing Company, 1886), 1076.

20. Anne M. Heinz and John P. Heinz, eds., *Women, Work, and Worship in Lincoln's Country: The Dumville Family Letters* (Urbana: University of Illinois Press, 2016), 59–60.

21. Tara McClellan McAndrew, "When Central Illinois Was King of Ceramics and Pottery," *Illinois Times*, September 9, 2010.

22. Theodore Calvin Pease, *The Frontier State, 1818–1848* (Springfield: Illinois Centennial Commission, 1919), 426–27.

23. Brett H. Smith, "Reversing the Curse," 273.

24. Richard Fox, *Reinhold Niebuhr: A Biography* (Ithaca: Cornell University Press, 1996), 7.

25. John E. Hallwas, *The Bootlegger: A Story of Small-Town America* (Urbana: University of Illinois Press, 1999), 34–35.

26. Hallwas, *Bootlegger*, 60–61.

27. Lowell N. Peterson, "Omer N. Custer: A Biography of a Downstate Political Boss," *Journal of the Illinois State Historical Society* 60 (1967): 37–63.

28. Hallwas, *Bootlegger*, 60–63.

29. Mark W. Sorensen, "Ahead of Their Time: A Brief History of Woman Suffrage in Illinois," Illinois State Historical Society, accessed Oct. 30, 2014, http://www.historyillinois.org/suff.html.

30. Thomas R. Pegram, "The Dry Machine: The Formation of the Anti-Saloon League of Illinois," *Illinois Historical Journal*, 83 (1990), 184. The counties were Macon, Shelby, Brown, De Witt, Mercer, Scott, Champaign, Douglas, Greene, Moultrie, Hamilton, Piatt, Coles, and Edgar.

31. William J. Menghini memoir, Oral History Collection, Archives/Special Collections, Norris L Brookens Library, University of Illinois Springfield, 4.

32. Julia Duncan Kirby, *Biographical Sketch of Joseph Duncan: Fifth Governor of Illinois* (Chicago: Fergus Printing Company, 1888), 45.

33. John Bartlow Martin, *Adlai Stevenson of Illinois: The Life of Adlai E. Stevenson* (New York: Doubleday, 1976), 444.

34. "I Wish't I Was in Peoria," words by Billy Rose and Mort Dixon, music by Harry Woods. MPL Communications, 1925.

35. "Report U.S. Plans to Close City to Men on Leave Unless Prostitution Is Checked," *Peoria Journal-Transcript*, Jan. 28, 1942.

36. Bernie Drake, "Peoria and the Shelton Gang," accessed Oct. 30, 2014, http://www.peoriamagazines.com/ibi/2012/apr/peoria-and-shelton–gang.

37. Elise Morrow, "Springfield, Illinois," *Saturday Evening Post*, Sept. 27, 1947.

38. Daniel J. Elazar, *Cities of the Prairie: The Metropolitan Frontier and American Politics* (New York: Basic Books, 1970), 314.

9. JIGGERY-POKERY: PRACTICAL POLITICS IN MID-ILLINOIS

1. J. N. Gridley, H. McHenry, J. B. Pearce and G. B. Thompson, "The County Seat Battles of Cass County, Illinois," *Journal of the Illinois State Historical Society* 7 (1914), 174.

2. Gridley et al., "County Seat Battles," 176.

3. Gridley et al., "County Seat Battles," 176.

4. Gridley et al., "County Seat Battles," 188.

5. Christiana Holmes Tillson, *A Woman's Story of Pioneer Illinois* (Carbondale: Southern Illinois University Press, 1995), 19.

6. *History of Pike County, Illinois: Together with Sketches of Its Cities, Villages and Townships, . . .* (Chicago: Chas. C. Chapman and Company, 1880), 197.

7. Versions of that kind of politics predated the arrival of the upland Southerners. In the late 1600s, French colonial authorities, eager to make Native

Americans more manageable, began insisting that chiefs take responsibility for the actions of tribal members, and by the 1760s, new chiefs in effect had to be approved by the French. Gifts and access to trade goods were granted or withheld according to how well a chief pleased the French in this new role. "The Illinois: Society," Illinois State Museum website, accessed Oct. 29, 2014, http://www.museum.state.il.us/muslink/nat_amer/post/htmls/il_soc.html.

8. Edward F. Dunne was born in Connecticut in 1853 but grew up in Peoria before making a career as a judge in Chicago. He served as a reformist mayor of that city before taking on the easier job of running the state, which he did for one term beginning in 1913, leaving office with a reputation as "far and away the most Progressive state executive Illinois ever had." Richard Allen Morton, *Justice and Humanity: Edward F. Dunne, Illinois Progressive* (Carbondale: Southern Illinois University Press, 1997), vii.

9. Richard Jensen, *Illinois: A History* (New York: W. W. Norton and Company, 1978), 57–58.

10. Rozann Rothman "Changing Expectations of Local Government in Light of the 1960s: The Cases of Champaign and Urbana" in *The Closing of the Metropolitan Frontier: Cities of the Prairie Revisited*, by Daniel J. Elazar et al. (Lincoln: University of Nebraska Press, 1986), 192–217.

11. Jeremy Atack, "The Evolution of Regional Economic Differences within Illinois," in *Diversity, Conflict, and State Politics: Regionalism in Illinois*, edited by Peter Nardulli (Urbana: University of Illinois Press, 1989), 73.

12. Samuel K. Gove and James D. Nowlan, *Illinois Politics and Government: The Expanding Metropolitan Frontier* (Lincoln: University of Nebraska Press, 1996), 10.

13. Robert P. Howard, *Mostly Good and Competent Men: Illinois Governors, 1818–1988* (Springfield: *Illinois Issues*, Sangamon State University, and Illinois State Historical Society, 1988), 101.

14. Roger D. Bridges, "Blacks in a White Society," in *Illinois: Its History and Legacy*, edited by Roger D. Bridges and Rodney O. Davis (St. Louis: River City Publishers, 1984), 91.

15. M. Swearingen, review of *A Conscientious Turncoat: The Story of John M. Palmer, 1817–1900*, by George Thomas Palmer, *Journal of Southern History* 8 (1942): 430–31.

16. Elbert Hubbard, *Little Journeys to the Homes of American Statesmen*, Project Gutenburg e-book 13911 (unpaginated), accessed Dec. 20, 2016, http://www.gutenberg.org/files/13911/13911-h/13911-h.htm.

17. Frederick Trevor Hill, *Lincoln the Lawyer* (New York: Century, 1906), 181.

18. Hubbard, *Little Journeys.*

19. Review of *Lincoln's Manager: David Davis*, by Willard L. King, *University of Chicago Law Review* 28 (1961), 586.

20. Willard L. King, *Lincoln's Manager, David Davis* (Cambridge: Harvard University Press, 1960), xi.

21. Robert W. Johannsen, review of *Lincoln's Manager: David Davis*, by Willard L. King, *Indiana Magazine of History* 57 (1961), 168.

22. Donald F. Tingley, review of *Adlai Stevenson and the World: The Life of Adlai E. Stevenson*, by John Bartlow Martin, *Journal of the Illinois State Historical Society* 71 (1978), 75.

23. Candace Summers, "Adlai Ewing Stevenson II," McLean County Museum of History 2014, accessed Jan. 13, 2015, http://www.mchistory.org/research/resources/adlai-stevenson-ii.php.

24. Clarence A. Berdahl, review of *Uncle Joe Cannon, Archfoe of Insurgency: A History of the Rise and Fall of Cannonism*, by William Rea Gwinn, *Journal of the Illinois State Historical Society* 51 (1958): 333–34.

25. Lance Morrow, "We Lose a Great Speaker, We Gain a Great Book," *Time*, May 24, 2000, accessed June 5, 2016, http://content.time.com/time/magazine/article/0,9171,45926,00.html.

26. Cited by William Barry Furlong, "The Senate's Wizard of Ooze: Dirksen of Illinois," *Harper's*, Dec. 1959, 44.

27. Edward L. Schapsmeier and Frederick H. Schapsmeier, "Serving under Seven Presidents: Les Arends and His Forty Years in Congress," *Illinois Historical Journal* 85 (1992): 105–18.

28. Springfield socialist Duncan McDonald was nominated for president by the Farmer-Labor Party in 1924 but did not run. Barack Obama, whose career lies outside the scope of this book, served his political apprenticeship in Springfield as a state senator from 1996 to 2004.

29. John J. Miller, "Eureka's Reagan," *National Review*, Oct. 14, 2011. The street on the south side of campus is now named Reagan Drive, there is an annual Eureka Reagan Fest, the college maintains a Ronald Reagan Museum, and visitors are provided with walking tours of Reagan sites.

30. Melvyn Dubofsky and Warren van Tine, *John L. Lewis: A Biography* (New York: New York Times Books, 1977).

31. Paul M. Angle, *Here I Have Lived: A History of Lincoln's Springfield, 1821–1865* (Chicago: Abraham Lincoln Bookshop, 1971), xiv.

32. K. J. Winkler, "The Voters of Lincoln's Springfield: Migration and Political Participation in an Antebellum City," *Journal of Social History* 25 (1995), 606.

33. Allen C. Guelzo, "Come-Outers and Community Men: Abraham Lincoln and the Idea of Community in Nineteenth-Century America," *Journal of the Abraham Lincoln Association* 21 (2000), 24–25.

34. Erika Nunamaker, "Lincoln's Pursuit of 'Egalitarian Refinement': Evidence from His Mahogany Sofa," *Journal of the Abraham Lincoln Association*, 28 (2007), 32.

35. Theodore Calvin Pease, *The Frontier State, 1818–1848* (Springfield: Illinois Centennial Commission, 1919), 317.

36. Howard, *Mostly Good and Competent Men*, 53.

37. Karl Schriftgiesser, *The Farmer from Merna: A Biography of George J. Mecherle and a History of the State Farm Insurance Companies of Bloomington, Illinois* (New York: Random House, 1996), 24–25.

38. Jane Wolf Hufft and Anne Nevins Loftis, "Reports of a Downstate Independent: Excerpts from the Letters of Lewis Omer to Allan Nevins, 1930–1953," *Illinois Historical Journal* 81 (1988), 28.

39. John Bartlow Martin, *Adlai Stevenson and the World: The Life of Adlai E. Stevenson* (New York: Doubleday, 1976), 532.

40. See Lowell N. Peterson, "Omer N. Custer: A Biography of a Downstate Political Boss," *Journal of the Illinois State Historical Society* 60 (1967), 37–63.

41. Daniel J. Elazar, *Cities of the Prairie: The Metropolitan Frontier and American Politics* (New York: Basic Books, 1970), 208.

42. David Donald, review of *Tyrant from Illinois: Uncle Joe Cannon's Experiment with Personal Power*, by Blair Bolles, in *Journal of the Illinois State Historical Society* 44 (1951): 358–59.

43. Joseph G. Gambone, review of *Fifty Years of Public Service: Personal Recollections of Shelby M. Cullom*, by Shelby M. Cullom, *Journal of the Illinois State Historical Society* 64 (1971): 230–31.

44. Leonard Schlup, "Gilded Age Politician: Adlai E. Stevenson of Illinois and His Times," *Illinois Historical Journal* 82 (1989): 218–30.

45. Frank H. Mackaman, introduction to *The Education of a Senator*, by Everett McKinley Dirksen (Urbana: University of Illinois Press, 1998), xxxi.

46. Arthur C. Cole, *The Era of the Civil War, 1848–1870* (Springfield: Illinois Centennial Commission, 1919), 177.

47. Robert M. Crunden, *A Hero In Spite of Himself: Brand Whitlock in Art, Politics, and War* (New York: Alfred A. Knopf, 1969), 35.

48. Howard, *Mostly Good and Competent Men*, 82.

49. Don Harrison Doyle, *The Social Order of a Frontier Community: Jacksonville, Illinois, 1825–70* (Urbana: University of Illinois Press, 1978), 64–65.

50. Michael Burlingame, *Abraham Lincoln: A Life* (Baltimore: Johns Hopkins University Press, 2008), 121.

51. "Veterans Affairs National Home for Disabled Volunteer Soldiers: Danville Branch, Danville, Illinois," National Park Service, accessed Oct. 29, 2014, http://www.nps.gov/nr/travel/veterans_affairs/Danville_Branch.html.

52. Don E. Fehrenbacher, "The Post Office in Illinois Politics of the 1850's," *Journal of the Illinois State Historical Society* 46 (1953), 60.

53. Frank B. Norbury, "Dorothea Dix and the Founding of Illinois' First Mental Hospital," *Journal of the Illinois State Historical Society* 92 (1999), 22.

54. Gene Callahan interview, Illinois Statecraft Oral History Project, Abraham Lincoln Presidential Library.

55. Hufft and Loftis, "Reports of a Downstate Independent," 29.

56. Paul M. Angle, *On a Variety of Subjects* (Chicago: Chicago Historical Society and the Caxton Club, 1974), 73–77.

57. Joan Gittens, *Poor Relations: The Children of the State of Illinois, 1818–1990* (Urbana: University of Illinois Press, 1994), 2.

58. Vachel Lindsay, *"The Golden Whales of California" and Other Rhymes in the American Language* (New York: Macmillan, 1920), 22–23.

59. Lynnita Aldridge Sommer, "Illinois Farmers in Revolt: The Corn Belt Liberty League," *Illinois Historical Journal* 88 (1995): 222–40.

60. Theodore Saloutos and John D. Hicks, *Agricultural Discontent in the Middle West, 1900–1939* (Madison: University of Wisconsin Press, 1951), 581.

61. David Dechenne, "Recipe for Violence: War Attitudes, the Black Hundred Riot, and Superpatriotism in an Illinois Coalfield, 1917–1918," *Illinois Historical Journal* 85 (1992): 221–38.

62. Quoted in Errol Wayne Stevens, "The Socialist Party of America in Municipal Politics: Canton, Illinois, 1911–1920," *Journal of the Illinois State Historical Society* 72 (1979), 262.

63. Stevens, "The Socialist Party of America in Municipal Politics," 272.

64. Elazar, *Cities of the Prairie*, 222–23.

65. Carl Sandburg, *Always the Young Strangers* (New York: Harcourt, Brace and Company, 1953), 286–87.

66. John D. Coats, "A Question of Loyalty: The 1896 Election in Quincy, Illinois," *Journal of the Illinois State Historical Society* 108 (2015), 127.

67. *Portrait and Biographical Record of Adams County, Illinois: Containing Biographical Sketches of Prominent and Representative Citizens . . .* (Adams County, Ill.: Chapman Brothers, 1892), 332.

68. Anne M. Heinz and John P. Heinz, eds., *Women, Work, and Worship in Lincoln's Country: The Dumville Family Letters* (Urbana: University of Illinois Press, 2016), 62.

69. Mark W. Sorensen, "Ahead of Their Time: A Brief History of Woman Suffrage in Illinois," *Illinois Heritage* 7 (2004), 5.

70. Mark W. Sorensen, "Ahead of Their Time: A Brief History of Woman Suffrage in Illinois," accessed Oct. 30, 2014, http://www.historyillinois.org/suff.html, 1.

71. "Women's Suffrage in Illinois," Sangamon County Historical Society, Sangamon Link, accessed Oct. 30, 2014, http://sangamoncountyhistory.org/wp/?p=2666.

72. Grace Wilbur Trout, "Side Lights on Illinois Suffrage History," *Journal of the Illinois State Historical Society* 13 (1920), 150.

73. "Women's Suffrage in Illinois."

10. ROLLOVER TERRITORY: GETTING FROM HERE TO THERE IN MID-ILLINOIS

1. Jeremy Atack, "The Evolution of Regional Economic Differences within Illinois, 1818–1950," in *Diversity, Conflict, and State Politics: Regionalism in Illinois*, edited by Peter Nardulli (Urbana: University of Illinois Press, 1989), 84.

2. Charles L. Dancey, "The Pekin Centenary, 1849–1949: A Souvenir Book Commemorating 100 years of Community Progress in the City of Pekin, Illinois" (Pekin Association of Commerce, 1949?), 3.

3. Betty I. Madden, *Art, Crafts, and Architecture in Early Illinois* (Urbana: University of Illinois Press, 1979), 186.

4. Robert F. Mazrim, *The Sangamo Frontier: History and Archaeology in the Shadow of Lincoln* (Chicago: University of Chicago Press, 2008), 58–61.

5. Gurdon Saltonstall Hubbard, *The Autobiography of Gurdon Saltonstall Hubbard: Pa-pa-ma-ta-be, "The Swift Walker"* (Chicago: R. R. Donnelley and Sons, 1911), 153–54.

6. Federal Writers' Project, *Illinois: A Descriptive and Historical Guide* (Springfield: State of Illinois, 1939), 474–75.

7. Paul M. Angle, *Here I Have Lived: A History of Lincoln's Springfield, 1821–1865* (Chicago: Abraham Lincoln Bookshop, 1971), 162.

8. "Beardstown to Bluff Springs in Cass County Plank Road," Illinois State Museum, accessed Oct. 30, 2014, http://www.museum.state.il.us/RiverWeb/harvesting/transportation/plankroad/beardstown_plank_road.html.

9. Earnest Elmo Calkins, *They Broke the Prairie* (Urbana: University of Illinois Press, 1989), 199.

10. *Transactions of the Department of Agriculture of the State of Illinois* 12 (1875), 148.

11. James E. Davis, *Frontier Illinois* (Bloomington: Indiana University Press, 2000), 230–31.

12. H. J. Stratton, "The Northern Cross Railroad," *Journal of the Illinois State Historical Society* 28 (1935), 23–25.

13. Robert P. Sutton, "From Trails to Rails," in *Illinois: Its History and Legacy*, edited by Roger D. Bridges and Rodney O. Davis (St. Louis: River City Publishers, 1984), 73.

14. Federal Writers' Project, *Illinois*, 163.

15. Robert D. Sampson, "'Honest Men and Law-Abiding Citizens': The 1894 Railroad Strike in Decatur," *Illinois Historical Journal* 85 (1992): 74–88.

16. Davis, *Frontier Illinois*, 378–79.

17. *History of McDonough County, Illinois* (Springfield, Ill.: Continental Historical Company, 1885), 825.

18. Thomas J. Brown, "The Age of Ambition in Quincy, Illinois," *Journal of the Illinois State Historical Society* 75 (1982): 242–62.

19. John Dowling, ed., *History of Iroquois County* (Iroquois County Board of Supervisors, n.d.), 13.

20. Robert P. Sutton, "Illinois River Towns: Economic Units or Melting Pots," *Western Illinois Regional Studies* 13 (1990), 30.

21. Thomas J. Brown, "The Age of Ambition in Quincy, Illinois," *Journal of the Illinois State Historical Society* 75 (1982), 256.

22. Charles Manfred Thompson, "The Farmers' Movement, 1872–1875" in *The Industrial State 1870–1893*, by Ernest Ludlow Bogart and Charles Manfred Thompson (Springfield: Illinois Centennial Commission, 1920), 82–84.

23. Atack, "Evolution of Regional Economic Differences," 89–90.

24. Thompson, "Farmers' Movement" in Bogart and Thompson, *Industrial State, 1870–1893*, 90ff; George H. Miller, *Railroads and the Granger Laws* (Madison: University of Wisconsin Press, 1971).

25. Thompson, "Farmers' Movement" in Bogart and Thompson, *Industrial State, 1870–1893*, 91–92.

26. *Prairie Farmer*, March 8, 1873, quoted in Thompson, "Farmers' Movement" in Bogart and Thompson, *Industrial State, 1870–1893*, 94.

27. Ernest Ludlow Bogart, "Waterways and Roads, 1870–1893" in *The Industrial State, 1870–1893*, 343.

28. C. C. [Cary Clive] Burford, "The Twilight of the Local Passenger Train in Illinois," in *The Prairie State: A Documentary History of Illinois, Colonial Years to 1860*, edited by Robert P. Sutton (Grand Rapids, Mich.: William B. Eerdmans Publishing Company, 1976), 334.

29. Madeline Smith, *The Lemon Jelly Cake* (Urbana: University of Illinois Press, 1997), 36.

30. Burford, "Twilight of the Local Passenger Train," 161.

31. *New York Times*, August 12, 1887.

32. Robert P. Howard, *Illinois: A History of the Prairie State* (Grand Rapids, Mich.: William B. Eerdmans Publishing, 1972), 486.

33. "Illinois Terminal Railroad," processed by Gary Iverson, McLean County Museum of History, accessed March 9, 2013, http://www.mchistory.org/research/resources/terminal/.

34. C. C. Burford, review of *The Electric Interurban Railways of America*, by George W. Hilton and John F. Due, *Journal of the Illinois State Historical Society* 53 (1960): 305–6.

35. Mark Van Doren, *The Autobiography of Mark Van Doren* (New York: Harcourt, Brace, 1958).

36. Burford, "Twilight of the Local Passenger Train," 177–80.

37. H. George Friedman Jr., "An Interurban for Urbana: The Kankakee and Urbana, 1906–1926," chapter 6 in *Twin Cities Traction: The Street Railways of Urbana and Champaign, Illinois*, accessed Oct. 30, 2014, http://www.cs.uiuc.edu/homes/friedman/champaign-urbana/Chapter06.htm.

38. "Illinois Terminal Railroad," McLean County Museum of History.

39. Bill Kemp, "First Brick Street in U.S. Myth Endures in Bloomington," *Pantagraph*, September 30, 2012, accessed Oct. 30. 2014, http://www.pantagraph.com.

40. Tom Emery, "Fading Away: Brick Streets Linger, but Disappearing Fast," *Jacksonville (Ill.) Journal-Courier*, January 3, 2016, accessed May 17, 2016, http://myjournalcourier.com/news/90121/fading-away.

41. *Transactions of the Department of Agriculture of the State of Illinois* 12 (1875), 142.

42. Lloyd Loving memoir, "Bates Experimental Road Project," Oral History Collection, Archives/Special Collections, Norris L Brookens Library, University of Illinois Springfield, 3. See also Clifford Older, "Bates Experimental Road or Highway Research in Illinois," Bulletin 21 (Springfield, Ill.: Department of Public Works and Buildings, ca 1937).

43. "1920–1928," *Journal of the Illinois State Historical Society* 69 (1976), 281.

11. GROWING FACTORIES: MID-ILLINOIS'S INDUSTRIAL HEYDAY

1. Raymond Wiggers, *Geology Underfoot in Illinois* (Missoula, Mont.: Mountain Press Publishing Company, 1996), 135ff.

2. "A Rambler's Notes," *Canton (Ill.) Weekly Register*, January 3, 1907.

3. Alonzo M. Swan, *Canton: Its Pioneers and History: A Continuation to the History of Fulton County* (Canton, Ill.: the author, 1871), 117.

4. "The A. E. Staley Story," Staley Museum website, accessed May 20, 2016, http://staleymuseum.com; David Satterfield, interviewed by Betty Turnell, Decatur Public Library, January 1983, accessed Oct. 30, 2014, http://www.decaturlibrary.org/wp-content/uploads/2012/08/Satterfield_David_interview.pdf.

5. David Foster Wallace, *A Supposedly Fun Thing I'll Never Do Again: Essays and Arguments* (Boston: Little, Brown, 1997), 10.

6. William Shurtleff and Akiko Aoyagi, "History of Soybean Crushing: Soy Oil and Soybean Meal—Part 5," SoyInfo Center website, accessed May 30, 2016, http://www.soyinfocenter.com/HSS/soybean_crushing5.php.

7. "Rushville," in *Combined History of Schuyler and Brown Counties, Illinois: 1686–1882* (Philadelphia: W. R. Brink and Company, 1882), 235.

8. *Paris Beacon-News*, March 3, 1999; "Paris, Illinois," Commercial Club of Paris, undated, accessed Oct. 31, 2014, https://archive.org/details/parisillinois00sln.

9. "Hummer Manufacturing Co.," Sangamon Link, Sangamon County Historical Society, accessed May 22, 2016, http://sangamoncountyhistory.org/wp/?p=1344.

10. Dave Reynolds, "Posted Keystone Transformed Itself and Came Back as Strong as Ever," *Peoria Journal-Star*, Aug. 28, 2013, accessed Oct. 30, 2014, http://www.pjstar.com/article/20130828/News/308289833.

11. Howard F. Dyson, "A Record for 'Jug Town,' Ripley," *Rushville Times*, reprinted at Illinois GenWeb Project, accessed Oct. 21, 2014, http://schuyler.illinoisgenweb.org/OldTimesInSchuyler/OTIStownsites.html.

12. From "The Town Clean Dirt Made Famous—Pottery Town," a typed memoir by Mrs. A. F. Worcester, 1960, accessed Oct. 12, 2015, http://www.bluewhitepottery.org/the-white-hall-pottery-center--greene-county--illinois.html.

13. Tara McClellan McAndrew, "When Central Illinois Was King of Ceramics and Pottery," *Illinois Times*, Sept. 9, 2010, accessed Oct. 31, 2014, http://illinoistimes.com/article-7722-when-central-illinois-was-king-of-ceramics-and-pottery.html.

14. *Souvenir: White Hall, Illinois* (White Hall, Ill.: Pearce Printing Company, 1911), 3, at Internet Archive, accessed Oct. 31, 2014, https://archive.org/stream/souvenirwhiteha100whit/souvenirwhiteha100whit_djvu.txt.

15. Federal Writers' Project, *Illinois: A Descriptive and Historical Guide* (Springfield: State of Illinois, 1939), 58–81.

16. Quoted by Betty Shaw, "The Coal Mine," Mining More in Moweaqua, 1889–1940, 58, accessed Dec. 22, 2016, miningmoreinmoweaqua.com/pdf/chap6.pdf.

17. Because overburden could not be dug when it was very cold outside, and coal couldn't be sold when it wasn't, operators had to expose the coal in summer and remove it in winter until steam-powered shovels made it possible to strip even frozen ground.

18. L. B. Sheley, "Story of Strip Mining in Illinois," in *Annual Coal Report* (Springfield: Illinois Department of Mines and Minerals, 1935), 117.

19. Sheley, "Story of Strip Mining," 118.

20. Lottie E. Jones, *History of Vermilion County* (Chicago: Pioneer Publishing, 1911), 1:376.

21. Michael Rice memoir, Oral History Collection, Archives/Special Collections, Norris L Brookens Library, University of Illinois Springfield.

22. Jason Nevel, "Benld's Coliseum Likely to Fade into History," *State Journal-Register,* Aug. 30, 2011, accessed Oct. 31, 2014, http://www.sj-r.com/article/20110830/News/308309923.

23. Amy Zahl Gottlieb, "British Coal Miners: A Demographic Study of Braidwood and Streator," *Journal of the Illinois State Historical Society* 72 (1979), 191.

24. "Minonk Coalmine," from History: A Look at Minonk's Past, Minonk Talk, accessed Oct. 31, 2014, http://www.minonktalk.com/coalmine.htm.

25. Louise C. Odencrantz and Zenas L. Potter, *Industrial Conditions in Springfield, Illinois; A Survey by the Committee on Women's Work and the Department of Surveys and Exhibits* (New York: Russell Sage Foundation, 1916), 70–72.

26. David Markwell, "A Turning Point: The Lasting Impact of the 1898 Virden Mine Riot," *Journal of the Illinois State Historical Society* 99 (2007), 219.

27. Drew VandeCreek, "1877: The Great Strike," Illinois during the Gilded Age Digitization Project, accessed Oct. 31, 2014, http://dig.lib.niu.edu/gildedage/narr4.html.

28. Robert D. Sampson, "'Honest Men and Law-Abiding Citizens': The 1894 Railroad Strike in Decatur," *Illinois Historical Journal* 85 (1992): 74–88.

29. Eleanor L. Hannah, *Manhood, Citizenship, and the National Guard: Illinois, 1870–1917* (Columbus: Ohio State University Press, 2007).

30. Bill Steinbacher-Kemp, "Mother Jones Played Key Role in 1917 Streetcar Strike," *Pantagraph,* May 12, 2007, accessed Oct. 31, 2014, http://www.pantagraph.com/news/mother-jones-played-key-role-in-streetcar-strike/article_c4866b75–0791–5edc-ae78-cdea2caaf8c0.html.

31. Melvyn Dubofsky and Warren van Tine, *John L. Lewis: A Biography* (New York: New York Times Books, 1977), 169.

32. Thomas B. Littlewood, *Horner of Illinois* (Evanston: Northwestern University Press, 1969), 123.

33. John H. Keiser, "The Union Miners Cemetery at Mt. Olive, Illinois: A Spirit -Thread of Labor History," *Journal of the Illinois State Historical Society* 62 (1969), 263.

34. Michael G. Matejka and Greg Koos, *Bloomington's C & A Shops: Our Lives Remembered* (Urbana: University of Illinois Press, 1988).

35. Earnest Elmo Calkins, *They Broke the Prairie* (Urbana: University of Illinois Press, 1989), 8–9.

36. Jeremy Atack, "The Evolution of Regional Economic Differences within Illinois, 1818–1950," in *Diversity, Conflict, and State Politics: Regionalism in Illinois*, edited by Peter Nardulli (Urbana: University of Illinois Press, 1989), 78.

37. Daniel J. Elazar, *Cities of the Prairie: The Metropolitan Frontier and American Politics* (New York: Basic Books, 1970), 82–83.

38. Elazar, *Cities of the Prairie*, 84.

39. Deborah Dougherty, "Peoria Union Stockyards: Gateway between the Corn Belt and the Packers," *InterBusiness Issues*, April 2012.

40. Elazar, *Cities of the Prairie*, 222.

41. "Industry," Peoria Historical Society website, accessed Oct. 31, 2014, http://www.peoriahistoricalsociety.org/!/History-Of-Peoria/Industry; Jerry Klein, "Made in Peoria: The Birth of Industry," Peoria Magazines website, January 2011, accessed Oct. 31, 2012, http://www.peoriamagazines.com/ibi/2011/jan/made-peoria-birth-industry.

42. Sam Moore, "Let's Talk Rusty Iron: Continuing the Avery Co. Story with the Development of the Avery Tractor Line," *Farm Collector*, June 2007, accessed Oct. 31, 2014, http://www.farmcollector.com/.

43. Sam Moore, "Robert Avery and Avery Co.," *Farm Collector*, May 2007, accessed Oct. 31, 2014, http://www.farmcollector.com.

44. Interview with Dan Fogelberg, Rock around the World, accessed Oct. 31, 2014, http://www.ratw.com/issues/13/fogelber.htm.

45. Autumn Stanley, *Mothers and Daughters of Invention: Notes for a Revised History of Technology* (New Brunswick, N.J.: Rutgers University Press, 1995), 124.

46. Karl Schriftgiesser, *The Farmer from Merna: A Biography of George J. Mecherle and a History of the State Farm Insurance Companies of Bloomington, Illinois* (New York: Random House, 1996), 40–41.

EPILOGUE

1. "History Corner: A Look Back (June 2009)," *Decatur Herald-Review*, accessed Oct. 30, 2014, http://herald-review.com/.

2. Jan Morris, *Lincoln: A Foreigner's Quest* (New York: Simon and Schuster, 2001), 70.

3. Earnest Elmo Calkins, *They Broke the Prairie* (Urbana: University of Illinois Press, 1989), 98.

4. Calkins, *They Broke the Prairie*, 98.

5. *Tales from the Trees: Profiles and Legends of Some Who Watched a Station-Stop Grow into a Little City on the Illinois Prairie; Mi-Nonk! Minonk!* (privately printed, 1981).

6. See Marjorie Rich Bordner, *From Cornfields to Marching Feet: Camp Ellis, Illinois* (Dallas: Curtis Media Corporation, 1993). See also the brochure produced by Dickson Mounds Museum in conjunction with the special exhibit *Reveille to Retreat—The Story of Camp Ellis in World War II*, Illinois State Museum website, accessed June 10, 2016, http://www.museum.state.il.us/ismsites/dickson/brochere.pdf.

7. William Furry, "Barely a Trace: What's Left of the Old Indian Trail Known as Edwards Trace," Sangamon County Historical Society, accessed July 31, 2013, http://www.sancohis.org/OLDER FILES/trace.htm.

INDEX

Page numbers in italics refer to illustrations.

James Krohe Jr. is an award-winning columnist, journalist, and historian who has written about the people, places, and events of mid-Illinois for more than forty years. A native of Beardstown and Springfield, Mr. Krohe is the editor of *A Springfield Reader: Historical Views of the Illinois Capital, 1818–1976* (1976) and the author of several works of Sangamon County history.